EYEWITNESS COMPANIONS

Whisky

CHARLES MACLEAN
EDITOR-IN-CHIEF

LONDON, NEW YORK,
MELBOURNE, MUNICH AND DELHI

Contributors: Dave Broom, Tom Bruce-Gardyne, Ulf Buxrud, Ian Buxton, Glenn Gillen, Peter Mulryan, Hans Offringa, Dominic Roskrow, Gavin D Smith

Produced for Dorling Kindersley by
Blue Island Publishing

Art Director	Stephen Bere
Managing Editor	Michael Ellis
Editors	Jane Simmonds, Michael Fullalove
Proof Reader	Pamela Giles
Senior Designer	Marisa Renzullo
Picture Research	Ben White, Chrissy McIntyre, Yumi Shigematsu, Taiyaba Khatoon

Dorling Kindersley

Senior Editor	Jennifer Latham
Senior Art Editor	Isabel de Cordova
Managing Editor	Dawn Henderson
Managing Art Editor	Susan Downing
Production Editor	Jenny Woodcock
Jacket Designer	Nicola Powling
Picture Research	Jenny Baskaya

First published in 2008 by
Dorling Kindersley Limited
80 Strand, London WC2R ORL
Penguin Group (UK)

2 4 6 8 10 9 7 5 3 1

ISBN 978-1-4053-2814-2

Colour reproduction by Colourscan, Singapore
Printed and bound in China by Leo Paper Group

Discover more at

www.dk.com

*Introduction by
Charles MacLean 10*

16
THE WORLD
OF WHISKY

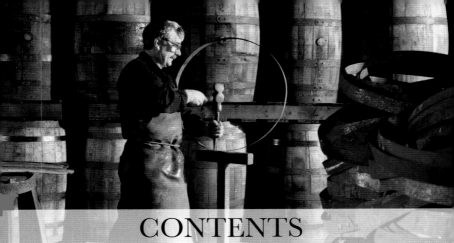

CONTENTS

INTEREST IN WHISKY HAS NEVER BEEN GREATER THAN IT IS TODAY, AND THE CURRENT LEVELS OF INVESTMENT IN ITS PRODUCTION AND MARKETING REFLECT THIS. WE ARE, INDEED, AT THE DAWN OF A GOLDEN AGE FOR WHISKY.

The secrets of distilling are likely to have been known by scholars, physicians, and monks throughout Europe in the early Middle Ages. It is possible that the knowledge had already been introduced to Scotland by the early 14th century, with the arrival from Ireland of the MacBeaths. The members of this clan, or family, were known to be "wise doctors", and they quickly became hereditary physicians to the Kings of Scots and to the Lords of the Isles.

The first written reference to making "aqua vitae" in Scotland, however, is from 1494, and we do not find references to it being taken for anything other than medicinal purposes until the early 1500s. By the end of that century, though, whisky drinking was perceived as a problem by the Scottish government, which sought to curtail it in the Western Isles.

References to distilling during the 17th century are few and sometimes contradictory, but it seems likely that whisky making was widespread in Scotland and Ireland. Farming communities throughout Scotland gave over large proportions of their best arable land to growing barley for brewing ale. To prevent this turning sour – preservatives such as hops were unknown – much of it must have been distilled.

Whisky making remained small-scale and in the hands of landowners and local communities until well into the 18th century. Such "private" distilling from grains grown by the community and for their consumption (rather than for sale) was perfectly legal until 1781.

The first excise duty on whisky – a cunning imposition, learned from the Dutch – was imposed as early as 1641, which demonstrates that, even by the mid-17th century, whisky was, to some extent, being made commercially. The earliest reference to an "industrial" distillery dates from 1689, and during the 1780s such enterprises began to proliferate in Lowland Scotland.

Parallel developments were taking place in America, where Evan

Glenfiddich took the groundbreaking step of marketing its single malt in the 1960s.

Easter Elchies House stands at the heart of the Macallan estate, which includes arable land given over to the cultivation of barley for whisky making.

Williams established a large-scale distillery in Louisville, Kentucky, in 1783. When the nascent government of the United States attempted to impose tax on commercial distilling eight years later, the farmer-distillers rebelled, and George Washington had to muster an army of 13,000 men to restore order and the rule of law *(see p209)*.

Similar unease was manifested in Scotland, where small-scale "private" distillers defied the law, becoming "smugglers" (illicit distillers). By 1800 large, well-organized bands of smugglers openly flouted the authorities to bring their whisky to market, and by 1820 the situation had become anarchic. Licensed distillers and landowners pressed the government to revise the law so as to encourage small distillers to take out licences, and make good whisky cheaply.

Glenlivet, a classic Speyside whisky

Lagavulin was founded in 1817, though illicit whisky was certainly made in this area of Islay, off the west coast of Scotland, well before that date.

THE WHISKY REVOLUTION

The 1823 Excise Act *(see p47)* laid the foundations of the modern Scotch whisky industry. Many more distilleries were opened, often on the sites of former smugglers' dens. Some lasted only a few years, but others are with us still. They made malt whisky and grain whisky – the latter mainly in the Lowlands. After 1830, grain whisky was made in continuous stills, which had been perfected and patented by a former Inspector General of Irish Excise, Aeneas Coffey *(see p172)*.

Grain whisky is lighter in style, higher in strength, and cheaper to produce than malt whisky. The malt whiskies of the day were generally heavy, pungent, and variable in quality. It was logical, therefore, to mix them together to produce a drink that was more generally acceptable, and from the 1860s "blended" whisky came to dominate the market, and blending firms to control the industry.

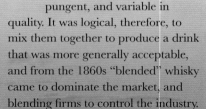

In its bricks and mortar, Bushmills, in Ireland, is very much a 19th-century distillery, but its whiskey-making origins go back to 1608.

BOOM AND BUST

The Scotch boom of the 1890s culminated in over-production and a collapse in confidence by 1900. The industry's self-assurance returned only in the 1920s, with the amalgamation of the leading blending houses into the Distillers Company Limited (DCL), and (paradoxically) with the banning of the manufacture and sale of spirits in the USA. Knowing that Prohibition could not last forever, the Scotch whisky companies made sure that America was supplied with good quality Scotch through adjacent countries such as Canada and the Bahamas, laying the foundations of what would become the largest export market soon after Prohibition was repealed in 1933.

In the early years of the 20th century Irish whiskey prospered as much as Scotch, but the Irish distillers had turned their backs on their countryman's invention, the Coffey still *(see opposite)*, and as blended Scotch became better, so the consumption of Irish declined.

Also, a taste for bourbon had been brought to Europe by American GIs in World War II. After the war, the demand for Scotch and bourbon was seemingly insatiable; Scotch, in particular, became the epitome of style and good taste in the Free World. Demand far-outstripped supply, and throughout the 1960s distilleries were expanded and modernized, and new ones built. The boom was not to last, however. By the mid-1970s – largely owing to changes in fashion away from brown spirits in favour of white

Maker's Mark Distillery was founded in Kentucky in 1805, though its distinctive brand of bourbon originated in the 1950s.

was little left over for bottling as single malt.

Though it still accounts for only around 8% by volume of total sales of Scotch (much less in the case of Japanese and Irish malts), malt whisky has spawned huge enthusiasm, appreciation, and enjoyment all over the world, demonstrated by the number of whisky festivals, clubs, publications, and websites devoted to the subject. Appreciation of malt whisky has seen a corresponding interest in "small-batch" expressions (notably of bourbon and rye in the USA).

spirits and wine – distillers contended with the potentially disastrous combination of a shrinking market and large stocks of mature whisky (known in Europe as "the Whisky Loch").

This had an upside, however, in that it led to a phenomenon that has done a great deal to increase interest in all kinds of whisky throughout the world: the discovery of malt.

THE DISCOVERY OF MALT

Led by William Grant & Sons with their Glenfiddich Distillery, followed by other independents such as Macallan and Glenmorangie, distillery owners began to bottle and market their own malts for the first time. Of course, Scotch malt whisky had been around for at least 500 years, and small amounts had been bottled by spirits merchants and occasionally by the distillers themselves, but it had rarely been promoted. Such was the demand for malt whisky from the blenders – 99.9% of the Scotch sold in the 1970s was blended – that there

CURRENT TRENDS

Recent years have seen a rise in the number of "wood-finished" whiskies – mainly malts, but also some blends and non-Scotch whiskies. These are simply whiskies that have been re-racked into different casks (usually fresh ex-wine barrels) for the last months or years of their maturation. The process was pioneered by Glenmorangie as a way of diversifying the range of products available from a single distillery.

Another trend has been the bottling of "non chill-filtered" whiskies, often at "cask strength" (typically around 60% ABV, as opposed to the more usual 40–43%). Chill-filtration removes certain compounds from the liquid in order to retain its clarity and brightness when ice or water is added. It is also called "polishing" and takes place just before the whisky is bottled, when the spirit's temperature is lowered to around freezing and the liquid pushed through a card filter. Most whiskies undergo such treatment, but some connoisseurs prefer the compounds to be left in, even if the liquid develops a haze when water is added.

BETTER WHISKY

There is an old Scots saying: "There's no bad whisky. Just good whisky and better whisky!" And this applies to any well-made whisky, from wherever in the world it comes. We are these days blessed with a great diversity of whisky styles available to us from around the world, and each has its intrinsic qualities. "An American whiskey is not a failed attempt to make Scotch, or vice versa", to quote my late colleague Michael Jackson (to whose memory this book is

Canadian Club, a classic blended whisky

respectfully dedicated by all of us who have contributed to it).

Over the past 20 years, the science underpinning the making and maturation of whisky has developed hugely – although, happily, there are still gaps in our knowledge, which allow us to debate the relative importance of raw materials, processes, wood, and the intervention of the artisans who make the spirit.

Whisky is the most complex spirit known to man. It rewards study and is worthy of contemplation – appreciation as well as simple enjoyment.

I hope this book will guide you, dear reader, on a rewarding journey of discovery into "the world's noblest spirit" – whisky!

Slainte!

CHARLES MACLEAN, EDINBURGH

When Masataka Taketsuru set up Yoichi Distillery in the 1930s, he looked for a site that mirrored the climatic conditions he'd experienced in Scotland.

THE WORLD
OF WHISKY

THE WORLD OF WHISKY

Many people drink whisky without knowing much about it. While it is not necessary to be familiar with the intricacies of its production in order to enjoy a dram, a degree of knowledge adds considerably to the drinker's pleasure and satisfaction.

The ingredients that go together to create whisky are few in number, and the basic processes that turn grain in a field into drink in a bottle are relatively simple. But the methods involved in the combination and interaction of the raw materials employed are full of subtle nuances and regional or national variations, all contributing to the particular style of the finished whisky.

In the following pages we explore just where sweetness, peatiness, heather, smokiness, and saltiness in the aroma and flavour of whisky come from, and address how such disparate characteristics are possible in something made only from grain, yeast, and water.

However, to these three ingredients can be added one more – wood – and, more specifically, the casks in which whisky is stored during maturation. The casks in question are far from passive vessels. The interaction between wood and new spirit leads to a mellower and more well-mannered drink, and the length of time over which the spirit is allowed to mature in the cask will play a major part in its ultimate character, as will any previous contents of the cask. What is sometimes perceived as simply a period of "storage", undertaken once the whisky is made, is actually crucial to the complex and multi-faceted business of creating whisky.

MAKING SPIRIT

At the core of the definition of "spirit" is the process of distillation, and there is a vast stylistic difference between whisky made in pot stills and that produced in continuous stills. And, particularly in the case of pot stills, variations in size, shape, and operational techniques play a major role in determining the whisky's make up.

Although sometimes seen as less important than distillation, the earlier stages of mashing and fermentation are vital in developing a variety of desirable aromas and flavours that will carry through right into the bottle.

At the very beginning, of course, there is the selection of grain. Whiskies are created from one or more of a number of different grains, and the choice of which type and which strain plays a central role in shaping the profile of the whisky into which it will eventually be transformed.

So, although the production of whisky from just three principal ingredients may initially seem to be a straightforward process, resulting in a spirit that we might imagine would possess little variation, the reality is really very different.

Whisky from the stills at Abelour is used in blends such as Clan Campbell and also released as both a 10-year-old and cask strength single malt.

INGREDIENTS

Making whisky is actually a reasonably simple process that uses a small number of ingredients. Yet the permutations of equipment, practice, and raw materials allow for an incredible number of variations in the whisky that finally finds its way into the bottle.

GRAIN

Of all the diverse factors that determine the ultimate character of the whisky we buy, none is as important as the type of grain from which that whisky is distilled. Whisky may be made from barley, corn, rye, and wheat, with only barley being used in isolation. All other whiskies embrace grains in various combinations and proportions.

Malted barley is used in Scotch malt whisky, and a percentage is included in the multi-grain mashbill of most whiskies, in order to promote fermentation. Malted barley is the most expensive grain, while corn gives the highest yield per tonne.

In terms of flavour, barley contributes malty, cereal, biscuit-like notes to whisky. Corn gives sweet, spicy, and oily notes, while rye contributes a full-bodied, pepper and spice character, along with dried fruit on the palate. Wheat provides mellow notes of honey, which balance the bolder characteristics of other grains when used in the production of bourbon. Of all the grains employed in the creation of

The grains used for whisky are barley and wheat, which are used for all Scotch and Irish whisky, and corn and rye, which are widely used in the States.

whisky, only corn is indigenous to North America. Barley, wheat, and rye were all cultivated in Europe prior to their introduction to America by European settlers. Barley is one of the longest-established grain crops to be grown in Britain and Ireland, and it is thought that Neolithic man was growing the crop between 5,000 and 10,000 years ago. Inevitably, from a historical perspective, distillers tended to work with whichever grain grew most successfully in their vicinity.

The permitted combinations and percentages of various grains within each designated type or style of whisky *(see p34)* are usually enshrined in law. For example, "straight rye" whiskey must legally be distilled using a minimum of 51 per cent rye *(see p186)*.

YEAST

Yeast is a single-cell organism that feeds on sugars and produces alcohol and carbon dioxide as a result. It is probably the least discussed element that affects a whisky's profile, yet it is essential, not only in the creation of alcohol but also in its contribution to a spirit's character. At one time, virtually all distillers in Scotland and Ireland used a mixture

Barley

Wheat

Corn

Rye

of a specific distiller's yeast and a much cheaper brewer's yeast (often collected from local breweries). Today, in the interests of greater bacterial control, some distillers use only distiller's yeast, while others believe that mixing the two improves the flavour of the spirit. Certainly, different strains of yeast contribute a variety of aromas and flavours to the final whisky.

Arguably, North American distillers have been aware of the importance of yeast in relation to spirit character for longer than their European counterparts, and many US distilleries pre-cultivate their own yeast strains on site. Modern yeasts are employed to promote a more predictable and less volatile fermentation than was sometimes the case in the past.

Yeast transforms the sugars in the grain into alcohol.

WATER

The production of malt whisky revolves around the addition and subtraction of water at various stages in the whisky-making process. Moisture is removed from newly-harvested malting barley; water is added to the malt during steeping; and moisture is taken away again during kilning. Water is added during the mashing process, removed during distillation, and once again added before bottling to reduce the strength of the spirit. Water is also used for condensing the distilled spirit.

It is fair to say that the single most important factor in distillery location has always been the availability of a reliable source of pure water. Everything else is secondary. The water must be pure, but it must also

Barley is one of the cornerstones of whisky making. It is not only the key ingredient of malt whisky, but is also used in the majority of mash bills.

be available in quantity. Distilleries take water from boreholes, natural springs, lochs, burns, and rivers, as well as from the public supply.

Illicit stills were frequently set up in isolated places, not just to hide them from the prying eyes of the excisemen, but also because such places were frequently where the best distilling water was to be found. If the distillers ultimately chose to operate within the law – as many did – they were often loath to leave their favoured locations, hence the remote settings of so many distilleries, especially in Scotland. If water is so crucial to whisky making, it follows that the character of the water used can have a significant impact on the profile of the final spirit. Salts dissolved in water used to make wort *(see p25)* affect its flavour and provide trace elements which are vital in the propagation of yeast. It is often said

Distilleries such as Glenfarclas are found in isolated locations because of the whisky maker's search for abundant supplies of pure water.

that the best whisky is made using soft water that flows over granite and peat. This is perhaps because granite is very insoluble, and so does not pass undesirable minerals into the water. Soft water is also a better solvent than hard water, and, because it contains very little calcium, yeast can work more vigorously in it and ferment the wort more efficiently. Nonetheless, it is not difficult to find examples of distilleries which make excellent whiskies using hard water. They include Glenmorangie, in the Scottish Highlands, and Highland Park, on Orkney.

The water of the Scottish Highlands is usually soft, however. It rises in red granite and often flows along its way through peat and heather, both of which can influence its character. It is sometimes argued that soft, peaty water, such as that used in distilling on Islay, makes for heavier whiskies, while the harder water of Speyside makes for a lighter style of spirit. This is a very broad generalization, however, for there are many other factors to consider, such as the size and shape of stills and the manner in which they are run.

The limestone that dominates the principal whiskey-producing states of the USA is rich in calcium, magnesium, and phosphate, and the hard water of Kentucky, for example, helps to promote efficient enzyme action during the mashing stage of production. The

The kilns at Balvenie Distillery are fired up with the addition of peat to create a distinctive, phenolic characteristic in the whisky.

layer of limestone is also pitted with caverns, which act as reservoirs.

Water temperature is another significant variable in whisky making. Even in the condensers this is the case, since the colder the water the more efficient the condensing, which speeds up the process of turning the alcohol vapour back into liquid. This may give a "cleaner" spirit than if the condensing process were slower. Water temperature, as well as availability, traditionally has been a factor in the existence of the "silent season" – the period when distilleries close down for a spell during the hottest and driest summer months.

Peat used to be dug by hand, but these days is usually cut by machine.

Once distillation is complete, water remains important, since most whisky is reduced to its optimum maturation strength prior to filling into casks. De-ionized water is also usually used to reduce the spirit to bottling strength after maturation is complete.

The Scottish Highlands provide an abundance of water from mountain springs and streams.

PEAT

Peat is vegetable matter decomposed by water and partially carbonized by chemical change over thousands of years. It is usually found in wetland areas. The use of peat during the kilning stage of malt production tends to be limited largely to Scotland, Japan, and occasionally Ireland. Peat is added to the kiln fire to provide what is known as "peat reek" in order to promote phenolic characteristics. The influence of peat is most apparent in the single malt whiskies of Islay.

The provenance of the peat used in malting is significant. Peat that has developed from sphagnum moss or grass roots differs in character from that composed of bog myrtle, which produces a sweet, citric aroma when burnt. It is sometimes argued that using peat which includes heather in its make up may add a "heathery" note to the whisky. Peat harvested close to the coast will be looser in composition than that further inland, due to the greater amount of sand it contains. It will also possess more salty, maritime aromas and flavours.

In the days before centralized, commercial maltings were a common feature of the industry, most distilleries cut their own peat or bought it from local suppliers to use in on-site kilns. It was said that the character of peat could differ significantly from distillery to distillery, even within one comparatively small island such as Islay.

Formerly cut manually, peat is almost invariably now harvested by machine. At one time, it was also used as fuel to fire the stills of rural Scottish and Irish distilleries, but now its use is restricted to kilning.

In addition to its malting role, peat may be an influence on whisky because the water used during production has previously flowed through peat,

Maple wood is burnt at Jack Daniel's Distillery to create maple charcoal, which is used for filtering the Tennessee whiskey produced there.

absorbing peaty characteristics as it passes. This is particularly the case on Islay, where peat comprises up to 25 per cent of the island's surface area. Indeed, the peatiness of the process water may influence the profile of the whisky produced even if the level of peating in its malt is comparatively low.

WOOD

With the exception of the type of grain used for distillation, the most significant factor that influences the character of the whisky we drink is the manner in which it is matured. In effect, the wood in which whisky is aged is one of the ingredients of whisky-making (see p30).

However, in the case of officially designated Tennessee whiskey, wood plays a vital part prior to the process of filling the spirit into barrels. Central to the designation is the Lincoln County Process (see p191) in which new-make spirit is filtered through tanks filled with up to 4 metres (12 ft) of maple charcoal. The process takes four days and removes many of the more dominant congeners, as well as adding a slightly sweet note to the spirit.

American white oak is used for the barrels at Jack Daniel's Distillery.

PRODUCTION

Despite the variation of grains used and techniques employed, whisky making the world over is remarkably similar. Its principal stages can be boiled down to malting, mashing, fermenting, and distilling.

MALTING

This is the first stage of the malt whisky distillation process in Scotland, where only malted barley may be used. In many other countries, whisky is produced using a variety of grains that are not malted. However, a percentage of malted barley is always used in their production in order to promote efficient fermentation.

The process of malting breaks down cell walls within the grains and activates enzymes which will convert the starch into sugar during the "mashing" stage. During malting, the grains are germinated by steeping in water and being spread onto a concrete floor. The grains then begin to sprout. Before they have the chance to develop further, the germination is stopped by drying the "green malt" in a kiln with hot air. Sometimes peat is burned during kilning to add smoky flavours to the whisky. The quantity of peat used will vary, depending on whether the whisky is to be heavily or lightly peated.

Phenol levels of peating are measured in parts per million (ppm). Many Speyside distilleries use malt peated to just one or two ppm, while the most heavily peated Islay whiskies

Not many distilleries still use old-fashioned "rake and plough" mash tuns, such as this one; most now use stainless-steel Lauter tuns.

will use malt with a phenolic level in excess of 50ppm. Once dried, the malt is ground in a mill to produce a rough "grist", after which the process of mashing can begin.

Today, only a handful of distilleries still malt their own barley, with the vast majority buying in malt prepared to their specification by commercial maltsters in large, automated plants. Although such facilities were developed in Scotland only from the 1970s onwards, commercial maltings have been used in the USA, Canada, Ireland and other European countries since the early 20th century.

MASHING

During mashing, the grist is mixed with hot water in a large vessel known as a mash tun. This is a circular, metal container, and since the 1960s, many

Mash tuns are used to mix grist (ground malt) with warm water to make worts; an inspection window (below right) is used to monitor the process.

On a traditional maltings floor, such as this one at Balvenie, the grain is turned by hand to aerate it and so promote an even rate of germination.

distilleries have adopted the "Lauter" tun. It is made from stainless steel, and has revolving arms to gently stir the mash. The starch in the grains is converted into a variety of sugars by enzymes within the grains, and the sugar goes into solution in the hot water, to be drained off through the base of the mash tun. This liquor is called "wort". The husks of the malt create a "bed" in the bottom of the mash tun, through which the sugary wort can drain.

Traditionally, three waters, or "extractions", were used for mashing in Scottish distilleries. The first water – which is, in fact, the third water from the previous mash – is heated to 63–4°C (145–7°F), then mixed with the grist. The temperature is crucial: if it is too hot, it will kill the enzymes; and if it is too cool, extraction from the malt will be limited. This liquid is drained off, then the second water is sprayed onto

the mash at around 75°C (167°F) and the remaining sugars in the wort are drained off. To ensure there are no useable sugars left in the mix, a third water, called "sparge", is then sprayed on, at around 85°C (185°F). This is then transferred to a tank to be used as the first water of the next mash.

Modern Lauter tuns continually spray water onto the bed of grist after the first water has been drained off. This is more efficient in extracting sugars, permits faster drainage, and creates clearer wort, with fewer solid particles. Clear wort allows for a greater range of flavours to be developed during the fermentation process.

The husks and other solids remaining in the mash tun are known as "draff", and are removed and, as they are rich in protein, are converted into cattle food. The wort passes through a heat exchanger to reduce its temperature to below 20°C (68°F), which is necessary in order to prevent the yeast being killed off immediately during fermentation.

Where non-malted grain, such as corn, is used in distillation, it is crushed in a mill and "cooked" in a cylindrical tank or pressure cooker to break down the cellulose walls and allow the starch within to absorb water during mashing. The starch then gelatinizes, enabling the grain's enzymes to convert the starch into sugar.

Traditional wooden washbacks are still in use in many Scottish and Japanese distilleries. In them, the wort is fermented to create wash.

The sight of smoke plumes from a distillery is now a rarity, being restricted only to those sites that still use kilns to malt their own barley.

FERMENTATION

From the heat exchanger, the wort is pumped into a number of fermenters, or "washbacks" as they are known in Scotland. Traditionally they are made of Oregon pine or larch wood, but are now often constructed of stainless steel.

As the wort enters the fermenter, a measured amount of yeast is added. Yeasts survive for years in a dormant state, but in the presence of sugars, warmth, moisture, and an absence of air, they multiply at an astonishing rate. The yeast consumes the sugars in the wort, and converts them into alcohol and carbon dioxide. At this point, the wort becomes what is known as "wash".

The reaction during fermentation is violent, with the temperature increasing to around 35°C (95°F). The wash froths dramatically, and mechanical "switchers" revolve over the surface, breaking the foam and preventing the wash from overflowing. The increasing temperature and rising alcohol level causes the yeast multiplication to slow down after some 12 hours. By this stage, there will be a considerable increase in the amount of bacteria present, principally lactobacillus.

There follows a period of bacterial fermentation, which is important for the development of flavour compounds and the degree of acidity in the wash. Longer fermentations produce a more acidic wash, which reacts beneficially with the copper in the wash still, producing a cleaner, more complex spirit. By the time fermentation is complete, the wash contains between six and eight per cent alcohol, its acidity has increased, and around 80 per cent of the solids in the wash have been converted into alcohol, carbon dioxide, and new yeast cells. The remaining solids pass over with the wash into the wash still.

In many US distilleries a "sour mash" process takes place during fermentation. An amount of residue from the still, known as "backset" or "stillage", is pumped back into the fermenter in order to maintain the desired level of acidity. This helps to control the level of natural bacteria.

DISTILLATION

The process of distillation takes place in pot stills or continuous stills. In both cases the principle is the same. Alcohol boils at a lower temperature than water, so when the wash is heated, alcohol vapours rise up from the still first to be condensed back into liquid ready for collection.

CONTINUOUS DISTILLATION

Virtually all bourbon, rye, Tennessee, and Canadian whisky, along with grain spirit for Scotch whisky blending, is produced using a method of continuous distillation. Irish distillers use both pot stills and continuous stills. Grain spirit, usually from corn, is produced in

"Man doors" are a feature of pot stills. They can be opened up to inspect and clean the insides between distillation batches.

In tall stills, such as these at Glenmorangie, the vapour has to climb a greater height, and consequently more falls back as "reflux".

continuous stills, while what is termed Irish "pure pot still whiskey" is made in pot stills from a mix of both malted and raw barley *(see p168)*.

Although there are technical differences between the many continuous stills in use around the world, they all work on the same basis, and none are far removed from the original Coffey still, patented in the early 1830s by Irishman Aeneas Coffey *(see p172)*.

Compared to malt whisky distillation in pot stills, the production of whisky in a continuous, column, or patent still – as it is variously known – is significantly closer to an industrial process. The stills making grain spirit are large, versatile, and highly efficient, as they can work continuously, whereas malt whisky distillation in pot stills is a "batch" process, requiring time-consuming cleaning between each period of production. A much greater quantity of grain whisky can be distilled in any given period, and the

Squat stills, such as these from Midleton in Ireland, allow more "congeners" to remain in the final spirit, as the degree of "reflux" is limited.

THE CRUCIAL ROLE OF COPPER

Pot stills are made from copper, as it is an excellent conductor of heat, and is malleable and therefore comparatively easy to fabricate into the many and varied shapes of pot stills. With the exception of the output of the Canadian Mist Distillery *(see p223)*, which employs stainless-steel distilling equipment, all whiskies produced in continuous stills are also exposed to copper during the whisky-making process.

It was not until the early 1980s that scientists began to fully comprehend just how important copper was in the creation of fine spirits. It acts as a catalyst in removing foul-smelling, highly volatile sulphur compounds, and also assists in the creation of desirable fragrant, fruity notes, which are known as "esters".

The more contact the spirit has with copper, the lighter and purer it will be. When the alcohol vapour reaches the head of the still, the still's design and the manner in which it is operated can either encourage the vapour to condense quickly, or to trickle back down into the body of the still and be re-distilled. This is known as "reflux", and makes for greater copper contact and therefore increased purity.

Column stills consist of two connected cylinders, a rectifier and an analyser: the rectifier performs the initial distillation, the analyser the second.

unmalted grain which is predominantly used is significantly cheaper than malted barley.

The continuous still consists of two large, connected, parallel stainless-steel columns, called the analyser and the rectifier. The fermented wash enters at the top of the rectifier column, where it is warmed by hot steam and is able to descend over a series of perforated copper plates. These plates serve the purpose of holding back heavier compounds, which flow from the bottom of the still.

The desirable volatile compounds are vapourized and pass over into the second column (the analyser) at a strength of between 10 and 20 per cent ABV. Here the vapours are cooled as they rise up the column, eventually condensing and being collected in liquid form. It is possible to distil spirit to a strength of just below 95 per cent ABV in a column still.

There are three basic shapes of pot still: plain (or onion) stills tend to create heavier spirits than the lamp-glass and boil-ball stills.

In North America, wash is referred to as "beer", and the first column of the continuous still is known as the "beer still". The second distillation takes place in what's called a "doubler" or "thumper" still, which is not dissimilar to a pot still. The beer or wash that enters the beer still contains solids, whereas in pot still distillation the wash enters the still in clear liquid form.

POT STILL DISTILLATION

In this traditional method of distillation, the wash is pumped into the first still, called the "wash still", and is brought to the boil. The boiling liquid forms a foam which climbs up the neck of the still. The stillman then adjusts the heat to make sure that the foam does not reach the top of the still and carry over into the condenser.

Plain still

Lamp-glass still

Boil-ball still

After a short while, the foam subsides and the operator can turn up the heat and drive off the spirit until the strength of the liquid left in the still (about half of the volume it was charged with) is down to around two per cent ABV. This is called "pot ale" and, after evaporation, can be used for cattle feed.

The vaporized spirit driven off the stills must be condensed back into liquid form, and this takes place in either modern "shell and tube" condensers or in "worm tubs". Shell and tube condensers are tall copper drums filled with dozens of narrow-bore copper pipes through which runs cold water. The spirit vapour enters the drum and condenses on the cold copper pipes. The worm tub is a coiled copper pipe of diminishing diameter, set in a deep vat of cold water outside the still house. Until the 1970s, all distilleries used worm tubs, but today only around a dozen Scottish distilleries still employ them.

In a spirit safe, samples from "the run" are taken and analysed to check the spirit's level of purity.

The liquid (condensed from the spirit produced by the wash still) is called "low wines". It is pumped into a "low wines receiver" before passing into the second "low wines" or "spirit" still, along with the residue of the previous distillation. The liquid is boiled in the same way as in the first distillation, but with two significant differences. The first spirits to come off are known as "foreshots". They are high in strength (around 75–80 per cent ABV), pungent, and impure, and are directed to a separate receiver tank. The later spirits, known as the "aftershots" or "feints", are also unpleasant in aroma and flavour, and go into the same receiver tank as the foreshots. Both are added to the next batch of low wines for re-distillation.

Only the "middle cut" of the run from the spirit still is directed to the "intermediate spirit receiver", to be filled into casks or barrels.

"Cut points" vary from distillery to distillery, and the skill of the stillman is to know when to start saving spirit and when to stop. In some modern distilleries, however, cut points are computer controlled.

The spirit from both stills passes through a locked brass box with a glass front called a "spirit safe". Inside are glass jars containing hydrometers to measure strength. The stillman manipulates handles on top of the safe to fill these jars and add water. When the spirit is impure it turns cloudy, but once it remains clear, he turns another handle and starts saving it. A similar operation is performed when the feints begin to flow, and the stillman comes "off spirit". This mix of pure spirit and impurities, or "congeners", is different in every distillery, and plays a vital role in determining the character of the whisky produced. The still continues to be run until its contents are around 0.1 per cent ABV. This final residue is called "spent lees", and is run to waste. The product of the spirit still is referred to as "new make" or "clearic". It is a perfectly clear liquid and around 70 per cent ABV. Before it can be put into casks or barrels, its strength must be reduced by diluting it with water to achieve an ABV of around 63 or 64 per cent, which is considered the optimum strength to begin the maturation stage.

A spirit safe is essential for monitoring "the run" and deciding on the dividing line between the foreshots, the middle cut, and aftershots.

MATURATION

The influence of maturation in the creation of good whisky cannot be over-emphasized. Indeed, some authorities consider that whisky acquires up to 80 per cent of its final character in the cask. The cask cannot make bad whisky good, but it can make a good whisky great.

THE IMPORTANCE OF OAK

Oak has long been the wood of choice for whisky maturation, and it is specified in the legal definitions of many whiskies around the world. The advantages of oak are that it is able to impart beneficial flavours and aromas to the contents of the cask, and its tight grain

The Glenfiddich Distillery uses a mixture of European oak and ex-bourbon American oak barrels to mature its range of whiskies.

prevents leakage while its pores allow the contents to breathe. It is also a very durable wood, and may be bent when heated without cracking.

Whisky is usually matured in casks constructed either of European oak *(Quercus robur)* or, more commonly, American white oak *(Quercus alba)*, which has largely superseded its European form. American oak is more widely available, and therefore considerably cheaper. Today, the Scotch whisky industry uses around 95 per cent American white oak.

EUROPEAN OAK

The most commonly-used form of European oak, especially in Scotland, comes from Spain, principally because of Britain's long association with shipping sherry from Spain in casks and bottling it in the UK. The desirability of "sherry wood" for the maturation of whisky is recorded as long ago as the 1860s, but as the popularity of sherry declined during the 1970s, fewer such casks were available. The problem was compounded in 1983 when shipping sherry in bulk was banned by the European Commission.

Today, whisky companies requiring Spanish casks sometimes buy their wood while it is still growing ("on the tree", as it is known), and have it staved and coopered in Spain. They must then make arrangements with Spanish *bodegas* to have casks "seasoned" with sherry before importing them.

AMERICAN WHITE OAK

The wide availability of casks made from American white oak has its origins in a deal brokered between the US coopers' unions and the country's distillers in the mid-1930s. The terms of the agreement were that whiskey must be filled into new casks if it was to be designated as bourbon or rye. The result of this was that large numbers of used American white oak barrels became available in the years after World War II.

Spanish sherry casks are made of European oak, which is richer in tannins than American oak and able to impart more complexity to the whisky.

Bourbon is matured in barrels (which hold around 200 litres, or 44 gallons). Some are shipped from the USA intact as "American Standard Barrels", but most are broken down into their staves and arrive in bundles called shooks. In Scotland they are re-assembled in a slightly larger, 250-litre (55-gallon) format called a re-made hogshead.

THE USE OF OLD CASKS

With the exception of whiskey made in the USA, very little spirit is filled into new casks. Most casks have previously contained other spirits or wine. Whisky matures better in a used cask, and the first contents "seasons" the wood by removing some of its most obvious woody flavours, while adding its own desirable traces of spirit or wine.

In Scotland, the first time a cask is filled with spirit, it is known as a "first-fill", and thereafter it is referred to as a "refill" cask. The more often it is refilled, the less impact the wood will have upon its contents. It will impart less colour and flavour, and extract fewer undesirable flavours from the

New American white oak is charred prior to use, the char acting as a purifier and removing unwanted compounds.

Penderyn Distillery in Wales uses top-quality American oak to mature its whisky, but, to add complexity, finishes it off in Madeira casks.

spirit. After being filled three or four times (depending upon how long it held whisky during each filling), the cask is considered to be exhausted, and is either discarded by the whisky industry or "rejuvenated".

Rejuvenation involves scraping out the inside walls of the cask, and scorching the wood again – a process called "de-char/re-char" in American casks. This serves to re-activate the layer of wood immediately beneath the charred walls of the cask, but it does

A MATTER OF AGE

Many legal designations of whisky around the world specify a minimum maturation period. In Scotland, Ireland, and Canada this is three years, and in the case of bourbon and rye in the USA, two. Scotch whiskies may be used for blending purposes at quite young ages, but very little single malt is bottled at less than eight years of age.

US whiskeys tend to be released at much younger ages, but the higher temperatures that they experience allow them to mature quicker. Whisky also matures at different rates depending on the cask in which it has been filled, where it has been stored, and on the character of the spirit itself. Some lighter bodied, less complex whiskies may reach their optimum level of maturity several years sooner than "bigger", more complex spirits.

There is a common belief that the older the whisky, the better it must be, but age does not necessarily guarantee quality. If left in a cask for too long, the wood can turn against the spirit, giving it sour and "woody" notes.

WHICH OAK IS BEST?

Casks made from European oak and American white oak affect their contents in significantly different ways. American white oak casks are higher in vanillin (giving sweet toffee and coconut notes to the spirit); European oak is higher in tannins (giving fruity, complex, and astringent notes). Also, European casks are usually twice the size of American white oak casks and mature their contents more slowly. The smaller the cask, the greater the surface area exposed to the spirit, and the more rapid the rate of maturation.

not make the cask as good as new. A rejuvenated cask will not mature its contents in the same way as a first-fill, and most of the whiskies matured in such casks are used for blending.

THE IMPORTANCE OF HEAT

In order to be bent into a barrel-shape, the staves must be heated, and that heating process alters the chemical structure of the inside surface of the cask. Indeed, without heating, the spirit will not mature, but merely acquire a "green", woody note. European casks are "toasted" to bend them into shape, while the carbon char on American white oak casks acts as a purifying

In the cooperage of Balvenie Distillery, casks are constructed from the staves of former bourbon barrels, shipped over from the USA.

agent, removing "immature" characteristics and extracting compounds from the new spirit, principally sulphur-based molecules.

The first time casks are filled with new make, residues of the previous filling will be present in the walls of the cask. These leech out into the maturing spirit, adding character to the whisky. Gradually, the colour also changes, principally due to tannins in the wood. European oak is more tannic than American white oak, and so imbues its contents with a deeper hue. The degree of colour becomes progressively lighter, the more times the cask has been filled.

Oak wood is semi-porous, which allows the contents of an oak cask to "breathe" and interact with the air outside. This leads to oxidation, which removes harshness, increases fruitiness, and enhances complexity. Over the years, a cask usually loses both volume and strength – volume loss being known in Scotland as "the angels' share".

STORING THE SPIRIT

The interaction between the wood and the atmosphere is the least understood aspect of maturation. It is also the one most affected by the micro-climate of the warehouse in which the cask is placed during maturation.

Racked warehouses, such as this one at Woodford Reserve in the USA, allow barrels of whiskey to be stored on their sides on multi-storey racks.

It follows that both the type and location of warehouses in which casks are stored are significant in terms of whisky maturation. During maturation there is evaporation of ethanol and water, and the ingress of oxygen through the cask. The amount of bulk loss depends upon temperature and humidity levels, as does the speed of maturation. In high temperatures spirit expands, causing it to extract flavours from the wood at a comparatively fast rate. In damp warehouses the amount of liquid in the cask remains high, while the alcoholic strength declines. In dry warehouses the opposite occurs.

In Scotland, traditional dunnage warehouses – usually constructed of stone, with an earth or cinder floor – hold casks stacked three high on wooden runners. Due to constraints of space, large, multi-storey warehouses have been constructed in more recent times. They are fitted out with steel racks to hold casks, up to 12 rows high, closely packed together. For ease of operation, palletization has also been introduced in many warehouses. Here casks are stacked not on their sides, as tradition has dictated, but on their ends on wooden pallets, up to six high. This facilitates handling by fork-lift trucks.

Compared to most modern facilities, dunnage warehouses have fewer temperature variations, as their heavy construction insulates them better. But, whatever the type of warehouse, there are also differences between casks stored close to the ground, where it tends to be cooler, and those stored near to the roof, where the warmth increases the pace of maturation. To ensure consistency, casks from different parts of a warehouse are often vatted together prior to bottling.

US distillers tend to use either brick or corrugated metal, racked warehouses. The latter are usually sited on exposed ground, which allows them to utilize the seasonal differences of temperature and humidity to the best effect.

In a palletized warehouse casks are stored in an upright position, rather than on their sides, so that several at a time can be moved by fork-lift trucks.

TYPES OF WHISKY

As whisky making has developed over time and in different parts of
the world, so distinct styles have emerged. These regional varieties are
often dictated by the most readily available grains, but they are also
based on climatic conditions and traditions too.

SCOTCH WHISKY

To be called Scotch whisky, a spirit must
conform to the standards of the Scotch
Whisky Order of 1990 (UK), which
states that it must be distilled at a
Scottish distillery from water and malted
barley, to which only other whole grains
may be added. It has to be processed at
that distillery into a mash, fermented
only by the addition of yeast, and
distilled to an alcoholic strength of less
than 94.8 per cent ABV to retain the
flavour of the raw ingredients used.
It also has to be matured in Scotland in
oak casks for no less than three years. It
should not contain any added substance
other than water and caramel colouring,
and may not be bottled at less than
40 per cent ABV.

SCOTCH MALT WHISKY

Malt whisky is distilled from 100 per
cent malted barley and is usually
distilled in a pot still. Single malt
Scotch whisky is the product of just
one distillery *(see p45)*.

BLENDED SCOTCH WHISKY

Blended Scotch whisky is a mixture
of single malt whisky and grain whisky.
The constituent whiskies are from a
number of different distilleries, and
any age statement given on the bottle
must refer to the youngest whisky in
the blend *(see p116)*.

BLENDED MALT WHISKY

Previously known as "vatted malts",
blended malts consist of two or more
single malt whiskies mixed together.
As with blended whiskies, any age
statement given has to refer to the
youngest whisky in the blend.

GRAIN WHISKY

Grain whisky may contain unmalted
barley or other malted or unmalted
grains, such as wheat and maize (corn),
and is generally distilled in a continuous
still. Most grain whisky is used for
blending. However, single grain Scotch
whisky is sometimes bottled, and is the
product of just one distillery *(see p110)*.

IRISH WHISKEY

Irish distillers use both pot and column
stills, producing grain spirit, usually
from corn, in the column stills, while
what is termed Irish "pure pot still
whiskey" is traditionally made in pot
stills from a mixture of both malted and
raw barley. Typically 40–50 per cent of

**Single Malt
Scotch**   **Blended
Scotch**   **Blended
Malt**   **Single Grain
Whisky**   **Single Malt
Irish Whiskey**   **Pot Still Irish
Whiskey**   **Blended Irish
Whiskey**

the mash bill is malted barley, though this isn't a legal requirement *(see p168)*. Traditionally Irish whiskey is triple-distilled. Blended Irish whiskeys are made from a mixture of pot and column still spirits. Like Scotch, Irish whiskey must be distilled and matured in the country of origin for at least three years.

BOURBON WHISKEY

By law, bourbon must be produced from a mash of not less than 51 per cent corn grain, and is usually made from between 70 and 90 per cent corn, with some barley malt plus rye and/or wheat in the mash bill. Legally, bourbon has to be matured in new, charred, white oak barrels for at least two years *(see p186)*.

TENNESSEE WHISKEY

Essentially bourbon-style spirits, Tennessee whiskeys do, however, undergo a distinctive filtration through sugar maple charcoal. This is known as the Lincoln County Process *(see p191)*.

RYE WHISKEY

Legally, rye whiskey has to be made from a mash of not less than 51 per cent rye and, as with bourbon, virgin charred oak barrels are required for maturation. To be called "straight rye" it must be matured for at least two years *(see p186)*.

CORN WHISKEY

Corn whiskey is distilled from a fermented mash of not less than 80 per cent corn at less than 80 per cent ABV. It is the one American whiskey that does not have to be aged in new charred oak barrels, and no minimum maturation period is specified *(see p186)*.

CANADIAN WHISKY

Virtually all Canadian whisky is distilled in column stills, and in most cases, rye is blended with a comparatively neutral base spirit – sometimes with the addition of bourbon-type whiskey and corn whiskey. Unlike US bourbon and rye, pre-used casks may be employed for maturation. As with Scotch and Irish, Canadian whisky must be matured for a minimum of three years. It is permissible to add small amounts of fruit or alcohols such as sherry to the whisky *(see pp222 & 225)*.

JAPANESE WHISKY

Japanese distillers take Scotland as their model, distilling malt whisky in pot stills and grain whisky in column stills. As with Scotch, blended Japanese whisky is a mixture of both malt and grain spirit, often containing a percentage of imported Scotch malt whisky *(see p241)*.

INDIAN WHISKY

Much of the "whisky" produced in India would not qualify as whisky elsewhere. Most Indian whisky is ENA (extra neutral alcohol) whisky, produced in continuous stills using buckwheat, rice, millet, or molasses, and generally sold unaged. A number of Indian single malts and blended malts are also produced, and these tend to conform to classifications widely used in the European Union *(see p276)*.

Bourbon Whiskey | **Tennessee Whiskey** | **Rye Whiskey** | **Corn Whiskey** | **Canadian Whisky** | **Japanese Single Malt** | **Indian Single Malt**

BLENDING AND BOTTLING

There remains an unwarranted degree of snobbishness regarding blended whiskies. Too often they are perceived as the poor relations of single malts, yet a well-made blend is at least their equal. And remember, over 90 per cent of all Scotch consumed is blended whisky.

If blends did not sell in such large quantities, many of the distilleries producing highly-prized single malts would surely have fallen silent long ago.

Sam Bronfman, head of the former Canadian distilling giant, Seagram, famously declared, "distilling is a science, blending is an art," and today's practitioners of the "art" of combining malt and grain spirit strive to maintain consistency in an ever-changing whisky world. Indeed, consistency and harmony are at the core of all good blending. It is no use creating the finest blended whisky in the world today if the blender is unable to reproduce it tomorrow.

WORLD BLENDING

In the USA, blends are produced using bourbon, rye, or other "heavy" styles of spirit, along with grain whiskey or neutral grain spirit. Unlike in Scotland, US distillers are allowed to add up to 2.5 per cent of sherry or wine to help enhance the character of the blend. Canadian blenders may legally mix the components of their blends prior to filling into cask for maturation. Irish and Japanese blenders face the problem of a comparatively small malt base with which to work, and the Japanese have, for many years, solved this by importing Scotch malt whisky to give greater variety to their blends.

Nosing whiskies at the Seagrams in the 1970s

Blending involves contending with many variables, including practical changes at distilleries, which might affect the spirit being produced and the overall stock position. It may be necessary to substitute some whiskies with others from the same stylistic "family" from time to time. The blender also has to take into account the different types and condition of casks in which the various whiskies are maturing, along with the manner and location in which they are stored.

Modern "wood management programmes", which are designed to monitor closely the casks in use by the whisky industry, give the blender greater confidence in the quality and likely character of component whiskies than used to be the case, and the increased consistency of new make spirit being produced also makes the task a little easier.

THE NOSE

The blender's principal tool is the nose, and only rarely are constituent whiskies actually tasted. The reason for this is that while humans have some 9,000 taste buds, our olfactory receptors number 50 to 100 million. Smell is undoubtedly the most important sense when it comes to analyzing whisky.

At one time, blenders would work with as many as 40 malts for any one blend, but today that number has been reduced to between a dozen and 25 in most cases. Of course, the quality of a blend does not depend on the number of malts in its composition. It need not even depend on the percentage of malt in its make-up, though, as a general rule, the higher the percentage

of malt in a blend, the better its flavour. Most of our best-known blended whiskies will have a malt content of between 30 and 40 per cent.

When producing a blended whisky, the blender will have to take into account not only the style of whisky but also economic factors. If developing a blend for a specific "price point", proportions of the component whiskies will be adjusted accordingly. As a basic rule, the more malt in a blend and the older the whiskies it contains, the higher its price. A "deluxe" blend will normally carry an age statement, usually 12 years or more, and can be expected to have a higher malt content than a "standard" blend.

Stylistically, there has been a gradual shift from full-bodied, peaty blends towards lighter-bodied whiskies such as Cutty Sark *(see p127)* and J&B *(see p137)*. The blender may use a higher proportion of lighter malts, perhaps from Speyside, in order to create such a blend, and may also reduce the percentage of malt used and increase the amount of grain spirit.

Most blenders are employed by comparatively large companies which own several distilleries. For the sake of economics and availability, they are expected to use sizeable amounts of their "house" malts in the blends they create. However, they will also acquire malts from other companies, usually by way of "reciprocal trading" of stocks,

In assessing whiskies, the nose is the blender's most valuable tool.

Blending whisky is all about balance – combining whiskies, often with markedly different characters, into a harmonious ensemble.

with no money changing hands. It is only a very few large distillers that are sufficiently well resourced to be self-sufficient in terms of both malt and grain whiskies.

The blender will usually utilize a number of different grain whiskies to help achieve harmony in the blend, and none of today's generation of blenders regard grain whisky as merely a cheap "filler" to bulk out the blend, as was sometimes the case in days gone by. Grains are recognized as crucially important in drawing together the various malts and allowing their best qualities to shine.

THE COMPONENTS OF A BLEND

Blenders tend to categorize the component malts in their blends as "packers", "core malts", and "top dressing". The "packers" may make up half the malt content of the blend and add bulk to it. They are chosen to combine well with the other malts, but without adding a great deal in terms of final flavour. "Core malts" are often from distilleries owned by the blender's own company, and tend to define the overall character of the finished blend. "Top dressing" malts are high-quality whiskies that are used for adding depth and "top notes" to the mix.

A traditional Scotch blend is normally constructed around a mix of high-quality Speyside malts, which may make up approximately 50 per cent of the malt total. Some 10 per cent of Highland and Islay malts are added to "dry out" the blend and add complexity, though the powerful Islays rarely contribute more than two per cent of the malt total or their effect is too dominant. The remaining 40 per cent of the malt component are "packers". These are decent malts, but have a low aromatic intensity – the "supporting cast" of the malt world.

In most instances, the selected casks of malt and grain whisky are "dumped" into a stainless-steel trough at the blending plant in accordance with the blend recipe. From there, they are transferred to a large blending vat, usually of around 25,000 litres (5,500 gallons), for thorough mixing. Demineralized water is then added to reduce the blend to bottling strength, generally 40 or 43 per cent ABV. "Rough filtration" to remove particles of char from the casks is followed, in most cases, by chill-filtration, during which the temperature of the spirit is reduced to around 0°C (32°F) and passed through a fine filter. This practice removes compounds in the whisky which might cause it to go slightly dull or cloudy when ice or water is added. Small quantities of spirit caramel are sometimes added to ensure consistency of colour from one batch of whisky to another.

Some companies will initially blend all their malts together and then add their blended grains. A number of firms maintain the old practice of "marrying" their blends for a number of months prior to bottling, either in well-used, inert casks or stainless-steel

Whyte & Mackay take the art of blending very seriously, marrying their malts before mixing with the grain, then marrying all prior to bottling.

vats. Whyte & Mackay take this a stage further, however, by maturing their component malts in wood for several months before blending them with the grain whisky. They then marry the resultant blend for a further period before bottling.

The blender is not able to nose every component cask destined for a blend, but in most cases, casks are nosed prior to dumping by a member of the company's "nosing panel", who will also assess each vatting. Samples of the whiskies will also undergo laboratory tests to ensure they are "fit for purpose".

INDEPENDENT BOTTLINGS

Today, most whisky, whether malt or blended, is bottled by its producers, in what are usually known as "house" bottlings. However, this practice is

THE BLENDER'S ART

"I compare a blender to a conductor or a musical arranger. The arranger will use his stringed instruments for melody, and the blender will use certain flavours such as fruity, floral, nutty, malty, fragrant, honey, for his theme. The arranger will use the woodwind section for his harmonies, and the blender's harmonies will be flavours such as leafy, grassy, spicy. The arranger also has his brass section and percussion to complete the composition. This could be compared to the blender's flavours such as peaty, smoky, and medicinal. Each arranger has in his own mind what his ear will hear as the finished symphony, so it is with the blender as to how his finished blend will impart aroma and flavour."
Retired Chivas master blender Jimmy Laing

Chivas Regal 18-Year-Old Blend

comparatively new. For a long time, it was principally independent bottling companies, such as Gordon & MacPhail in Elgin *(see p52)* and Cadenhead in Campbeltown, that undertook the bottlings of malt – sometimes on behalf of distillers, but more usually on their own initiative.

With the renaissance of malt whisky in the past two decades, the number of independent bottlers has grown, and now includes well known names such as Adelphi, Duncan Taylor, Signatory and the Scotch Malt Whisky Society, in addition to long-established companies like Hart Bros and Douglas Laing of Glasgow.

One effect of this development is that, with increasing competition among "independents" and a tendency for large distillers to bottle more of their own malt themselves, good casks of malt whisky have become increasingly scarce and hard to purchase. This has led bottlers like Signatory and Ian Macleod Distillers Ltd to acquire their own distilleries – Edradour *(see p82)* and Glengoyne *(see p84)*, respectively – in order to secure supplies for their own use and for reciprocal trading.

In order to differentiate their expressions from those of the major distillers and offer consumers a greater degree of choice, a number of independents have opted to bottle "single cask" whiskies, taken, as the name, implies, from just one cask. These are usually individually numbered and are often bottled at natural cask strength.

Some bottlers also make a virtue of not chill-filtering their whiskies, as the process removes compounds produced during distillation or extracted from the cask during maturation, and in so doing also removes some body and flavour. In order to emphasize the "natural" credentials of their product, independents also tend to avoid the addition of caramel. Many of the whiskies bottled by independents come from silent or demolished distilleries or

CLASSIC COCKTAILS

The purists may shake their heads in dismay, but let them – a great whisky cocktail is a joy and a revelation as new layers of flavour in your favourite dram are there to be discovered, complemented by the other ingredients. You probably won't use your finest single malt, but don't economize on ingredients. A number of well-known brands and whisky styles lend themselves admirably to the cocktails we've selected, and their recipes can be found in the section on Whisky Nations, close to the whiskies that have been recommended for use:

Blue Blazer *(see p130)*
Buffalo and Ginger *(see p189)*
Canada Day Cocktail *(see p224)*
Flying Scotsman *(see p141)*
Game Bird *(see p132)*
Irish Coffee *(see p161)*
Ladies *(see p233)*
Maker's Mark Bourbon Manhattan *(see p198)*
Maple Leaf *(see p231)*
Mint Julep *(see p201)*
Rabbie Burns *(see p150)*
Rob Roy *(see p151)*
Turkey Collins *(see p199)*
Williamstown *(see p165)*

are marketed at ages significantly greater than is commonly the case.

A few whisky producers object to independent bottlers using their distillery names, reckoning that they have insufficient control over the quality of the whisky. In response, some independents bottle whiskies with code numbers rather than names, along with information that hints at their origins. This practice was first adopted by the Scotch Malt Whisky Society of Edinburgh, which was set up in 1983 to offer cask strength, single cask malts at a time when the notion of such "pure" bottlings was still rare.

NOSING AND TASTING

There is an enduring school of thought that considers that whisky should only be drunk neat. It tends to prevail more in Scotland than elsewhere, but still has the status of received wisdom. In fact, a modest amount of pure still water is beneficial.

Water served at room temperature can help to tease out aromas and flavours that might otherwise remain hidden in the whisky. But, apart from adding water, just how should whisky be drunk? The short answer is any way you choose. You paid for it, so you can consume it however you wish. One of the principal growth markets for Scotch whisky is China, where a fashion has developed for drinking whisky with green tea. Nonetheless, many connoisseurs consider an expensive malt whisky or small-batch bourbon to be spoilt by the addition of anything but a small amount of water.

Nosing is the best way to evaluate whisky, as our sense of smell is greater than our sense of taste.

For distillers there are many checks and comparisons to make beyond aroma and taste, including the viscosity and colour of the whisky.

It is important to serve whisky in a glass that will do it justice, and for purposes of evaluation and comparison a stemmed *copita*, or tulip-shaped glass that tapers towards the top, is ideal. This serves to hold in the aromas, making it much easier to detect and analyse components by smell.

COLOUR, NOSE, PALATE, AND FINISH

Professional tasters usually evaluate whisky using four factors: colour, nose, palate, and finish. The colour of a whisky should give clues to the type of cask in which it has been matured. If it is a deep rich copper colour, it has probably come from a European oak cask, formerly used to hold sherry. A pale, straw-coloured whisky is likely to have been matured in an American white oak cask that previously held bourbon. Look at the "legs" of the whisky as it rolls down the side of the glass. A well aged, full-bodied whisky will have "longer" legs than a younger, light-bodied style of spirit.

A vocabulary of eight broad terms has been developed to describe aromas: namely cereal, fruity, floral, peaty, feinty, sulphury, winey, and woody. However, for the untrained nose, this part of the process may be principally about evocation: for example, a whiff of worn leather that transports the sampler back in time to childhood trips in an old car, or the smell of seaweed and tarry ropes that evoke the memory of a harbour.

In terms of taste and what is termed "mouth-feel", professionals may use the adjectives sweet, sour, salty, bitter, warming, cooling, prickly, viscous, and cloying. The "finish" is the lingering flavour of the whisky in the mouth after it has been swallowed. Generally speaking, a long, lingering finish is a desirable feature, though some light-bodied whiskies benefit from a finish that is short and crisp.

During a tasting lids are put on top of the glasses to hold in the aromas eminating from the whisky.

After an initial nosing, it may pay to take a small, preliminary sip of whisky undiluted, in order to give a "baseline". Then add just a few drops of water before nosing again. Follow up with a second, comparative sip. It is also often instructive to leave the whisky to stand for a few moments after your initial assessment. Sometimes it is surprizing just how much the sample changes after exposure to the air.

When diluting whisky, try to be consistent and dilute to the same degree. Comparisons can be made much more accurately that way. Younger and lighter-bodied whiskies will usually stand up to less dilution than older and big-bodied spirits. Also, beware the power of suggestion. If undertaking an informal tasting session with friends, it is advisable to ask each sampler to write down his or her reactions before discussing them. Smoking and wearing perfume should be discouraged, and it is advisable not to eat garlic or chilli sauce before tasting! The more you practise, the keener your skills of whisky assessment will become. And, most importantly, remember that the whole process should be about enjoyment and fruitful experimentation.

Whisky tasting glasses hold in the aroma of the spirit and also echo the shape of a pot still.

WHISKY AND FOOD

For many years it was widely held that whisky was too strong, assertive, and complex a drink to accompany food. But an increasing number of connoisseurs have come to realize that this need not be the case. Many whiskies can enhance meals, provided careful choices are made.

Consider the essential characteristics of a specific whisky and decide which dishes it is likely to complement. A fresh, light-bodied Lowland single malt would probably pair well with a fish dish, while a heavier, more aromatic whisky may be the perfect partner for beef or duck. Some of the lighter, fruitier Japanese whiskies, such as Yamazaki, are now being successfully pared with tuna and salmon in sushi and sashimi dishes – often being served slightly chilled. The secret to getting it right is in balancing the competing flavours and not allowing either the food or the whisky to dominate. A smoky, peaty, or peppery whisky is ideal with oysters and smoked fish, but contrasts such as "sweet and sour" may be equally effective. Chilli heat can be matched to sweetness, or an acidic whisky can cut through a very sweet dish. The same acidic match will also serve to neutralize excessive fat or richness.

A big, smoky, peaty, peppery whisky such as Talisker, from Skye, is ideal with seafood like oysters and smoked fish.

GREAT WHISKY NATIONS

SCOTLAND

"A compound distilled spirit, being drawn on aromaticks; and the Irish sort is particularly distinguished for its pleasant and mild flavour. The Highland sort is somewhat hotter and by corruption in Scottish they call it whisky."

This early description of whisky appeared in Dr Johnson's famous dictionary of 1755. The word came from the Gaelic *uisge beatha* (pronounced "oosh-key-ba"), meaning water of life, which the Scots had been making for years. With a long tradition of brewing, they may have discovered distilling by accident, while boiling up some heather ale that had gone bad perhaps. Or maybe they learnt it from the Irish monks, who brought the secret with them when they sailed to Iona with St Columba in the 6th century.

The first official mention of spirit produced in Scotland came in an exchequer roll of 1494, and concerned Friar John Cor, of Fife. There were soon references from across the country, as distilling spread to wherever there was access to grain, water, and fuel to fire the stills. Whisky making developed on the farm as a seasonal activity, whenever there was grain to spare after the harvest.

Drunk neat and unaged, the whisky would have been extremely rough, hence the need to compound it with sugar, herbs, and spices. Yet, it was definitely malt whisky, in the sense that it was distilled in a copper pot still. It was by no means exclusive to the Highlands either – there were said to be 400 stills in Edinburgh by the late 18th century – though it started to move that way as the Government sought to control whisky making through licences and taxes.

When Scotland and England were joined under the Act of Union in 1707, it was decided that excise duty would be the main source of revenue. The English authorities proceeded cautiously at first, waiting 10 years after the Jacobite Rising of 1715 before they increased the tax on malt, which provoked rioting on the streets of Glasgow. With each subsequent move to raise revenue and stamp out smuggling, whisky became more and more the spirit of defiance.

LOWLANDS v HIGHLANDS

In the Lowlands, distilling was part of the early industrial revolution, as commercial distilleries grew in scale to provide whisky for the masses. Laws came in to increase the minimum size of the stills, presumably to make them more visible to the authorities, while taxation was so heavy that many distillers had to run their stills flat out to make any profit at all. The result, according to one contemporary, was a spirit suitable only for "the most vulgar and fire-loving palates".

Granite, heather, and location all play their part in creating the extraordinary diversity of Scottish malt whisky.

Macallan Distillery began to market its single malt in 1978; in keeping with trends in the industry, it now produces a variety of oak finishes for its malts.

The Highlands were another world, a place untouched by revolutions in farming or the industrial world, where distilling remained a cottage industry. From a weak wash slowly distilled in relatively small stills, the Highlanders produced whisky that would have been infinitely superior to the industrial spirit pumped out by the big Lowland distillers. The production was on a very small scale, just enough to provide for family, neighbours, and any passing trade. The more successful farm distilleries were often near droving routes, where cattle were taken from high pastures to market.

This national difference was recognized by the Government in the Wash Act of 1784. Henceforth, Highland distillers would be excused malt tax and could use smaller stills so long as they did not try to export their whisky below the "Highland Line". Inevitably, it did seep southwards as demand grew. The licensed, tax-paying distillers were incensed and claimed that the production of moonshine was 10 times that of legal whisky.

The crackdown that followed, as the Government tried to claw back its lost revenue and bring the Highlands to heal, only served to raise the price of illicit whisky. A nefarious activity turned into a profitable business. In the early 1800s, Glenlivet became a one-industry glen almost overnight, with plumes of smoke rising from every isolated bothy.

CHANGES IN THE LAW

The odds seemed firmly in favour of the illicit whisky makers rather than the poorly paid excisemen who were drafted in from outside to stamp out smuggling. The Government's initiatives were often not rigorously enough thought through, and the offer of £5 to anyone who handed in a piece of distilling equipment

Glenfiddich Distillery, founded by William Grant in the 1880s, pioneered the sale of malt whisky to an international market in the 1960s.

was quickly seized upon by the makers of moonshine as a way to pay for replacement parts. But, with more troops, the authorities gradually began to drive the underground industry deeper into the Highlands.

The real change came with the Excise Act of 1823, when illicit distillers were offered the chance to go straight by taking out a £10 licence. Within two years, the number of licensed distillers leapt from 111 to 263. Smuggling continued for some time, but the balance now lay in favour of legal whisky, and it was in the interests of the majority of distillers to create what became the modern whisky industry.

Suddenly, it was no longer an advantage to be hidden in some desolate farmstead. It was far more important to be near a market. As a result, the first building boom of new distilleries was in Campbeltown, on Kintyre, which was a short boat ride up the Firth of Clyde to Glasgow.

By the second half of the 19th century, the "market" for malt whisky had become the blenders, who were often licensed grocers, such as the Chivas brothers in Aberdeen. Using a base of grain whisky made in a continuous still, the blenders mixed in malt whisky and developed their own house style. With entrepreneurial flair, the advent of mass communication, and modern bottling lines, some of these early blends became internationally recognized brands.

THE BIRTH OF SINGLE MALTS

The story of Scotch is often portrayed as a conflict between blended whisky and malts, but the reality was rather different.

The blenders created the demand for Scotch, first in England and then abroad, and it was this that inspired the late-Victorian distillery boom that engulfed the Highlands, particularly Speyside. The big blenders often bought or built their own distilleries as their brands grew – though they were rarely, if ever, self-sufficient in malt.

The long-lived Black & White brand once had Dalwhinnie malt at the heart of its blend.

Malt distilleries became part of the food chain supplying the blends. Apart from friends of the distillery manager and a tiny band of devotees, the world never got to hear about single malts. Malt whisky had, of course, been made in Scotland for over three centuries before anyone had even thought of blending it, but in the modern, commercial sense it was an invention of the 1960s.

Glenfiddich led the way, selling its first bottle of malt in England in 1965. Slowly, other distilleries, such as Macallan and Glenmorangie, began to bottle their single malts, until eventually the great white whale of the whisky business – DCL (now Diageo) – decided to create their own "Classic Malts" in the late 1980s.

Even then, there were plenty who thought the robust flavours of malt whisky would be too much for anyone beyond the wilds of Scotland. The thought that it would catch on among American bankers, Spanish students, and Taiwanese businessmen seemed absurd. Yet, that's exactly what happened.

REGIONAL STYLES

If early distilleries developed a regional style, it was because they were supplying the local market. Whisky had somehow to reflect the environment. A distillery like Talisker, on Skye, could have produced a gentle, understated malt like Glenkinchie, but few would have bought it – the windswept people of the Western Isles needed something more robust.

It was the blenders who split Scotland into different styles of malt, to help standardize their blends. This "regionality" endures today, even if there are plenty of exceptions.

Skye's Talisker Distillery produces a strong tasting whisky that's peppery and smoky.

SPEYSIDE

Whisky distilleries are scattered throughout the Highlands, but when you reach Speyside they come at you thick and fast, with around 50 distilleries. Some are set in open country, while others cluster together in towns such as Rothes, Keith, and Dufftown.

There are several reasons why this region has become so synonymous with whisky making, and the first lies in the landscape itself. In winter, traditionally the best time for making whisky, Speyside seems to close in on itself behind the granite bulk of the Cairngorms. Not so long ago, isolated glens like Glenlivet would be cut off for months. But there was plenty of fresh spring water, sufficient barley, and enough peat with which to malt the barley and fire the stills for whisky making.

To these raw ingredients was added the incentive of defiance. After the Jacobite Rising of 1745 *(see p45)*, the Catholic religion and wearing national dress such as the kilt were suppressed. It was, therefore, not surprising that the Scots turned to whisky – and that meant illicitly produced whisky that the excisemen would find hard to trace. The fact that this home-produced spirit contributed not a penny in tax to prop up the regime "down south" made it taste all the sweeter. As an Irishman once said of poteen, it is "superior in sweetness, salubriety, and gusto to all that machinery, science, and capital can produce in the legalised way." Doubtless this was true of the Highland spirit also.

Demand for smuggled Speyside whisky, particularly if it came with the magic word "Glenlivet" attached to it, only increased as the Government cracked down on illicit stills elsewhere.

THE INDUSTRIAL AGE

This romantic image endured long after whisky making moved out of the farm and became a serious industry after the Excise Act of 1823 *(see p47)*. In truth, however, it was the advent of the railways that really led to Speyside's distillery boom in the late 19th century. Before then the region was seriously disadvantaged by its distance from the major blenders. Those in Glasgow had a much closer source of malt whisky in Campbeltown on the Kintyre Peninsula.

Eventually the quality and consistency of Speyside won the blenders over and, since the 1890s, the region has provided the lion's share of Scotch malt whisky.

Glenlivet was one of the first Speyside distilleries to forge a strong identity, and to this day its malts are among the most famous in the world.

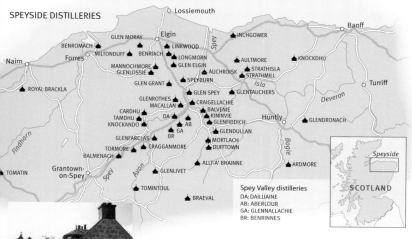

SPEYSIDE DISTILLERIES

Lossiemouth
Elgin
Banff
GLEN MORAY
BENROMACH
LINKWOOD
INCHGOWER
Forres
MILTONDUFF
BENRIACH
LONGMORN
AULTMORE
KNOCKDHU
Nairn
MANNOCHMORE
GLEN ELGIN
AUCHROISK
STRATHISLA
GLENLOSSIE
STRATHMILL
ROYAL BRACKLA
GLEN GRANT
SPEYBURN
GLEN SPEY
GLENTAUCHERS
Turriff
GLENROTHES
CRAIGELLACHIE
MACALLAN
BALVENIE
CARDHU
DA
KININVIE
GLENDRONACH
TAMDHU
AB
GLENFIDDICH
Huntly
KNOCKANDO
GA
GLENDULLAN
GLENFARCLAS
BR
MORTLACH
TORMORE
CRAGGANMORE
DUFFTOWN
BALMENACH
ALLT-A' BHAINNE
ARDMORE
TOMATIN
Grantown-
on-Spey
GLENLIVET
TOMINTOUL
BRAEVAL

Findhorn · Spey · Avon · Spey · Isla · Deveron · Bogie

Spey Valley distilleries
DA: DAILUAINE
AB: ABERLOUR
GA: GLENALLACHIE
BR: BENRINNES

Speyside

SCOTLAND

Aberlour was rebuilt at the end of the 19th century, after a fire destroyed the previous distillery.

ABERLOUR

✉ Aberlour, Banffshire
⌨ www.aberlour.co.uk
⛴ Open to visitors

The village of Aberlour was established in 1812 on the east bank of the Spey, close to where it is joined by the Lour, or "chattering burn". A Druid community based here and dating back to the Bronze Age was converted to Christianity by St Drostan in the 6th century. He is said to have used the local well to baptise his flock, and, centuries later, it was the pure spring waters of St Drostan's Well that attracted the first whisky makers.

What was originally the Aberlour-Glenlivet Distillery was founded by James Fleming in 1879. The son of a tenant farmer born in 1830, Fleming knew the local distilleries well, having been a grain merchant supplying them with barley. With the growing popularity of Scotch whisky, he decided to set up on his own. He soon found himself up before the High Court in London, along with half the distillers on Speyside, to defend his use of the "Glenlivet" suffix – a case that was eventually won.

Despite Aberlour being described as "a perfect modern distillery" following a visit by the eminent whisky writer Alfred Barnard *(see p50)* in the 1880s, Fleming sold out to his agent R Thorne & Sons of Greenock a few years later. Fleming became a local benefactor, paying for the village community hall and leaving money to fund a hospital and a bridge across the Spey. His motto, "Let the Deed Show", is displayed on every bottle of Aberlour.

In 1898 the distillery was badly damaged in a fire, most of its stocks being lost in the process. Charles Doig of Elgin *(see p59)*, the architect responsible for so many distilleries on Speyside, was commissioned to rebuild Aberlour into more or less what you see today.

Since World War II, as part of Campbell Distillers and now Pernod Ricard, Aberlour has supplied the heart of the Clan Campbell blend. In recent decades more emphasis has been put on Aberlour as a 10-year-old single malt, aged in a mix of bourbon and sherry casks. Sold in over 60 countries, it is particularly popular in France – the biggest malt whisky market in the world.

🍶 **ABERLOUR 10-YEAR-OLD** 40% ABV
Clean and fresh on the nose with a trace of pears and bubblegum, smooth and slightly spicy in the mouth, drying on the finish.

🍶 **ABERLOUR A'BUNADH**
A cask strength from selected Oloroso sherry butts, this is a rich, sumptuous full-bodied malt, with notes of ginger and dark chocolate.

ALLT A' BHAINNE

✉ Glenrinnes, Dufftown, Banffshire

From a distance, there is little to suggest any whisky is made in this modern, flat-roofed building a few miles south of Dufftown. It could be a sports centre or executive flats, but surely not a distillery? The name is Gaelic for

Aberlour a'bunadh

"the milk burn", which flows close by and is the place where local dairy farmers used to wash their equipment after milking – which presumably turned the water cloudy.

Allt a' Bhainne was built by Seagram in 1975 for £2.7 million as a super-efficient production unit. Its purpose in life is to supply malt for blends, specifically Chivas Regal (see p124) and 100 Pipers (see p118), though there are occasional independent bottlings of Allt a'Bhaine as a single malt. The distillery's current owners, Pernod Ricard, found it surplus to requirement in 2002, and its was closed. But three years later it was cranked back to life and is now running at full capacity.

AUCHROISK

✉ **Mulben, Banffshire**

Like Allt a'Bhainne Distillery, Auchroisk – pronounced "Ath-rusk", and meaning the "ford across the red stream" in Gaelic – is another modern plant, having been built in 1975. For this one, however, the

---

architects went for a more interesting design. At the front of the building is a curious, small turret where the yeast is stored; it pokes through the roof like the head of a rocket. Auchroisk was built to supply malt for the top-selling J&B blend, and its location, like that of all distilleries, was dictated by having a reliable source of pure water – in this case a spring called Dorrie's Well above Rothes.

A decade later it was decided to bottle the malt as a 10-year-old – called "The Singleton of Auchroisk" to help whisky drinkers get their tongue round the name. Now branded simply as "Auchroisk", it continues as a relatively rare single malt that is mellow, medium-bodied, and faintly herbal in style.

AULTMORE

✉ **Keith, Banffshire**

With the late Victorian whisky boom in full swing, Alexander Edward established the Aultmore Distillery in 1895 on the flatlands between Keith and the sea. He was already well-established in the business, having, with Peter Mackie,

---

Aultmore's stills provide whisky for John Dewar & Sons, and occasional single malt bottlings.

built Craigellachie Distillery (see p55). Before that, he had helped his father run Benrinnes Distillery.

Aultmore 12-Year-Old

In 1898 he acquired Oban, and renamed his company Oban and Aultmore-Glenlivet Distilleries Ltd. His aim was to supply malts to big blenders such as Pattisons (see p142), but the timing proved terrible. Pattisons went bankrupt at the end of the same year, almost destroying the entire Scotch whisky industry. Aultmore had barely recovered before distilling was banned during World War I, and in 1923 the distillery was bought by John Dewar & Sons, with whose blends it has been associated ever since. Occasional independent bottlings of a gentle, smoke-scented, aromatic single malt can be found.

BALMENACH

✉ **Cromdale, Grantown-on-Spey, Morayshire**

In the early 1800s James McGregor and his two brothers took a lease on

Balmenach farm. It lay in a dip in the hills between the Upper Spey and its tributary the Avon, near the village of Cromdale – scene of an early Jacobite battle in 1690. James is said to have established an illicit still before taking out a license in 1824. The distillery was described as "among the most primitive in Scotland" by Alfred Barnard after his visit in the 1880s.

Its chimney stack blew down on 28 December 1879, crashing through the roof and rupturing the stills. Miraculously the whole place did not explode, though if it had it would hardly have made the front page the next day – the same storm blew down the Tay Bridge sending all 75 passengers and crew aboard the Edinburgh train to their death.

Today, after a period in "mothballs" in the 1990s, the distillery is back in action, supplying blends and the occasional independent bottling as a single malt.

BALVENIE

✉ Dufftown, Keith, Banffshire
🖰 www.balvenie.com
🚪 By appointment only

Within six years of building Glenfiddich in 1886, William Grant felt ready to invest in a new distillery next door.

Balvenie, which cost £2,000 to build, was a measure of Grant's confidence in the whisky trade. He knew that there were many blenders now desperate for Speyside malts, as a fire at Glenlivet Distillery in 1891 had destroyed all its stocks. He also knew that he needed to protect his water supply, having heard that a local man was considering taking a lease on land next to Glenfiddich to build a distillery. Had he succeeded he would have been entitled to half the available water.

As with Glenfiddich, whose stills were bought second-hand from Cardhu, Grant looked around for a bargain. On hearing that there might be an old mash tun for sale, if somewhat larger than he wanted, Grant scribbled a gruff note to his son: "Don't be afraid of the depth of the mash-tun if otherwise suitable – a man does not need to piss his pot full unless he likes."

The stills came from Glen Albyn in Inverness and Lagavulin on Islay. Their tall-necked design has been faithfully copied ever since.

Balvenie Doublewood 12-Year-Old

Balvenie was originally distilled within Balvenie House – a Georgian manor house that was eventually knocked down in the 1920s.

By then William Grant & Sons were bottling their own blends, such as Grant's Finest and Standfast (named after the battle cry of Clan Gant). The stones from the old manor house were used to build a new malt barn, where the grain was malted and dried above a kiln.

Today Balvenie is the only distillery on Speyside to have retained its floor maltings. As a result, smoke still seeps out from the original pagoda roof, giving the distillery a real traditional feel, even if most of the barley is brought in already malted to supply the needs of the eight stills.

🍸 **BALVENIE DOUBLEWOOD**
12-YEAR-OLD 43% ABV
After years in a bourbon barrel, the whisky is finished off in a first-fill sherry cask to give a sweet, sumptuous malt with a nutty-spicy character. Doublewood has replaced the original 10-year-old. Plenty of older expressions are aged in different casks.

Balmenach Distillery is working once again, having fallen silent in the 1990s.

BENRIACH

✉ Longmorn, Elgin, Morayshire
🖥 www.benriachdistillery.co.uk

Having built Longmorn near Elgin in 1894, John Duff decided to add a sister distillery four years later. Benriach operated for just three seasons, supplying malt whisky to the Pattisons *(see p142)*, the biggest blenders of their day. When Pattisons went bust, Benriach promptly shut down and remained closed for the next 65 years.

It only survived because no-one wanted to build a supermarket or car park on the site, and because its floor maltings were kept going in order to supply Longmorn next door. The distillery was brought back to life in the 1960s only to be mothballed again in 2002.

It was bought two years later by an independent consortium led by Billy Walker, a veteran of the whisky industry. Today Benriach is available as a floral, honey-scented 12-year-old and richer, darker malts up to a 40-year-old. There are also a couple of heavily peated, Islay-style whiskies called "Curiositas" and "Authenticus".

Benriach Authenticus

Glenfarclas *(see pp59 & 61)*. Its six stills are worked in tandem in a type of triple distillation that, after 15 years of maturation in sherry casks, produces a sumptuous, plum-pudding style single malt, occasionally available in the Flora & Fauna range.

BENROMACH

✉ Forres, Morayshire
🖥 www.benromach.com

Whatever else one can say about Benromach, this small distillery in the market town of Forres is certainly a survivor. It was established in 1898 by FW Brickmann, a spirit broker from Leith, and Duncan Macallum of the Glen Nevis Distillery in Campbeltown. Together they hired the famous distillery architect Charles Doig *(see p59)*. Benromach struggled on through the great whisky crash of 1900, two world wars, US Prohibition, and the 1930s Depression more or less in one piece. It changed hands many times along on the way, however, at one point being owned by National Distillers of America, whose stable included Old Crow and Old Granddad *(see p216)*. In 1953 it became part of the Distillers Company (DCL), Benromach's sixth owner.

With just two stills and a production of half a million litres (110,000 gallons) of pure alcohol a year, it always suffered from its size, and on 24 March 1983 it shut down, seemingly for good. The eight distillery workers on duty that day signed their names on the

GORDON & MACPHAIL

Benromach Distillery was bought and reopened by Gordon & MacPhail in 1993.

Founded in 1895, Gordon & MacPhail is a food and wine merchants based in Elgin on Speyside. Part of that business has always been the supply of quality whisky, and for Gordon & MacPhail that means independent bottling. More or less since its inception, the company has had a policy of buying new make spirit from distilleries and maturing it themselves – at least partly in their own warehouses – in casks that they have selected. The whisky is bottled only when they consider it to be at its best level of maturation. Currently, they work with around 80 different malts and offer somewhere in the region of 400 expressions of single malts, as well as some of their own blends.

BENRINNES

✉ Aberlour, Banffshire

The hump-backed shape of Ben Rinnes, heather-clad in summer and bare and bleak-looking in winter is a prominent landmark on Speyside. For years its many springs have provided local whisky makers with crystal-clear water, so it is only right that this hill should have a distillery named after it.

The original distillery was called Lyne of Rutherie and was first licensed by Peter McKenzie in 1834. It was renamed Benrinnes in 1842, and after various changes in ownership was bought by David Edward in 1864. His son Alexander later founded the Craigellachie *(see p55)* and Aultmore *(p50)* distilleries.

Being located 200 m (700 ft) up on the north-facing slope of Ben Rinnes, it shares the same feeling of remoteness as Glenlivet and

Benromach Traditional

Cardhu, once the spiritual home of Johnny Walker, now releases most of its output as a single malt.

filling room wall. The stills were ripped out and the building left empty to await potential developers. Ten years passed before the distillery was finally bought by Gordon & MacPhail, one of Scotland's leading independent bottlers.

Eventually, having overcome some major structural problems –which included having to dig up most of Forres to repair the pipe supplying spring water – the distillery was officially reopened by Prince Charles in its centenary year, 1998.

🎗 **BENROMACH TRADITIONAL**
40% ABV • Launched in 2004, this straw-coloured whisky has a herbal, malty flavour with a whiff of peat smoke.

BRAEVAL

✉ Nr Dufftown, Keith, Banffshire

The Braes of Glenlivet were a hotbed of smuggling in the twilight years before whisky came in from the cold and went legal in the 1820s. It was the name chosen in the 1970s by Seagram for a modern distillery, over 300 m (1000 ft) up and a short drive from Tomintoul. In keeping with the romance, the outside design is traditional, with a decorative pagoda strapped to the roof. This may, in part, have been to

emphasize that it was Scotch not bourbon being made here – its then sister distillery was Four Roses in Kentucky.

Edgar Bronfmann, heir to the mighty Seagram empire, cut the soil in 1972 and within a year the first spirit flowed. The name became Braeval when the company acquired Glenlivet five years later, and since then it has remained somewhat in the shadow of its more famous neighbour. Now part of Chivas Brothers *(see p126),* little if any Braeval is bottled as a single malt.

CAPERDONICH

✉ Rothes, Morayshire

Major James Grant decided to build Caperdonich in Rothes in 1897. It was to be a replica of its successful neighbour Glen Grant Distillery, which had been built by his father and uncle in 1840. Indeed it was initially called Glen Grant No. 2, and used the same shaped stills and source of grain to replicate the exact same spirit. The authorities even insisted that it had to pass through Glen Grant's spirits safe via an overhead

pipe, which, according to folklore, was occasionally tapped into by thirsty locals.

If true, that only happened for three years, because the new distillery shut down in 1901, as if for good. It finally reopened as Caperdonich in 1965, and capacity was doubled to 4 stills two years later. Its owners have never bottled it as a single malt, though there are occasional offerings from independent bottlers.

Cardhu 12-Year-Old

CARDHU

✉ Knockando, Aberlour, Banffshire
⛴ Open to visitors

In around 1810, John Cumming took a lease on Cardow farm near Knockando and soon began making whisky as a sideline to the farming. His wife, Helen, was in on the act too, and used to sell flagons of illicit whisky through the farmhouse kitchen window. She was said to be forever baking cakes known as bannocks to disguise the smell of fermenting barley, as well as to have something to offer any visiting excisemen. While they were tucking in

CARDHU AND THE PURE MALT RUMPUS

Thanks to its huge following in Spain, Cardhu almost became a victim of it own success in recent years. Between 1997 and 2002, sales grew by 100,000 cases and demand was set to outstrip supply. Rather than raise the price to restrict demand, Cardhu's owners, Diageo, embarked on a different course – one that was to cause the biggest storm to hit the whisky industry for decades, with public cries of betrayal and questions raised in Parliament.

Cardhu Distillery and its prized malt whisky were at the heart of the dispute between Diageo and Glenfiddich.

It centred on the decision to re-christen the brand Cardhu Pure Malt and allow similar Speyside malts into the mix. Unleashed from being tied to a single distillery, it could expand production and potentially overtake Glenfiddich within 10 years to become the biggest selling malt of all. Not surprisingly Glenfiddich's owners were extremely alarmed and led a full-scale campaign to force Diageo into a humiliating climb-down and the removal of Pure Malt in March 2003.

to their tea, Helen would run into the yard and raise a red flag to warn any passing trade not to approach.

Meanwhile, her husband was often out smuggling and had a string of convictions to prove it. Years after he went legal and started operating as a licensed distiller in 1824, these convictions were framed and hung on the walls of the distillery manager's office. Cardhu continued to operate as a small farm distillery for the next 60 years.

By then, John's daughter-in-law Elizabeth Cumming was in charge. She remained so even after selling the distillery to John Walker & Sons in 1893. She was known as the "Queen of the whisky trade", and reached the ripe old age of 95. In the 1880s, Elizabeth oversaw the complete rebuilding of Cardhu. The old stills, badly worn and patched up, were taken out and sold to William Grant to start his own distillery. That was Glenfiddich, the distillery with whom Cardhu would have a very public spat some 120 years later (see above).

Cardhu was rebuilt in the 1960s, more or less in keeping with the original design, and was known as the spiritual home of Johnnie Walker, since that is where most of the malt ended up. Today barely a teaspoon escapes into blends, such is the demand for Cardhu as a single malt, which, in the UK, is only available at the distillery.

🍶 **CARDHU 12-YEAR-OLD** 40% ABV
This smooth sweet-scented Speyside malt is very approachable, if not overly complex.

CRAGGANMORE

✉ **Ballindalloch, Banffshire**
🖥 **www.malts.com**
🚪 **Open to visitors**

When John Smith decided to set out on his own, he was one of the most experienced distillers on Speyside. Said to be the illegitimate son of George Smith – the man who founded Glenlivet in 1824 – John had managed

both Glenfarclas and Macallan. By 1870, he clearly felt ready to establish a distillery of his own, which he positioned at an old smuggler's bothy (hut) on the east bank of the Spey.

His plans were well-conceived, starting with the water source, which was the pure spring-fed Craggan burn (which also provided the distillery's power, via a water wheel, right up until 1950). He was close to good-quality barley and peat with which to malt. Crucially, he was also near Ballandalloch station, and Cragganmore became the first distillery in Scotland to be built beside a railway with its own siding.

Besides whisky, trains were the other great passion in Smith's life – though, weighing in at 22 stone (140 kilos), he was a little too large to squeeze through the carriage doors, and so

Cragganmore 12-Year-Old

sat in the guard's van instead. Sadly he

died in 1886, a year before the first Whisky Special rolled out of Ballandalloch laden with Scotch.

John's son, Gordon Smith, took over, and in 1901 hired the leading distillery architect of his day, Charles Doig of Elgin *(see p59)*, to rebuild Cragganmore. But for a few new warehouses and a doubling of the original pair of stills, the place has changed little over the years. With its outbuildings arranged in a compact cluster, it has the self-contained feel of a small Highland distillery. Inside is the curious feature of two spirit stills, whose necks, rather than rising up like an elegant swan's, are lopped off halfway up. In the past, people speculated that this was to fit them in under the roof, but it seems unlikely that Smith made such an obvious mistake. Whatever the case, the design is always faithfully copied every time a still needs replacing for fear of altering the spirit's character.

Nor would anyone tamper with the old-fashioned worm tubs outside, which are used for condensing the spirit. With less copper contact than a modern condenser, a meatier, more complex spirit is derived. Today Cragganmore represents the

region within Diageo's six Classic Malts, which is quite an accolade given how many Speyside distilleries the company owns.

CRAGGANMORE 12-YEAR-OLD
40% ABV ● An intriguing herbal bouquet with a trace of honey and vanilla gives way to malty flavours in the mouth and a whiff of smoke on the finish.

CRAIGELLACHIE

✉ Craigellachie, Banffshire

In 1891 Peter Mackie joined a partnership to build Craigellachie with the highly experienced Alexander Edward as master distiller. Of all the great Victorian whisky barons, Mackie was definitely closest to the actual production of malt whisky, having completed his apprenticeship at Islay's

Craigellachie supplies whisky for John Dewar & Sons, whose White Label is a big seller in the USA.

Lagavulin Distillery. Craigellachie paired with Lagavulin provided the foundations of his famous White Horse blend, although some Craigellachie has always been sold as a single malt.

Mackie died in 1924, having bought the distillery outright, and three years later, his business was swallowed up by the Distillers Company (DCL), the forerunner of Diageo.

Today the distillery is hardly recognizable, after a comprehensive makeover in the 1960s which gave it a shiny metal chimney that rises high above the rooftops like a silver mast. All that remains of its Victorian roots are parts of two of the

Cragganmore was built by the renowned distillery architect Charles Doig.

Craigellachie 14-Year-Old

original warehouses. It seems strange that Craigellachie – named after a high crag where the River Fiddich flows into the Spey – has only the one distillery. It is certainly right in the midst of whisky-making country, and its size grew five times on the back of Speyside's late Victorian rise to become the pre-eminent whisky region in Scotland.

Craigellachie became part of the stable of distilleries supplying malt for Dewar's White Label – the most popular blend in America. Both were bought in 1998 by Bacardi, who released Craigellachie as a 14-year-old single malt six years later.

DAILUAINE

✉ Carron, Aberlour, Morayshire

The small hamlet of Carron lies between Ben Rinnes and the Spey, near Aberlour. It was here, beside the approach road, that a local farmer called William Mackenzie built Dailuaine in 1852. When he died, his widow leased it to James Fleming, who went into partnership with her son Thomas Mackenzie in 1879. Later it teamed up with a famous whisky from the Western Isles to form Dailuaine-Talisker Distilleries Ltd.

In 1884, Fleming and Mackenzie found the means to rebuild Dailuaine into one

of the biggest malt distilleries in the Highlands, and the first in Scotland to have a pagoda roof – designed to draw smoke through the malting barley above the kiln. It was solidly built, and in 1917 survived a bad fire with its crenulated, mould-blackened warehouses intact – you can still see them to this day.

The ground beside the distillery was flattened to make room for a siding attached to the main railway line that ran through Carron. The distillery had its own steam train, or "puggie", which meant all the raw materials, from the barley to the empty casks, could be delivered right to the door. When it was ready to leave, laden with casks of whisky, a call would be put through to the station master at Carron.

Most of what comes off Dailuaine's six stills goes

into blends such as Johnnie Walker. There are occasional limited release bottlings of a single malt, most recently of a sumptuous, heavily sherried 16-year-old.

DUFFTOWN

✉ Dufftown, Keith

It was James Duff, the fourth Earl of Fife, who founded Dufftown in 1817, on a site where the Dullan water meets the River Fiddich. At first its plentiful supplies of pristine cold water attracted mill owners, who used it as a source of power to grind oatmeal. It was on the site of one such mill that the Dufftown-Glenlivet Distillery was built in 1896. By then the town already had five distilleries and was on its way to eclipsing Campbeltown *(see p47)* as Scotland's whisky metropolis.

DALLAS DHU

In the pit of winter when other distilleries are radiating warmth and whisky, Dallas Dhu in Forres, Morayshire, remains cold. It has been that way since 1983, the distillery being a victim of widespread cuts to drain the "whisky loch" that was then full to the brim. Five years later, it was opened as a museum by Historic Scotland, who provide an audio-visual guide to the distillery's history. At the end of the tour you can even sample a drop of Dallas Dhu in the Roderick Dhu blend.

The distillery's name, meaning "black water valley" in Gaelic, was built by Alexander Edward in 1898 to supply malt for this once popular brand owned by Wright & Greig in Glasgow. Edward sold up after a year and the distillery struggled on, almost disappearing in a fire in 1939. With just two stills and a water wheel that provided the power up until 1971, the distillery never quite embraced the 20th century, which is perhaps why it became a museum – information about which you can find at www.historic-scotland.gov.uk.

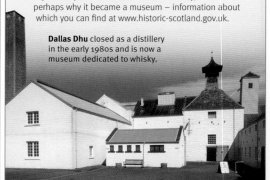

Dallas Dhu closed as a distillery in the early 1980s and is now a museum dedicated to whisky.

The site of Glenallachie Distillery was chosen so that it could source its water from a snow-fed burn.

The partners who owned Dufftown included two Liverpool businessmen, a local solicitor, and a farmer who owned the nearby farm of Pittyvaich, which supplied the barley. Soon the solicitor had his work cut out in a protracted dispute over water rights with the distillery's neighbour, Mortlach *(see p72)*, where whisky had been made since 1824. Angry letters were traded by day, while at night the water course from Jock's Well in the Conval hills was constantly redirected.

In year two the distillery was bought outright by one of the Liverpudlians, Peter Mackenzie, who also owned Blair Athol. Most of the malt disappeared into Bell's – the popular brand owned by Arthur Bell & Sons of Perth, and they eventually bought both distilleries in 1933 *(see p122)*. When not performing for Britain's best-selling blend, Dufftown does make an occasional appearance as a green, herbal, slightly oily single malt.

GLENALLACHIE

✉ **Aberlour, Banffshire**

In 1967 Charles Mackinlay & Co., part of Scottish & Newcastle Breweries, decided they needed their own distillery for their Mackinlay blend. Having chosen a site near Aberlour,

months were spent locating the perfect water source. In the end, a pipeline was built to draw water from a snow-fed burn which rises among the deep granite springs on Ben Rinnes. The distillery's architect was William Delmé-Evans, who was also responsible for Tullibardine and Isle of Jura. Glenallachie is a contemporary, gravity-flow distillery on one level, with a pond which steams up in the winter months when warm water is pumped in from the condensers.

Its brewery owners decided it was time to sell up in 1985 and Glenallachie passed to Invergordon and then to Chivas Brothers *(see p126)*. Though its owners have always used it solely for blending purposes, there are a fair number of independent bottlings.

GLENBURGIE

✉ **Forres, Morayshire**

Those travelling on the busy A96 to Inverness could easily miss Glenburgie, with just its blackened rooftops poking above the trees in a wooded valley between Forres and Elgin. Originally called the Kilnflat Distillery, it was established in 1829, though unconfirmed reports place it as early as 1810. The fact that it did not survive in its original form may have had something to do with its size.

If the stillroom really was below ground in the curious stone hut beside what is now the manager's office, little more than a trickle of Scotch can ever have been produced here. The trickle had already dried up by the time it was sub-let to Charles Hay, who rebuilt and re-named it Glenburgie.

The distillery passed through various hands until it was bought by the owners of Ballantine's *(see p121)* in the 1930s. At the time, it had the almost unique distinction of having a female manager – Miss Nicol. In the 1950s a pair of Lomond stills were installed. These were squat, round-necked, and quite unlike the existing pair, and produced a very different malt to the light, apple-scented Glenburgie. The new malt was called Glencraig after Ballantine's then production manager, Willie Craig – one of the few men ever to have had a malt named after him. However, this whisky disappeared when the Lomond stills were replaced with conventional stills in the early 1980s.

In his monumental book on distilleries of 1887, Alfred Barnard *(see p50)* described Glenburgie as "about as old-fashioned as it is possible to conceive." The old distillery was levelled in 2004 and replaced by an elegant, state-of-the-art distillery, which opened in June 2005.

GLENFIDDICH

William Grant founded Glenfiddich Distillery in 1887, and named it after the nearby River Fiddich. Having developed his knowledge of whisky at Mortlach Distillery, Grant set up Glenfiddich in good time to catch the late Victorian swell of interest in whisky.

Born in 1839, William Grant worked for a brief stint in a local lime quarry, after which he joined Mortlach, Dufftown's only distillery at the time, eventually rising from bookkeeper to manager. Despite having a wife and nine children to support on a salary of £100 a year, plus £7 he received as the precentor of the Free Church of Dufftown, he nursed ambitions to set up in business on his own. Initially he wanted to open a lime works, but slowly over time his dreams turned to whisky.

After 16 years at Mortlach he had saved enough to build a distillery for £650 using stones dug from the bed of the River Fiddich. For another £120 he acquired a pair of second-hand stills, a set of washtuns, a worm, and a water mill from Cardhu's lady distiller, Elizabeth Cumming. With the Robbie Dhu spring to provide water and a nearby burn diverted to power the malt mill, the site was well chosen.

Glenfiddich 18-Year-Old

The first spirit from Glenfiddich flowed on Christmas Day 1887. Now all Grant needed was a buyer.

Luckily there was a shortage of Speyside malt at the time, thanks to a fire at Glenlivet, and Grant began supplying a big blender in Aberdeen. Later he developed brands of his own, including "Stand Fast" – the battle cry of the Clan Grant. By the time of his death in 1923, the company's blends were being sold from Adelaide to Vancouver. They survived American Prohibition and began to thrive in the postwar whisky boom.

Today Glenfiddich is geared almost entirely to its own single malt, particularly the standard 12-year-old. Fans appreciate its smoothness. As one wrote, "it slips down the throat like Elizabeth Taylor in velvet trousers". It may not be the most complex of whiskies, but it has introduced millions to the world of single malt.

Glenfiddich pioneered the sale of single malt, and the whisky produced at this vast distillery remains the world's biggest selling brand.

GLENDULLAN

✉ Dufftown, Keith, Banffshire

By the end of the 19th century, the townsfolk of Dufftown were host to no fewer than six distilleries. Yet the Aberdeen-based blenders William Williams & Sons decided there was still room for one more whisky-making plant, and began building Glendullan in 1897. The distillery opened the following year and by 1902 had secured a Royal warrant from Edward VII.

In comparison to its neighbours, Glendullan fared well, only stopping production in the 1940s, when grain was rationed during World War II. By then, Glendullan whisky had become a key filling in Old Parr (*see p143*), a Macdonald Greenlees blend named after a certain Thomas Parr, who died in 1635 at the age of 152 – or so it was claimed. The blend, which comes in a raft of age statements, still sells well in East Asia and Paraguay.

In 1962, a new distillery was built next door. Architecturally, it resembles either an office block or perhaps, better still, a secondary modern school, with its flat roof and large plate-glass windows. For the next 13 years the old and the new worked in tandem, with their own mash tuns, wash backs, and stills. The spirit was then vatted together, filled into casks, and used for blending. Then, in 1985, the old Glendullan was quietly dismantled. Its successor now has six stills and is Diageo's second-largest malt distillery after Dufftown.

As a malt, Glendullan has been bottled at various ages, from 8 years upwards. As a straw-coloured 12-year-old, it has a rich malty character, sweetened with oak.

GLEN ELGIN

✉ Longmorn by Elgin, Morayshire

The distinguished architect Charles Doig witnessed the late Victorian whisky boom at first hand. He had designed many of the region's distilleries, and, when called upon in 1899 to create yet another on the road from Elgin to Rothes, he predicted it would be the last on Speyside for 50 years. In fact, it was not until 1958 that another distillery was built – that being Glen Keith.

Doig's client was William Simpson, a former manager at Glenfarclas, whose timing was terrible given that the market was awash with whisky at the time.

Having spent £13,000 on it, he recouped just £4,000 when he sold the distillery in 1900. Glen Elgin also suffered from sharing the same water supply as its near neighbour Coleburn. Once this dispute was resolved and the distillery connected to the National Grid in the 1960s, Glen Elgin's future was assured as a key filling for the White Horse blend (*see p153*).

Glen Elgin 12-Year-Old

GLENFARCLAS

✉ Ballindalloch, Banffshire
🖥 www.glenfarclas.co.uk
⛴ Open to visitors

From a distance, Glenfarclas resembles a remote farmstead more than a distillery, lying in open farmland beneath the hump-backed slopes of Ben Rinnes to the northeast. This gives a clue to its origins as a small rural distillery on the Rechlerich Farm near Ballindalloch, where Robert

Hay, a tenant farmer, began making whisky to supply the cattle drovers who would stop there on their way to market in Elgin.

Having been licensed by Hay in 1836, the Glenfarclas distillery passed to John Grant when he took the tenancy of Rechlerich in 1865, adding to several farms he had nearby. The Grants have owned it ever since, making it virtually unique in an industry that is dominated by big corporations. That said, Glenfarclas was valued at only £511 in 1865, and was immediately sublet to a relative called John Smith. This left John Grant to concentrate on what he did best – breeding champion Aberdeen Angus cattle.

Five years later Smith left to set up Cragganmore, leaving Grant and his son George to run the distillery alongside the farm. By the time George's two sons inherited in 1890, the whisky making side of the business had become a lot more important. The brothers formed the Glenfarclas-Glenlivet Distillery Co. in partnership with Pattison

Glenfarclas, with its low-lying medley of buildings, resembles a farmstead more than a distillery.

Brothers of Leith, into whose blends most of the malt went. However, a little was bottled as "Pure Old Glenfarclas-Glenlivet Malt Whisky" from as early as 1899.

Disaster struck a year later when Pattisons went bankrupt *(see p142)*. As the Pattison brothers were sent to jail for fraud, the prospects for Glenfarclas looked decidedly grim. Somehow the distillery managed to survive as a private business called J&G Grant & Sons, which by 1914 was being run solely by John Grant's grandson, George. Perhaps the trauma of the Pattisons' crash taught the Grants never to go into partnership again, for the business has remained fiercely independent ever since.

Yet unlike other privately-owned distilleries, Glenfarclas is no boutique operation. Its six stills are the biggest on Speyside, and it also boasts a large visitor centre, which opened in 1973. The centre's reception room resembles one of the state rooms on the ship *Empress of Australia*, as Glenfarclas's former chairman, George Grant, heard it was about to be broken up and decided to buy the panelling.

GLENFARCLAS 10-YEAR-OLD
40% ABV ● Straw-coloured, gently spicy malt with notes of pear drops and sherry.

GLENFARCLAS 12-YEAR-OLD
43% ABV ● Distinct sherried nose with spicy flavours of cinnamon and stewed fruit.

GLENFARCLAS 105 60% ABV ● This intense, cask-strength whisky is infused with liquorice, molasses, and smoke.

GLENFIDDICH

✉ Dufftown, Banffshire
🖥 www.glenfiddich.com
🚪 Open to visitors

Although it comes from a late-Victorian distillery, the world's top-selling single malt is really a child of the 1960s. It was in 1964 that William Grant & Sons decided to launch an 8-year-old in a distinctive triangular bottle and market it in England.

It struggled at first because shopkeepers and barmen were reluctant to stock a drink that no-one had ever asked for by name, but soon Glenfiddich was receiving plenty of media coverage. There were endless articles explaining how this "new" drink called single malt

Glenfiddich 12-Year-Old

whisky was made. It hardly mattered whether they mentioned Glenfiddich or just the word "malt", since the two became synonymous for a time.

By 1970, UK sales had passed 24,000 cases and the whisky was beginning to venture further afield through duty-free sales. Only a year earlier the Scotch Whisky Association had questioned the wisdom of selling unblended whisky to the "Sassenachs", and many in the industry thought it would be a short-lived fad. Instead Glenfiddich pioneered the whole reinvention of single malts, and established a lead it has never lost.

GLENFIDDICH 12-YEAR-OLD
40% ABV ● A pale straw-coloured malt with a trace of pears, drying on the finish.

GLENFIDDICH 15-YEAR-OLD
40% ABV ● The use of sherry wood adds texture and colour in the 15-year-old.

GLENFIDDICH 18-YEAR-OLD
43% ABV ● An altogether richer, more complex style, with flavours of spicy baked apples and cinnamon.

GLENFIDDICH 21-YEAR-OLD 40% ABV
A rich, indulgent malt finished off in rum casks to give a toffee sweetness.

Glenfiddich whisky is matured in the cool, damp conditions of traditional warehouses.

GLEN GRANT

✉ Rothes, Morayshire
⛴ Open to visitors

With its thick, red sandstone walls and pair of pepperpot turrets, the oldest surviving distillery in Rothes appears reassuringly solid. Glen Grant was founded in 1840 by two brothers – James Grant, a solicitor in Elgin, and John Grant, a local grain merchant whose knowledge of whisky making allegedly came from supplying the region's illicit distillers.

They certainly picked a good site with the Glen Grant burn to provide water for the mash and power for the machinery, and plentiful supplies of good-quality barley from the flatlands of Moray nearby. Before long the distillery also benefited from the railways, which reached Rothes in 1858. Three years later Glen Grant became the first industrial works in the Highlands to install electric lighting.

James Grant's son, known to everyone as "the Major", took over in 1872. He was the quintessential Victorian gent, clad head-to-toe in tweed with a superb walrus moustache. At the time the distillery was primed to ride the surge in whisky's popularity; Scotch was still very much a local vice with per capita consumption in England one third that of Scotland.

Glen Grant remained in family hands until 1977 when it was sold to Seagram. As a 5-year-old single malt it became hugely successful in Italy, and the distillery now belongs to the Italian group Campari. Visitors should explore the beautifully restored gardens after seeing the distillery. The Major used to take after-dinner guests to a narrow ravine in the garden where he would unlock a safe embedded in the rock to produce glasses and a bottle of Glen Grant. If anyone required water, they had only to dip their glass in the burn as it rushed past in the moonlight.

GLEN KEITH

✉ Keith, Banffshire

In 1958 Seagram decided to build a new distillery in Keith across the road from Strathisla, its recently acquired flagship. As this was the first new malt distillery on Speyside for almost 60 years, it was a significant move by the Canadian giant, seeming to signify the end of postwar austerity and the start of a golden age for Scotch.

It was built on the site of an ancient malt mill in a fairly traditional style, using local stone and a decorative pagoda on the roof. Almost the entire production of Glen Keith disappears into blends, notably Chivas Regal *(see p124)* and Passport

The gardens at Glen Grant have recently been restored to their late Victorian glory.

(see p146). Given the success of both in Asian markets – with Chivas booming in China – the distillery's role seems set to continue.

GLENLIVET

✉ Ballindalloch, Banffshire
🖰 www.theglenlivet.com
⛴ Open to visitors

Today Glenlivet is the second-biggest-selling single malt in the world and is especially popular in the US. New French owners, Pernod

THE GHOST OF BIAWA

With the day-to-day running the distillery delegated to others, James Grant ("The Major") spent many months big-game hunting in Africa. On one trip he returned with an orphan boy. The Major christened him Biawa and sent him to the local school, prior to employing him as his butler. The Major died in 1931, and Biawa lived for another 40 years. He is buried in the town cemetery, opposite Glenrothes Distillery, and his ghost has occasionally been spotted in the vicinity. He left his gun and fishing rod to his beloved Rothes Football Club, for whom he had once played.

Ricard, who acquired the distillery in 2000, seem keen to challenge William Grant's leviathan for poll position. They have some way to go.

Glenlivet entered the 20th century as by far the most famous distillery in Scotland, yet it then appeared to rest on its laurels while others traded on the Glenlivet name. It was only after US Prohibition that it was finally sold in bottle rather than cask.

Glenlivet formed a partnership with Glen Grant and Longmorn until all three distilleries were bought by Seagram in 1977.

GLENLIVET 12-YEAR-OLD 40% ABV
Light and delicate, with an oaky sweetness and a faint hint of apple peel.

GLENLIVET 15-YEAR-OLD 43% ABV • Riper floral notes are here underplayed by the sweet smack of vanilla.

GLENLOSSIE AND MANNOCHMORE

✉ Elgin, Morayshire

These two distilleries lie just beyond Elgin and have worked side by side, sharing the same workforce, since Mannochmore was built in the 1970s. Glenlossie was built a century earlier in 1876 by Glendronach's former distillery manager, John Duff. From the start it was an efficient, self-contained unit with its own reservoir to supply cold water to condense the spirit and power the waterwheel. There was a railway siding to connect to the line from Rothes to Elgin, and houses were supplied for Duff's staff – employed not only to run the distillery but also to look after his herd of cattle, which were fed on draff from the distillery.

Glenlossie was gobbled up by the giant DCL in 1919 and over the years the number of stills has been

Glenlossie has worked with neighbouring Mannochmore since the 1970s.

increased to six, with purifiers on each of the stills to produce a more delicate spirit than its neighbour. Mannochmore was briefly responsible for a "black whisky" called Loch Dhu, the result of heavy tinting with caramel.

GLEN MORAY

✉ Bruceland Road, Elgin
⌂ www.glenmoray.com
🚶 Open to visitors

The Ancient Royal Burgh of Elgin is the official capital of Speyside, though it sits slightly on the edge of the main bustle of whisky-making activity, which is concentrated closer to the river itself. Glen Moray Distillery stands far from the Spey on the banks of the River Lossie on the western edge of Elgin, beneath Gallow Hill where executions were carried out until the end of the 17th century. Like its sister distillery Glenmorangie, Glen Moray was originally a brewery.

Having brewed ale for over 60 years, it was a small matter to take the process one step further and turn the beer into whisky. Glen Moray was converted into a distillery in 1897 with buildings clustered round a courtyard in the style of a traditional farmstead. The timing could have been better, with Speyside already bristling with new distilleries eager to cash in on the late-Victorian whisky boom. Glen Moray survived the ensuing crash at the start of the 20th century, but had spluttered to a halt by 1910.

Glenlivet 12-Year-Old

That was the year it closed down, seemingly for good. There were occasional signs of life afterwards, but by the end of World War I the distillery was in liquidation.

Glen Moray was bought in 1920 by Macdonald & Muir, a large firm of whisky blenders in Leith, for £12,000, "less £700 for repairs to the roof".

Macdonald & Muir had been buying Glen Moray whisky for some time for their top-selling blend Highland Queen (see p136). More recently, this classic Speyside malt has been a key filling in the newly reconstructed blend Bailie Nicol Jarvie (see p119). Glen Moray was modernized in the 1950s. A pair of new stills were added, doubling capacity, and, shortly after, the distillery won a contract to supply single malt to Japan's All Nippon Airways.

Since then, however, Glen Moray has sunk back into the shadows of its stable mate, its fate forever to be "brother of the more famous Glenmorangie". The owners have certainly lavished a lot more time and money on their "glen of tranquillity" than on Glen Moray. Yet, mostly through supermarket sales, it remains a top-selling introductory malt in the UK.

GLEN MORAY CLASSIC 40% ABV
Pale gold, smooth, light-bodied with traces of oatmeal and shortbread

GLEN MORAY 12-YEAR-OLD 40% ABV
As above, with sweeter, floral notes coming through.

GLEN MORAY 16-YEAR-OLD 40% ABV
A richer, more honeyed expression of Glen Moray.

GLENLIVET

As one Victorian visitor to the Glenlivet Distillery wrote in the late 1800s, "a more lonely spot in winter, or a more delightful one in summer could not be found and, for those who like quietude and rest, truly it is very far from the 'madding crowd'."

This sense of isolation remains largely intact as you stare south across an open bowl to the barren hills and braes of Glenlivet beyond. The romantic image is hard to sustain once you turn to face the distillery, however. This is no lonesome farm distillery. Today's Glenlivet is a substantial industrial unit, clad in shiny, corrugated steel, and with a large, steaming dark grains plant on site.

Yet, in the history of Speyside, there are few words so evocative as Glenlivet. As Government troops attempted to clamp down on illicit Highland distilling from the late 19th century on, whisky became a spirit of defiance. Nowhere was this more true than in Glenlivet, where "there were not three persons", according to a local farmer, "who were not engaged directly or indirectly in the trade".

Glenlivet was one of the first distilleries in Speyside to turn legitimate, and operate as a legal, tax-paying whisky producer.

Glenlivet 25-Year-Old

George Smith was no doubt making whisky on the side at Upper Drummin farm when he established Glenlivet Distillery in 1824. As the first distiller to go legal in a glen dedicated to producing moonshine, he made a lot of enemies and had to carry a pair of hair-trigger revolvers for his own protection. Meanwhile others on Speyside bolted the name "Glenlivet" on to their distilleries in the hope of a little reflected glory.

Smith began supplying Andrew Usher in Edinburgh, who pioneered the idea of blended Scotch with his "Old Vatted Glenlivet", launched in 1853. Soon afterwards, Glenlivet slipped down the glen to its present site and increased in scale. At the time of Smith's death in 1871, the distillery was producing 18,200 litres (4,000 gallons) of whisky a week. While other distilleries were almost wholly anonymous, Glenlivet had established a real identity for itself – one that lives on to this day.

The Spey is Scotland's longest river, and gives its name to the the nation's foremost whisky-producing region.

GLENROTHES

✉ Rothes, Morayshire
🖥 www.glenrotheswhisky.com

The small town of Rothes is strangely reticent about what it does best. It produces enough malt whisky to fill the equivalent of 50 million bottles a year, yet you wouldn't know it driving down the narrow High Street by day. Only by night do you get an idea of the scale of production, as clouds of steam billow up from the town's five distilleries. Among them, hidden in a tree-lined gorge beside the Rothes burn, is Glenrothes.

Once established *(see below)*, Glenrothes became a key filling in the Cutty Sark and Famous Grouse blends. The distillery expanded to keep pace, building a huge new stillroom in pink granite to house its eight stills. This has since been increased to 10, giving an impressive capacity of 5 million litres

**Glenrothes
Select Reserve**

(1.1 million gallons) of alcohol. The flipside of being so popular with the blenders was that there was never any spare Glenrothes to bottle as a single malt. This finally changed in 1987 when a 12-year-old was released, followed by the first critically acclaimed Vintage Malt in 1994.

🍶 **THE GLENROTHES SELECT RESERVE** 43% ABV
Sweeter on the nose than in the mouth, this malt develops into a long, creamy, and seriously smooth dram on the tongue.

GLEN SPEY

✉ Rothes, Aberlour, Banffshire

Having decided to pull out of the partnership behind Glenrothes in 1878 *(see below)*, James Stuart returned to Rothes to build a new distillery to add to his Macallan a few years later. He owned an oatmeal mill on the opposite bank of the Rothes burn beneath the

ruined Castle of Rothes, and took a decision to make whisky on the site. Inevitably this led to disputes with Glenrothes as to who owned the water rights.

At some point it became a fully fledged distillery, and registered as Glen Spey in 1884. Three years later it was sold to the London-based gin distiller Gilbeys in one of the first moves into Scotch by a firm from the south. Years later, Gilbey's merged with Justerini & Brooks, by which time Glen Spey had become a key ingredient in their top-selling blend J&B *(see p137)*. Its 12-year-old malt is relatively rare.

🍶 **GLEN SPEY 12-YEAR-OLD** 43% ABV
A light, herbal Speyside with notes of vanilla ice-cream.

GLENTAUCHERS

✉ Mulben, Keith, Banffshire

Unlike many distilleries that only went in search of a market once they were built, Glentauchers was destined from the offset to supply malt for Buchanan's Blend (later known as Black & White, *see p123*). The distillery was built in a partnership between the whisky baron James Buchanan and the Glasgow-based spirits brokers WP Lowrie in 1897 on the edge of the Craigellachie forest, just beyond Keith.

Standing beside what is now the A95 and with a siding at the back that joined the main east-coast rail line from Aberdeen to Inverness, Glentauchers was certainly well connected. Once Buchanan took over the distillery completely in 1906, its future looked secure so long as Black & White continued to thrive. It suffered during the distillery closures of the 1980s, but was rescued by new owners in 1988. Today, as part of Pernod Ricard, its main role is to supply malt for Ballantines *(see p119)*.

GLENROTHES FALTERING START

Built in 1878 by James Stuart of Macallan Distillers, Glenrothes almost collapsed right at the outset. An economic recession hit in the summer of that year, and Stuart pulled out to concentrate on Macallan. His partners, Robert Dick and Willie Grant, struggled on, and the first spirit flowed on 28 December 1879. Somehow the pair staved off bankruptcy through loans from local supporters, and within five years Glenrothes was turning a profit. But for one lost season during World War I, it kept working right up until the start of the Great Depression in the 1930s, when it fell silent. Just a few years later, US Prohibition ended, and Glenrothes was cranked back to life to capitalize on the American market. It has been distilling ever since.

**Glenrothes Select
Reserve 1975**

IMPERIAL

Thomas Mackenzie built Imperial in 1897, siting it close by Dailuaine Distillery near Aberlour. Its name was intended to honour Queen Victoria in her diamond jubilee year, but sadly for Mackenzie his impressive red brick distillery proved less durable than the British Empire and fell silent within six months. It was reopened in 1919 by DCL (the Distillers Company), but they promptly closed it again because its mighty stills produced too much waste in the form of draff. For the next 30 years just the maltings operated. It was not until a method of compressing the draff into cattle cake was found in the 1950s that Imperial's stills were fired up once again. Since then, it has experienced both productive times and further silent periods. In 2005 it was taken under the wing of Pernod Ricard.

INCHGOWER

✉ Buckie, Banffshire

Inchgower is right on the edge of the region near Spey Bay and the town of Buckie, though in terms of style it produces a classic Speyside malt. Originally the plant was situated at Cullen and known as the Tochineal Distillery. It had been founded in 1824 by John Wilson, and it was his son Alex who decided to move it a few miles west in 1867 to escape a doubling of the rent by his landlady, the Countess of Seafield, who disapproved of distilleries.

As a family business it survived until the recession of 1930. The stills remained cold for the next six years when the distillery was bought by Buckie Town Council for the princely sum of £1,000. Two years on, they sold it to Arthur Bell &

Sons for £3,000, and ever since then much of the malt has disappeared into the Bell's blend (see p120). There are periodic bottlings of Inchgower as a dense, creamy vanilla malt.

KININVIE

✉ Dufftown, Banffshire

If few of the many thousands of visitors to Glenfiddich Distillery each year have heard of its sister distillery Balvenie, virtually none knows of Kininvie, despite the fact that all three share the same site at Dufftown. Kininvie is by far the smallest, and began life in 1990, with the first spirit flowing on 4 July. This being American Independence Day was probably no accident, since William Grant & Sons are fiercely proud of being an independent family business.

In reality, Kininvie consists of little more than a stillroom, as its washbacks and other distillery paraphernalia are housed at Balvenie. Its whisky is a sweet, floral malt, with a distinct note of barley sugar. It can

Despite its proximity to the river, like all Speyside distilleries, Knockando uses water from a spring to make its whisky.

mostly be found in William Grant whiskies, such as the recently launched Monkey Shoulder.

KNOCKANDO

✉ Knockando, Morayshire
🖥 www.malts.com

The distillery was set up by John Thompson in 1898 and was run on a seasonal basis as though it were an old-style farm distillery that only made whisky after the harvest. In other respects Thompson was up with all the latest technological advances, for Knockando had electric lighting at a time when most distilleries did not.

Sadly he was caught in the speculative bubble that engulfed the whisky trade at the start of the 20th century, and was forced to sell.

The new owners were the London gin distillers Gilbeys. Knockando has remained in their hands since, though Gilbeys is now under the Diageo umbrella.

Knockando 12-Year-Old

The low, stone-built dunnage warehouses at Knockdhu help it to retain a traditional feel.

Until recently, the entire production went into blends, particularly for J&B *(see p137)*. Since the distillery ceased malting its barley in 1968, the malt barns have hosted endless sales conferences for the J&B global team. Whether its one-time salesman turned film star David Niven ever came here for a spot of corporate bonding is unclear, but the brand was certainly big in America by the time he hit Hollywood in the 1930s. J&B began to slip in the US in the 1970s, but later surged in Spain, prompting a distillery visit from Mrs Thatcher in 1985. The then Prime Minister handed over the Queen's Award for Export and received the billionth bottle of J&B in return.

Knockando is an Anglicized version of the Gaelic Cnoc-an-Dhu, "dark hillock", which guards a bend in the Spey. Despite being so near the river, it draws its water from a spring like all Speyside distilleries. In colour it is noticeably pale, due to the use of American oak casks and a refusal to use caramel to tint the whisky and give an impression of age.

🍶 **KNOCKANDO 12-YEAR-OLD** 40% ABV • Light-bodied, almost "Lowland" in style with a delicate, creamy texture in the mouth and a trace of toffee and hazelnuts.

KNOCKDHU

✉ Knock, by Huntly, Aberdeenshire
🖰 www.inverhouse.com

Opened in 1894 in the village of Knock on the edge of Speyside, Knockdhu is small and traditional in style. It was the first of a handful of distilleries acquired by Inver House Distillers in 1988. The company have strived to preserve the character of Knockdhu by keeping its wooden washbacks, its worm tub, and granite, old-style dunnage warehouses. Of these, the most important is the worm tub, which tends to produce a richer, more meaty spirit than modern condensers that strip out sulphur compounds with great efficiency to give a fresher, clean-tasting spirit.

**Knockdhu's anCnoc
Single Malt**

🍶 **KNOCKDHU'S AN-CNOC SINGLE MALT** 40% ABV • This is a relatively full-bodied Speyside, with notes of heather honey and lemon peel, named anCnoc after the Gaelic for the nearby "black hill", whose springs supply the water.

LINKWOOD

✉ Elgin, Morayshire

Whisky makers tend to be conservative by nature and adverse to change. Their mantra of "if it ain't broke, don't fix it" was taken to extremes by one distillery manager at Linkwood in the 1930s. He was convinced that everything played its part in forming the character of the whisky, and that nothing, not even a cobweb, should be removed. The poor man would be spinning in his grave if he could see what has happened to Linkwood since – not that the lack of spiders has had any adverse effect on the quality of the whisky. It is a fine Speyside malt, much in demand from blenders.

Named after Linkwood House on the Seafield estate, the distillery was established in 1821 by the estate manager, Peter Brown, in what was then open country, but is now within Elgin. Today it is one of a cluster of distilleries between the town and the lower reaches

JOHN DUFF, LONGMORN'S PIONEER

John Duff had dedicated his life to making whisky before he set up Longmorn on the road to Rothes from Elgin, but it was a circuitous route, taking him from Scotland first to South Africa and then to America before returning home.

After a solid grounding in distilling at Glendronach, where he was distillery manager for years, Duff initially left to run a hotel. Before long, however, he was back making whisky as John Duff & Co. at Glenlossie Distillery, which he set up with two partners in 1876.

The Benriach to Longmorn train was a shuttle service for ferrying whisky casks between the two sister distilleries.

Twelve years later he found himself in Cape Town with his family, and, after failing to set up a distillery there, he crossed the Atlantic to try his luck in America. When that failed, he returned home in 1892, aged 50, to be the manager at the Bon Accord Distillery in Aberdeen, where he also became a partner in a local wine and spirit merchants.

In 1894, having seen all sides of the trade and witnessed the potential for Scotch whisky abroad, Duff felt the timing was right for yet another distillery on Speyside. Longmorn had plentiful supplies of spring water, access to some of the best barley from the Laich o' Moray, a waterwheel to provide all the power, and peat to kiln the barley from the nearby Mannoch hill. It also had its own station connected to the Great North of Scotland line, along which the raw ingredients came in and the finished whisky left. It cost £20,000 to build and had four stills, producing spirit that, according to the National Guardian, "jumped into favour with buyers from the earliest day on which it was offered."

In a word, Longmorn was well-conceived from the start, and its early success encouraged Duff to buy out his partners and build Benriach next door in 1897. Unfortunately he was a major supplier to the Pattison brothers, and when they were forced out of business and into jail in 1901 (see p142), Duff soon followed them into bankruptcy.

Longmorn remained in private hands until the 1970s, when it was bought by Seagram; it is now owned by Pernod Ricard.

THE MACALLAN BACK STORY

The Macallan, with its famously sherried nose and rich mahogany colour, has become one of Scotland's most highly rated single malts. It was not a reputation formed overnight, however, for the Macallan evolved slowly out of a small-scale 19th-century farm distillery.

Situated on the west bank of the Spey, Macallan was originally called the Elchies Distillery. It was first licensed to Alexander Reid in 1824, but was almost certainly distilling before then to supply drovers who would pass by on their way from Moray to the cattle markets of Falkirk and Perth. As a staging post, it was somewhere to gather before crossing the Spey and, no doubt, to pick up a few casks for the journey.

Macallan Eleganzia

Macallan was bought in 1892 by Roderick Kemp, a wine merchant in Elgin and former distiller at Talisker. He was determined to make the most of Macallan, and six years later refused an offer of £80,000 to sell it. The bid came from its previous owners, two of whom set up Highland Distillers. That company did eventually buy Macallan – nearly 100 years later in 1996, and this time at a price of £180 million.

The distillery remained more or less as it had been in 1896 until after World War II, passing through family hands to Gordon Shiach, an intelligence officer who interrogated Herman Goering at the Nuremberg trials. The distillery was completely rebuilt in the 1950s, and by 1970 had trebled production to over 4.5 million litres (1 million gallons). By now stocks were being laid down in preparation for the Macallan 10-Year-Old Single Malt, which was launched in 1978. Two years later Allan Shiach took over at the distillery, while continuing his career as a successful Hollywood scriptwriter. As Allan Scott, his scripts include *Castaway*, *Regeneration*, and *Don't Look Now*, in which Donald Sutherland pours himself a generous slug of Macallan after making love to Julie Christie.

Since its launch, the Macallan single malt has developed a loyal following.

The stills at Macallan have been producing whisky for their respected and popular single malt since the 1970s.

The Macallan uses a mix of European and American ex-bourbon casks for maturation.

of the Spey that have never received the recognition they are due. Far more attention is given to those upstream at Rothes, such as Macallan and Glenfiddich.

Under Brown, Linkwood was remarkably self-sufficient, growing its own barley in the adjoining fields and having its own cattle to gobble up the draff produced in the process. It was rebuilt in the 1870s by Brown's son William, who doubled the output to 227,500 litres (50,000 gallons) a year and re-christened the business the Linkwood-Glenlivet Distillery Co. Ltd. The company remained independent until 1933, when it finally sold out to DCL for £80,000 – far more than most malt distilleries were worth at the time.

Having radically changed its layout in the early 1960s, Linkwood gained a whole new distillery alongside it with two pairs of stills in 1971. The operations ran in tandem until the Victorian stillhouse was closed down in

1985. Since then the original set of stills have been fired again and the spirit produced is vatted with that produced from the new stills.

🍷 **LINKWOOD 12-YEAR-OLD** 40% ABV
A supple and complex malt with the scent of fresh-cut grass and orchards. Sweet and then savoury on the tongue, finishing long with a satisfying smoky twist at the end. There are a host of older expressions available from independent bottlers.

LONGMORN

✉ Elgin, Morayshire

From the distillery's outset *(see p69)*, Longmorn has maintained a reputation with blenders, and so has been in almost constant production since the late 19th century – unlike its sister distillery Benriach, which struggled from the start *(see p52)*. Having remained in private hands for over 60 years, Longmorn became part of Seagram in the 1970s. It has now passed to Pernod Ricard, who have started to promote Longmorn as a single malt in its own right.

Longmorn 16-Year-Old

🍷 **LONGMORN 16-YEAR-OLD**
A beautifully balanced cask-strength malt with a ripe, floral scent and honeyed texture that dries gently on the long finish.

MACALLAN

✉ Easter Elchies, Craigellachie
🖰 www.themacallan.com
⚓ Open to visitors

Since 2000, building on its strong history *(see over)*, Macallan has launched a number of new lines. For older vintages there is the Fine & Rare collection, including a bottle from 1926, which sold for £36,000 at auction. For those wanting a less heavily sherried Macallan, the distillery released its Fine Oak range in 2004. The Macallan has always taken maturation very seriously. Wood is bought "on the tree" in Spain, where it is seasoned, turned into butts, and filled with sherry in Jerez. After a few years, the butts are shipped to Speyside and filled with Macallan whisky. For Fine Oak, a mix of American and European oak is used.

🍷 **MACALLAN SHERRY OAK** 40% ABV ● The

Macallan 10-Year-Old

original 10-year-old has a mid-amber colour and a scent of spice, orange peel, and fruit cake. The colour and intensity of aroma deepen with older expressions, which include 12, 18, 25, and 30 year-old bottlings. The 12-year-old Eleganzia is aged in Oloroso and Fino sherry casks.

🍷 **MACALLAN FINE OAK** 40% ABV
Available in a raft of ages from 8 to 30 years, this is a lighter style of Macallan, with notes of coconut and vanilla to complement the richer sherry flavours.

MILTONDUFF

✉ Elgin, Morayshire

With plentiful supplies of water and some of the best barley grown on Speyside, the area south of Elgin was said to be home to over 50 illicit stills during the 19th century. One of the first to go legal and take out a licence was Miltonduff in 1823. It is claimed that the distillery stands on the site of an old mill that belonged to Pluscarden Abbey, where the monks made ale of such sublime quality that "it filled the abbey with unutterable bliss". Whether the monks ever went further and distilled their beer into whisky is unclear, but they certainly used the same spring-fed water as the distillery. This flows into the Black Burn, which was blessed by an Abbot in the 15th century.

For over 60 years, ever since the Canadian distillers Hiram Walker took over the distillery in 1936, Miltonduff has been a key ingredient in

Mortlach Distillery was founded on the site of a well where it is said moonshine used to be made.

Ballantine's blend *(see p119)*. This role keeps the six stills busy pumping out over 5 million litres (1.1 million gallons) of whisky a year, leaving little available for bottling as a single malt. Examples do appear from independent bottlers such as Gordon & Macphail *(see p52)*, together with the odd, extremely rare bottle of Mosstowie. This curiosity, which used special Lomond stills, was begun by Hiram Walker in the 1960s in an attempt to broaden their repertoire. The experiment was abandoned in 1981.

MORTLACH

✉ Dufftown, Keith, Banffshire

Mortlach was established by James Findlater in 1823 on the edge of Dufftown around a well that had been used to make moonshine, or so it was said. Seven years later Findlater was forced to sell up for a mere £270 and there followed long periods of inactivity. When it was owned by J&J Grant of Glen Grant, the distilling equipment was removed and the disused granary given over to the local Free Church of Scotland in which to hold services. Later Mortlach became a brewery until it was finally converted back into a distillery by George Cowie in 1897, who turned it into one of the largest in the Highlands by doubling the number of stills to six. Within a year it was also probably the most modern,

with a railway siding connecting it to the main line, electric light, and a series of hydraulic lifts.

The distillery's most famous employee was William Grant, who spent nearly 20 years as Mortlach's loyal book-keeper, then manager before handing in his notice in 1886 to strike out on his own at Glenfiddich *(see p58)*. This was the second distillery in town and was quickly followed by a stampede of others. Today there are seven distilleries here, making Dufftown the unchallenged whisky capital of Speyside.

Mortlach was effectively rebuilt in the 1960s, though much of its outside character as a late-Victorian distillery has been preserved, along with the use of an old-fashioned worm tub, which helps give the malt a richer flavour than many Speysides.

🍶 **MORTLACH 16-YEAR-OLD** 43% ABV
Well-rounded with notes of spice and a toffee sweetness that finishes dry.

SPEYBURN

✉ Rothes, Aberlour, Morayshire
🖥 www.inverhouse.com

Yet another classic Victorian distillery designed by Charles Doig *(see p59)*, Speyburn was built in 1897, as Queen Victoria was entering her twilight years. Despite not

being finished by the end of that year, the distillery manager ordered the stills to be fired up. With snow swirling in from the outside, as the stillroom lacked doors or windows, and the workers buttoned up against the cold, the first spirit began to flow. This was all to have at least one butt bearing the date of the Queen's Diamond Jubilee.

The distillery stands on the edge of Rothes in a narrow tree-lined glen. As a result, Doig had to adapt his design and build upwards to create a distillery on three floors, with its elegant pagoda roof peaking above the pines and clearly visible from the road to Elgin. The result is one of the most picturesque distilleries from the period. Unlike many, it survived the 1960s unscathed, partly because the cramped setting made any attempted makeover difficult to achieve. It fell silent during the 1980s when the "whisky loch" was full to the brim, and remained so until bought by Inver House in the early 1990s.

**Speyburn
10-Year-Old**

SPEYBURN'S MALT WHISKY

The majority of the malt is tankered away to Airdrie, where Inver House is based, though what is left is aged on site for bottling as a delicately fruity, aromatic 10-year-old and an altogether richer, more complex 25-year-old.

SPEYSIDE

✉ Glen Tromie, Kingussie,
Inverness-shire

🖰 www.speysidedistillery.co.uk

At first sight, this tiny, boutique distillery could be one of those late-Victorian survivors that make up so many of the distilleries in these parts. Only the discreet modern smoke stack gives away its age. Speyside opened in 1991 with a solitary pair of stills able to produce 600,000 litres (132,000 gallons) a year, making it the second-smallest distillery in the region. It was no overnight creation, however, and took almost 30 years to build stone by stone on the insistence of its owner

George Christie, a Glasgow-based whisky man. Sadly the funds ran out and the venture had to be sold to a Swiss firm four years after it went into production. Since 2000 it has been back in Scottish hands, with the Christie family still involved, producing a delicate 12-year-old with pronounced cereal notes and a slight trace of smoke on the tongue.

ROSEISLE

In 2007, Diageo announced they were building a new £40-million distillery on Speyside at Roseisle near the Moray Firth, between Elgin and Forres. Having talked up the huge potential for Scotch in countries such as China and India for some time, the whisky industry was finally putting its money where its mouth is. With an annual capacity of 10 million litres (2.2 million gallons) of alcohol from 14 stills, Roseisle is no boutique distillery. As the first of any scale since Seagram built Allt a'Bhaine in 1975, it will be Diageo's largest malt distillery by far.

After the grim years of whisky lochs and distillery closures in the early 1980s, it is a heartening declaration of faith in the future of Scotch whisky. It is also an example of real long-term planning, since it will be 2021 at the earliest before the first drop of Roseisle goes into deluxe blends such as Johnnie Walker Black Label. This is likely to be its main role, though there is bound to be some Roseisle set aside for a single malt.

Speyburn's stills remain intact, but the distillery no longer has its original maltings.

STRATHISLA'S BEGINNINGS

What drew the early distillers to a particular site was the same as what attracted the brewers before them – a reliable source of good, clear water. In the 12th century Dominican monks in Keith used a well that was fed by the Broomhill spring to brew a potent heather ale. Whether they ever distilled the ale into something stronger is anyone's guess, but it is one theory about how distilling came to Scotland. What is known for sure is that since 1786 the well has been used to make whisky at Strathisla – though the distillery was originally called Milltown. It began as a tiny operation, with a pair of stills able to produce just 150 litres (40 gallons) of spirit at a time. The name was changed to Strathisla in the 19th century, and the distillery was bought by William Longmore. The distillery was destroyed by fire in the 1870s, but rebuilt by William's son-in-law.

Strathisla suffered two fires in the 1870s, but was rebuilt into the distillery you see today.

STRATHISLA

✉ Keith, Banffshire
⛴ Open to visitors

With its high-gabled roofs topped with twin pagodas, and its speckled stone walls like nougat, Strathisla is one of the most handsome distilleries in the Highlands, and boasts a venerable history *(see above)*. Before 1900 the whisky was available by the bottle from wine and spirit merchants, who bought it in 23-litre (5-gallon) stone jars direct from the distillery, while bars sold it on tap from glass decanters that were engraved "Strathisla Whisky".

To raise money for rebuilding following fire damage, William Longmore & Co. was floated, which allowed in outside investors. Eventually this meant ceding control to a crooked theatrical impresario, George Pomeroy, who was jailed for tax evasion in 1949. A year later it was sold to a church organist from Aberdeen for £70,000. The organist was simply a front for Seagram, who had recently bought Chivas Brothers and needed supplies of malt whisky. Strathisla has been the spiritual home of Chivas Regal ever since, and most of the production disappears into the famous blend.

🥃 **STRATHISLA 12-YEAR-OLD** 43% ABV
As a single malt, Strathisla is a soft-centred, syrupy whisky, with rich, fruitcake notes.

STRATHMILL

✉ Keith, Banffshire

For most of the 19th century the Strathisla mill in Keith had been milling oatmeal, though it may well have occasionally produced something a little stronger on the side. In 1891 it began officially producing whisky as the Glenisla-Glenlivet distillery – a name that rather stretched credibility, what with Glenlivet being 24 miles (39km) away by road. Four years later it was bought by the London gin distiller Gilbey and was re-christened Strathmill.

While most of the output has always gone into blends, a first Strathmill single malt was released as early as 1909, though the second official bottling was not until 1993. The distillery was sympathetically modernized in the 1960s when it was the headquarters of Gilbey's Highland Distilleries.

TAMDHU

✉ Knockando, Aberlour
⛴ www.edrington.com

In 1863, the Strathspey railway opened from Craigellachie on the Spey to Boat of Garten and soon distilleries were springing up along the line like homesteads across the American Midwest. The train chugged upstream for 30 miles (48km), stopping at all the tiny stations en route, including one for the private Knockando House. Knockando's old station building is now the reception centre at Tamdhu, which began distilling in 1897. The following year it joined Glenrothes and

The elegantly shaped twinned-pagoda roof of Strathisla was built in the 1870s.

Bunnahabhain to form Highland Distilleries Co., which is now part of the Edrington Group, which also owns Macallan.

After 20 years lying idle in the first half of the 20th century, Tamdhu was brought back to life and then expanded in the 1970s into a modern six-still distillery, which uniquely malts all its own barley on site.

TOMINTOUL

✉ Kirkmichael, Ballindalloch, Grampian
⌂ www.tomintouldistillery.co.uk

Of all the Speyside distilleries that bolted the magic word "Glenlivet" onto their names in the hope of added lustre, Tomintoul-Glenlivet has the best case, being a virtual next-door neighbour. Yet the real

heyday of Glenlivet was aleady long past when this distillery was built in 1965. Situated 5 miles (8 km) from the village of Tomintoul, it is the highest distillery in the Highlands at 350 m (1,150 ft).

The village was a staging post on the old military road from Corgaff to Fort George, and was built after the Jacobite Rising of 1745 *(see p45)* in an attempt to bring the Highlands to heel. At first it was little more than a village inn, where travellers would rest and numb the cold with whisky at a penny a dram. By 1823, it had its first licensed distillery called Delnabo.

The Tomintoul Distillery was sited on the Glenlivet estate beside the River Avon to take advantage of the crystal clear water from the Ballantruan spring. It was first bottled as a single malt in 1972, though its main role was to supply whisky for blending by parent company Whyte & Mackay. Now owned by Angus Dundee distillers, Tomintoul's range of bottlings is set to increase.

🍶 **TOMINTOUL 10-YEAR-OLD** 40% ABV
A gentle, vaguely spicy malt, with nut and cinnamon notes.

🍶 **TOMINTOUL 16-YEAR-OLD** 40% ABV
A more ample, sweet-centred texture in the mouth than the 10-year-old expression.

Tomintoul, a near-neighbour of the more famous Glenlivet, is the highest distillery in Speyside.

TORMORE

✉ Grantown North Spey, Moray
⌂ www.Tormore.com

After the spate of distilleries that flooded the region at the end of the 19th century, there was a long wait for the next one. It was not until 1960 that Tormore was built on Speyside. The design, by architect Sir Albert Richardson, president of the Royal Academy, was nothing if not bold, and the original drawings even featured a chimney stack shaped like a giant whisky bottle and a clock that chimed *Highland Laddie* on the hour. The chimney was rejected by the clients – Shenley Industries of America – but the clock survived into the final build, as did the massive stillhouse, clad in pale granite, which houses eight stills.

Tormore 12-Year-Old

After years as a fairly anonymous blending malt and key ingredient in the Long John brand *(see p141)*, Tormore has more recently rediscovered itself as a single.

🍶 **TORMORE 12-YEAR-OLD** 40% ABV ● A caramel-scented, creamy whisky, with some light spicy notes.

HIGHLANDS AND ISLANDS

As you drive northwards from Stirling, leaving behind the Lowlands and entering the Scottish Highlands, the scenery suddenly changes dramatically. If it feels as though you are entering a different world, imagine what it was like before tarmac roads and petrol stations.

The mountainous landscape may have lost some of its stature in the last 400 million years, having once been as high as the Himalayas, but it is still a real and inspiring force of nature.

From the outset, this was prime whisky-making country. There was no shortage of water, and fuel was plentiful in the form of peat. If the quality of the barley was somewhat poorer than that grown along the fertile east coast, there was an added incentive to distil it into something more valuable, something powerful enough to numb the depressing effects of a long Highland winter.

Whenever the authorities tried to suppress unlicensed whisky, they only added to its allure. For a ferociously independent Highlander of the 18th century, this forbidden fruit suddenly tasted all the sweeter. It was there to toast the Jacobite "King O'er the Water" and raise two fingers to the bloated Hanoverian on the throne.

The trouble with the Highlands as a whisky region is its vastness. It extends from Glengoyne, half an hour's drive

north of Glasgow, to Old Pulteney, just south of John O'Groats, or to Highland Park, on Orkney, if you want to stretch it even further. Taste these three whiskies blind and you would be hard pressed to say they were from the same region.

A MISCELLANY OF STYLES

Those distilleries designated "Highland" have never had the critical mass to create a house style. There are clusters of them on the Black Isle; the northeast corner of Aberdeenshire and the Perthshire glens are dotted with them, but there has never been the concentration that there is in Speyside or on Islay. As a result, Highland distilleries have usually evolved in isolation – they were there to satisfy a local demand and any passing trade.

Perhaps "Highland" whiskies can only be defined by what they are not. They tend not to use heavily peated malt like Islay, though they often carry more of a smoky fragrance than Speyside. Unlike Lowland whiskies, which tend towards dryness on the tongue, Highland whiskies are richer and more robust.

Plentiful supplies of water and peat mean there is a high concentration of distilleries in the Highlands and Islands.

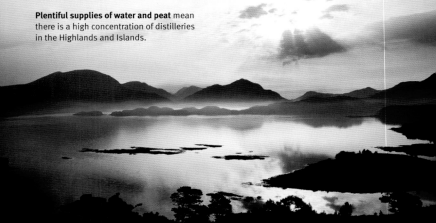

HIGHLANDS AND ISLANDS DISTILLERIES

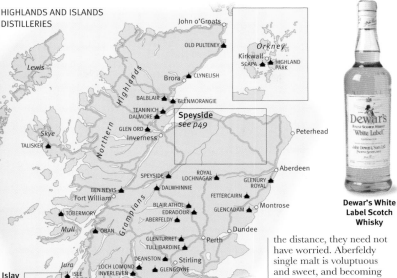

John o'Groats

OLD PULTENEY

Orkney

Kirkwall
SCAPA ◆ HIGHLAND PARK

Brora ◆ CLYNELISH

Lewis

Highlands

BALBLAIR ◆ GLENMORANGIE

TEANINICH
DALMORE

GLEN ORD

Inverness

Skye

TALISKER

Northern

Speyside
see p49

Peterhead

SPEYSIDE
ROYAL LOCHNAGAR

GLENURY ROYAL

Aberdeen

BEN NEVIS
Fort William

DALWHINNIE

Grampians

FETTERCAIRN

BLAIR ATHOL
EDRADOUR
ABERFELDY

GLENCADAM

Montrose

TOBERMORY

Mull

OBAN

Dundee

GLENTURRET
TULLIBARDINE

Perth

Jura

DEANSTON
INVERLEVEN
LOCH LOMOND

Stirling

GLENGOYNE

Islay
e p99

ISLE OF JURA

Glasgow

ARRAN

Arran

GLEN SCOTIA
SPRINGBANK

Campbeltown
GLENGYLE

At Aberfeldy, there are eight large washbacks made of Siberian larch, with two additional state-of-the-art stainless-steel washbacks nearby.

Dewar's White Label Scotch Whisky

ABERFELDY

✉ Aberfeldy, Perthshire
🖰 www.dewarswow.com
⛴ Open to visitors

Most of the malt whisky distilleries that sprang up in late-Victorian Scotland were built as an act of faith, in the hope that there would be a ready market among the big blenders once the spirit began trickling off the still.

The story of Aberfeldy is rather different. It was established in the Perthshire town of Aberfeldy by John Dewar & Sons in 1898 and its role – then as now – was to supply malt for the firm's top-selling blend, Dewar's White Label. Unless the brand falls from grace as the most popular Scotch in the United States, Aberfeldy's purpose in life is unlikely to change.

The site for the distillery was chosen partly for sentimental reasons – it was close to the bothy where John Dewar was born and from where – so legend has it – he walked to Perth in 1828, with his eyes set on making his fortune. More importantly, the chosen site also had a good consistent source of water, as well as a railway link to Dewar & Sons' head office in Perth.

Aberfeldy's village elders had grown up in the days of illicit whisky making and had later witnessed the town's first licensed distillery close for good in 1867. If they had doubts about Dewar's venture and whether it would last

the distance, they need not have worried. Aberfeldy single malt is voluptuous and sweet, and becoming increasingly available as 12 and 18-year-old expressions.

ARDMORE

✉ Kennethmont, Aberdeenshire

By the time its creator William Teacher died in 1876, Teacher's Highland Cream had become a popular blend in Scotland, with its own network of bars, known as Teacher's Dram Shops, in Glasgow.

His son Adam expanded the business at home and abroad until he felt the need for his own distillery, to ensure a steady supply of malt for his blend. At some point in the 1890s, he stayed at Leith Hall, a fine Georgian house

Ardmore is one of Scotland's biggest distilleries, and most of its malt is used for blending.

by Kennethmont, in the northeast of Aberdeenshire, and found a suitable site nearby, with its own source of spring water.

The result was Ardmore (named after the Teachers' ancestral home on the west coast), which was finished in 1898, a year before Adam died.

One of the early advertisements for "Teacher's Old Scotch Whiskies" shows Ardmore as a huge industrial distillery, right beside the tracks on the main Aberdeen-to-Inverness line. It was ambitious in scale, but left the business saddled with punitive interest charges for

Ardmore Highland Single Malt

years, at a time when whisky sales were deep in the doldrums.

Both the distillery and the family firm managed to survive intact until 1976, when the company was bought up by Allied Distillers. By this time, it had expanded – there were now eight stills, with a production of 4.5 million litres (1 million gallons) a year. Today, the Ardmore Distillery is owned by the makers of Jim Beam, in America.

Occasional bottlings of a smoky, oily single malt appear, but Ardmore's principal role remains that of supplying malt for blends – notably Teacher's.

DEWAR'S WORLD OF WHISKY AT ABERFELDY

After a £2 million refit in 2000, Aberfeldy's new American owners, Bacardi, reopened the distillery as the all-singing, all-dancing "Dewar's World of Whisky". Visitors receive the full brand experience, as well as an insight into the life of the Edwardian whisky baron Tommy Dewar. Within the exhibition, there is a re-creation of his London office and of the Perth blending room, circa 1929. Outside, standing guard over the distillery is a life-size statue of the famous Pipe Major, whose image appears on every bottle of "White Label".

The distillery gets a little lost in all of this, though the view from the still room is definitely worth seeing. In summer, when the weather is fine, the shutters are pulled up, leaving the room open to the elements, so cool air can blow in and mix with the heat radiating off the stills. To underline the fact that this is all about the blend, at the end of the tour, visitors are given a dram of White Label. You can, however, try the silky-textured single malt, with its aromas of pear drops and vanilla.

The visitor centre at Aberfeldy is a celebration of the Dewar's brand.

BALBLAIR

✉ Edderton, Tain, Ross-shire
🖐 www.inverhouse.com

The original Balblair was built in 1790, making it the second-oldest working distillery in Scotland, according to the claims of its current owners, Inver House.

In truth, Balblair moved from its original site in 1872, but only by a stone's throw and still with the Ross family, who had been in charge almost since day one. The decision to move was to allow for the expansion of the distillery and to site it right beside the railway line.

After three generations, the Ross family line petered out and Balblair was acquired by Alexander Cowan in 1894. Cowan promptly rebuilt it into pretty much what you can see today from the east coast train line.

Balblair 1[
Single M[

Over the years, the malt has played its part in many blends, notably Bells, Whyte & Mackay, and – more recently – Ballantine's.

Balblair has recently been relaunched as a vintage malt, in much the same vein as Glenrothes – even the squat bottles are similarly shaped.

BEN NEVIS

✉ Lochy Bridge, Fort William
🖐 www.bennevisdistillery.com
⛰ Open to visitors

The west coast's island distilleries have tended to flourish, while those on the mainland opposite are few and far between. When Glen Lochy closed for good in 1983, Ben Nevis became the only distillery in Fort William and the most northerly one on the west coast.

Ben Nevis was founded beside Loch Linnhe by

Nestled at the foot of Ben Nevis, Britain's highest mountain, is the distillery of the same name.

"Long John" Macdonald in 1825. By the 1880s, when the distillery was producing 680,000 litres (150,000 gallons) a year, the Macdonald family had their own fleet of steamers to carry the whisky down the loch. They also had their own farm, sawmill, and workshops, which, together with the distillery, employed some 230 people. The farm was integrally involved, with barley at one end and 200 head of cattle at the other to hoover up the draff produced.

The whisky was called "Long John's Dew of Ben Nevis", a name that was to resurface years later as a popular blend owned by Whitbread. In 1981, the brewer bought the distillery outright, owning it until they decided to get out of Scotch whisky altogether a decade later. Since then Ben Nevis has belonged to the Japanese drinks giant Nikka.

Today, the distillery incorporates "The Legend of the Dew of Ben Nevis" visitor centre and it is one of the few where you can buy your own cask of malt whisky and have it kept under bond in the warehouse until it is ready for bottling. Over 15 years a sherry butt of Ben Nevis will have lost about a fifth of its contents through evaporation, leaving enough for around 600 bottles.

BLAIR ATHOL'S ASSOCIATION WITH BELL'S

When Arthur Bell bought Blair Athol Distillery in 1933, a year after it was forced to shut, it was the start of a close association. Blair Athol was a key component of the Bell's blend *(see p120)*, and in 1970 another pair of stills was added and production was cranked up by 300 per cent, as Bell's sought to increase its market share. Some in the industry felt Bell's was working its stills too hard and was causing heavier, unpleasant compounds to rise up the neck and into the condensers, thereby adversely affecting the spirit. Bell's attained its goal, but by the 1980s had conceded its Scottish market leadership to Famous Grouse.

Subsequently, Bell's became embroiled in one of the most bitter takeover battles in the industry's history, when it was acquired in 1985 by Guinness (which later merged with Grand Met to become Diageo, the present owners).

Since the mid-1980s, life at Blair Athol has calmed down considerably. Production has settled at around 38,000 litres (8,400 gallons) a week. Meanwhile, Bell's has been turned into an 8-year-old blend. It is still a big brand in South Africa and the UK, where it shares the lead position with Famous Grouse.

Comedian Eric Morecambe *(left)* presents football manager Don Revie with a bottle of Bell's in the 1970s, the brand's heyday.

BLAIR ATHOL

✉ Pitlochry, Perthshire
🖥 www.discovering-distilleries.com
🏛 Open to visitors

When the Perthshire town of Pitlochry was little more than a village, and long before the Victorian tourists first arrived, John Stewart and Robert Robertson opened the Aldour Distillery here in 1798. The name came from the Gaelic *allt dour*

Much of the Blair Athol 12-Year-Old produced is consumed here at the distillery, by the 30,000 visitors who turn up each year.

(meaning "burn of the otter"). In an area heaving with illicit stills, business proved tough for this licensed tax-paying distillery, and Aldour soon closed.

In 1826, Alexander Connacher resurrected the distillery, calling it Blair Athol, even though it was some distance south of the village of Blair Atholl. Whether the spelling was different by accident or by design is unclear.

During the second half of the 19th century it belonged to Peter Mackenzie & Co. and had close ties with the Perth blender Arthur Bell & Sons. Bell steadfastly refused to divulge the recipe for his blends, except to say that they included whiskies from Glenlivet, Stirlingshire, and Pitlochry. The latter was almost certainly Blair Athol.

Some Blair Athol malt is bottled today as a dark, rich, plummy 12-year-old.

CLYNELISH

✉ Brora, Sutherland
🖰 www.discovering-distilleries.com
⛴ Open by appointment only

Established in 1819 by the 1st Duke of Sutherland *(see below)*, Clynelish was first let to James Harpur, from Midlothian, and then in 1846 to George Lawson, who expanded the distillery by adding a new kiln and a new set of stills.

During the salmon season, trade was brisk, with hordes of fishermen sipping flasks of whisky on the banks of the River Brora, the town's main tourist attraction.

In 1896, Clynelish was transformed into a classic late-Victorian distillery, with a pair of pagoda roofs and an enclosed courtyard. It was state of the art, except for the lack of electricity.

Clynelish became the "old" Clynelish when it was shut down in 1967 and a brash, box-shaped "new" Clynelish sprang up alongside it. Two years later, the old distillery was back. Operating under the name Brora Distillery, it was charged with

One of the most northerly distilleries in Scotland, Clynelish was completely rebuilt in 1967.

making a peat-soaked, Islay-style whisky that was much in demand by blenders.

For a while, Brora and the "new" Clynelish bubbled away in tandem, until the former was shut down for good in 1983. You can still see it more or less intact; though, with most of its guts ripped out, it appears rather empty and forlorn.

Traditionalists may find it more pleasing on the eye than the plate-glass 1960s unit next door, but it was probably cramped and drafty to work in. It is unlikely anyone at the "new" Clynelish Distillery would swap their warm well-lit space for one in the "old" building. Besides,

Clynelish 14-Year-Old

on a good day the views from the still room can be truly magnificent.

🥃 **CLYNELISH 14-YEAR-OLD** 46% ABV
This is relatively rare and has a fragrant, maritime style, a whiff of smoke, and a unique waxiness on the palate.

DALMORE

✉ Alness, Ross-shire
🖰 www.thedalmore.com
⛴ Open to visitors

The name Dalmore is part Gaelic and part Norse and means "the big meadowland". The distillery was set up in 1839 on the banks of the Cromarty Firth, and looks out across the water to the Black Isle, where some of the best barley in Scotland can be found. With good-quality grain, no shortage of peat, and water from the nearby River Alness, the site was well chosen.

Dalmore took a while to get into its stride, however. Its founder, Alexander Matheson, lasted less than a decade, and his successor, Mrs Margaret Sutherland, had other engagements, to judge from her job title as "sometime distiller".

This all changed in 1886, when Dalmore was bought by the local Mackenzie family, who were soon supplying James Whyte and Charles Mackay, in Glasgow, with malt for their blends.

DISSIPATION AND VICE

The 1st Duke of Sutherland was a landowner on an epic scale, with estates that stretched right across the northern Highlands. Keen to entice his crofting tenants off the land, he started a series of ventures, including a salt factory and a brick works. In 1819, he added a distillery, Clynelish, on the outskirts of Brora.

The duke's other reason for building a licensed distillery was to wean his tenants off moonshine. According to his land commissioner, James Loch, this had caused "every species of deceit, vice, idleness, and dissipation". If the people would not sober up and leave the land, then they needed encouraging. In the same year Clynelish was built, 250 crofts were burnt down in the Highland Clearances, and it is claimed that 15,000 tenants were "persuaded" to make room for sheep on the Sutherland estates.

1st Duke of Sutherland

THE AMERICANS ARE COMING

In 1905, Dalwhinnie was bought by Cook & Bernheimer, the largest distilling company in America. This was the first US venture into Scotch whisky and it fuelled industry fears that this was the start of a giant takeover bid. Flying the Stars and Stripes above their warehouse in Leith can have done nothing to allay those fears. With US Prohibition, however, Dalwhinnie slipped safely back into Scottish hands in 1919.

The bond between the distillery and the firm of blenders has endured ever since, being formalized in 1960, when Dalmore officially became part of Whyte & Mackay.

During the First World War the distillery was used as a place to prepare mines, when a contingent of the US Navy was stationed here. It survived unscathed and, despite a major expansion in the 1960s, the two-storey stone buildings retain their solid Victorian feel.

The three spirit stills are clad in copper cooling jackets, and one of them dates back to 1874. What makes them look even more

Picturesquely set on the banks of the Cromarty Firth, Dalmore looks out towards the Black Isle.

eccentric is the way their necks have been abruptly cut off, like those at Cragganmore, on Speyside. Whether this was by accident or by design is unclear, but they certainly seem to work and no one has since dared tinker with the shape whenever the stills have needed replacement. Beside the stills and the gleaming brass spirits safe, there is a giant control console that could have come from a 1950s sci-fi movie.

The Victorian feel of the distillery is enhanced by the dark panelling in the offices above the visitor centre, which came from an old shooting lodge that was being pulled down on the Black Isle. There is also the use of the Mackenzie's family crest, with its 12-point stag's head, on the Dalmore label.

🍸 **THE DALMORE 12-YEAR-OLD** 40% ABV ● A distinct sherried nose, in keeping with its polished mahogany colour, gives way

to a creamy texture and fruit-cake notes on the tongue.

🍸 **THE DALMORE 21-YEAR-OLD** 43% ABV ● Ripe and floral on the nose, with a rich, nutty, spicy character in the mouth.

DALWHINNIE

✉ Dalwhinnie, Inverness-shire
🖰 www.discovering-distilleries.com
🚪 Open to visitors

Just past Drumochter Pass, right beside the A9, is one of the highest whisky distilleries in Scotland. Dalwhinnie lies in an empty, wind-swept bowl 327 m (1,073 ft) above sea level. Photographs often show the distillery half-buried in snow, and tour guides tell of the time the workers once had to crawl from their cottages via top-floor windows to get to work, such were the drifts that day. In truth, the snow has been much less reliable of late, as visitors to the country's ski resorts will readily confirm.

Yet, thanks to the wind-chill factor, Dalwhinnie can claim to be one of the coldest inhabited places in Britain, with a mean annual temperature of just 6°C (43°F) – perfect conditions for making whisky.

The water that feeds the distillery is equally chilled, coming from the Allt an t-Sluic spring, 610 m (2,000 ft)

Despite Dalwhinnie's apparent isolation, it has always had vital transport links close by.

up in the Drumochter Hills. Having cold, pure water was crucial to John Grant, Alex Mackenzie, and George Sillar, who established what was originally the Strathspey Distillery here in 1897. Equally important was the proximity of the railway and the Great North Road, which passed right in front of the distillery at the time. This allowed easy access for the raw ingredients coming in and the filled casks going out.

Within a year, Strathspey had been sold and re-named Dalwhinnie. The distillery was then in American hands for 14 years at the beginning of the 20th century *(see p81)*. After that, it was acquired in 1919 by the blenders Macdonald Greenlees, who sold it on to the Distillers Company, who (as Diageo) still own it today.

From the early 1920s, Dalwhinnie was a key filling for the Black & White blend. In fact, it was the brand's spiritual home until it was picked to be one of Diageo's "Classic Malts".

Dalwhinnie is a true Highland thoroughbred, with a dense creamy texture, thanks in part to the use of old-fashioned copper worms to condense the spirit. These sit in outdoor tanks, steaming away like giant hot tubs in the cold air.

🍸 **DALWHINNIE 15-YEAR-OLD** 43% ABV
Sweet, aromatic, and subtly infused with smoke, this complex malt is thick on the tongue.

Dalwhinnie 15-Year-Old

Etradour is Scotland's smallest distillery. The whisky is made here by hand by just three men.

expanded, with the number of stills doubling or tripling. In the process, whisky making lost some of its charm, as it became apparent just how far this industry had come from its artisan roots.

Anyone feeling nostalgic to see how whisky emerged from the farm should head for the hills beyond the Perthshire town of Pitlochry to find Scotland's smallest working distillery.

Founded in 1823, Edradour seems hardly to have changed at all since, with its rough, whitewashed walls giving the building the feel of a farmstead.

It fills just 12 casks of whisky a week from its tiny stills, to produce a raft of different ages and finishes down the line for its owner Andrew Symington, who bought the distillery in 2002 from the drinks company Pernod Ricard.

Edradour played a bit part in the House of Lords blend, one of many smuggled into the United States during Prohibition. Later, it was a signature malt in King's Ransom, a super-deluxe blend from William Whitely, who bought the distillery in 1933. It was the world's most expensive whisky when a consignment of 200,000 bottles went down with the

EDRADOUR

✉ Pitlochry, Perthshire
🖥 www.edradour.co.uk
🏛 Open to visitors

During the postwar boom for blended Scotch a few new distilleries were built, but many more were

SS Politician in 1941, an event that inspired the novel *Whisky Galore* by Compton Mackenzie *(see p140)*.

That the distillery has survived into the 21st century suggests it was simply overlooked by its big-industry bosses. Now back in independent hands, its doll's-house size is very much prized as a virtue.

🍸 **EDRADOUR 10-YEAR-OLD** 40% ABV
Clean peppermint nose with a trace of smoke; richer, nutty flavours on the tongue.

FETTERCAIRN

✉ Laurencekirk, Kincardineshire
🏛 Open to visitors

Despite the abundance of good-quality barley, there are very few distilleries along the east coast of Scotland south of Aberdeenshire. One lone survivor, in the Mearns of Kincardineshire, is Fettercairn, which was an old grain mill converted to distilling in 1823. The village itself stands below the Cairn o'Mount, the high, hump-backed hill that guards the old road over the Grampian Mountains to Deeside.

After various false starts and different owners, the Fettercairn Distillery Co. was formed in 1887, with Sir John Gladstone as chairman. His son, William, was the

Liberal Prime Minister who enshrined the "angels' share" in law, this being the 2 per cent of spirit that is lost through evaporation from the casks each year, and which distillers would no longer be taxed on.

Fast-forward to the present and Fettercairn is now part of the Indian corporation United Breweries (UB Group), who bought it along with then owners Whyte & Mackay in 2007.

GLENCADAM

✉ Brechin, Angus
🖰 www.glencadam.com
🚪 Open by appointment

When Allied Distillers closed down Glencadam in 2000 and made all but one of the distillery workers redundant, no one really believed the distillery would be able to survive.

Established in 1825 by George Cooper, it had played a minor role in Ballantine's and in Stewarts Cream of the Barley *(see p152)*, a blend that seems to have faded away somewhat, at least in Scotland. Being out on a limb as the only distillery in Angus must have fuelled this sense of vulnerability.

But, in 2003, a white knight was found in the shape of Angus Dundee Distillers. After 50 years in the whisky business, they decided it was time to acquire a distillery. As fully matured stocks come on stream, expect to see more Glencadam as a single malt.

GLENDRONACH

✉ Forgue, Huntly, Aberdeenshire
🖰 www.theglendronach.com
🚪 Open to visitors

Like its near neighbour Ardmore, Glendronach has been a part of the Teacher's story almost from the day the famous blend was created in the late19th

Stewarts Cream of the Barley

century, though it was only bought by William Teacher & Sons in 1960.

It began life in 1826 as Glendronach Distillery, a partnership of local farmers and traders run by James Allardice. The business was still going strong when the great whisky writer Alfred Barnard visited in the 1880s. He described the distillery, nestled among rolling hills beside the Dronach Burn, as "quaint and picturesque".

Glendronach was producing 227,000 litres (50,000 gallons) of pure Highland malt a year when it was sold to a firm of blenders in 1899, and the distillery struggled on until 1920, when it was bought by Captain Charles Grant, the son of William Grant, of Glenfiddich. It remained in family hands until the 1960s, and, but for a doubling of the stills to four, little has changed since.

On the distillery tour, visitors are shown the old floor maltings, where, until quite recently, the barley was spread out and laboriously turned by hand. All the washbacks are of Oregon pine, and the copper stills have been kept true to the original 19th-century design. Even the dunnage warehouses, with their traditional earthen floors, are evocative of a simpler, bygone era.

GLEN GARIOCH

✉ Oldmeldrum, Aberdeenshire
🖰 www.glengarioch.co.uk
🚪 Open to visitors

The town of Oldmeldrum, on the road to Banff from Aberdeen, has had its own distillery since 1798. Given how many distilleries have come and gone in the northeast, Glen Garioch's survival into its third century is no small achievement.

With no stainless steel in sight, a visit to Glendronach Distillery is like a step back in time.

Inevitably, a successful blend was involved – in this case, Vat 69, the brand created by William Sanderson (*see p153*), of Aberdeen.

Sanderson first encountered Glen Garioch (pronounced "glen geerie") when it was owned by a firm of blenders in Leith. In 1886, he bought a half-share in the distillery, and by 1921 his son, together with other investors, gained full control of the business.

After numerous changes in ownership since, and extended periods of lying idle, Glen Garioch is now in good hands with Morrison Bowmore. Having bottled a single malt as early as 1972, it now produces a range of smooth-textured malts, aged at 10, 15, and 21 years, and a complex 46-year-old rarity.

Glen Garioch 46-Year-Old

GLENGOYNE

✉ Drumgoyne, Stirlingshire
🖰 www.glengoyne.com
⛴ Open to visitors

In the sentimentalized view of the Highlands propagated by the Victorians, the epicentre of whisky smuggling was Glenlivet, on Speyside, where every bothy supposedly gurgled with an illicit still. In fact, the production of

Having fallen silent in the mid-1990s, Glen Garioch Distillery is working once again.

moonshine flourished right across the Highlands, just about anywhere there was ease of concealment and plentiful water.

The Campsie Fells, east of Loch Lomond, were ideal, especially the hidden glen beneath Drumgoyne Hill. The hill represents the first volcanic outcrop of the Campsies, and down its steep, southern flank runs a burn, which ends in a waterfall. Whether it was the sound of the cascade that attracted the first whisky makers is unknown, but once here there was plenty of foliage to provide cover.

Before the 1823 Excise Act changed the whisky industry for good in the following years, there were at least 18 illegal distillers in this pocket of Stirlingshire. Among them was probably George

Connell, who finally took out a licence for his Burnfoot Distillery (later renamed Glengoyne) in 1833.

With nearby Glasgow expanding at breakneck speed, the timing was good. Before long, the whisky was being sold there by Hugh Lang, who ran a pub in the Broomielaw district.

From selling jugs of Glengoyne malt, the Langs progressed to blending, which they did with considerable success, such that in 1876 they were able to buy the distillery, which was then called Glen Guin (Gaelic for "glen of the wild geese").

The distillery was rebuilt in the mid-1960s, having been taken over by the Robertson Trust, part of the group that now owns Famous Grouse and Macallan. It lost its tall chimney, and smoke no longer billowed from its handsome pagoda roof.

Other than that, the distillery has changed little. It has always fitted snugly into its tight-sided glen, and further expansion is not an option. Due to lack of space, the eight warehouses, where 2 million litres (440,000 gallons) of Glengoyne lie in cask, are across the road and officially in the Lowlands, the distillery being situated right on the Highland Line.

After years in the shadow of its stablemate Macallan,

Originally called Burnfoot, the distillery at Glengoyne has had a licence since 1833.

Glengoyne was bought by Ian Macleod Distillers in 2003, and, as their only distillery, it is clearly a cherished asset.

GLENGOYNE 10-YEAR-OLD
43% ABV ● Appealing cut-grass aromas with notes of apple peel, nuts, and caramel.

GLENGOYNE 12-YEAR-OLD
57.2% ABV ● A cask-strength take on the above, using the same unpeated malt and some sherry casks to give a marzipan-scented, mouth-filling dram.

GLENMORANGIE

✉ Tain, Ross-shire
🖥 www.glenmorangie.com
🏛 Open to visitors

The "Glen of Tranquillity" suggests a bucolic valley hidden deep in the Highlands. Instead, Glenmorangie is down by the shore of the Dornoch Firth and positively bustling these days as the top-selling malt in Scotland, with increasingly ambitious plans abroad now that it is part of the French luxury goods group LVMH.

The distillery has come a long way since its farmyard roots in the mid-19th century, when it was converted from a brewery by William Matheson, who had been involved in Balblair since the 1820s. It had been an adjunct to the old Morangie farmhouse, and probably operated on a seasonal basis whenever there was grain to spare after the harvest. By the time the great whisky writer Alfred Barnard visited in the 1880s, he declared it was "the most ancient and primitive [distillery] we have seen" and "almost in ruins".

William's eldest son, John Matheson, was now in charge, and before the distillery collapsed altogether, he dragged in outside investors to form the Glenmorangie Distillery Company.

They rebuilt the distillery, and production doubled to satisfy demand down south, with the odd cask making its way as far as San Francisco, on the west coast of the United States. When the local newspaper discovered that a shipment had been sent to Rome, the townspeople wondered whether the Pope himself had asked to sample "the Mountain Dew of Easter Ross".

One of Glenmorangie's main customers was the prominent firm of blenders Macdonald & Muir, in Leith, who bought the distillery and its stocks for £74,100 in 1918. Production was stepped up to 500,000 litres (110,000 gallons) a year, much of which went into blends like Highland Queen and Martin's VVO. But for a five-year period in mothballs during the Depression of the 1930s, the distillery was kept busy by the US market, where most of Macdonald & Muir's brands were sold. As long as sales there continued to flourish, Glenmorangie's future looked secure.

Unfortunately, in the 1970s, the United States began to fall out of love with blended whisky, as sales of vodka there began to boom. This persuaded the owners of the distillery to follow Glenfiddich into the brave new world of single malt.

It turned out to be the best decision they could ever have made, and today all but a drop is bottled as Glenmorangie, mainly as a 10-year-old, though surrounded by a family of different finishes.

The use of special casks to "finish off" the whisky for a few months before bottling was pioneered by the company. Today, after its relaunch in 2007, there are three main whisky finishes: La Santa, (from sherry casks), Quinta Ruban (from port casks), and Nectar d'Or (from Sauternes casks).

GLENMORANGIE'S STILLS

When William Matheson first obtained his licence to distill at Glenmorangie in 1843, he bought a pair of second-hand gin stills from a firm in London. These have been endlessly reproduced ever since, in the sure knowledge that to change their unique design would be to alter Glenmorangie for good. The necks are the tallest in Scotland and start with a boil ball (*see p28*) that rises almost 5.2m (17ft) into the air. This increases the reflux, so the alcoholic vapours condense on the inside of the neck and run back into the still. The result? A particularly fresh and clean final spirit.

Glenmorangie's stills have the longest necks of any pot stills in Scotland.

GLEN
GARIOCH

WASH STILL

CONTENTS
25,000
LITRES

GLEN
GARIOCH
SPIRIT STILL
N° 1
CONTENTS
11,000
LITRES

GLEN
GARIOC
SPIRIT S
N° 2
CONTENT
11,000
LITRES

Glen Garioch's stills have provided whisky for the famous Vat 69 blend for much of their lives, but now the distillery's output is geared towards a range of smooth single malts.

GLEN ORD

✉ Muir of Ord, Ross-shire
🔗 www.discovering-distilleries.com
⛴ Open to visitors

Despite the name, Glen Ord lies not in a valley but in the fertile flatlands between the mountains and the sea, 15 miles (24 km) northwest of Inverness at Muir of Ord. Not far away, Ferintosh Distillery once stood – the first one of any size in Scotland. It closed in the late 18th century, and some 50 years later Alexander Mackenzie built Glen Ord in 1837.

With issues over water rights, which it shared with a mill, and fierce competition from nine rival distilleries nearby, Mackenzie's venture stumbled at first, until the widow of his successor married a local banker, who had the funds to maintain it.

In 1923, Glen Ord was swallowed up by the joint forces of Johnnie Walker and John Dewar & Sons, along with Pulteney and the now-defunct Parkmore, in a deal worth £2 million.

The total stocks of maturing whisky were put at 36 million litres (8 million gallons) – something of a whisky loch on its own. With the vast US market out of bounds because of Prohibition, supply was fast outstripping demand, and the industry was heading for decline.

Singleton of Glen Ord

Glen Ord can boast its own maltings on site, though not in the sense of traditional floor maltings, where the grain is turned by hand and then malted over a peat fire. Those at Glen Ord are on an industrial scale, to supply not just this distillery, but its Diageo stablemates in the north of Scotland also.

Renovated and expanded to six stills in the 1960s, Glen Ord can produce 3.4 million litres (750,000 gallons) of whisky a year.

Various single malts have appeared, from Ord, to Glenordie, to Singleton of Glen Ord, which was launched in 2006. After ageing in predominantly European oak, it has a fragrant marzipan nose and a silky texture in the mouth.

GLEN SCOTIA

✉ Campbeltown, Argyll

Springbank was almost the only surviving distillery of Campbeltown's spectacular boom and bust, but not quite. Much smaller and far less well known is Glen Scotia, which was first licensed in 1835, to Stuart Galbraith & Co. The family firm retained control until 1895, giving Glen Scotia the same sense of continuity as Springbank. After that, it was passed around between various owners.

In 1930, at the low point of Campbeltown's whisky trade, the distillery manager committed suicide in Campbeltown Loch. His name was Duncan MacCallum and his ghost is said to haunt the still room to this day.

After periods of inactivity recently, Glen Scotia's pair of stills is back in action under its present owners, the Loch Lomond Distillery Co. The malt is lightly smoked, with a rich, silky texture.

GLENTURRET

✉ Crieff, Perthshire
🔗 www.thefamousgrouse.com
⛴ Open to visitors

As well as its claims to be the oldest working distillery in Scotland, Glenturret is the spiritual home of Scotland's favourite blend of Scotch whisky, The Famous Grouse. This fact is made clear before you even enter the Perthshire distillery by a grouse that acts as a road sign pointing the way just beyond Crieff, and by a giant 5.2-m (17-ft) sculpture of the same bird in the car park.

In the past, the only animal visitors were told about was Towser, the distillery cat. As the celebrated catcher of nearly 30,000 mice from 1963 to 1984, she secured a place in the *Guinness World Records*. A small statue of her stands by the entrance. In comparison, Brooke, the current distillery cat, is a much less accomplished mouser.

For today's visitors, though, it is the full grouse and nothing but the grouse, with the cheeky cartoon version of the bird popping up just about everywhere on the official distillery tour.

Glenturret was licensed in 1775 and was one of the very first farm distilleries to go legal in a region that brimmed with illicit stills.

Glenturret is not only the oldest distillery in Scotland, it is also the most visited.

DISTILLING ON ORKNEY

To early explorers, Orkney was the "Ultima Thule", the most northerly fringe of the known world. Far from the watchful eyes of the excise men, it was the perfect place for distilling, and, whenever there was barley to spare, whisky making thrived in a small, underground way.

Having secured the grain, outwitting the law was a relatively easy matter for one Magnus Eunson, whose day job gave him the perfect cover. Eunson was an elder of the Kirk in the island's capital, Kirkwall. He began distilling in 1798 on land known as the "High Park" and used to stash the barrels of whisky under his pulpit. Once, he was allegedly almost caught in a raid, when the casks were still out in the aisle, but, so the story goes, he quickly covered them with a coffin lid and white sheet just before the troops burst in. Then, he "let up a great wail for the dead" as one of the congregation whispered the dreaded word "smallpox" and the excise men fled.

Eunson was finally caught in 1813 by John Robertson, the chief excise officer, who decided to turn distiller himself. The illicit still became the

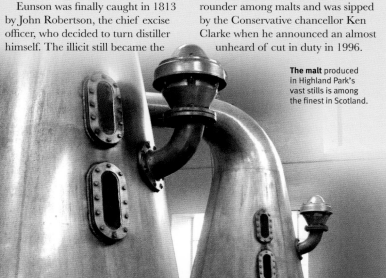

Highland Park 30-Year-Old

Highland Park Distillery under Robertson's partner, John Borwick, who died in 1860. The business passed to a relative in Fife, the Reverend James Borwick, for whom whisky making caused the sort of moral dilemmas that had never troubled Eunson, and the distillery was sold for £450 to a firm of brokers called Stuart & Mackay, who supplied the big blenders.

The quality of the whisky was put down to the use of "bere" – a primitive strain of barley – and to the tradition of laying heather on top of the smouldering peat in the kiln. Though the practice has long been abandoned, Highland Park retains a subtle heathery sweetness. It has been praised as the greatest all-rounder among malts and was sipped by the Conservative chancellor Ken Clarke when he announced an almost unheard of cut in duty in 1996.

The malt produced in Highland Park's vast stills is among the finest in Scotland.

Highland Park 15-Year-Old

Wedged in by the landscape and unable to expand, the distillery would probably not have survived without its link to the popular blend.

It was closed in 1921 and remained so until the late 1950s, when it was restored and reopened by a new owner, James Fairlie, who later sold it to one of his biggest customers, the French group Cointreau, in 1981.

Ten years later, it joined Highland Distillers, now the Edrington Group, who spent millions in 2002 creating "The Famous Grouse Experience" visitor centre.

Of what little Glenturret is bottled as a gentle, aperitif-style single malt, most is drunk at the distillery itself.

THE JEWEL IN THE CROWN

When the Bangalore-based billionaire Vijay Mallya bought Whyte & Mackay in 2007, the main attraction was doubtless the stocks of maturing Scotch whisky in bond for bottling in India and for blending with his own Indian whiskies. (India is the largest "whisky" market in the world, depending on your definition of what constitutes whisky.) Yet, there was also a sentimental element to Mallya's £560 million purchase. Whyte & Mackay's portfolio included the small Jura Distillery (see right), whose malt was also a much-loved favourite of his father's.

HIGHLAND PARK

✉ Kirkwall, Orkney
🖐 www.highlandpark.co.uk
⛴ Open to visitors

Founded in 1798, Highland Park (see also p89) is the most northerly of all Scotland's distilleries. Perhaps its greatest triumph is to have survived at all, given the distance from the big blenders, who have long dominated the whisky industry. Yet, survive it has, and with some aplomb, producing one of Scotland's very finest malts.

Highland Park is a favourite dram of Inspector Rebus – Ian Rankin's hard-boiled fictional cop – whose 20th anniversary in print was celebrated with a special single-cask bottling of Highland Park in 2006.

🍾 **HIGHLAND PARK 12-YEAR-OLD**
40% ABV ● Smooth and well rounded with a smoky, orange-peel sweetness and a trace of heather.

🍾 **HIGHLAND PARK 15-YEAR-OLD**
40% ABV ● Sweetly aromatic, fading to dry on the palate.

ISLE OF ARRAN

✉ Lochranza, Isle of Arran
🖐 www.arranwhisky.com
⛴ Open to visitors

In 1995, Harold Currie, previously MD of Chivas Brothers, achieved his dream of building a new distillery. The site was Lochranza, on the northern tip of Arran. It marked the return of whisky making to an island that once had almost 50

distilleries, most of them illegal, in the 19th century.

The first spirit flowed from the solitary pair of stills on 29 June, and at the opening ceremony a pair of golden eagles soared high above the distillery. This unanticipated fly-past was taken as a very good omen. Two years later, the Queen herself turned up to open the visitor centre.

The distillery has survived into its second decade thanks to sales through the distillery shop and a raft of different releases, including malts as young as three years – the absolute legal minimum. There was some criticism of releasing such youthful whisky, but maybe whisky does mature quicker here, in the slightly warmer and often wetter climate of Arran. The island is tucked down the Firth of Clyde, protected from the west by the sheltering arm of the Kintyre peninsula.

JURA

✉ Isle of Jura, Argyllshire
🖐 www.isleofjura.com
⛴ Open by appointment only

Like every Hebridean island of any size, there was a long established tradition of illicit whisky making on Jura before the first distillery was licensed in 1831. It had been built 20 years earlier by the local laird, Archibald Campbell, and, after many false starts, the distillery was finally leased to James Ferguson, who rebuilt it in 1875.

Hampered by the harsh conditions of the lease, the Fergusons decided to abandon the business in 1901. Having first ripped out all the distilling equipment, they sold it off. The laird pursued them in the courts for the next 20 years.

Meanwhile, the roofs of the distillery were removed

One of the last few independent distilleries in Scotland, Arran uses only traditional distilling methods.

to avoid paying rates. With each passing year, hopes that malt whisky would ever be made again on the island of Jura appeared to be fading away.

In the late 1950s, two of Jura's estate owners met to see what could be done to halt the ever-declining population on the island, due to lack of regular employment. With the aid of investment from Scottish & Newcastle, they recruited the architect and engineer William Delmé-Evans to resurrect the Jura Distillery.

Though on the same site, the distillery was to produce whisky that was totally different from the powerful, phenolic spirit made in the past. Using lightly peated malt and particularly large stills, which increased the ratio of copper to spirit, they created a softer Highland-style of whisky.

Lying just off the northeast tip of Islay, Jura has always lived in the shadow of its more famous neighbour, especially when it comes to malt whisky. It was not surprising then that its distillery chose to offer the world something different from Islay's muscular, peat-smoked whiskies.

🍶 **ISLE OF JURA 10-YEAR-OLD** 40% ABV • Relatively light bodied for a west coast whisky, with a trace of almonds and the faintest wisp of smoke on the tail.

🍶 **JURA SUPERSTITION** 43% ABV • A bigger, more succulent malt, with nutty, woody flavours of pine and marzipan.

Jura Superstition

LOCH LOMOND

✉ Alexandria, Dumbartonshire
🏠 www.lochlomond distillery.com
⚓ Open to visitors

The malt whisky favoured by Captain Haddock in the *Tintin* books comes from a large distillery by the southern shores of Loch Lomond. The original Loch Lomond Distillery existed for just a few years in the early 19th century and it was only resurrected in name in the 1960s.

It was bought in 1985 by Glen Catrine, a massive bottler of own-label whisky, which found itself needing malt for its blends.

With its mix of equipment – two conventional pot stills and four with rectifying heads – Loch Lomond can play many tunes. It can produce grassy, Lowland-style whiskies alongside meaty, full-bodied malts.

To complete the sense of self-sufficiency, there is also a continuous still for producing grain whisky. Two malts are produced – an unaged version that is popular in Germany,

Rebuilt in the 1960s, Jura Distillery uses lightly peated malts to produce Highland-style whiskies.

and the 21-year-old Black Label; there are occasional single-cask releases too.

OBAN

✉ Oban, Argyll
🏠 www.discovering-distilleries.com
⚓ Open to visitors

Now dubbed "The Gateway to the Isles", Oban was a tiny west coast fishing village in 1794, the year when John and Hugh Stevenson arrived here, having moved from Port Appin. They built a fine Georgian house and set up wa distillery next door. The Stevensons' original distillery

THE SCOTI FIND

Being hemmed in while the town grew up around it, Oban Distillery has always been hampered by lack of space. In the late 19th century, owner J Walter Higgen was forced to blast into the rock face behind the distillery to create a new warehouse. When he did so, he discovered a secret chamber, with tools and bones from a prehistoric tribe. These were identified as Scoti, cave-dwellers from around 5000 BCE. The remains are now on display in Edinburgh's Museum of Scotland, while the cave was blocked up again.

The still house at Oban was rebuilt in the 1960s and 70s, but its single pair of stills was left untouched.

was right by the water's edge, supposedly, but, if this is true, it means that the sea has retreated a good few hundred metres since then.

Oban was always a sideline to the Stevensons' main business interests, which included shipping, property, and quarrying slate. The distillery remained in family hands for three generations, until it was sold to J Walter Higgen in 1883. Oban had recently been connected by train down the west coast to Glasgow and this no doubt boosted demand. To maintain supply, Higgen kept his two stills working while carefully rebuilding the distillery over the next four years. What he created is more or less what you can still see today.

Oban was impressively self-sufficient, with water coming from two lochs in Ardconnel, a short distance behind the distillery, and a shed containing two years' supply of peat. The only problem it has ever had is one of space (*see p91*).

By the start of the 20th century, Oban was already being sold as a single malt, though with a production of just 160,000 litres (35,000 gallons) a year it was never in huge supply.

Oban 14-Year-Old

The distillery later joined forces with Glenlivet and Aultmore, before the three were bought out by John Dewar & Sons and then became part of the Distillers Company in 1930.

Given its size, Oban was never the first distillery the big industry bosses sought to close during periods of overproduction. But for a few years in the 1930s and 1960s, when the still house was rebuilt, Oban Distillery has been in continuous production.

Since 1990 it has been one of Diageo's "Classic Malts", which has done nothing to dampen the demand for it. Today, it is sold on allocation in selected markets.

🍶 **OBAN 14-YEAR-OLD** 43% ABV ● A mix of sea spray and citrus fruits on the nose, luscious and oily in the mouth, drying to a smoky finish.

OLD PULTENEY

📫 Huddart Street, Wick, Caithness
🖥 www.oldpulteney.com
⚓ Open by appointment only

The most northerly distillery on the Scottish mainland once stood in the midst of a late-19th century boom town. In its heyday, Wick had the feel of the Wild West,

especially in summer, when a 10,000-strong, itinerant workforce assembled to process the catch landed by Europe's largest herring fleet. At its peak, there were as many as a thousand fishing boats crammed into the harbour, such that you could walk from one side to the other from deck to deck.

Gutting fish was thirsty work, as James Henderson soon realized when he set up the town's first licensed distillery in 1828.

Henderson had made whisky on the side before and he decided to name his new venture after Sir William Johnstone Pulteney, who had helped establish the town in 1801 on behalf of the British Fisheries Society.

The distillery took its water from the Loch of Hempriggs, which was famously peaty – a characteristic that was enhanced in the whisky by malting the barley over a peat fire. The result, drunk unaged, would have been a robust, tarry spirit that perfectly reflected its maritime environment.

Coming from a town so impregnated with the reek of fish and the tang of the sea, a whisky that was gentle and understated would never have caught on. With a captive audience and no fear of illicit competition, thanks to a strong and active contingent of excisemen, Old Pulteney seemed ideally placed. There was also ready access to markets across the North Sea, in Russia, Germany, and the Baltic States, where most of the pickled, salted herring ended up on sale.

By the start of the 20th century, however, Wick was slipping into a decline, along with its herring fleet, while whisky was taking the rap for all manner of social ills

Old Pulteney 12-Year-Old

in the town. In 1922, the citizens voted to go dry – a state that remained until after World War II.

It did splutter into life once again in the 1950s, but only as an anonymous supplier of malt for blends such as Ballantine's. In 1957, it was rebuilt in a functional, bare-bones style, losing its original pagoda roof and gaining a modern chimney stack.

Royal Brackla 10-Year-Old

By the 1990s it was looking distinctly unloved when it was bought by its current owners, Inver House. In 1997, playing heavily on the whisky's maritime roots, they launched it as a single malt.

OLD PULTENEY 12-YEAR-OLD
40% ABV • Clean, bracing style, with a faint nutty sweetness that dries on the tongue.

ROYAL BRACKLA

✉ Cawdor, Nairn
🖥 www.dewarswow.com

Whisky had barely moved in from the cold to become a legitimate business when Captain William Fraser managed to secure the first-ever royal warrant for a whisky distillery in 1835.

He had built Brackla 23 years earlier between the River Findhorn and the Murray Firth. Being near Cawdor Castle, where Macbeth allegedly murdered King Duncan, perhaps gave it a royal connection anyway. Whether this helped persuade King William IV to bestow his blessing on Brackla we will never know, but Fraser wasted no time in promoting his malt as "The King's Own Whisky".

Soon, much of the production was heading south to Andrew Usher, in Edinburgh, the original pioneer of blended whisky.

The distillery was rebuilt in the 1890s and again in the 1970s, when the brief was clearly functionality. Whatever Prince Charles might think of its aesthetics, the modern, box-shaped Brackla, with its corrugated-steel roof, is still "royal".

Brackla was the first distillery to be granted a royal warrant, by King William IV.

LOCHNAGAR'S ROYAL WARRANT

In 1848, John Begg, of Lochnagar, decided to invite the neighbours round to his three-year-old distillery on the banks of the River Dee. These were not just any old neighbours, however, but Queen Victoria and Prince Albert, who had acquired Balmoral Castle the same year. Begg walked the short distance from Lochnagar to drop them a note. Life was clearly pretty relaxed in those days – the invitation was only issued at 9pm, but the very next day the royal entourage arrived at the distillery door. "We have come to see through your works, Mr Begg," boomed Albert.

And so began possibly the first-ever official distillery tour, followed by a dram for all, including the children. As the party moved from the still house, Prince Albert noted the spirits safe, as Begg recorded in his diary: "'I see you have got your locks there,' he said. On my replying, 'These are the Queen's locks,' Her Majesty took a very hearty laugh".

Lochnagar received a royal warrant shortly after the visit of Queen Victoria and Prince Albert.

Production at Royal Lochnagar is on a small scale. Most of its whisky is used in Johnnie Walker blends.

ROYAL LOCHNAGAR

✉ Ballater, Aberdeenshire
🏛 www.discovering-distilleries.com
🚪 Open to visitors

Royal Lochnagar Distillery was originally called New Lochnagar, as it was the replacement for a distillery that had stood on the opposite bank. It had been established in 1825 by James Robertson, but had burnt down and then been swept away in a flood.

The new distillery was built in 1845 by John Begg, and, once he had obtained a royal warrant *(see p93)*, both distillery and whisky were renamed Royal Lochnagar.

Begg prospered and soon set up an office in Aberdeen, where he developed a blend to satisfy a wider audience. Meanwhile, he made sure he had plenty of casks on site to supply nearby Balmoral

Scapa Distillery produces only single malts, with a flavour of heather and honey all their own.

Castle and keep John Brown's hip flask topped up. John Brown was the loyal manservant of Queen Victoria (he was portrayed by Billy Connolly in the 1997 film *Mrs Brown)*. John's relationship with Victoria aroused plenty of gossip. When he fell flat on his face after one dram too many, the Queen leapt to his defence, pronouncing that she too "had felt the earth move".

As John Begg & Sons, the business remained in family hands until 1916 when it was bought by John Dewar & Sons. By then, Lochnagar was a key component in Vat 69, the blend created by Begg's friend William Sanderson.

With its solitary pair of stills, Royal Lochnagar is almost a boutique distillery, but one highly cherished by its owners, Diageo.

🥃 **ROYAL LOCHNAGAR 12-YEAR-OLD**
40% ABV ● A ripe sherried nose with notes of fruit cake, spice, and old leather.

SCAPA

✉ St Ola, Orkney
🏛 www.scapamalt.com

Besides Highland Park, the only other surviving distillery on the Orkney Islands is Scapa, whose origins go back to 1885. Its prospects had not looked so good, however, when the distillery was closed – seemingly for ever – in 1994. It was rescued a decade later, and its future now appears secure as a boutique distillery determined to make a virtue of its far-flung location. Its then owner, Allied Domecq, embarked on a rebuilding programme that restored Scapa to full operation, before selling it to Pernod Ricard in 2005.

🥃 **SCAPA 14-YEAR-OLD**
40% ABV ● Rich, spicy fruit-cake notes, with an impressive lingering finish.

**Scapa
14-Year-Old**

SPRINGBANK

✉ Campbeltown, Argyll
🏛 www.springbank
distillers.com
🚪 Open by appointment

When Springbank was founded just five years after the Excise Act of 1823, there were 13 licensed distilleries in Campbeltown. By the 1830s, the number had jumped to 20, encouraged by the ever-expanding, ever-thirsty Glasgow, just a short sail up the Firth of Clyde.

Later, when the railways gave Speyside the chance to seduce the big blenders with

TALISKER

The story of Talisker begins with the MacAskill brothers – a pair of farmers from the Isle of Eigg. They arrived on Skye to take a lease on Talisker House and were soon encouraging the locals to emigrate to make room for sheep, this being the time of the Highland Clearances.

When the MacAskills built Talisker in 1830, it was much to the distress of the local minister, who preached against the evils of drink. His prayers were finally answered when the brothers sold up 24 years later.

Two million litres (440,000 gallons) of whisky are made at Talisker Distillery each year.

Talisker limped on until the 1880s, when it was bought by Roderick Kemp, from Aberdeen. Unhappy that it had no jetty – which meant the barrels of whisky had to be floated out to the puffers waiting offshore – Kemp wrote desperate letters to his landlord at Dunvegan Castle, begging him to build a proper pier. Although the laird happily accepted Kemp's rent of £45 a year and a 46-litre (10-gallon) cask of Talisker every Christmas, he did nothing about the pier until 1900. By which time, Kemp had given up and left Skye to run Macallan.

The distillery teamed up with Dailuaine, on Speyside, to form a limited company in 1898, which was bought by the Distillers Company in 1925. At the time, Talisker was triple distilled, like an Irish whiskey. The new owners changed back to double distillation, but otherwise left things as they were, including the use of coal fires under the stills. In 1960, this almost caused the end of Talisker, when someone left the manholes off one of the wash stills, causing the liquid to bubble over. The blackened stills were replaced using the same design, only this time they were fitted with internal steam coils.

One thing that has never changed is the curious lyne arms. These wide copper pipes poke through the wall of the still house, kink upwards in a large U-bend, and then plunge into the worm tubs. What this does for Talisker is hard to say, but judging by the accolades heaped on this "Classic Malt", it cannot be all bad.

There were once seven distilleries on Skye but, without barley crops on the island, they struggled, and Talisker is the only one that remained.

its softer, gentler malts, the town's distillers looked west to the United States. When the US market shut down as a result of Prohibition, Campbeltown's demise was swift. By the mid-1930s the only distilleries left were Glen Scotia and Springbank.

Part of the reason that Springbank survived was that its malt was a little less heavy than the usual Campbeltown style, of which blenders had grown weary. Also, the distillery never compromised on quality – unlike many of its rivals, who had grown complacent through years of supplying Glasgow blenders. People in the business began referring to the "stinking fish" aroma of the region's malts, though it seems extremely unlikely that anyone really did use old herring barrels to mature their whisky, as was the implication.

The other factor that has been instumental in Springbank's success is continuity. It has been in the same family's hands since the very start. In 1992, the Mitchells decided to restore the floor maltings, in a bid to control the whole whisky-making process from start to finish and be more self-sufficient. The rest of the industry, meanwhile, was busy contracting into an ever-declining number of ever-larger corporations.

That same year, it was also decided not to sell the distillery's whisky as fillings for blends, but to concentrate on releasing it as single malt.

Alongside its namesake whisky, Springbank also produces Hazelburn and the heavily peated Longrow. In 2004, its owners opened a new distillery in the town, on the site of what was the Glengyle Distillery. Its single malt – to be called Kilkerran – will be available in 2014.

🍾 **SPRINGBANK 10-YEAR-OLD** 46% ABV
Notes of leather, nutmeg, and orange peel, with a tang of salt and smoke on the finish.

🍾 **LONGROW 10-YEAR-OLD** 46% ABV • Initial spicy, sherry notes are soon enveloped by dense aromatic smoke.

TALISKER

✉ Carbost, Isle of Skye
🌐 www.discovering-distilleries.com
🚪 Open to visitors

In 1823, there were seven licensed distilleries on Skye. Today, there is only one – Talisker. Unlike the more fertile Islay, the island lacked barley of its own, which meant the early distillers on Skye always struggled.

The grain now all comes from Scotland's east coast, and, with the advent of tarmac roads and the Skye Bridge, life is considerably easier these days.

🍾 **TALISKER 10-YEAR-OLD** 45.8% ABV
A feisty, bracing malt that is initially sweet on the palate and then hot and peppery on the finish.

Talisker 10-Year-Old

🍾 **TALISKER 18-YEAR-OLD** 45.8% ABV • Candied fruit and toffee on the nose, with a beguiling, mellow smokiness in the mouth.

🍾 **TALISKER 21-YEAR-OLD** 57.8% ABV • A giant, brooding malt that crashes over the tongue like breakers on the beach.

TEANINICH

✉ Alness, Ross-shire

Hidden on the outskirts of town in an industrial estate beside the Cromarty Firth is Dalmore's neighbouring distillery, in Alness.

It was founded by Captain Hugh Munro in 1817 and was named after his estate of Teaninich (pronounced "chee-an-in-ick"). In the 1850s, Munro was posted off to India, and the distillery was leased out.

When the whisky writer Alfred Barnard (see p50) paid a visit in 1885, it was said to be the only distillery north of Inverness to boast "telephonic communication". By then, it was producing up to 365,000 litres (80,000 gallons) of "pure Highland malt" a year, which went straight off to the blenders down south.

Little changed until the 1960s, when the still house was refitted and then expanded in 1970 to fit six stills, losing whatever old-world charm it once had in the process.

TOBERMORY

✉ Tobermory, Isle of Mull
🌐 www.tobermory.co.uk
🚪 Open to visitors

If the art of distilling came to Scotland from Ireland, then it was perhaps on Mull that the first Scotch whisky was made. After all, it was to Iona, the small island off the southwest tip of Mull, that

Springbank uses a variety of oak casks, some having previously contained sherry or bourbon, to mature its whisky.

Tobermory markets two whiskies – a malt and a blend – as well as a single malt bottled under the site's old name of Ledaig.

St Columba sailed in his coracle in 563, although there is no actual mention of him bringing a still, and it seems unlikely the islanders would have kept it secret for so long if he did.

Whatever the truth, there is now just one distillery on Mull. It was officially founded in 1823 by John Sinclair, whose first application to the powers that be was turned down. The Fisheries Society of the British Isles, who created Tobermory as a model village at the end of the 18th century, suggested Sinclair build a brewery instead. Once his distillery was up and running, he gave it scant regard as he dwelt on his main business of supplying kelp for making soap and glass. When Sinclair died in 1837, the distillery at Tobermory closed for the next 40 years.

But for grain, which came from the mainland, Mull had everything else. It had plentiful water, peat, and a ready market, with the island population approaching its peak of 10,600. Yet, the distillery was only brought back to life in 1878. It then tottered on until 1916, when it was acquired by the Distillers Company. During the Depression of the 1920s and 30s, it was shut down, as if for good.

The next lull in trading was even longer, and when a business consortium took it on in 1972 there was precious little left. Armed with a hefty development grant, they put in new stills and all the equipment needed. The timing was terrible, however, with the industry awash with whisky in search of a home. Their venture failed, but at least they had done enough to save the distillery, and in 1993 it was once again kicked into life by Burn Stewart Distillers, who own it today.

🍸 **TOBERMORY 10-YEAR-OLD** 40% ABV • A crisp, tangy unpeated malt that dries on the finish.

🍸 **LEDAIG 10-YEAR-OLD** 42% ABV The strong, peat-smoked big brother of Tobermory.

TOMATIN

✉ Tomatin, Inverness-shire
🖥 www.tomatin.com
🍺 Open to visitors

Situated halfway between Aviemore and Inverness, Tomatin attracts a steady stream of passing trade, which rattles past on the A9. It has always been a staging post on the main road north, if not always with a gift shop and car park.

Long before there was a licensed distillery here, there was an illicit still attached to the laird's house, supplying whisky to the drovers on their slow journey from upland grazing land to the cattle markets down south.

As with most Scotch whiskies, the wash at Tomatin is distilled twice in copper pot stills.

Though it was a long way from Speyside, the original distillery called itself the Tomatin Spey District Distillery Company when it opened in 1897. It survived for just eight years before going under.

It quickly resurfaced as Tomatin Distillers Ltd and grew to become a monster distillery, with 23 stills and a production of 546 million litres (12 million gallons) by 1974, putting it second only to Glenfiddich in scale.

Twelve years later, Tomatin was bought by the Takara Co. Ltd and became the first distillery in Scotland to be owned by a Japanese firm.

TULLIBARDINE

✉ Blackford, Perthshire
🖥 www.tullibardine.com
🍺 Open to visitors

Writ large on the side of this modern-looking distillery beside the A9 are the words "Tullibardine 1488", the year being a reference to when King James IV bought beer from an old brewery sited here for his coronation at nearby Scone.

The brewery survived into the 20th century, and was bought in 1947 by the noted distillery architect William Delmé-Evans, who was also involved with Glenallachie and Jura. His real passion was Tullibardine, however, and he successfully converted the brewery to a distillery. Sadly, failing health forced him to sell up in 1953.

The distillery spent the 1990s in mothballs and, as each year passed, the chances of resuscitation appeared to fade. A rescue package was finally agreed in 2003, and in December that year the boiler was fired up once again. The new independent owners are doing everything they can to sustain the business through tours, a restaurant, and a shop until they deem that the new spirit has reached maturity.

ISLAY

Of all Scotland's whisky regions, Islay has the strongest identity. Being an island helps, but there is also its signature tune of peat smoke. Apart from Bunnahabhain, which "gracefully declines to run with the pack" (to quote its website), all Islay's whiskies are peated.

This was never a collective decision. It was simply that peat was the only source of fuel to be found on the island. It was how people heated their houses, with a fire in the middle and the smoke wafting up through a hole in the roof. Peat's uniquely pungent aroma would have impregnated people's hair, clothes, bedding, and food. As such, the idea of an unpeated whisky would have been totally unimaginable – it just wouldn't have been whisky.

In addition to the plentiful supplies of peat to malt the grain and fire the stills, there was no shortage of soft, pure water. Yet, this was true of other islands. What set Islay apart was that it was the most fertile of the Hebrides, and the presence of barley gave its distillers a head start. With gale-force winds and no shelter to speak of, the barley harvest was often meagre, but there was usually enough to make whisky. The first imports of grain on to Islay did not arrive until 1815, by which time distilling was there to stay.

The pier at Bunnahabhain was built shortly after the distillery was founded in the 1880s, so boats could easily dock to load up with whisky.

No one knows when whisky making began, though with Ireland just 20 miles (32km) away it may have been very early, if Irish monks really did convert the west coast to whisky as well as Catholicism in the 6th century. Yet until some evidence is unearthed from a peat bog, we will never know for sure.

What we do know is that Islay's first licensed distillery was Bowmore, which was established in 1779. It was joined by more than 20 distilleries during the 19th century, of which six survive today. The most recent casualty was Port Ellen, in 1984, though its maltings continue to supply most of the distilleries on the island with malt. The peat used is entirely from Islay and is said to give whiskies like Ardbeg their uniquely medicinal, mildly antiseptic tang.

Not long ago, the prospects for Islay looked bleak, and many feared that Ardbeg or Bruichladdich would also have to close for good. Even Lagavulin was once on a three-day week. Today, the situation is far healthier, as more and more whisky lovers gravitate to this beautiful island, hooked on the strange, bitter-sweet taste of peat.

ISLAY DISTILLERIES

virtually unknown outside the industry and the heavily peated malt it produced was not sufficiently different.

In 1989, with demand for blended whisky about to recover after the bad years of the early 1980s, production resumed on a small scale. Whether those re-employed at Ardbeg felt secure is unlikely. Somehow, there was already an unofficial "For Sale" sign over the door. The eventual sale did not take place until 1997, when the owners of Glenmorangie beat off seven rival bids and bought the distillery for an estimated £7 million. They then spent a further £1.4 million on repairs, to crank Ardbeg fully back to life. Today, Ardbeg is a famous single malt with an ever-growing band of admirers.

🥃 **ARDBEG 10-YEAR-OLD** 46% ABV
Notes of creosote, tar, and smoked fish on the nose, while any sweetness on the tongue quickly dries to a smoky finish.

🥃 **ARDBEG "UIGEADAIL"** 54.2% ABV
Fragrant notes of pot-pourri and leather give way to an intense earthy character in the mouth, tempered with sweet sherry notes.

Ardbeg 10-Year-Old

Ardbeg Distillery – in a precarious state for much of the 1980s and 90s – is now very much on the up.

ARDBEG

✉ Port Ellen, Isle of Islay
🖥 www.ardbeg.com
⛴ Open to visitors

Ardbeg took out a licence in 1815, the same year as Laphroaig and a year before Lagavulin. These three distilleries on the coast road from Port Ellen, in the parish of Kildalton, produce big, pungent malt whiskies reeking of peat; and none more so than Ardbeg.

This is not a whisky to drink beneath a smoke alarm, unless you enjoy upsetting the neighbours. Besides, it is a real outdoor whisky, and – like all malts – is best enjoyed in situ, next to the distillery that produced it.

Having visited Ardbeg in the 1880s, the whisky writer

Alfred Barnard wrote that its "isolation tends to heighten the romantic sense of its position". Yet by then, as Alexander MacDougall & Co., it was fully connected to the whisky industry. Its four stills produced 1.1 million litres (250,000 gallons) of "Pure Islay Malt", which was then sold on by Buchanan's, in Glasgow, to blenders keen to add weight and texture to their blends.

Like most other remote distilleries, Ardbeg supported a whole community, providing not just jobs, but a social life for the village. From a peak of 60, Ardbeg's workforce declined to just 18 in 1981, when the distillery was mothballed by Allied Distillers. The workers were laid off and the last vestiges of a community crumbled away. Being in the same stable as Laphroaig (also owned by Allied Distillers) had not helped. Ardbeg was

BOWMORE

✉ Bowmore, Isle of Islay
🖥 www.bowmore.co.uk
⛴ Open to visitors

Bowmore stands right on the shore of Loch Indaal, whose salt-laden breezes blow into the warehouses and presumably seep into the casks. As with the majority of Islay distilleries, however, most of the whisky produced at Bowmore is transported off the island for maturing on the mainland. This is due to lack of space, which

Bowmore Legend

With waves crashing on to the shore at the feet of the distillery, Bowmore produces characterful whisky that echoes its position.

shrank even further in 1991, when warehouse No.3 was converted into Islay's only public swimming pool, its water warmed by recycled heat from the distillery.

Bowmore's own water comes from the River Laggan via a 7 mile (11km) aqueduct and is used to mix with the mash, cool the stills, and steep the barley, this being one of the few distilleries to have its own floor maltings.

The majority of the barley arrives pre-malted, but part of what makes Bowmore

Distillery different is having a proportion created here on a stone floor, turned by hand and dried over a peat fire. Whether it really affects the quality of the whisky would be hard to prove, but it certainly makes the distillery, with its blue smoke wafting from its pagoda roof, well worth a visit.

BOWMORE: ISLAY'S OLDEST DISTILLERY

The oldest distillery on Islay was founded in 1779, when there was little more to Bowmore than a curious round church. It was started by part-time distiller and farmer David Simpson. Like all early distillers, Simpson would have relied on local barley, and in 1800 he and a neighbouring distiller complained that Islay's illicit distillers were denying them their share of barley. This coupled with Simpson's farming interests ensured that Bowmore remained tiny. It was producing just 3,640 litres (800 gallons) a year when it was bought by the Glasgow firm of W&J Mutter in 1837. Some 50

A W&J Mutter's poster

years later, the distillery was greatly expanded and annual production soared to 900,000 litres (200,000) gallons. The whisky was shipped off the island to be stored and bottled beneath the arches of Glasgow's Central Station.

In 1890, W&J Mutter were forced to sell the distillery, which was then passed from one owner to the next until the Glasgow-based whisky firm Stanley P Morrison Ltd bought Bowmore in 1963. Production was cranked up again, this time reaching 4 million litres (880,000 gallons) by the end of the 1960s. It became the flagship distillery of Morrison Bowmore, which itself became part of the Japanese Suntory group in the mid-1990s.

The round church was the focal point of the village when Bowmore was founded.

Twenty years later, its four stills went cold once more and Bruichladdich was back on the market. It was finally rescued at the end of 2000 by a consortium led by Mark Reynier, an independent whisky bottler. At his side was Bowmore's former manager, Jim McEwan, who was charged with the job of bringing Bruichladdich Distillery back to life again.

While the new spirit has been maturing in cask, a raft of regular bottlings and special editions has been released for sale from inherited stocks. The traditional style, using lightly peated malt – in contrast to most other whisky distilleries on the island – was not dissimilar to Bunnahabhain.

In 2002, Bruichladdich's new owners decided to expand the range with a heavily peated whisky, called Port Charlotte after a nearby village. They have since added Octomore, named after an Islay distillery that closed in 1852. Available at some point after 2010, it promises to be one of the most pungent, smoky whiskies yet made.

With its solitary distillery, Bruichladdich has always had to try to punch well above its weight to compete against much bigger rivals. But the ever-growing interest

🍾 **BOWMORE LEGEND** 40% ABV • A dry, bracing malt whisky with a faint citrus flavour that develops into a smoky finish.

🍾 **BOWMORE 12-YEAR-OLD** 43% ABV • The smoke comes through on the nose and mingles with citric notes of lemon zest and barley sugar on the tongue.

Bowmore 12-Year-Old

BRUICHLADDICH

✉ Bruichladdich, Isle of Islay
🖥 www.bruichladdich.com
⛴ Open to visitors

Set on the shores of Loch Indaal, facing Bowmore, the oldest established distillery on Islay, Bruichladdich was built in 1881 by Robert, William, and John Harvey. Their family had been making whisky for over a century and already owned Yoker and Dundashill, in Glasgow, the latter being the largest malt whisky distillery in Scotland at the time.

From the start, their new operation was a serious venture, boasting cavity walls and a prototype form of concrete made from pebbles on the beach. This was radical stuff in those days.

The Harvey family remained involved until 1929, when the distillery shut down for a decade. It was then bought and sold repeatedly until owners Invergordon Distillers took it on in the mid-1970s.

Bruichladdich "1986"

in single malts, and in Islay in particular, means that for the moment Bruichladdich is definitely in the right place at the right time.

🍾 **BRUICHLADDICH 10-YEAR-OLD** 46% ABV • Fresh, floral nose, with a malty, cereal aroma, a trace of brine, and a light oily texture.

Stored two-high on an earth floor, Bruichladdich's oak casks are regularly checked to see how well the whisky is maturing.

MODEST BEGINNINGS

The distillery at Bunnahabhain was established beside a shingle beach by two farmers in 1881. At the time, there was no infrastructure of any kind, and the contractors had to start by building a road and then cottages for the workers, followed by a schoolroom and a pier. The total venture, including distillery, cost £30,000, yet it was making a profit of £10,000 by its second year. It was then called the Islay Distillery Company, and its directors were delighted with the manager and asked him to name his terms. It seems his only request was that "not less than £30" be spent on furnishings for his cottage. His bosses were happy to oblige.

A signpost to Bunnahabhain Distillery.

BUNNAHABHAIN

✉ Port Askaig, Isle of Islay
🖥 www.bunnahabhain.com

Of the seven distilleries on Islay, Bunnahabhain has always been the least typical, It forsook the use of peated barley, with a view to creating something a little more gentle. This point of difference is now marketed as a virtue, though the original motives for it were rather different.

Famed for their "hair-on-the-chest" style, Islay malts have long been used as a top dressing in blended Scotch. Although highly regarded, they were added sparingly, since more than a few

spoonfuls per bottle might unbalance the blend, especially if it was predominantly Speyside.

Bunnahabain's decision to forsake peated barely meant it now offered a low-tar alternative, which, it was hoped, blenders would use more generously.

A few years after it was established *(see above)*, the distillery was gobbled up by Highland Distillers, which later became part of the Edrington Group; they owned it until recently. Whether Edrington

ever really appreciated what they had is unclear. So much attention was being paid to their flagship malts – The Macallan (on Speyside) and Highland Park (on Orkney) – that their outpost on Islay may at times have felt neglected. But Bunnahabhain played an important role in The Famous Grouse *(see p132)* and Black Bottle *(see pp123)*, a strong, fulsome blend that includes whiskies from every distillery on Islay.

A single malt was made available, but it never quite rode the wave of popularity that engulfed the island's whiskies, largely because it lacked the signature tune of peat. If you were expecting a huge smoking volcano of a malt whisky that would erupt on your tongue and leave a trail of ash, Bunnahabhain was bound to disappoint.

Aware of this problem, the new distillery owners, Burn Stewart, began filling casks with a well-peated version, alongside the existing style, for those who don't want hairs on their chest.

Bunnahabhain whisky label

🍶 **BUNNAHABHAIN 12-YEAR-OLD**
40% ABV • A bracing, maritime malt on the nose which displays a malty sweetness on the tongue.

Bunnahabhain Distillery produces the sweetest and least peaty of Islay's malts.

CAOL ILA

✉ **Port Askaig, Isle of Islay**
🖰 **www.discovering-distilleries.com**
⛴ **Open to visitors**

Until recently, few people outside the whisky industry knew about Islay's largest distillery. While its island stablemate, Lagavulin, basked in the limelight as one of Diageo's "Classic Malts", Caol Ila kept a low profile. Its role in life was simply to provide backbone and peat smoke to blends created on the mainland. There were occasional independent bottlings, it is true, but on the whole it was unknown as a single malt.

This has all begun to change, partly because Lagavulin can barely keep up with demand and partly as a result of the ever-growing interest among whisky drinkers in Islay malts.

Caol Ila is Gaelic for the Sound of Islay, the narrow channel that separates the island from Jura, to the north. The distillery stands on the shore, just beyond Port Askaig, where the Caledonian Macbrayne ferry calls from the mainland.

It was built by Hamish Henderson in 1846, on the site where people used to wash lead ore in a burn that flows down from Loch nam Ban. Henderson had been looking for a suitable spot for six years, and perhaps it was the sound of running water that brought him here. Either way, he was soon using it to mash the grain, condense the spirit, and power the distillery via a set of turbines.

In 1863, Caol Ila was bought and then extended by the Glasgow distillers Bulloch Lade, who built a pier in front of the distillery. Within 20 years, two steamers a week were calling to deliver the grain and take away the filled casks. Caol Ila later acquired its own "puffer", the Pibroch, which was only decommissioned in 1972, when the distillery was shut down for large-scale refurbishment. When it reopened, some two years later, the only building still standing from the past was the warehouse. The still room was completely new and now had six stills and a capacity of 3 million litres (660,000 gallons) of alcohol a year. It also had a huge, almost floor-to-ceiling window that gives the stillman on duty one of the

**Caol Ila
12-Year-Old**

Caol Ila's east-facing windows offer views across the sea to the neighbouring Isle of Jura.

best views in the whisky industry. Often, there will be seals playing on the rocks, alongside cormorants and eider duck. Beyond are the Paps of Jura – the famous breast-shaped peaks of Islay's neighbour.

🥃 **CAOL ILA 12-YEAR-OLD** 43% ABV
The fresh citrus tang on the nose gives way to gentle aromatic smoke in the mouth.

🥃 **CAOL ILA 18-YEAR-OLD** 43% ABV
Sweeter than the 12-year-old, with a more creamy texture in the mouth that develops a smoky edge before the finish.

KILCHOMAN

This boutique operation, which began distilling in the summer of 2005, models itself on an old farm distillery. It was the first to be built on Islay for 124 years and is the most westerly. Every stage of the process is highly traditional, from the use of locally grown barley to maturation on site. The distillery aims to release bottlings at various ages, starting with a 5-year-old in 2010. It is open to visitors. For more information, visit www.kilchomandistillery.com.

LAGAVULIN

✉ Port Ellen, Isle of Islay
🔗 www.discovering-distilleries.com
🏛 Open to visitors

Every summer a flotilla of yachts sails past the ruins of Dunyvaig Castle into Lagavulin Bay for the climax of the Classic Malts Cruise. Those who have arrived early can sit back and watch latecomers negotiate their way in over the submerged rocks. Often, someone will come to grief with an expensive scraping sound. Consolatory drams are offered and any damage is forgotten until the morning, as the farewell ceilidh heats up.

Many centuries ago, these rocks protected the Lord of the Isles, whose power-base was Dunyvaig. If invaders came too close, they risked being shipwrecked, an event the islanders doubtless celebrated with whisky.

Illicit distilling had been endemic here in the parish of Kildalton for years when a number of smuggling bothys merged to form Lagavulin in 1817.

In 1836, Alexander Graham took on the lease of Lagavulin, whose whiskies were sold through The Islay Cellar, his shop in Glasgow.

The rocky shoreline where Lagavulin is based once offered protection from invaders; it still catches out an occasional yacht.

Later, his partner's nephew, Peter Mackie, created the White Horse blend *(see p153)*, with Lagavulin at its heart. To meet demand for the blend, he relied on neighbouring Laphroaig, and when that distillery stopped supplying him, he decided to build a Laphroaig of his own and call it The Malt Mill. The distillery stood within the grounds of Lagavulin, which Peter Mackie finally acquired in 1921, three years before he died.

The Malt Mill was said to produce one of the most heavily peated malts of its day, though whether it ever resembled Laphroaig is unclear. The mill was demolished in the 1960s, leaving only a couple of millstones painted with a white horse beside the gate. The design of its pear-shaped stills, however, was copied for two of Lagavulin's four stills. These are run at a slow pace, just five hours for the first distillation, but nine for the second. All that contact with the copper helps lighten and polish what might be a very heavy, phenolic spirit, given the amount of peat used on the barley. All the grain is malted at nearby Port Ellen. The whisky then mellows for

**Lagavulin
16-Year-Old**

16 years in cask before being bottled as one of Diageo's Classic Malts.

🥃 **LAGAVULIN 16-YEAR-OLD**
43% ABV ● Beneath the layers of peat smoke that first dominate the nose and palate lurks a beguiling sweetness and complexity.

🥃 **LAGAVULIN DISTILLER'S EDITION** 43% ABV ● The 16-year-old whisky "finished" in a sherry cask, to give an initial sweetness that fades to a long smoky, salt-flecked finish.

LAPHROAIG

✉ Port Ellen, Isle of Islay
🔗 www.laphroaig.com
🏛 Open to visitors

Laphroaig has always revelled in its harsh, peat-smoked character – a seemingly unappetizing mix of hemp, bonfires, iodine, and seaweed, wrapped in peat smoke. With a flavour profile as far as it is possible to be from a sweet, crowd-pleasing drink like Baileys Irish Cream, there is nothing gentle about Laphroaig. Yet, every day whisky drinkers new to this uncompromising malt break through the pain barrier and become hooked.

Laphroaig's origins go back to the Johnston brothers, who arrived from the mainland to graze cattle on the southern shores of Islay.

PRINCE CHARLES' FONDNESS FOR PEAT

Prince Charles numbers among the fans of Laphroaig, and his crest appears on the label of the bottle. In 1994, he dropped in on the distillery after overshooting Islay's tiny airstrip. The heir to the throne had made the near-fatal mistake of landing with a tail wind. All four tyres went pop before the plane came to a halt nose-down in a peat bog. Fortunately, no one was hurt in the incident.

Laphroaig uses American oak to mature its whisky, with plenty of sea air seeping into the wood.

They were soon making whisky on the side and in 1815 Laphroaig was officially born. Donald Johnston was in sole charge from 1836 until his death 10 years later, when, tragically, he fell into a vat of his own partially made whisky and drowned.

The distillery stayed with the Johnstons and the Hunters – who they married in to – for over a century. During this time there was a bitter and often litigious dispute with neighbouring Lagavulin Distillery, or rather its owner, the whisky baron Sir Peter Mackie, who used to buy half of Laphroaig's production for his blends. When the contract was rescinded, he reacted with spite, ordering Laphroaig's water supply to be cut off. This resulted in yet another court case, which Mackie lost.

Relations had improved by the time Ian Hunter took over in 1927. He was the first to bottle Laphroaig and began to build its reputation abroad, including in the USA, despite Prohibition there. Helped perhaps by its mildly antiseptic taste,

Laphroaig was accepted as a "medicinal spirit" and could be acquired on prescription from a sympathetic doctor *(see p211)*.

In the 1930s, Ian Hunter recruited a young Glaswegian woman called Bessie Williamson to help out in the office. The arrangement was originally just for one summer, but Bessie never left and she eventually inherited the distillery when Hunter died without an heir in 1954.

In the 1960s, Laphroaig became part of Allied Domecq, and remained so until the distillery was sold to Fortune Brands (owners of Jim Beam) in 2005.

🍶 **LAPHROAIG 10-YEAR-OLD**
43% ABV ● An intense, smoky mix of hemp and sea spray, with a little malty sweetness on the tongue.

🍶 **LAPHROAIG 15-YEAR-OLD**
43% ABV ● A richer, more-rounded flavour than the 10-year-old; the smoke does still dominate, but it is more aromatic.

Laphroaig 10-Year-Old

The stills at Laphroaig are small and onion-shaped, and seem to maximize the tarry smokiness.

Ardbeg Distillery provides some of the most coveted malts for use in blends.

LOWLAND DISTILLERIES

The overriding image of malt whisky is of a Highland spirit made against a backdrop of barren peaks or heather-clad hills in a remote glen, or on the west coast lashed by wind and rain. The soft, rolling farmland south of Edinburgh somehow just doesn't fit the bill.

The whisky industry has been bedevilled by periodic lean times, and many a far-flung outpost of whisky making has survived decades of inactivity, only to sputter into life in the good times. A silent distillery in the Lowlands, however, faces a much higher risk of being redeveloped into executive flats or a supermarket car park. Not so very long ago, there were more than 20 licensed distilleries in the Lowlands. Now, there are just two of any size – Auchentoshan and Glenkinchie, with two others, Bladnoch and Daftmill, recently in resurgence. All but Daftmill are open to the public.

LOWLAND DISTILLERIES

Edinburgh
AUCHENTOSHAN   GLENKINCHIE
Glasgow
Ayr   SCOTLAND
LADYBURN
Dumfries
Stranraer
BLADNOCH

SCOTLAND
Lowlands

of times, but still retained the feel of a farm distillery. When Alfred Barnard *(see p50)* paid a visit in 1878, he described Auchentoshan as a "little distillery… situated in a romantic glen, with a stream of water running past it." The romantic glen subsequently disappeared in Glasgow's expansion, leaving Auchentoshan at the end of the Great Western Road, close to the Erskine Bridge. Its proximity to the city meant that its whisky could almost be piped into the warehouses of the Glasgow blenders direct from the still.

At some point, Auchentoshan increased its pair of stills to three and began triple-distilling its spirit, as though it were making Irish whiskey. The whisky has been triple-distilled ever since. Morrison Bowmore took over the distillery in 1984.

Auchentoshan Select has a fresh approachable style, with citrus aromas and an Ovaltine sweetness on the palate.

AUCHENTOSHAN

Originally built as the Duntocher Distillery by John Bulloch in 1817, Auchentoshan (www. auchentoshan.co.uk) stands on land once owned by Paisley Abbey, whose monks might have been the first distillers in these parts. Bullogh's son renamed the distillery Auchentoshan (Gaelic for "corner of the field") before it was sold to a local family. It then changed hands a number

Bladnoch 15-Year-Old

BLADNOCH

Founded in 1817, tiny Bladnoch Distillery (www. bladnoch.co.uk), near Wigtown, remained in the same family hands – the McLelland's – until 1930.

It was then repeatedly bought and sold, spending prolonged periods lying idle until it was finally rescued in 1994 by Raymond Armstrong, from Northern Island, who spent a small fortune restoring it to a tiny boutique distillery.

Bladnoch is available bottled, or by the cask for around £1,000, which includes eight years' storage but not the tax.

DAFTMILL

A tiny farm distillery near Cupar in Fife, Daftmill was created within a converted mill house dating from the late 17th century. The creators were Francis and Ian Cuthbert, whose family had farmed the land here for generations. The distillery went into production in December 2005, and can produce 20,000 litres (4,400 gallons) per annum – as much as a large distillery produces each day.

GLENKINCHIE

Founded at Pencaitland in East Lothian in 1825, Glenkinchie (www.discovering-distilleries.com) was originally known as the Milton Distillery. The stills ran cold in the mid-1850s and for the next 30 years it became a saw mill. It was resurrected by an Edinburgh brewer and a pair of Leith wine merchants, who rebuilt Glenkinchie as a highly efficient, state-of-the-art operation. It had a siding connected to the railway, its own overhead rails inside the distillery to carry the barley to the malting floor, and mechanical rakes in the mash tun.

Glenkinchie was also totally connected to the land, with fields of barley close at hand to supply the grain, which was malted on site until 1968. It provided whisky for Haig – Britain's biggest whisky brand until the mid-1970s – but with Haig's sharp decline of fortunes in the UK, Glenkinchie faced an uncertain future. Until, that is, it was elevated by current owners Diageo to sit alongside the likes of Lagavulin and Oban in their "Classic Malts" series.

Glenkinchie 10-Year-Old has a malty, cut-grass sweetness on the nose with vanilla notes on the palate leading to a faint spiciness on the finish.

**Glenkinchie
10-Year-Old**

Bladnoch, near Wigtown, is a small boutique distillery, with an annual production of just 51,000 litres (11,250 gallons).

GRAIN DISTILLERIES

There is a common misconception that grain whisky is virtually neutral alcohol, lacks character, and is produced principally to provide comparatively cheap spirit to bulk out blends. Ask any Scotch whisky blender, however, and they will tell you that this is far from the case.

Every grain whisky available varies significantly in style and adds different dimensions to the particular blend that is being constructed.

We rarely get the opportunity to sample single grain whiskies in their own right because almost all the grain output is destined for blending, and few bottlings are made available by the distilleries. However, independent bottlers offer a surprisingly wide selection of older single grains, many of which come from distilleries that have fallen silent *(see p111)*.

Grain whisky is a mix of cereals, including some malted barley.

In 1980, there were 12 working grain distilleries in Scotland, but today just seven survive, with five in the industrial

Until 20 years ago, shipments of maize from North America were disembarked at the port of Girvan. They were then transferred by road to Grant's grain distillery nearby.

"Central Belt", one at Invergordon, in the Highlands, and one at Girvan, on the west coast of Ayrshire.

GRAIN WHISKY DISTILLATION
Grain whisky is distilled in column stills in a continuous process, as opposed to malt whisky, which is made in batches in pot stills.

Scottish distiller Robert Stein pioneered continuous distillation, but it took the Dublin-born, former exciseman Aeneas Coffey to perfect the process in 1830 *(see p172)*.

Coffey's invention revolutionized the production of grain whisky – not only could cheaper raw materials be used, but the alcohol content of the spirit distilled was higher, too. It paved the way for the creation of blended whisky later in the century. To this day, most of the stills used in the manufacture of Scotch grain whisky are called Coffey stills.

CAMERONBRIDGE

✉ Windygates, Leven, Fife

Founded in 1824 by John Haig, Cameronbridge was the first distillery in Scotland to produce grain whisky in column stills. It was also one of the six founding distilleries of the Distillers Company in 1877. Today, Cameronbridge has three Coffey stills, and, along with Port Dundas, is one of the two grain whisky distilleries wholly owned by Diageo.

Cameronbridge does not only distil grain whisky, however; a further nine stills also make "grain neutral spirit" for use in gin and vodka distillation. As such, it is the largest grain distillery in Scotland, with a capacity of 70 million litres (15.5 million gallons) of grain whisky a year and a further 30 million litres (6.6 million gallons) of grain neutral spirit.

Cameronbridge is a key component of Bell's, Johnnie Walker, and White Horse blends, and is considered to be one of the fuller-bodied grain whiskies on the market.

🍾 **CAMERON BRIG SINGLE GRAIN WHISKY** 40% ABV ● Bottled by Diageo, Cameron Brig is the most readily available of the Scottish single grains. A clean, grassy nose, smooth and elegant, sweet and slightly spicy, with perhaps a more sherried character than might be expected.

meron Brig 2-Year-Old ingle Grain

HEDONISM BLENDED GRAIN WHISKY

One of the most interesting developments in the world of grain whiskies in recent years has been the release of the first blended (vatted) grain whisky. Going by the name of Hedonism, it was the brainchild of innovative whisky entrepreneur John Glaser and his Compass Box company. It comprises a blend of grains of varying ages from the Cambus and Caledonian distilleries.

"I believe that great grain whiskies from well-chosen casks are the undiscovered treasures of Scotland's whisky kingdom," says Glaser. And, indeed, Hedonism is a smooth, silky, and eminently drinkable whisky – soft and sweet with a comparatively complex palate, displaying vanilla, toffee, coconut, and cocoa notes.

For John Glaser, "grain whisky is one of the most elegant, delicious whiskies on the planet".

GIRVAN

✉ Grangestone Industrial Estate, Girvan, Ayrshire
🖥 www.williamgrant.com

After Bladnoch *(see p108)*, Girvan is the southernmost working distillery in Scotland. It was constructed in 1963 by William Grant & Sons, its west-coast location chosen partly to facilitate the import of maize by sea from North America. However, since

The industrial appearance of Cameronbridge is a stark contrast to Scotland's malt distilleries.

the mid-1980s, Girvan has distilled from wheat, in common with most Scottish grain distilleries.

The original Coffey stills have been superseded by a complex, five-column vacuum-distillation plant, unique to Girvan, which produces some 50 million litres (11 million gallons) of grain whisky and grain neutral spirit a year.

Girvan is also now a major blending and warehousing centre for Grant's operations. Between 1966–1975, the Girvan site was home to the Ladyburn malt distillery.

Girvan grain whisky is one of the lighter grains used by blenders, and is at the heart of Grant's Family Reserve.

🍾 **BLACK BARREL SINGLE GRAIN WHISKY** 40% ABV
Delicate and fragrant on the nose, fruity, with vanilla and a hint of spice. Soft on the palate, with sweet cereal notes.

INVERGORDON

✉ Cottage Brae, Invergordon, Ross-shire
🖑 www.whyteand mackay.com

Invergordon's eastern Highlands location, far from the blending halls of central Scotland, was chosen to boost the area's flagging economy. Built between 1959 and 1961, the distillery belongs to Whyte & Mackay, who purchased the Invergordon Distillers Group in 1993, principally to acquire the Invergordon grain distillery and thereby secure a guaranteed supply of grain spirit for its own blending requirements. A small malt facility was installed in the Invergordon complex in 1965 and operated for 11 years.

Invergordon grain distillery has four Coffey stills and a capacity of 40 million litres (8.8 million gallons) a year.

For some years, a 10-year-old expression of Invergordon single grain was marketed. It was soft, clean, and straightforward, with big, sweet toffee notes.

LOCH LOMOND

✉ Alexandria West, Dunbartonshire
🖑 www.lochlomond distillery.com

Loch Lomond is the newest recruit to the line-up of Scottish grain distilleries and is the only one that produces both malt and grain whisky. The distillery dates from 1965, and was initially constructed to produce just malt whisky. The grain distillery was built alongside the malt plant in 1993–4 and its single Coffey still turns out some 10 million litres (2.2 million gallons) a year.

An early bottling of Girvan Single Grain

The whole complex is owned by the Bulloch family, who can trace their involvement in the Scotch whisky trade back to 1842, when Gabriel Bulloch partnered JH Dewar in a Scotch wholesaling business in Glasgow.

🍾 **LOCH LOMOND DISTILLERY SELECT SINGLE HIGHLAND GRAIN WHISKY** 45% ABV • In 2005, Loch Lomond released Scotland's first single cask, organic, single grain whisky, which was matured in French organic wine hogsheads.

When it came on stream in 1887, North British produced 114,000 litres (25,000 gallons) a week. Today, it turns out 10 times that.

Initial wine notes on the nose, then fresher vanilla and cereals emerge. Well mannered on the palate, with caramel, vanilla ice cream, and a hint of ginger. Malty caramel notes linger in the finish, with a sting of pepper in the tail.

NORTH BRITISH

✉ Wheatfield Road, Gorgie, Edinburgh
🖑 www.northbritish.co.uk

North British is Edinburgh's only surviving distillery and is located in the capital's Gorgie suburb. It was set up in 1885 by a group of influential blenders, and the "NB", as it is affectionately known, retained its independence until 1993, when it was jointly acquired by Diageo and The Edrington Group.

Three Coffey stills turn out around 64 million litres (14 million gallons) a year. North British is unique among grain distilleries in that it operates its own maltings and continues to distil from maize, rather than the cheaper alternative of wheat. Additionally, it uses around 15 per cent of "green malt", compared with the more usual 10 per cent of dried malt content used in other grain distilleries.

The result is a rich, full-flavoured whisky, much

tangier and sharper than that made from wheat, and with a more obvious vanilla note that is characteristic of maize distillation.

PORT DUNDAS

✉ **North Canal,
Bank Street, Glasgow**

One of Glasgow's two grain distilleries, Port Dundas stands beside the Forth & Clyde Canal and dates back to the early 19th century. Until the 1860s, when they amalgamated, there were two neighbouring Port Dundas distilleries, one founded in 1811 and the other established two years later. Both began to produce grain whisky using Coffey stills in 1845.

Port Dundas operates under the auspices of Diageo, who boast between 35–40 per cent of Scotland's total grain whisky output. Port Dundas contributes significantly to all the principal Diageo blends, including Haig, Johnnie Walker, and White Horse.

Traditionally, Port Dundas was considered one of the heavier, more full-bodied, and characterful grain whiskies, but has become rather lighter in recent years. Three Coffey stills are in operation, producing around 39 million litres (8.6 million gallons) of whisky a year.

STRATHCLYDE

✉ **Moffat Street, Glasgow**

The first grain spirit flowed from Strathclyde in 1928. The distillery was constructed by Seager Evans & Co., the owners of Long John blended whisky, in the Gorbals district of Glasgow. Through a series of takeovers, it passed to Allied Domecq, and the plant has been owned by Chivas Brothers since its acquisition of Allied Domecq assets in 2005.

Having closed Dumbarton grain distillery in 2002, Allied

FOUR GRAIN DISTILLERIES THAT ARE NOW SILENT

Caledonian
Along with North British, Caledonian was one of two working grain distilleries in Edinburgh, until its closure in 1988, two years after Guinness took over its owner, the Distillers Company. Established in 1855, in the Haymarket area, Caledonian was the largest grain distillery in Britain for some years. Some of the warehouses survive, while the still house has been converted into apartments. Caledonian's tall, brick chimney continues to act as a landmark in the Scottish capital.

Cambus
Located at Tullibody, in Clackmannanshire, and dating from 1806, Cambus was well-regarded by blenders for the quality of its spirit. Part of the Distillers Company, it became surplus to requirement when Guinness took over, and closed in 1993. The site is now used by Diageo for cask filling and maturation.

Carsebridge
Like Cambus, Carsebridge was a large-scale Clackmannanshire distillery. It was built by the Bald family in 1799, and switched from malt to grain whisky production in the early 1850s. Carsebridge closed in 1983. From the site, Diageo now runs its "Spirits Supply, Scotland" operation, which is responsible for the company's entire UK spirits production.

Dumbarton
The vast, red-brick Dumbarton Distillery was constructed on the Clyde coast in 1938 by the Canadian distiller Hiram Walker, though it ultimately became part of the Allied Domecq empire. It is the most recent Scottish grain distillery to close, falling silent in 2002. Dumbarton distilled with maize rather than wheat and produced a full-bodied and distinctive grain whisky.

spent more than £7 million increasing Strathclyde's capacity from 32 million litres (7 million gallons) a year to 39 million litres (8.6 million gallons) a year. The facility is equipped with two column stills, which manufacture grain whisky, and five that make grain neutral spirit.

Strathclyde is considered to be one of the fullest-bodied and most "meaty" of the grain whiskies, especially when young. As at Girvan and Invergordon, a small malt distillery operated within the Strathclyde complex between 1958–1976 under the name Kinclaith.

Port Dundas was modernized in the 1970s, gaining new, up-to-date whisky-making facilities.

The Scottish Lowlands
produce top quality cereal
crops for whisky making.

BLENDED WHISKY

"The art of combining meticulously selected, mature, high-quality whiskies, each with its own flavour and other characteristics, with such skill that the whole is better than the sum of its parts, so that each makes its contribution to the finished blend without any one predominating."

These were the words of David MacDonald, the last member of the MacDonald family to be chairman of Glenmorangie, before its sale to LVMH, the French-based luxury goods conglomerate, in 2004. It is a definition of blending that has seldom been bettered. Yet, it is perhaps somewhat idealized, ignoring as it does the pricing pressures that drive the creation of so many standard and secondary (cheaper) blends. It also reflects only the skill of blending and not its troubled history.

Grant's Premium 12-Year-Old

Despite the fact that the whisky industry makes much play of its roots in the 15th century, few distilleries can trace their history back beyond the 1820s. The reason

for this is that for much of the 18th century there was an ongoing battle between legal and illegal distilling. By the 1780s, large-scale distilling from grain had been developed in the Lowlands by the Haig and Stein families. In contrast, it was the smaller, pot still production, largely artisanal in nature, that characterized the Highland output. Disputes between the two were constant.

NEW LAWS

In the 1820s, new legislation helped the whole industry to legitimacy *(see p47)*, and its potential was transformed in 1827 by Robert Stein, who invented a method of continuous distillation. Rapidly perfected by Aeneas Coffey *(see p172)*, the continuous still allows the production of a more lightly flavoured spirit from cheaper ingredients. It is a more consistent

In the blending room of John Walker's and Sons' Barleith complex, barrels of whisky are poured into 16 troughs in readiness for blending.

method of distillation, too, and achieves a higher alcohol content in the spirit than the product of a pot still.

Yet, blending as we understand it today did not emerge until after the Spirits Act of 1860. Importantly, this legislation permitted whiskies from different distilleries to be blended "under bond" (before the payment of excise duty). By reducing the amount of cash tied up in stock, the blender was able to experiment more freely, and, in an unforeseen but wholly beneficial consequence, it became possible to "marry" (age) the resultant blend, thus further improving its flavour.

The first man to realize the full potential of blending was Andrew Usher, who, since 1853, had been selling Usher's Old Vatted Glenlivet, a blended malt. He could see the possibilities of a consistent and repeatable product that combined the full flavour of the Highland single malts with the lightness and economy of grain whisky.

Haig Gold Label and The Dimple

SCOTCH SUPREMACY

At about the same time, several trends combined to favour blended Scotch whisky. Scotland had become popular with the English. The opening of rail links to the Highlands began the development of mass tourism, initially with the upper classes (strongly influenced by Queen Victoria and Prince Albert), who came for the field sports. They were subsequently followed by middle-class tourists, who saw Scotland as fashionable, its rugged landscape more grand and romantic than any English vistas. Sir Edwin Landseer's painting *Monarch of the Glen* (1851) expresses this relationship.

The role of Scottish regiments, administrators, and traders in the creation of the British Empire helped spread whisky's fame, and the fashion for drinking whisky with soda water helped the new blends. The depredation of the French cognac industry, caused by the destructive phylloxera louse in the 1880s, opened a gap in the market that was quickly exploited by innovative, energetic entrepreneurial whisky blenders such as Usher, Alexander Walker, John and Tommy Dewar, and James Buchanan. Their names live on in the names of some of the famous brands, even if the companies they created have long since been absorbed in the ruthless consolidation that followed the Second World War.

ANTI-BLEND FEELINGS

But not everyone cared for the impact of "silent spirit", as grain whisky was known. Sir Walter Gilbey, proprietor of Glen Spey, Strathmill, and Knockando Distilleries, railed against it as "nearly free from taste and smell", and the Irish distilling industry, in a commercially suicidal move, turned their face against blending *(see p159)*. The North of Scotland Malt Distillers' Association also fought a long rearguard action against the incursions of grain.

Nosing has always been the key to creating great blended whisky.

The argument was settled, at least in a legal sense, by the 1908–1909 Royal Commission on Whiskey. In a landmark decision, it resolved that both grain and single malt spirit could be sold as "whisky", clearing the way for the modern industry.

Today, more than 90 per cent of all the Scotch whisky sold in the world is a blend, with the great brands each selling well over a million cases annually.

As the foundation stone of the Scotch whisky industry, blended whisky is today in good heart and its future seems assured. The whole is indeed better than the sum of its parts.

SCOTCH BLENDS

The general trend in recent decades has been towards rationalization, with fewer and fewer companies controlling more and more brands. But there are signs of a renaissance in craft blending, too, with both independent companies and large players producing limited edition blends.

100 PIPERS

Owner: Chivas Brothers

The sight of 100 pipers in full flow would undoubtedly be an awe-inspiring one, and it did indeed inspire a well-known Scottish air, which commemorates the march of Bonnie Prince Charlie on the city of Carlisle. As the song relates, the English army reacted as you might expect: "Dumfoun'er'd they heard the blaw, the blaw; Dumfoun'er'd they a' ran awa', awa'."

When the Seagram Company was looking for a contender in the "value" sector of the Scotch whisky market in 1965, they too drew inspiration from the song and named their brand 100 Pipers. No doubt, they had similar hopes that the competition would flee in fear.

With a competitive price tag, 100 Pipers proved an immediate success in many markets, but not in the UK, where it was rather looked down upon, perhaps unfairly. The blend contains Braeval and Allt a' Bhainne among its fillings, and probably some Glenlivet and Longmorn as well, and it may be that its pale colour affected the perceptions of some UK drinkers accustomed to darker coloured blends.

Seagram's developed the brand very effectively and it has continued to grow under its new owners, Chivas Brothers (the spirits division

100 Pipers

of Pernod Ricard), so that today it is one of the world's top 10 selling blends. It is the best-selling whisky in Thailand, a dynamic market for Scotch, and is growing rapidly in many other countries, especially Spain, Venezuela, Australia, and India.

🍸 **100 PIPERS** 40% ABV
A light and very mixable whisky, with a smooth, subtly smoky taste.

THE ANTIQUARY

Owner: Tomatin Distillery

This famous old blend, first introduced in 1857 by John and William Hardie, takes its name from a novel by the early 19th-century writer Sir Walter Scott. For many years this blend was the product of William Sanderson (of VAT 69 fame), until it was sold by United Distillers (forerunners of Diageo) in 1996. Today, it is owned by The Tomatin Distillery Co., which is itself a subsidiary of Takara Shuzo and Okura Ltd of Japan.

For many years, The Antiquary was a well-regarded luxury blend, packaged in a handsome faceted bottle that looked similar to a decanter.

Sadly, it was not regarded as a priority by United Distillers and sales fell away, until the name and blend recipe were eventually sold.

The new owners now offer 12 and 21-year-old versions of the brand, and appear to be making some effort to

The Antiquary 12-Year-Old

re-establish The Antiquary. New packaging that harks back to the old bottle has been introduced.

🍸 **THE ANTIQUARY HOUSE STYLE**
As befits its deluxe status, there is at the heart of The Antiquary a very high malt to grain ratio, which includes some of the finest malts from Speyside and the Highlands. Their flavours are balanced by Lowland malt, which adds gentleness to the profile. The subtle fruitiness has a hint of apples. The result of the high malt content is depth of flavour, outstanding smoothness, and a long aftertaste.

🍸 **THE ANTIQUARY 21-YEAR-OLD**
40% ABV ● This is a premium blend that combines the

PERCENTAGE ABV

The vast majority of Scotch blends are bottled for the market at 40 per cent ABV (alcohol by volume). Malt whiskies tend to be a little higher, commonly 43 per cent, while cask-strength whisky is bottled at a strength of between 50–60 per cent ABV.

signature style with a dash of Islay malt to create an exceptional dram. A light maltiness with muted peaty notes allows the heather, dandelion, and blackcurrant notes to flourish. A smooth, full-bodied whisky with a lingering taste.

ASYLA

Owner: Compass Box Whisky Company

Asyla is a blended whisky produced by the Compass Box Whisky Company, headed by self-styled "whisky zealot" John Glaser, who works rather in the manner of a *negociant*, aiming to create some of Scotland's premier whiskies through the art of blending.

The name Asyla comes from the plural of the word "asylum". As Glaser explains: "It is simply a word I like because of the various connotations it can have. Are we talking sanctuary, madhouse, a little of both?"

From this you may discern that Compass Box is not your average whisky maker. In fact, though the company is relatively small, it enjoys a disproportionate influence on current thinking within the industry and has won a high number of awards.

Compass Box whiskies are not cheap, for which Glaser makes no apology. They are, however, beautifully packaged and very, very good.

🍸 **ASYLA** 40% ABV • The blend comprises equal proportions of single grain and malt whiskies, containing Cragganmore, Linkwood, and Glen Elgin malts, and Cambus and Cameron Bridge grains, all from first-fill bourbon barrels, naturally coloured, and non chill-filtered. Asyla is a *tour de force* from a true lover of whisky.

Asyla from Compass Box

BAILIE NICOL JARVIE

Owner: Glenmorangie

Bailie Nicol Jarvie, or BNJ as it is commonly known in Scotland, is produced by Glenmorangie and has long been rated by enthusiasts as a particularly fine blended whisky. Accordingly, it has acquired something of a cult following, with its acolytes torn between wishing the company would promote the brand a good deal more enthusiastically and savouring the idea of being one of the cognoscenti.

Reputedly first produced in 1893 by Alexander Muir and Roderick Macdonald (the predecessors to the Glenmorangie Company), Bailie Nicol Jarvie is named after a character in Sir Walter Scott's novel *Rob Roy*. In one famous incident in the book, the Bailie, a Scottish magistrate, distinguished himself by tackling a fierce Highlander with a red-hot poker. The poker itself (actually a plough coulter) remains on display outside the Bailie Nicol Jarvie Hotel, in Aberfoyle.

Long reputed to contain a healthy measure of both Glenmorangie and Glen Moray single malts, Bailie Nicol Jarvie has one of the highest malt contents of any blended whisky on the market, and contains only "first-class" ranked malts in the blend.

The bottle label has a delightful period feel, apparently untouched by the hand of marketing – though in fact it was subtly revamped in the mid-1990s.

🍸 **BAILIE NICOL JARVIE** 40% ABV
Smooth, subtle, and full of character, it has a delicate balance of sweet Speyside, aromatic Highland, and peaty Islay malt whiskies blended with only the finest grain whisky. Definitely one to show off to your friends.

BALLANTINE'S

Owner: Chivas Brothers

Ballantine's may have the most extensive range of blended Scotch in the world today. It includes Ballantine's Finest and a host of blends with various age statements, among them 12, 17, 21, and 30-year-old versions.

Ballantine's were pioneers of aged blends and first produced their flagship 30-year-old in the late 1920s, from special stocks of malt and grain Scotch that had been set aside years before, with the idea of creating a super-premium product already in mind.

This foresight enabled the brand to establish a strong, competitive position at the top of the market, which, despite various changes of ownership *(see p121)*, has stood the company in good stead ever since.

Relatively hard to find in the UK market, Ballantine's Finest has long been popular elsewhere in Europe, and the more premium expressions enjoy huge success in the Far East, especially in China, Japan, South Korea, and Asian duty-free markets.

The range now sells nearly 5.5 million 9-litre (2-gallon) cases a year, making it the world's third-biggest selling Scotch whisky by volume.

The blend is noted for its complexity, with

Ballantine's Finest

more than 40 different malts and grains being used in the mix. The two Speyside single malts from Glenburgie and Miltonduff form the base for the blend, but malts from all parts of Scotland are also employed. For maturation, Ballantine's favour principally the use of ex-bourbon barrels, for their vanilla influences and sweet creamy notes.

BALLANTINE'S HOUSE STYLE
In keeping with Ballantine's distinguished pedigree, there is a specific Ballantine's family signature style flowing through the range. All Ballantine's aged, blended whiskies are elegant and superbly balanced, with a distinctive soft and sweet flavour.

However, care is also taken to ensure that each product throughout the range has its own individual personality. All are characterized by some degree of complexity, but the younger versions are fresher, with more immediate appeal.

BALLANTINE'S 17-YEAR-OLD 40% ABV
In this expression, a deep, balanced, and elegant whisky announces itself, with a hint of wood and vanilla. The body is full and creamy, and has a vibrant, honeyed sweetness, with hints of oak and peat smoke on the palate. Some tasters have detected a hint of salt in this whisky, and in the 12-year-old expression too.

BALLANTINE'S 21-YEAR-OLD & BALLANTINE'S 30-YEAR-OLD 40% ABV
Such older expressions are characterized by a deeper colour and traces of heather, smoke, liquorice, and aromatic spice on the nose and body. The medium to heavy palate is complex yet harmoniously balanced, with rich, mellow sherry, honey, and floral notes.

BELL'S

Owner: Diageo

Brand leadership in the emotionally charged Scottish market was conceded to The Famous Grouse *(see p132)* in 1980, but Diageo has taken a number of steps to consolidate the position of Bell's as the UK's overall best-selling Scotch. Visitor facilities at the Blair Athol Distillery in Pitlochry *(see p79)* – the spiritual home of Bell's and the source of the single malt at the heart of the blend – have been enhanced, and, in 1994, the blend itself was upgraded. Bell's Extra Special is now an 8-year-old, the only major blend to be matured for that length of time.

Besides Blair Athol, the two original Bell's distilleries, Dufftown and Inchgower, are key components of the blend, along with Caol Ila, from Islay, and the Lowlander, Glenkinchie.

Bell's also produces exclusively for the UK a premium blended malt called Special Reserve, in which a touch more Islay may be detected in the blend.

Even rarer are the collectable Bell's decanters. They were first produced in the 1930s, and since 1988 a

Bell's 8-Year-Old

decanter has been produced each Christmas. The most sought-after is the Charles and Diana decanter that commemorates their 1981 marriage. It fetches up to £2,500 (when full, naturally).

BELL'S 8-YEAR-OLD 40% ABV
A medium-bodied blend, with a nutty aroma and a lightly spiced flavour.

BENMORE

Owner: Diageo

In response to the growing market for blended Scotch in Thailand, Diageo launched Benmore in 2005. Meaning "the big hill" in Gaelic, Benmore is a revival of an old name that was acquired by the Distillers Company (DCL) in 1929, when they bought Benmore Distillers.

Benmore operated Dallas Dhu, Lochindaal, and Lochhead distilleries, all of which have now been silent for many years.

This latest incarnation of Benmore contains 18 malts and grain whiskies and is offered as a 5-year-old.

> ### BAXTER'S BARLEY BREE
>
> The wonderfully named Baxter's Barley Bree is today owned by Diageo, but, despite efforts to revive the brand in the 1990s, it appears to be currently moribund. For traditionalists, this is a matter of some regret, as Baxter's Barley Bree was once an important brand of the large Dundee-based distiller James Watson & Co., which was eventually absorbed into the Distillers Company in the 1920s. The name carries enormous resonance for those who care to look below the surface. "Barley" is, of course, the raw material of whisky and "bree" is the old Scots word for broth or liquor and, by extension, a synonym for whisky.

Blair Athol Distillery provides the malt at the heart of Bell's, and is home to the Bell's vistor centre.

THE BALLANTINE'S STORY

In 1827, at the age of 19, George Ballantine opened his first grocery and whisky business in Edinburgh. Proving to be an exceptional entrepreneur, he had a growing reputation by 1837 and moved to a prestigious address at the very heart of this prosperous city.

Edinburgh was one of the richest cities in the world at the time, and Ballantine's new address on South Bridge, near Princes Street, showed that he was a man with ambition and confidence.

He began innovative experimentation, blending different whiskies from different distilleries to produce something lighter and more sophisticated. This led him to create a consistent house style for his customers, and so Ballantine's became one of the very first whisky brands.

By 1869, Ballantine had expanded his business into Glasgow, and from these premises he and his two sons gained international status as purveyors of the finest-quality blended whisky. He continued to experiment – the effects of maturation on whisky, and the importance of first-fill cask selection were typical of Ballantine's innovation and imagination, which were key to

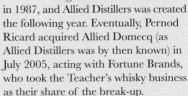

Ballantine's 12-Year-Old

establishing blended Scotch as the leading international drink.

By 1881, Ballantine's was already exporting blended whisky to a worldwide market.

A royal warrant to Queen Victoria and subsequently to King Edward followed, but in 1936 Ballantine's was bought by the Canadian firm Hiram Walker, as one of their first moves into the Scotch whisky market. Hiram Walker merged with Allied Vintners in 1987, and Allied Distillers was created the following year. Eventually, Pernod Ricard acquired Allied Domecq (as Allied Distillers was by then known) in July 2005, acting with Fortune Brands, who took the Teacher's whisky business as their share of the break-up.

Pernod's whisky division, Chivas Brothers, has effectively relaunched the brand, and sales are now growing rapidly, after a period of stagnation under the previous ownership.

Ballantine's Distillery, by the River Leven in Dumbarton, is soon to be turned into modern apartments.

THE BELL FAMILY

"Several fine whiskies blended together please the palates of a greater number of people than one whisky unmixed," wrote Perth blender Arthur Bell, and the total confidence he had in his products led him to appoint a London agent as early as 1863.

Despite this, Bell's remained a little-known brand for another 50 years or so, and didn't really hit its stride until as recently as the 1970s. This was in great part due to the religious beliefs that shaped Arthur Bell, and to his innate modesty.

He refused to allow the family name to appear on a bottle, explaining that he preferred "the qualities of my goods to speak for themselves". His sons, Arthur Kinmond (AK) and Robert, were considerably less idealistic and self-effacing, and, soon after their father's death in 1900, set about making up for lost time.

The prohibition on the use of the Bell name was abandoned by 1904 and a healthy export business in Australia and New Zealand was quickly established. Agents were appointed in India, Ceylon, Italy, and France. AK

Arthur Bell

made a lengthy trip to North America, especially Canada, and the brand became the most popular in South Africa.

The slogan "Afore Ye Go", which has served the company so well, dates from around this period, though it was not registered as a trademark until 1925. After a period in abeyance, it made a welcome return to the brand's revamped packaging, launched in 2006.

Bell's acquired the Blair Athol and Dufftown Distilleries in 1933 and, three years later, added Inchgower. The family connection was severed in 1942 with the death of both Bell brothers, and William Farquharson took over as chairman – a post he held until his demise in 1973.

This portrait of the Bell's staff was taken in the early 1900s, in the period when Arthur Bell's sons had taken over and were not averse to branding the family name.

THE CRITICS SAY...

IN a game where virtually every stroke affords an opportunity for critical judgement, it is not surprising that opinions are almost as numerous and varied as the strokes themselves.

Connoisseurs of Scotch Whisky, on the other hand, are unanimous in their appreciation of " Black & White"— as fine a whisky as ever came out of Scotland.

"BLACK & WHITE"
SCOTCH WHISKY

James Buchanan & Co. Ltd., Glasgow and London

Advertising for Black & White whisky always made use of two dogs: a black Scottish terrier and a white West Highland terrier.

BLACK & WHITE

Owner: Diageo

A long-lived and much-loved brand from the Buchanan's stable (see p124), Black & White is today marketed by Diageo in France, Brazil, and Venezuela, where it continues to enjoy a popularity that it has long since lost in its homeland.

There are two accounts of how the brand came to have its name and carry the distinctive symbol of two terrier dogs, one black and the other white.

One version has it that James Buchanan, the brand's owner, was an ardent animal lover and conceived the idea for one of the world's most famous trademarks in the 1890s, when he was returning home from a dog show. Soon after, the black Scottish terrier and the white West Highland terrier were adopted as the brand's motif.

The alternative and equally plausible version is that James Buchanan supplied his whisky to the UK's House of Commons, where, in a very dark bottle with a white label, it was sold under the name "Buchanan's Special". Supposedly incapable of memorizing the whisky's real name, British parliamentarians would call instead for "Black and White". The name eventually stuck and, instinctive marketer that he was, Buchanan adopted the name and subsequently adorned the label with the two dogs.

Perhaps both accounts are true. Either way, it is a pleasant memory of a gentler age, far removed from the focus groups and brand strategies of today.

BLACK BOTTLE

Owner: Burn Stewart Distillers

Another well-loved blend with a long history, Black Bottle was first created by C D & G Grahams, an Aberdeen firm of tea blenders, in 1879. After surviving various vicissitudes, the company was sold to Long John International in 1964. Allied Lyons acquired the brand in 1990 and started to invest in it, but in turn sold it on to Highland Distillers in 1995.

That was not the end of its travels, however, because in April 2003 Highland then sold Black Bottle – along with the Bunnahabhain Distillery on Islay – to the current owners, Burn Stewart Distillers, who are themselves part of CL WorldBrands Ltd, a multinational drinks group based in Trinidad.

There are two excellent variants, Black Bottle and Black Bottle 10-Year-Old. Great efforts have been made by Burn Stewart to invest in the packaging and, more importantly, the blend quality. Many commentators agree that the blend profile now resembles, as nearly as can be determined, that of the original 19th-century whisky.

🍶 **BLACK BOTTLE** 40% ABV
The blend contains malts from seven Islay distilleries, along with hefty helpings of the company's Deanston malt. The nose is fresh and fruity, with hints of peat, while the palate is full, with a slightly honeyed sweetness, followed

Black & White

by a distinctive smoky flavour. The finish is long and warming, with a smoky, Islay character.

🍸 BLACK BOTTLE

10-YEAR-OLD 40% ABV

This expression again contains malt from seven Islay distilleries. Accordingly, "peat freaks" will find this very much to their taste. But steer away if you are not a fan of the traditional peaty and phenolic Islay character. Black Bottle 10-Year-Old is a big, no-nonsense whisky that takes no prisoners.

THE BLACK DOUGLAS

Owner: Chivas Brothers

The first Black Douglas was a 14th-century Scottish soldier and knight who fought with King Robert the Bruce in the Scottish Wars of Independence.

The Black Douglas Scotch was created by Seagram's, and thus eventually acquired by Chivas Brothers/Pernod Ricard, who in 2002 signed a supply arrangement with Carlton United Breweries of Australia to support their local bottling of The Black Douglas.

The Black Douglas is described as "a well-balanced grain and malt blend Scotch whisky, a soft, well-aged product with a smooth finish that appeals to Australians."

As well as a standard non-age bottling, 8-year-old and 12-year-old versions are offered.

BUCHANAN'S

Owner: Diageo

Buchanan's is an excellent example of a brand that has survived the ups and downs foisted upon them by changes of ownership and consolidation within the whisky industry. Indeed,

Buchanan's today is once again showing signs that it is prospering.

The original James Buchanan was one of the most notable "whisky barons" and a larger-than-life character. Starting in London in 1879 as an agent for Mackinlay's, he soon began trading on his own account, with capital loaned from a friend. A born salesman, he repaid the loan within a year and rapidly saw his whisky, then called Buchanan's Special *(see p124)*, adopted in the House of Commons. His genius for publicity also led him to be an early pioneer of newspaper advertising.

His main rival at the time was Tommy Dewar *(see p131)*. This extended beyond the world of whisky, and in direct competition with Dewar, Buchanan's horses won the Derby twice.

However, Buchanan's later merged with Dewar's in 1915, before they both joined the Distillers Company (DCL) in 1925. Wrapped up with the fortunes of DCL, Buchanan's is now a Diageo brand.

Today, the name is mainly seen in Venezuela, Mexico, Colombia, and – to a lesser extent – the United States, where, fittingly, it is positioned as a premium style that reflects the prestige and tradition that suits the taste and values of the Latin community. One feels that Buchanan himself would have approved.

Two variants are produced: a 12-year-old and Buchanan's Special Reserve, an 18-year-old expression.

Buchanan's 12-Year-Old

CATTO'S

Owner: Inver House Distillers

Aberdeen-based whisky blender James Catto set up in business in 1861 and his whiskies soon achieved international distribution on the shipping lines White Star and P&O, both of which were founded by former schoolfriends.

Ownership passed to Gilbey's after the death of James's son Robert during World War I. More recently, it was acquired by Inver House Distillers, who are themselves owned by the Thai Beverage Public Company (ThaBev).

Chivas Regal 25

Catto's is a deluxe, fully matured, and complex blend, fresh and clean with a lingering, warm finish. Two versions are available: a non-age standard and a 12-year-old style.

🍸 CATTO'S 40% ABV

The standard Catto blend is aromatic and well-rounded in character with a smooth, mellow finish.

CHIVAS REGAL

Owner: Chivas Brothers

Said to be a favourite of the late author and gonzo journalist Hunter S Thompson, Chivas Regal is among the top five best-selling Scotch blends in the world, and is one of the few truly global brands in terms of distribution.

Speyside's micro-climate is perfect for producing the single malts that are major components of the Chivas Regal blends, and special mention should go to Strathisla, whose rich and full malt whisky has long been at the heart of them.

Hunter S Thompson, the writer and journalist, was reputed to be a huge fan of Chivas Regal.

Chivas Regal 18 was launched in 1997 and is a super-premium blend with Strathisla 18-Year-Old (an expression that's not available as a single malt) contributing to its memorable warm finish.

For many years, Chivas Regal was positioned as a luxury good, and consistent and heavy advertising ensured its leading position. Today, under the Pernod Ricard umbrella, innovative marketing, such as an online broadband TV channel in partnership with Microsoft, has brought success in new markets.

CHIVAS REGAL 12 40% ABV • An aromatic infusion of wild herbs, heather, honey, and orchard fruits, with a radiant warm amber colour. Round and creamy on the palate, with a full, rich taste of honey and ripe apples, and notes of vanilla, butterscotch, and hazelnut. Rich and lingering.

CHIVAS REGAL 18 40% ABV An intense dark amber colour, with multi-layered aromas of dried fruits, spice, and buttery toffee. Exceptionally rich and smooth, with a velvety, dark chocolate palate, elegant floral notes and a wisp of sweet mellow smokiness.

CLAN CAMPBELL

Owner: **Chivas Brothers**

Another million-case-selling brand from Pernod Ricard's Chivas Brothers, Clan Campbell is a leading standard brand in the dynamic French market. In fact, it is something of a phenomenon, having only been launched as recently as 1984. The brand is not available in the UK, but may be found in Italy, Spain, and some Far Eastern markets, as well as in France.

Prior to this, the House of Campbell can trace its history to 1879, when it was based in Glasgow. In 1945, the company acquired Aberlour Distillery, later adding Perthshire's tiny Edradour, which it subsequently sold.

In 1988, a series of mergers and acquisitions brought Clan Campbell into the ownership of Pernod Ricard, and substantial growth followed.

Despite its relative youth, its origins are now inextricably entwined with Scottish heritage, thanks to clever marketing and a link to the Duke of Argyll, head of the clan.

CLAN CAMPBELL 40% ABV
The blend largely comprises Speyside malts (Aberlour and Glenallachie in particular) and selected grain whiskies. It is a smooth, light whisky with a fruity finish.

Clan Campbell

CLAN MACGREGOR

Owner: **William Grant & Sons**

It is unlikely that you will come across a bottle of Clan MacGregor in the UK, because this "secondary" (low-priced) blend is sold largely in North America and in more than 60 countries around the world, from Venezuela to the Middle East and Thailand, but not – to any noticeable extent at least – in Scotland.

For all its anonymity in its homeland, however, Clan MacGregor's sales approach a very respectable 1.5 million cases annually, and it is claimed by its owners, William Grant & Sons, to be one of the world's fastest-growing major Scotch whisky brands.

The bottle label proudly carries the Clan MacGregor badge and motto, and, with his kind permission, the personal crest of the 24th Clan Chief, Sir Malcolm MacGregor of MacGregor.

Clan MacGregor

Given its parentage and price point, the blend would seem likely to contain Grant's own malts (Glenfiddich, Balvenie, and Kininvie) and grain whisky from Grant's substantial Girvan operation.

THE CLAYMORE

Owner: **Whyte & Mackay**

Derived from *claidheamh mòr*, a Gaelic term meaning "great sword", a claymore is a Highland broadsword. The name was deemed an appropriate one to use by the Distillers Company (DCL) when, in 1977, they attempted to recover market share lost by the withdrawal from the UK of their Johnnie Walker Red Label. Driven largely by price, this was an immediate success, and The Claymore was for a while one of the best-selling whiskies in the country.

In 1985, during the battle for ownership of the Distillers Company, the brand was sold to Glasgow-

THE CHIVAS BROTHERS

Though a link can be traced to wine merchant William Edward's grocery store in Castle Street, Aberdeen, and the owner's partnership with a young farmer called James Chivas, in 1837, the story of the Chivas Brothers really starts some 20 years later.

In 1857, James Chivas dissolved his partnership with William Edward and joined his brother John to form Chivas Brothers. They planned to develop an already successful trade, which had begun to prosper with an order to supply nearby Balmoral Castle, Queen Victoria's Highland home. In 1843, James Chivas had been granted a royal warrant as grocers.

With the advantage of this regal connection, the business expanded dramatically. In imitation of Queen Victoria, many members of the British gentry came to Scotland to hunt, shoot stags, fish for salmon, and, of course, drink Scotch. Order books from the 1880s proudly list emperors, princes and peers, admirals and generals, bishops and professors among the company's customers.

James and John Chivas were pioneers of the art of blending,

Created in 1909, Chivas Regal was a top seller around the world by 1949.

producing consistently smooth, high-quality blended whiskies.

Their standards were carried forward by James Chivas's assistants, Alexander Smith and Charles Howard, and, in 1909, the company went on to create the Chivas Regal premium blend.

In 1949, the firm was acquired by Seagram's, of Canada, by which time Chivas Regal 12-Year-Old was one of the best-selling premium brands of whisky in the world. In 1950, Seagram bought Strathisla Distillery and, seven years later, to keep up with demand, constructed new facilities at Glen Keith *(see p61)*. The redoubtable Sam Bronfman, of the owning family, took personal responsibility for guiding the re-blending of Chivas Regal.

In the latter years of Seagram's ownership, the brand faded somewhat, but has been successfully re-invigorated under Pernod Ricard's energetic management, and is once again a major and dynamic force in whisky.

Chivas Brothers bought Strathisla Distillery in 1950 to safeguard supplies of the malt whisky that was at the heart of their blend.

based Whyte & Mackay (now owned by the UB Group). The Claymore continued to sell well for some time, but the sales volume has declined in recent years and it is now principally seen as a "secondary" (low-priced) brand.

Dalmore is believed to be the principal malt whisky in the blend.

Claymore figurine

CLUNY

Owner: Whyte & Mackay

Cluny is produced by Whyte & Mackay and supplied in bulk to Heaven Hill Distilleries of the USA, who have imported it since 1988. It is one of the United States' top-selling, domestically bottled, blended Scotch whiskies, and is sold primarily on its competitive price. It does, however, contain more than 30 malt whiskies from all regions of Scotland, along with grain whisky, presumably sourced largely from Whyte & Mackay's Invergordon plant.

CRAWFORD'S

Owner: Whyte & Mackay/Diageo

The old-established Leith firm of A & A Crawford had developed their Crawford's 3 Star brand into a Scottish

favourite by the time they joined the Distillers Company (DCL) in 1944. The brand continued to sell well, but was not of strategic significance to its owners, hence the decision to license the brand to Whyte & Mackay in 1986, though Diageo, successors to the Distillers Company, retain the rights to the name Crawford's 3 Star Special Reserve outside the UK. Benrinnes single malt was a long-time component in the blend. A 5 Star version was also produced but later discontinued.

CUTTY SARK

Owner: Berry Brothers & Rudd Ltd

Blended and bottled in Glasgow by The Edrington Group (proprietors of The Famous Grouse), who supply much of the whisky for the blend, Cutty Sark is owned by London wine merchants Berry Bros & Rudd.

It was created in 1923 by Charles Julian, of London blenders Porter, Dingwall & Norris, for the partners of Berry Bros & Rudd, who were looking to produce an innovative whisky. Cutty Sark was just that – the first naturally pale-coloured

whisky in the world, and one of great character and quality. The name was inspired by the fastest and most famous of all the Scottish-built clipper ships, itself named after the young witch dressed in a "cutty sark" (a sort of short shirt) in Robert Burns's celebrated poem "Tam O'Shanter".

The nautical reference also echoes the brand's early days, when Captain William McCoy, a famous American bootlegger, supplied Cutty Sark to customers in the United States during Prohibition (hence the phrase "the real McCoy"). Cutty Sark remains an important brand in the United States and is also enjoyed in Southern Europe and the Far East.

One of the acclaimed blended whiskies of the world, Cutty Sark uses some 20 single malts for the blend, many from the renowned distilleries of Speyside, such as Macallan and Glenrothes.

Cutty Sark

Maturation and marrying the blend contribute to the distinguishing qualities, and wood for the casks in which the blend is matured is carefully selected to bring out the flavour and aroma, as well as to impart colour gently during the lengthy ageing period. As well as the non-age expression, there is a deluxe range, aged at 12, 15, 18, and 25 years.

🍶 **CUTTY SARK** 40% ABV ● Golden, clear, and bright, Cutty Sark is notably pale. The aroma is light and fragrant with hints of vanilla and oak. The taste is of medium intensity, with a sweet, creamy, vanilla note evident. Cutty Sark has a crisp and clean finish.

THE CUTTY SARK LABEL

The label was designed by James McBay, a Scottish artist friend of the owners. McBay named the brand and designed the distinctive label over lunch in the parlour at the back of Berry Brothers' shop in fashionable St James Street, London. Presumably, it was a jolly lunch, as for many years the label carried the idiosyncratic descriptor "Scots Whisky", though sadly this has reverted to the standard "Scotch" in recent years.

Cutty Sark's original "Scots" whisky label

Blended whiskies are about mass appeal, and for big players like J&B that means finding ever new ways to promote the brand.

This Dewar's advertising poster of 1935 allies its whisky with the silver jubilee of King George V.

DEWAR'S

Owner: John Dewar & Sons (Bacardi)

Following Bacardi's purchase of Dewar's in 1988, the brand was re-packaged, with considerable investment being made throughout the business, from the distilling process to the warehousing and bottling.

To augment the standard White Label, new products were developed. The first of these was a 12-year-old version, Special Reserve. Then came the 18-year-old Founder's Reserve, and finally an ultra-premium non-age style known as Signature.

The main single malt in the Dewar's blends is Aberfeldy, though the group's other malts – Aultmore, Royal Brackla, Craigellachie, and, to a lesser extent, MacDuff –

are also used. Given the history of the company and the brand *(see opposite)*, it is reasonable to assume that a contribution from the Diageo stable of malts is also still present in the blend.

Dewar's is seldom seen in the UK, but is a dominant presence in the United States. It is also important in some European markets and of growing significance in Asia.

Bacardi has increased global distribution for Dewar's, greatly expanded the marketing budget, and raised the brand's profile while maintaining the quality standards. In fact, some would say the blend quality has been enhanced, especially in the new products, which have won many awards and medals.

BLUE BLAZER

Often made with bourbon, but perfectly at home with good Scotch, the Blue Blazer was created by Jerry Thomas, a San Francisco bartender. Watching Thomas making the drink, President Ulysses S Grant was reportedly so impressed that he presented him with a cigar. Thomas's bartending skills are an acquired art, so you may want to practise making the drink in the garden first.

Ingredients
1 measure (25ml) blended Scotch whisky
1 measure (25ml) boiling water
1 tsp powdered sugar
lemon peel

Method
Use two large metal mugs with handles. Warm the whisky and put it in one mug. Put the water in the other. Set the whisky alight and, as it burns, combine with the water, pouring the mixture from one mug to the other. Your audience (and you should have one) should see a stream of liquid fire. Sweeten and serve in a stemmed glass with a piece of lemon peel.

Dewar's 12-Year-Old

Dewar's future seems quite secure under the ownership of Bacardi, who, in August 2007, announced a further £120 million investment in their Scottish production facilities.

A state-of-the-art visitor centre, which celebrates the life of the Dewar family and the firm's long history of whisky making, was opened at Aberfeldy *(see p77)*, one of the four distilleries acquired by Bacardi when they bought the Dewar's brand nine years ago.

DEWAR'S – PIONEERS OF BLENDING

The firm of Dewar's was established in Perth in 1846 by John Dewar. Like so many other founders of a great whisky dynasty, he was working as a wine and spirit merchant when he decided to start out on his own. He then proceeded to develop the business in slow and careful steps.

John Dewar was experimenting with blending in the early 1860s, making him something of a pioneer. The whisky he produced was sold in stoneware crocks known as "pigs", and later he was among the first distillers to sell branded whisky by the bottle instead of by the cask.

By the time of his death in 1880, his business had really taken off. His sons, John and Thomas, rode the Victorian whisky boom with conspicuous success. John was a shrewd businessman, while Tommy, a born salesman, was responsible for the world's first whisky commercial in 1896, when he projected a film on to a New York skyscraper.

Together, the brothers transformed the firm from a local concern into a global business, hiring the renowned Elgin-based architect Charles Doig *(see p59)* to build Aberfeldy Distillery in the 1890s, thus turning themselves from whisky blenders into distillers.

The flagship White Label blend was launched around 1899, after experiments by Dewar's master blender, Alexander Cameron, to perfect the practice of marrying, which was still in use for premium whisky blends. Dewar's was also an early proponent of the benefits of ageing whisky.

By the 1920s, however, the whisky boom had passed and Dewar's entered into a merger, first with Buchanan's and subsequently with the Distillers Company (DCL). The business was managed as a separate concern until rationalization in the 1980s, after which it was reduced to the status of just one brand among many. With the formation of Diageo in 1998, regulatory concerns forced the sale of Dewar's to Bacardi.

Dewar's plate

Dewar's was a prosperous independent company, enjoying great success right up until the 1920s.

GAME BIRD

Created for The Famous Grouse, this is a refreshing summer cocktail.

Ingredients
2 measures (50ml) of The Famous Grouse
1 measure (25ml) of Sourz apple schnapps
½ measure (about 10ml) of elderflower cordial
½ measure (about 10ml) of freshly squeezed lemon juice
½ measure (about 10ml) of sugar syrup
Ginger ale to taste

Method
Shake all the ingredients apart from the ginger ale with ice. Strain into a flute glass. Top up with ginger ale.

DEWAR'S HOUSE STYLE
The signature note in all Dewar's blends is a heather-honey sweetness derived from the Aberfeldy single malt. Dewar's has always been renowned for the smoothness of its blends, which are easy to drink without being bland. Older versions and the ultra-premium, non-aged blend, Signature, are especially highly regarded for their complexity and finesse.

DIMPLE

See Haig

THE FAMOUS GROUSE

Owner: Edrington Group

The Famous Grouse has been the number one whisky in Scotland since 1980 and is also the best-selling Scotch in Sweden, Denmark, Iceland, and Mozambique. It is the fastest-growing Scotch whisky in the Greek market, where it outsells *ouzo*, while the USA, France, Portugal, and worldwide duty-free sales are also important markets.

Remarkably, in an industry characterized by consolidation and the creation of global drinks companies with wide-ranging portfolios, The Famous Grouse comes from an independent Scottish company that focuses exclusively on one product: Scotch whisky.

The Edrington Group, owners of Highland Distillers (proprietors of Famous Grouse), also owns some of the finest malt distilleries, such as Macallan, Highland Park, and the less well-known but no less excellent Glenrothes. They are also co-owners of the North British grain distillery in Edinburgh.

It is the high proportion of these excellent whiskies contained in the blend to which The Famous Grouse owes its reputation among connoisseurs. Today, there are a number of variations to explore, mainly a selection of aged blended malts available as 10, 12, 15, 18, 21, and 30-year-old expressions, depending on the individual market.

The standard blend, The Famous Grouse Finest Scotch Whisky, is the dominant seller. In its production, the company attaches a great deal of significance to the marrying process, whereby, after blending, the whisky is reduced to around 45 per cent ABV and returned to the cask to allow the malt, grain, and water interactions to reach an equilibrium. This creates a consistent product, which is then filtered at a very gentle temperature of 4°C (40°F), using a wide filter, to retain as much as possible of the original flavour and texture of the whisky. Early in 2007, the company launched The Black Grouse in Sweden – a blend of The Famous Grouse with the

The stills at Glenturret Distillery produce one of the key malts for the Famous Grouse blend.

addition of some more strongly flavoured Islay malt whiskies to create a smooth, blended whisky with a peated note. This is said to be an addition to the core range, the implication being that if The Black Grouse is successful, it will be seen much more widely. In 2002, The Famous Grouse Experience was opened at the company's tiny Glenturret Distillery (see p88) near Crieff. This highly interactive visitor centre also has a restaurant and a large shop.

The Famous Grouse Finest Scotch Whisky

🍸 **THE FAMOUS GROUSE FINEST SCOTCH WHISKY**
40% ABV ● Highly regarded as a fine example of a standard blend that punches above its weight. With a healthy measure of The Macallan and Highland Park, there is oak and sherry on the nose, with a citrus note. Nothing dominates or offends, and this is a well-balanced and appealing whisky. On the palate, it is mature, easy-going, and full of bright Speyside fruit, with a clean, medium-dry finish.

SCOTLAND'S FAVOURITE BLENDED WHISKY

"Goback, goback, goback", the distinctive call of the red grouse is heard across much of upland Britain, but the bird is particularly associated with Scotland and the sporting traditions of its great Victorian estates, where gun smoke filled the cold morning air.

Like so many other celebrated names in whisky, The Famous Grouse has its roots in a Victorian grocer's shop – in Perth in this case, where Matthew Gloag set up in business. His nephew, also called Matthew, shrewdly recognized the opportunities for a local product to supply to the growing numbers of upper-class gentlemen being lured to the Highlands by the choice of sporting activities available there. In 1896 he decided upon "The Grouse Brand", and set his daughter the task of sketching the label. Before long, it was known as "The Famous Grouse".

A red grouse has adorned the label of The Famous Grouse since 1896.

By 1970, sales had developed, but death duties obliged the Gloags to sell the company to Highland Distillers. Over the next 20 years, sales were well ahead of the market, and The Famous Grouse increased its visibility, becoming first the best-selling blend in Scotland and then an increasingly important brand in world markets. A much-loved advertising campaign featuring an animated grouse began in 1996 and continues to prove popular.

While clever marketing has played its part, the company's strict adherence to the highest standards of quality has also been key to building Grouse's reputation. The company asserts that they perform a remarkable 8,735 quality checks from distillation to bottling. If that seems excessive, the result can be easily ascertained.

Today, with sales approaching three million cases annually, The Famous Grouse is firmly established in the top 10 of global brands and seems set for further growth.

Glenturret Distillery is the spiritual home of The Famous Grouse, not only supplying malt for the blend but also housing its visitor centre.

"When you are cold and wet, what else can warm you?" wrote Ernest Hemingway about whisky. Grand Macnish was his favourite.

FINDLATER

Owner: Whyte & Mackay

The firm of Findlater Mackie Todd & Co. began with Alexander Findlater, who set up business in 1823 to bring Findlater's whiskies to the world. Things unwound in the 1960s, and the firm was bought by Bulmers in 1966. It was later sold to Beechams, who tried to use it to launch a whisky brand using the Findlater name. Beechams sold out to a management buy-out team, who in turn were bought by John Lewis in 1993, since when the firm has been the mail-order arm of Waitrose's Wine Department.

Rights to the Findlater whisky brand, however, were sold to Invergordon Distillers (today Whyte & Mackay), with whom they still rest. Boisset America import the brand into the United States, which appears to be the remaining significant market for this long-serving whisky.

Invergordon Distillery acquired the rights to the Findlater name, and supply whisky for its blend.

GRAND MACNISH

Owner: Macduff International

Recommended by Ernest Hemingway, a man who knew his drinks, the Grand Macnish has a long and distinguished history. Robert McNish (an "a" was added to the brand name at some point later on) was a licensed grocer in Glasgow who took up whisky blending in 1863. His early success was built upon by his two energetic sons, John and George, who joined the family firm in 1887 and greatly expanded the business's turnover.

Like many other firms, however, the McNishes found trading conditions very difficult after World War I, and in 1927 they sold the company to Canadian Industrial Alcohol (later Corby Distilleries). Further transfers of ownership eventually brought Grand Macnish to Macduff International in 1991, where it appears to be having a modest revival.

There are two blended expressions: Grand Macnish Finest, which still uses up to 40 whiskies in the blend, as was the practice of Robert McNish; and a 12-year-old, which is described by the

company as "more mature, fruity, and malty" than its younger sibling.

The distinctive bottle gives Grand Macnish splendid "on shelf" presence, and the label is graced by the motto of the McNish clan: *"Forti Nihil Difficile"* (to the strong, nothing is difficult).

GRANT'S

Owner: William Grant & Sons

William Grant & Sons are famously family owned and resolutely independent. As such, is not too surprising to discover that the base for their range of blended whiskies is their own Glenfiddich single malt, together with The Balvenie, and the little-known Kininvie, the third distillery on their sprawling Speyside complex.

What may not be so widely appreciated is that Grant's also produce their own grain whisky, and have done since 1963, when a difference of opinion with the Distillers Company led Charles Gordon, great-grandson of the founder, to believe that supplies of grain whisky might be vulnerable. Determined not to be held to ransom, he resolved to build a grain distillery of his own at Girvan, close to the championship golf course at Turnberry.

Historically, this was not a major centre for distilling. Gordon chose the site for the ease of access it afforded to the nearby port,

Grant's Ale Cask Reserve

so that shipments of North American maize could be easily and reliably delivered. Ironically, such has been the success of the Grant's blends that a new distillery is currently under construction at Girvan, to provide additional malt whisky.

David Stewart, master blender at William Grant & Sons since 1974, is the longest-serving master blender in the Scotch whisky industry. He has created a varied and interesting range of whiskies. The fact that the company is privately owned, and thus not subject to pressures from the City, has enabled him to work with a remarkable depth of mature stock, some dating back 40 or more years.

The best-selling blend in the stable is Grant's Family Reserve, which enjoys virtually global distribution.

Grant's Rare Old 18-Year-Old

🍸 **GRANT'S FAMILY RESERVE** 40% ABV An unmistakable Speyside nose, with fluting malty notes. It has a firm mouth feel, with banana-vanilla sweetness balancing sharper,

malty notes. Clean, but very complex. A long, smooth lingering finish.

🍸 **THE GRANT'S PREMIUM RANGE** 40% ABV • A unique combination of aged premium whiskies and distinctive wood finishes. It is said to be the first range of blended whisky to be finished in specially selected virgin bourbon barrels and sherry and port casks. This time spent in the wood finishes acts exactly like a marrying period.

🍸 **GRANT'S PREMIUM 12-YEAR-OLD** 40% ABV • Only the finest single malt and grain whiskies, which have matured for at least 12 years in oak casks, are used. They are blended and finished in bourbon barrels. This ensures a warm and full-bodied Scotch whisky of great richness.

🍸 **GRANT'S RARE OLD 18-YEAR-OLD** 40% ABV • In 2001, Grant's Cask Reserves were created. Before bottling, these whiskies are "finished" in either ale or sherry casks, where the aged spirit absorbs some of the key notes and flavours of the barrels. In the Rare Old 18-Year-Old, some of the whisky is finished in port casks, and the end result is an appealing Scotch, perfectly balanced, with considerable depth of taste.

🍸 **GRANT'S ALE CASK RESERVE** 40% ABV • This is the only Scotch whisky to be finished in casks that have previously been used to contain beer. The ale casks give the whisky a distinctively creamy, malty, and honeyed taste.

🍸 **GRANT'S SHERRY CASK RESERVE** 40% ABV • Prepared in exactly the same way as the ale cask finish, but Spanish oloroso sherry casks are used instead, giving a distinctively warm, rich, and fruity palate.

Grant's pays a great deal of attention to casks, for marrying blends and giving special finishes.

Haig dominated the UK market for decades through a combination of distinctive packaging and strong advertising campaigns.

HAIG

Owner: Diageo

A whisky of distinguished pedigree owned by Diageo, Haig is a memory of the oldest distilling family in Scotland and the winner of numerous awards throughout the years. In its glory days, Haig was the best-selling whisky in the UK, but is now mainly found in Greece, Germany, the Canary Islands, Korea, the United States, and Mexico.

The Haig company can trace its history back to one John Haig, who is believed to have started distilling the produce of his farm at Throsk, in Stirlingshire, in 1627. His descendants married into the Stein family, notable distillers in their own right, and later built a grain distillery at Cameronbridge, in Fife. Eventually, in 1877, they were one of the founders of the Distillers Company, but continued their own independent blending operations until 1919.

The company's best known brand, Dimple (or Pinch in the US), was launched in 1890. The blend consists of more than 30 whiskies, including a number of rare whiskies from Diageo's treasured reserves of the most matured Highland malts. The distinctive bottle for this deluxe brand was introduced by G O Haig and was noted for the hand-applied wire net over the bottle, introduced to prevent the cork popping out in warm climates or during sea transport.

The unique three-sided pinched decanter was the first three-sided bottle to be registered as a trademark in the US, though it took the company until 1958 to make the application.

There are three variants: a 12-Year-Old, a 15-Year-Old, and an 18-Year-Old.

HANKEY BANNISTER

Owner: Inver House Distillers

The unusually named Hankey Bannister takes its name from a partnership formed in 1757 by Messrs Hankey and Bannister, who became established as suppliers of some of the finest wines and spirits in the UK. Their customers included royalty such as the Prince Regent, William IV, the Duke of Norfolk, and the Duke of Queensberry. In the 1940s and 50s, Hankey Bannister also enjoyed a privileged position

Haig's Glenleven

at No. 10 Downing Street as a favourite drink of the UK prime minister Sir Winston Churchill.

Now owned by Inver House Distillers (a Thai Beverage Company business), Hankey Bannister is exported to over 40 countries worldwide. It has a presence in all major European markets and in other key markets, too, including Australia, Latin America, and South Africa. Hankey Bannister also now performs well in the worldwide duty-free sector.

There are three expressions: the standard carries no age declaration, but there are two aged versions – a 12-Year-Old and a 21-Year-Old. The style is best described as light and subtle. A clean, sweet, slightly spicy whisky, giving a full flavour with honeyed tones and a pleasant, lasting finish.

HIGHLAND QUEEN

Owner: Glenmorangie

Originally created by the Leith blenders MacDonald & Muir in 1893 and named in homage to Mary Queen of Scots, Highland Queen Blended Scotch Whisky honours Leith's connection with the ill-fated monarch, who arrived here from France in August 1561, aged 18, to take the crown of Scotland. The brand's logo includes a vignette of Mary on a white stallion.

Produced today by The Glenmorangie Company, this standard blend's key markets are Australia, Venezuela, India, Africa, the Middle East, and Japan.

🍶 **HIGHLAND QUEEN** 40% ABV Heather-honey, plum, and apple notes provide a fresh, clean taste. The blend has a gentle, warming finish.

Hankey Bannister

Whiskies from more than 20 distilleries are selected to make Inver House Green Plaid.

INVER HOUSE GREEN PLAID

Owner: Inver House Distillers

With its tartan-clad label, Inver House's Green Plaid has long been a familiar sight on American shelves and bars. The brand was first launched in the United States in 1956, since when it has enjoyed consistent success, remaining among the top 10 sellers in this important market. It is also sold in Europe and Latin America.

Green plaid itself is even more ancient than the distilling of Scotch whisky. Plaid is the traditional Scottish heavy woollen tartan material used to make kilts. It is thought that a green plaid was worn by the first Lord of the Isles, a 12th-century Viking warrior by the name of Somerled. The Lord of the Isles tartan pattern is incorporated into the label of the whisky bottle that carries its name.

Inver House uses more than 20 malts and grains to blend Green Plaid, which is available as a competitively

Inver House Green Plaid

priced non-aged version, and as 12 and 21-year-old expressions as well.

J&B

Owner: Diageo

Together with Johnnie Walker, the J&B brand gives Diageo the enviable responsibility of owning the two best-selling blended Scotch whiskies in the world (third-placed Ballantine's is number two in terms of value, however).

J&B Rare is the number one Scotch whisky in Europe, with its major markets being Spain, France, Portugal, and Turkey. Important markets outside Europe include South Africa and the United States. In all of these combined, around two bottles of J&B are sold every second.

The original owners of the company started by buying up stocks of old whisky in Scotland in the mid and late 1800s, but it was not until the 1930s that they developed J&B Rare. Its light colour was designed specifically with the United States in mind, where it flourished after the end of Prohibition. For the next 40 years, success continued unabated, with sales reaching three million cases a year during the 1970s. Ownership passed by way of United Wine Traders to IDV, then to Grand Metropolitan, United Distillers, and ultimately to today's largest whisky corporation, Diageo. Like so many brands, the family connections have long since been severed, but the distant memory of their now-faded drinks dynasty still lingers on.

J&B Jet

Current expressions of J&B include J&B Rare, Jet (the leading brand in South Korean bars), and the 15-year-old Reserve, which is only sold in Spain and Portugal. A blend aimed at the younger market called J&B -6°C, which seeks to make a virtue of its chill-filtering, was recently withdrawn.

J&B RARE 40% ABV

A highly distinctive blend, using some 42 individual malt and grain Scotch whiskies. Top-class Speyside single malts such as Knockando, Glen Spey, and Auchroisk are at the heart of J&B, but the delicate smokiness suggests an Islay influence. An apple and pear fruitiness, with vanilla notes and a honeyed sweetness, is set off by a background of restrained peat.

JUSTERINI & BROOKS

In 1749 Giacomo Justerini travelled from his native Italy to London in pursuit of an opera singer with whom he'd fallen in love. His journey was unsuccessful romantically, but Giacomo, who was from a family of liqueur distillers, stayed on in London and paired up with George Johnson to form Justerini and Johnson Wine Merchants. In 1779 they placed the earliest recorded advert for Scotch whisky in the London Morning Post.

Giacomo later returned to Italy and George Johnson was killed by a runaway horse. The firm passed through Johnson's family until 1831, when Alfred Brooks, an entrepreneur who had spotted the potential of blended whisky, bought the business and renamed it Justerini & Brooks.

THE BEST-SELLING SCOTCH WHISKY IN THE WORLD

The firm of John Walker & Sons can be traced back to a Kilmarnock grocery store in 1820, but it did not enter the whisky industry in a serious way until the 1860s. Indeed, it was not John Walker but his son and grandson who developed the whisky business.

With the legalization of blending "under bond" in the 1860s, John Walker's son and grandson, both named Alexander, progressively launched and developed their range of whiskies. These were based around the original Walker's Old Highland blend, which was launched in 1865 and is the ancestor of today's Black Label. The distinctive square bottle followed in 1870.

Alexander Walker, the elder

Trade developed phenomenally in the late 19th century, for the Walkers and their rivals. The British Empire was expanding, Scotland was growing ever more fashionable, and Scotch whisky was displacing cognac as the preferred drink of the smart set.

Alexander passed on the business to his two sons, George and Alexander junior, in 1889. In 1893 the brothers acquired Cardhu Distillery on Speyside. Now, they were distillers – a proud distinction – and immediately proclaimed their confidence in "the precise nature and quality of the principal components of their blend."

In 1908 their whiskies were first branded Johnnie Walker, as opposed to Kilmarnock Whisky. But, by 1925, the pressure of difficult trading forced a consolidation of the industry. Like many others, Johnnie Walker joined the Distillers Company, though the dynamic Sir Alexander Walker remained at the head of the firm.

By 1945 Johnnie Walker Red Label was the world's best-selling Scotch whisky, a status it retains to this day. Under Diageo, the brand has continued to grow and prosper, with a number of new variants being introduced.

Johnnie Walker has always promoted its brand prominently, as seen here on an office building in Bucharest, Romania.

JOHNNIE WALKER

Owner: Diageo

The Johnnie Walker brand offers a range of whiskies from Diageo's ample larder, and comprise Johnnie Walker Red, Black, Gold, and Blue, as well as the Johnnie Walker Green Label, which is a blended malt. From time to time, the firm also releases a number of one-off, limited, or regional expressions, including Swing, Quest, Honour, Excelsior, Old Harmony, Cask Strength, and 1805. Swing was devised while Sir Alexander Walker (junior) was in charge of the company, and was created for the affluent passengers on the great Atlantic liners of the 1930s. It remains popular in the Asian markets.

Johnnie Walker Red Label is the most successful brand of Scotch whisky in the world, and the total sales of all Johnnie Walker expressions amount to close on 12 million cases annually, far outstripping its nearest Scotch rival, Ballantine's. Both have enjoyed significant growth in developing markets in China, Asia, and Russia.

Johnnie Walker has long been characterized by its strong packaging and brand identity, symbolized by the character of the striding man. Another factor in its early success was the square bottle, which enabled the firm to pack more bottles in a given volume and thus reduce the transport costs.

The company has always used distinctive advertising and kept a high promotional profile. Currently, it is a major golf sponsor (supporting the Johnnie Walker Classic and the Johnnie Walker Championship at Gleneagles)

and a high-profile backer of the Team McLaren Mercedes Formula One racing team.

As the world's biggest producer of Scotch whisky, Diageo has the largest number of distilleries and access to unrivalled stocks. In fact, the firm claims that at any point in time Johnnie Walker has at their disposal more than seven million casks of whisky in maturation – and that is worth more than all the gold in the vaults of the Bank of England.

🎙 **JOHNNIE WALKER BLACK LABEL** 40% ABV • The flagship Johnnie Walker blend, recognizable by its smoky kick, is acknowledged as a classic blended whisky. With a base of Cameron Brig grain whisky, it uses single malts that include Glendullan, Mortlach, and Talisker, from Skye. The hint of smoke, contributed by Talisker and Diageo's Islay malts (Caol Ila and Lagavulin), distinguishes the Walker blends and runs through all the expressions, though less noticeably so in the smoother Gold and Blue styles.

🎙 **JOHNNIE WALKER RED LABEL** 40% ABV • Served as the basis of a mixed drink in many markets, Red is more

A bottle of Johnny Walker 1805, an incredibly rare whisky, was auctioned at Bonham's in 2007.

"up-front" in taste. Direct, fresh, and fruity, with smoky and chilli spice notes.

🎙 **JOHNNIE WALKER GOLD LABEL** 40% ABV • In an older style such as Gold, look for honey, fresh fruits, and toffee notes, with smoke very much in the background. Perhaps controversially, Diageo recommends chilling this in the freezer before serving, maintaining that the flavours are intensified in this way.

🎙 **JOHNNIE WALKER BLUE LABEL** 40% ABV • Unusually, the super-premium Blue does not carry an age statement. This blend was created in tribute to the style of 19th-century blenders and so uses a relatively tight group of grain and malt whiskies, some of great age and rarity. The whisky is remarkably smooth and mellow, with traces of spice, honey, and the signature hint of smoke. These older styles are more complex and layered than Red, but a clear family resemblance can be detected throughout the range.

🎙 **JOHNNIE WALKER 1805** 40% ABV Available in a very few selected bars at £1,000 a glass, the 200-bottle ultra-limited 1805 edition used whisky from a number of closed distilleries and cannot be repeated. It is a subtle, rich, and spicy blend, with an exceptionally long and consistent finish that lingers pleasantly on the palate.

Johnnie Walker Black Label

Johnny Walker created this tasting room to launch their Green Label brand in Taipei.

JOHNNIE WALKER BLUE LABEL – KING GEORGE V EDITION

Owner: Diageo

As the ultimate Johnnie Walker expression, the King George V Edition deserves its own entry. An exemplary demonstration of the blender's art, King George V is handcrafted using the original techniques practised during the 1930s, arguably a golden age for whisky. Only whiskies from distilleries operating during the reign of George V (many of which are now closed) have been selected, and oak casks dating back to the 19th century have been used to age these precious whiskies.

When these whiskies run out, it will not be possible ever again to achieve the taste of Johnnie Walker Blue Label King George V Edition, and the blend will cease to exist. As such, it has been released only in Asian markets, where gift-giving and display have greater importance than in the West.

Owners Diageo plan that the edition will be available until around 2016, but this is obviously dependent on the volume of sales. Only between three and five outlets in any one country have been allocated stock.

The Queen Mother was able to grant a Royal Warrant to Langs whisky in the 1980s.

The blend, which retails at around three times the price of its super-premium brother Johnnie Walker Blue Label, is described as having "a rich, profound smoky taste, followed quickly by sweet fresh fruit flavours developing into deep fruit, spicy complexity, and a long, mouth-warming, and lingering peaty finish."

LABEL 5

Owner: Jean-Pierre Cayard

The French blender and bottler La Martiniquaise was founded in 1934 by Jean-Pierre Cayard and moved its production facilities from France to Scotland in 2004. Label 5 is a big seller in the French market, recording sales of well over one million cases annually in the "secondary" (that is, low price) market.

There are three expressions: a standard, un-aged version; a 12-year-old and an 18-year-old.

LANGS

Owner: Ian MacLeod

Alexander and Gavin Lang were whisky merchants and blenders in Glasgow from 1861. In 1876 they bought the attractive little distillery of Glengoyne (see p84), which has remained a principal component in the Langs blends ever since.

In 1965, the firm was purchased by the Glasgow blenders Robertson & Baxter, who attempted to develop the brands, with some success, in the UK, Europe, and the Far East, acquiring in 1984 a Royal Warrant from the Queen Mother in the process.

However, Robertson & Baxter's interests in The Famous Grouse and Cutty Sark took precedence, and the Langs brand and Glengoyne Distillery were sold to Ian MacLeod in 2003.

Today, the principal Langs products are Langs Supreme and Langs Select 12-Year-

---

WHISKY GALORE!

Martin's was one of the brands of whisky on board the *SS Politician*, which was lost off the coast of Eriskay in February 1941. The event formed the inspiration for Compton Mackenzie's novel *Whisky Galore*, in which a group of islanders spirit away the cases of whisky that wash up on the shore. The novel went on to inspire a 1949 film of the same name.

Whisky Galore was adapted into a British film with enduring appeal by Ealing Studios.

Old blended whiskies, both noted for their relatively high malt content. The Select 12-Year-Old recently won a Gold Medal in the *Scottish Field* magazine's Merchants Challenge, in the Deluxe Blended Scotch category.

LAUDER'S

Owner: MacDuff International

A famous Glasgow landmark, Lauder's Bar on Sauchiehall Street dates from 1836. It is named after Archibald Lauder, the landlord who took over the licence in 1871 when it was the Royal Lochnagar Vaults. Lauder produced a blended whisky, Lauder's Royal Northern Cream, which was exported worldwide.

Today his name is recalled not only in the eponymous public house but also in Lauder's Scotch whisky, which, it is claimed, is one of the oldest brands of whisky still being made.

With perhaps just a touch of whimsy, the proprietors, MacDuff International, trace production back to 1834, and propose that Lauder himself was an early exponent of market research. Supposedly, development of the original blend took two years, during which time Lauder "invited many good friends of cheer to taste and remark upon each concoction" – a formula long established as finding favour with Glasgow drinkers.

Certainly Lauder's was a popular whisky and a prolific medal winner in the 19th century, since when it has largely slipped from public view in its homeland. However, it is imported by Barton Brands into the USA, where it continues to be bought by value-conscious consumers to this day.

LOCH FYNE

Owner: Richard Joynson

The label depicts the Glendarroch Distillery sited on the Crinan Canal, which links Loch Fyne with the Sound of Jura. Also known as Glenfyne, the distillery was built in 1831 but, sadly, no trace remains.

The name has been continued by Richard Joynson, proprietor of Inverary's award-winning Loch Fyne Whiskies and well-known piscatorial enthusiast, for his own-label whisky.

The blend was created by Professor Ronnie Martin, OBE, former production director with United Distillers (now Diageo). It is described as slightly sweet and smoky – an easy-drinking, well flavoured blend, but one to simply drink and enjoy rather than concentrate on.

Loch Fyne

LONG JOHN

Owner: Chivas Brothers

With annual sales in excess of 500,000 cases, Long John remains a significant brand, yet one that is apparently

Long John is a competitively priced blend, but the brand is not marketed heavily by its owners.

Tormore on Speyside is the brand distillery for Long John and provides the whisky's key filling.

very much in the shadow of its Chivas Brothers' stablemates, Chivas Regal and Ballantine's (all of which ultimately come under the Pernod Ricard umbrella).

Named in honour of Long John MacDonald of the original Fort William Distillery, Long John was for many years owned by the founder's family. However, it eventually passed to a London wine and spirit merchant and thus to Long John International, the distilling arm of brewers Whitbread.

Such is the way of these matters, however, that the brief reunion of brand and distillery under Whitbread was short-lived, the distillery passing in 1989 to its present owners Nikka of Japan and

PATTISONS

It may seem somewhat academic to include whiskies that have not been available for more than 100 years, but the influence of the firm of Pattisons of Leith was to shape the whole structure and development of the Scotch whisky industry as we know it today.

By 1890, the "whisky barons" of Victorian Scotland had never had it so good, and two brothers stood above all. Robert and Walter Pattison inherited partnerships in a small whisky blending business in Leith. In 1896 they floated it as a company. Just as in our own dotcom boom, the share offer was six times oversubscribed and the directors abilities seemed mercurial.

Pattisons' marketing reflected the firm's dynamic approach.

"The Doctor", "Morning Gallop" and "Morning Dew" brands were blends, but Pattisons also owned a distillery at Aultmore, a share in Glenfarclas, and office and blending premises in Leith and London.

One of their promotional schemes was a stroke of genius: Pattisons gave 500 African Grey parrots to publicans and licensed grocers, only for their proud owners to discover that they'd been trained to squawk, "Pattisons Whisky is best!" and "Buy Pattisons Whisky!" at customers!

When in 1898 the company went bankrupt, the collapse was initially greeted with incredulity. Slowly, the truth emerged: Pattisons had massively

Pattisons' downfall was described as the "the most discreditable chapter in the history of the whisky trade".

over-valued their stock and inflated their profits, often by selling the same whisky (on paper) several times over.

Moreover, they had also been adulterating their whisky, mixing cheap grain spirit with a dash of malt and passing it off as good malt. Following a well-publicised trial, the brothers were jailed, Robert for 18 months, Walter for nine.

It wasn't only Pattisons and their creditors who suffered. Ten other firms were brought down in the collapse that followed. The reputation of blending, indeed of the whisky trade in general, was hard hit, and its recovery did not even begin for another 10 years.

THE RISE OF DCL

While Pattisons charged towards their ignominious end *(see opposite),* others benefitted from their collapse, most conspicuously DCL (the Distillers Company Ltd). Their financial prudence in the late Victorian boom years stood them in good stead as trade tightened. They were able to purchase a number of Pattisons' assets at knock-down prices and steadily came to assume a pre-eminent position in the Scottish whisky industry.

the brand going to Allied Distillers. Allied Distillers was subsequently purchased by Pernod Ricard, whose spirits subsidiary Chivas Brothers controls the brand today.

The Scottish Whisky Association's Directory of Member's Brands lists a non-age version of Long John and two older styles: a 12 and a 15-year-old. So far as can be established, the bulk of sales are to Scandinavian and various Spanish-speaking markets.

MACARTHUR'S

Owner: Inver House Distillers

The ancient MacArthur Clan of Argyllshire fought alongside Robert the Bruce in the struggle for Scottish independence. The blend, which can be traced back to 1877, takes its name from this clan. MacArthur's enjoyed a brief spell of fame in the 1970s, due to its aggressive pricing in UK supermarkets, which led to a price war. Today it is owned by Inver House Distillers, a subsidiary of ThaiBev, and they describe it as having a "light, smooth flavour with toffee and vanilla from cask ageing."

MARTIN'S

Owner: Glenmorangie

The Martin's blends are today owned by Glenmorangie but derived from the old James Martin & Co. business, originally established in Leith in 1878. That firm formed part of MacDonald Martin Distillers.

In its heyday, Martin's VVO was a very significant brand in the USA and is still prominent there today, especially in eastern states. The initials stand for "Very Very Old" but this is stretching the point – in its standard expression, VVO is no more than a 5-year-old blend, albeit one with a significant contribution from Glenmorangie single malt.

Older 20 and 30-year-old versions sell very well in Portugal. Martin's VVO is described as "smooth and sweet, with notes of orange peel and vanilla, followed by a subtle floral peatiness". So the Glenmorangie influence would seem to predominate.

Martin's 20-Year-Old

MacArthur's

OLD PARR

Owner: Diageo

"Old Parr" was Thomas Parr, who was born in 1483 and, according to folklore, lived for 152 years. A move to London to be presented to King Charles I proved his undoing, and he died in November 1635. The king ordered that he be buried in Westminster Abbey, where his tomb may be seen to this day.

Parr's recipe for a long life was a simple one: "Keep your head cool by temperance and your feet warm by exercise. Rise early, go soon to bed, and if you want to grow fat [prosperous] keep your eyes open and your mouth shut".

He did, however, drink ale and even cider on special occasions, so we may presume that he would not have been upset when, in 1871, Samuel and James Greenlees appropriated his name for their deluxe whisky.

After several changes of ownership, the Old Parr brand was acquired by DCL (the Distillers Company Ltd) in 1925 and is thus now controlled by Diageo.

It is distinguished by its unique bottle design and, as a premium blend, sells steadily in Japan, Mexico, Colombia and Venezuela.

There are three Old Parr expressions: Grand Old Parr (12-year-old), Old Parr (15-year-old), and Old Parr Superior (18-year-old). By tradition, Cragganmore is the mainstay of the blend.

"Old Parr", who is said to have lived to the age of 152, abstained from whisky but did drink ale.

The Speyside region provides some of the most coveted malts for use in blends.

QUEEN OF QUEENS

Once a leading name from the distinguished Edinburgh blenders Hill, Thomson & Company, Queen Anne has suffered the kind of fate that calls to mind Shelley's sonnet *Ozymandias*, in which a traveller encounters the ruins of a once mighty empire:

"My name is Ozymandias, king of kings:
Look on my works, ye Mighty, and despair!
Nothing beside remains. Round the decay
    Of that colossal wreck, boundless and bare
    The lone and level sands stretch far away."

Like so many once-famous and proud brands, consolidation in the Scotch whisky industry has left Queen Anne bereft and isolated. As its new owners (Chivas Brothers, in turn owned by Pernod Ricard) concentrate on the "strategic" components of a "key brand portfolio", orphan brands like Queen Anne become casualties. Clinging on perhaps in one or more regions where once they were loved, they linger, offering their faint shreds of faded glory to the student of whisky's history, while awaiting the inevitable *coup de grâce*.

Queen Anne

OLD SMUGGLER

Owner: Gruppo Campari

Old Smuggler was first developed by James and George Stodart in 1835 when they launched their whisky business, taking a name that acknowledged the superior quality of illicitly distilled whisky prior to the 1823 Excise Act *(see p47)*. The Stodart name is also recorded in whisky history as being, reputedly, the first to marry their whisky in sherry butts.

Several changes of ownership later, Old Smuggler was acquired by Italy's Gruppo Campari in 2006, along with its sister blend Braemar and the Glen Grant Distillery (Glen Grant is the single malt market leader in Italy).

Today Old Smuggler is sold in more than 20 markets worldwide and continues to enjoy a significant presence in the USA, historically its principal sales destination. It is the number two selling whisky in Argentina, and developing strong sales in Eastern Europe.

Its partner in the Campari stable, Braemar, is distributed throughout Eastern Europe, Greece, Turkey, Thailand and the Caribbean.

PASSPORT

Owner: Chivas Brothers

Although Chivas Brothers/Pernod Ricard intended to sell off Passport as soon as they had acquired Seagram's whisky brands in 2002, they evidently had second thoughts and decided to retain ownership, their ruminations no doubt influenced by annual sales of some 850,000 cases.

Despite being unavailable in the UK, Passport is one of Scotch's success stories, with sales climbing rapidly towards the elite "millionaire's club" (those with sales of one million or more cases per annum). Passport's main strongholds are the US, South Korea, Spain and Brazil, where its fruity taste lends itself to being served on the rocks.

The brand claims that it is "designed to appeal to younger, independently minded consumers", attracted by the distinctive rectangular green bottle. Passport's publicity suggests that it is "a unique Scotch whisky, inspired by the revolution of 1960s Britain, with a young and vibrant personality."

Certainly, no other Scotch is packaged like it today, and the bottle is evocative of the 1960s, when the brand was created.

Whilst it initially benefited from aggressive pricing, Passport is today more of a standard brand, and its drinkers can enjoy such distinguished and famous malts as The Glenlivet and others from the Chivas stable in the blend.

🍸 **PASSPORT** 40% ABV
An unusually fruity taste and a deliciously creamy finish.

The Old Smuggler brand still enjoys success abroad but is no longer seen in its homeland.

Passport Scotch

It can be served straight or, more usually, over ice or mixed. Medium-bodied, with a soft and mellow finish.

PIG'S NOSE

Owner: Spencerfield Spirits

This unusually named blend is the partner to the Sheep Dip blended malt. The two brands were the brainchild of a West Country publican, M Dowdeswell, who first introduced Pig's Nose whisky in 1977.

For some years the brands enjoyed reasonable success, but, having passed through the hands of several owners, they ended up with Glasgow-based Whyte & Mackay and there languished (presumably at the back of a stable somewhere), receiving little attention or sales effort.

In 2005, a senior Whyte & Mackay executive, Alex Nicol, left the company to set up his own business, Spencerfield Spirits. He acquired both brands and set about relaunching them.

Pig's Nose has been reformulated under the watchful eye of Whyte & Mackay's master blender Richard Paterson, and has been repackaged in an attractive new livery. The result is a full-flavoured

and very drinkable blend, which more than lives up to the claim that "our Scotch is as soft and smooth as a pig's nose."

PINWINNIE ROYALE

Owner: Inver House Distillers

In its handsome and distinctive patterned green bottle, Pinwinnie Royale cuts a dapper figure to accompany the blend's unusual name, the derivation of which is, alas, obscure.

The blend is the product of Inver House Distillers of Airdrie, who are themselves part of the Thai Beverage Public Company Limited (ThaiBev). From this, it would seem likely that Inver House's Old Pulteney, Speyburn, anCnoc, and Balblair single malts are to be found in the blend.

The standard expression is described as "aromatic and well rounded, with a smooth, dry finish", whereas the 12-year-old version is initially dry and medium-

Pig's Nose was bought in 2005 by Spencerfield Spirits, who are very adept at marketing the brand.

bodied, but augmented by a gradual release of richer, oilier notes and a smooth, sweet finish.

Pinwinnie Royale

PRÀBAN NA LINNE

Owner: Pràban Na Linne / The Gaelic Whisky Company

The redoubtable Sir Iain Noble, former financier and champion of all things Gaelic, established his Pràban na Linne business (supposedly Gaelic for "a smugglers den by the Sound of Sleat") in 1976.

It was part of a project designed to create employment in the south of Skye, as so many young people were then leaving the island. The business has grown steadily over its 30 years, with its reputation being spread by word of mouth.

The company – which is also known as the Gaelic Whisky Company – markets a range of blended whiskies,

Pig's Nose

with sales concentrated in Scotland, France, Holland, Italy, and Canada.

TÉ BHEAG 40% ABV

Pronounced "chey vek", Té Bheag means "the little lady" and is the name of the boat in the company's logo. The name also means a "wee dram" in colloquial Gaelic. Smooth and slightly peated from its west coast origins, this is a connoisseurs' whisky, with a high malt content. It is aged for between 5 and 11 years, and offers a hint of sherry from the casks in which it has been matured. Unusually for a blend, Té Bheag is not chill filtered.

MAC NA MARA 40% ABV

Literally meaning "son of the sea", Mac Na Mara was introduced in 1992 and quickly became popular. Being competitively priced, it is now the company's biggest seller, especially in the French market.

The company do not make whisky themselves, all Pràban na Linne's output being blended for them by a well-established whisky broker in Scotland's Central Belt. However, the company have plans to open their own distillery on Skye.

Isle of Arran Distillery is the home of the Robert Burns blend, and its visitor centre (pictured) stocks a range of Burns whiskies.

THE REAL MACKENZIE

Owner: Diageo

Today a Diageo blend, The Real MacKenzie is named after Peter MacKenzie & Co., established in 1897 with the vision of producing high quality whisky. The "stag head" embossment on every MacKenzie bottle symbolizes the MacKenzies' consistent loyalty and courage.

The original company owned Blair Athol (quixotically located in Pitlochry) and Dufftown-Glenlivet distilleries on Speyside. Then in 1933, the whole lot was acquired by Arthur Bell & Sons (today part of Diageo).

At one time, various aged expressions were popular in Greece and South Africa, but in 2005 Diageo re-launched the brand with an emphasis on Taiwan, a rapidly growing market for premium blends.

Robert Burns

ROBERT BURNS

Owner: Isle of Arran Distillers

Given the industry's deep love affair with traditional Scottish imagery, it is rather

Royal Salute 21-Year-Old

surprising that no-one had previously marketed a brand named after Scotland's national bard.

Isle of Arran Distillers is one of the few remaining independent distilleries in Scotland. The company was set up in 1995 by Harold Currie, who was previously managing director of Chivas (then owned by Seagrams).

The Robert Burns blend contains a significant proportion of Isle of Arran single malt, and is claimed by the company to "capture the character of our beautiful island of clear mountain water and soft sea air."

ROYAL SALUTE

Owner: Chivas Brothers

There are a number of brands with "Royal" in the title, but in a competitive field, Royal Salute is undoubtedly *ne plus ultra*. A "royal salute" is, in military terminology, a 21-gun tribute to royalty, fired on a special occasion, such as the Queen's birthday.

Royal Salute, which was arguably the first whisky to launch in the super premium sector, was originally produced in 1953 by the Seagram Company. It was a 21-year-old whisky and its release was in celebration of the coronation of Queen Elizabeth II. Royal Salute is still the world's leading super premium aged Scotch whisky.

Now controlled by Pernod Ricard's Chivas Brothers, the Royal Salute "family" includes a range of expressions, each one comprising a special blend of very rare whiskies.

ROYAL SALUTE 21-YEAR-OLD
40% ABV ● Bottled and launched on Coronation Day in June 1953, the original Royal Salute 21-year-old was made using whiskies laid down in the 1920s and 30s. Planning for the sumptuous Royal Salute 21-year-old can begin up to 30 years before it is sealed in porcelain flagons, each one of which is embellished by craftsmen at the Wade pottery over four days. A deep gold colour; soft fruity aromas balanced with a delicate floral fragrance and mellow honeyed sweetness.

ROYAL SALUTE 50-YEAR-OLD 40% ABV
A very limited edition, launched in June 2003 in honour of the 50th anniversary of the Queen's

Royal Salute, The Hundred Cask Selection

coronation (and Royal Salute itself). It also celebrated the 50th anniversary of the first ascent of Mount Everest. Royal Salute 50-year-old is a limited edition of just 255 bottles and, accordingly, is so rare that very few have ever tasted it!

ROYAL SALUTE, THE HUNDRED CASK SELECTION 40% ABV
This is specially blended from a strict selection of 100 casks. First introduced to the market at the end of 2004, Royal Salute, The Hundred Cask Selection is elegant, creamy, and exceptionally smooth.

ROYAL SALUTE 38-YEAR-OLD STONE OF DESTINY 40% ABV
By tradition, the Stone of Destiny is supposed to be the pillow used by Jacob in the Bible. It is also the name given to the sandstone block used in the coronations of Scottish, and subsequently British, monarchs. Chivas used this name for their exclusive selection of powerful 38-year-old

The immaculate, modern Isle of Arran Distillery provides the heart of the Robert Burns blend.

whiskies first released on a permanent basis in February 2005.
Royal Salute 38-year-old Stone of Destiny offers rich notes of cedar wood and almond, with a sherried oakiness on the palate. Dried fruits linger with an assertive spiciness. An experience – even for the connoisseur!

The coronation of Queen Elizabeth II in 1953 inspired the creation of Royal Salute.

SCOTCH BLUE

Owner: Lotte Chilsung

Lotte Chilsung, part of the Lotte Group leisure and retail company – South Korea's fifth-biggest conglomerate – owns the Scotch Blue brand, which has grown very rapidly from its launch some 10 years ago.

It now records sales of more than 500,000 cases, based on spirit supplied by Burn Stewart Distillers. This is not a "value" brand and, indeed, in 2001 Burn Stewart's supply deal was challenged by Allied Domecq, who saw Scotch Blue threatening their Ballantine's brand and raised an action for "passing off" (copying the blend).

This failed to dent the brand's progress and in June 2007 The Korea Times reported that "Scotch Blue is no longer limited to the domestic boundaries, but is being exported to Malaysia, Japan, Thailand, and other Asian countries where its popularity is growing."

The line includes Scotch Blue (with non-age, 17, and 21-year-old variations), Scotch Blue International, and New Scotch Blue Special.

RABBIE BURNS

Dedicated to Scotland's national bard, and particularly enjoyable on 25 January, celebrated the world over as Burns' Night – the anniversary of the great man's birthday.

Ingredients:
1 Measure (25 ml) of blended Scotch Whisky
1 Measure (25 ml) Noilly Prat dry vermouth
Dash of Benedictine

Method:
Shake all the ingredients well with cracked ice until a froth forms, then strain into a chilled glass. Finish with a twist of lemon peel.

SCOTTISH LEADER

Owner: Burn Stewart Distillers

This is the flagship blend of Glasgow-based Burn Stewart Distillers, which in turn is part of CL World Brands, an offshoot of CL Financial of Trindad – thus are the tentacles of the global drinks industry spread far and wide.

The blend's heart is single malt from Perthshire's Deanston Distillery, which was formerly a cotton mill.

Initially targeted at the value-conscious supermarket buyer, Scottish Leader has recently been repackaged and shows signs of an attempted move towards a more upmarket territory. The range of Scottish Leader expressions includes two blended (vatted) malts.

🥃 **SCOTTISH LEADER**
40% ABV • The nose shows hints of peat, while on the palate the whisky is sweetish, with

The stills at Deanston provide the "honeyed" malt at the heart of the Scottish Leader blend.

honey notes in the Perthshire style. The peat smoke returns in the finish.

SIR EDWARD'S

Owner: Bardinet

A competitively priced "secondary" (low price) brand, Sir Edward's is unknown in the UK but popular nevertheless, especially in France, where it is the 10th best-selling brand. Industry statistics show that sales of Sir Edward's passed the one million case mark in 2005. The whisky is provided by Leith Distillers, a subsidiary of Whyte & Mackay, and supplied to the brand owner Bardinet, of Bordeaux, where it is bottled. There never was a "Sir Edward". Apparently, the late Paul Bardinet, who started the company at the end of the 19th century,

Scottish Leader

Longmorn Distillery supplies one of the distinguished malts in the Something Special blend.

named his imported brand of whisky after his son, Edward. He then added the "Sir" to make it sound more authentic and aristocratic.

Sir Edward's is sold as a non-age bottling and a 12-year-old version.

SOMETHING SPECIAL

Owner: Chivas Bros

Under this bold name, Something Special is a leading deluxe Scotch blended whisky in South America, and is particularly popular in Venezuela and Colombia.

First introduced in 1912 by Hill Thompson and Co. using casks specially selected by the directors themselves, the Something Special brand is today owned by Pernod Ricard's whisky subsidiary Chivas Brothers.

As befits its premium positioning, the whisky is presented in a distinctive, diamond-shaped bottle, apparently the inspiration of an Edinburgh diamond cutter.

Something Special

❦ **SOMETHING SPECIAL** 40% ABV
A distinctive blend of dry, fruity, and spicy flavours, with a subtle smoky sweetness. The highly regarded Longmorn malt is at the heart of the blend.

ROB ROY

Modelled on the Manhattan *(see p198)*, the warm red colour of this cocktail reminds us of the legendary Rob Roy McGregor, outlaw, folk hero, and Scotland's own Robin Hood.

Ingredients:
1 measure (25 ml) of blended Scotch Whisky
½ measure (about 10 ml) of Noilly Prat sweet vermouth
Dash Angostura bitters

Method:
Mix all the ingredients over ice. Stir and strain into a chilled glass. Finish with a twist of lemon peel.

❦ **SOMETHING SPECIAL 15** 40% ABV
This is a blend made with up to 35 of the better Speyside and Islay malt whiskies, and soft grain whiskies, aged in a mixture of European and American oak casks. So while it retains the distinctive style of Something Special, the 15-year-old expression is of greater intensity, complexity of character, and depth of flavour.

Whisky from Islay's distilleries is used sparingly in blends to impart depth and smokiness.

STEWART'S CREAM OF THE BARLEY

Owner: Chivas Brothers

First produced in the early 1830s by Alexander Stewart at Dundee's Glengarry Inn, Cream of the Barley quickly attained considerable popularity in Scotland.

By 1969 it was owned by Allied Lyons and enjoyed good distribution in their chain of public houses. The blend was also closely associated with Glencadam Distillery in Brechin, the sole remaining distillery in Angus. However, in total, the blend contains around 50 malts. It is now owned by Chivas Brothers (part of the Pernod Ricard stable) and is a top-selling blended Scotch whisky in Ireland.

TEACHER'S

Owner: Fortune Brands

The Teacher's firm was established in 1830, when William Teacher opened a grocery shop in Piccadilly Street, Glasgow. Like other whisky entrepreneurs, such as John Walker of Kilmarnock, William soon branched out into the spirits trade and began to develop his business. It became famous for its dram shops – so stern and austere in character that the licensing magistrates congratulated the firm on its work in temperance reform! There was absolutely no danger of adulterated whisky in a Teacher's establishment, even if laughter and general merriment were in short supply.

William Teacher died in 1876 and control of the firm passed to his sons William and Adam. Blending became increasingly important to the firm, and 1884 saw an event of great future significance: the trademark registration of Teacher's Highland Cream.

Originally beginning as "a very small item", Highland Cream came to dominate the firm to such an extent that business and brand became inextricably linked.

As with many independent Scottish companies, Teacher's found it hard to resist offers of outside capital. Under the sustained pressures of World War II, death duties, high taxation, and the need for continual investment and modernization, many families threw in the towel.

Teacher's was fortunate. It survived on its own until 1976, then its owners shrewdly negotiated a deal with Allied Brewers, instead of waiting for the inevitable hostile takeover. By doing so, the family held on to an important role, even if ownership passed out of their hands.

Allied Brewers, along with the rest of the brewing industry, had its own set of challenges and pressures, and it wasn't long before Allied Brewers evolved into Allied Lyons and then Allied Domecq. That firm was acquired by Pernod Ricard in 2005, then sold, along with Laphroaig and various other wine and spirit brands, to Fortune Brands of the USA for a reported £2.8 billion.

Teacher's Highland Cream

Ardmore Distillery is one of the essential, characterful malts in the Teacher's blend.

At its mid-20th-century peak, Vat 69 made it into the world's top 10 best-selling whiskies.

TEACHCHER'S HOUSE STYLE

From its earliest days, Teacher's has always been a full-flavoured blend, strongly built on the company's characterful single malts from Glendronach and, more particularly, Ardmore. In fact, more than 35 single whiskies go into the Highland Cream blend to this day – an individual whisky, with a silky texture and quite a quick finish that leaves the palate refreshed.

VAT 69

Owner: Diageo

Though this blend is still selling more than one million cases annually in places such as Venezuela, Spain, and Australia, it might not be entirely unreasonable to suggest that the glory days of VAT 69 are behind it.

Once this was the flagship of the independent South Queensferry blenders William Sanderson & Co.

and the name came from the fact that vat number 69 was the finest of 100 possible blends tested by Sanderson on trade colleagues. Accordingly, Sanderson launched his whisky as VAT 69 in 1882.

At its peak, VAT 69 was the 10th best-selling whisky in the world and even starred in an early example of product placement. In the 1959 film *Our Man in Havana*, one of James Wormold's agents is found dead with a bottle of Vat 69 clutched in his hand.

Today its owners, Diageo, give global precedence to the Johnnie Walker and J&B brands.

VAT 69

WHITE HORSE

Owner: Diageo

White Horse is named after one of Edinburgh's famous coaching inns, The White Horse Cellar Inn, place of embarkation for the eight-day coach trip to London. Once selling around two million cases annually and holding a position as one of the 10 best-selling Scotch

whiskies in the world, White Horse has slipped down the global sales league table. Despite this, it remains a significant brand in its areas of strength, especially Japan, Brazil, Greece, Africa, and parts of the USA, and the blend is still marketed in more than 100 countries.

Its heyday came under the ownership and direction of Peter Mackie, who, from 1890, was one of the most famous characters in the whisky trade. He took over the family business from his

SHACKLETON'S THIRST

Sir Ernest Shackleton took along with him on his 1907 Antarctic Expedition bottles of Whyte & Mackay, which turned up 100 years later encased in polar ice. For his Imperial Trans-Antarctic Expedition of 1914, however, he took supplies of VAT 69, stating that it would be used "for medicinal emergencies and for feast days in the Antarctic". This evidently was his more favoured dram for boosting morale, as Shackleton opted for further supplies of VAT 69 on his 1921 expedition.

FALL OF THE HOUSE OF USHER

Today you can buy a bottle of Usher's Green Stripe in the US for $12.99 (about £6.50). The brand, now controlled by Diageo, is among the lowest priced Scotch available, yet, despite such aggressive pricing, volumes have fallen steadily for the last 10 years. It is perhaps doubtful that today's Usher's drinker either knows or cares that this was once one of the foremost companies in Scotch whisky, and arguably the father of blending.

With a family business established in Edinburgh in 1813, the Ushers established themselves as successful agents. By 1840 it was noted that

Usher's Green Stripe

"Messrs Usher controlled the whole output of the famous Glenlivet Distillery".

Andrew Usher II was a blending pioneer, having learnt the necessary skills from his mother, as was the family tradition. Usher's Old Vatted Glenlivet is recognized as the first modern blended whisky. Such was the firm's success that by the late 19th century the Ushers were established as generous philanthropists.

The firm joined the Distillers Company (DCL) in 1919 and the Usher's brand slowly faded, eventually reduced to the indignity of bulk export for local bottling and today's bottom shelf discount offers.

Glenlivet was where blending started, in a sense, with Usher's Old Vatted Glenlivet, introduced in 1853.

uncle and soon made an impression on all who met him. Sir Robert Bruce Lockhart famously described him as "one-third genius, one-third megalomaniac and one-third eccentric". Mackie's nickname was "Restless Peter", and his favourite aphorism, "Nothing is impossible".

The art of blending may be about balancing flavours, but it is also vital to know the value of whiskies and understand potential markets.

The firm's reputation rested on the quality of its blending, and Mackie shrewdly commissioned the noted journalist and whisky authority Alfred Barnard *(see p50)* to write for them the handsome pamphlet entitled, "How to Blend Scotch Whisky".

🍷 **WHITE HORSE** 40% ABV

A complex and satisfying blend, White Horse retains the robust flavour of Lagavulin, assisted by renowned Speysiders such as Aultmore. With its long finish, this is an elegant and stylish whisky.

WHYTE & MACKAY

Owner: Whyte & Mackay

Whyte & Mackay traces its history back to 1844, when it was founded by James Whyte and Charles Mackay. By the late 19th century they had begun blending and had launched the company's flagship "Special" brand,

which has been a long-standing Scottish favourite.

Having been through a bewildering number of owners in recent years, this venerable Glasgow company was acquired in May 2007 by the Indian conglomerate UB Group for some £595 million. Plans to expand capacity at Invergordon, Whyte & Mackay's grain whisky distillery, have already been announced, so blending will presumably be of increased future importance.

Today the firm offers a range of expressions: the Special – which is, in fact, a standard blend – and five other blends aged at 13, 19, 22, 30, and 40 years. Though the more cynical drinker might view the unusual age statements as being driven by the need to stand out on the shop shelf, the company claim "the extra year gives the whisky a chance to marry for a longer period, giving it a distinct graceful smoothness".

Certainly, Whyte & Mackay's master blender Richard Paterson, who joined the firm in 1970, is very highly regarded in the industry and has received a large number of awards and citations. He created the "new" 40-year-old blend, which enjoys a very high malt content – 70 per cent malt to 30 per cent grain – but is available only in limited quantities.

The main market for Whyte & Mackay has historically been the UK, though the older styles, especially the 13-year-old, are popular in Spain, France, and Scandinavia. This may well change under the new ownership, however, with Asian sales likely to grow rapidly thanks to the India-based UB Group.

THE WHYTE & MACKAY STYLE

The "backbone" of the company's blends emanates from Speyside and the Highlands, though small quantities from Islay, Campbeltown, and the Lowlands are also used. For many years, Jura produced whisky in a "Speyside" style,

Whyte & Mackay Special

and the vast majority of the distillery's output was reserved for blending. In recent years, however, Jura's eponymous single malt has enjoyed growing sales in its own right.

Great stress is laid on marrying the blend at Whyte & Mackay, and the company has long been an adherent to the time-consuming process in which first the malts are married, before combining with the grain whisky and marrying again in sherry butts. The resulting blends, it must be said, are noticeably smooth and well-balanced.

WILLIAM LAWSON'S

Owner: John Dewar & Sons (Bacardi)

The William Lawson's range of whiskies is blended and bottled in Coatbridge and Glasgow by John Dewar & Sons *(see p130)*, and is thus ultimately owned by Bacardi. However, the brand can be traced back to 1849, when it

was blended in Liverpool by William Lawson; the trademark was registered in 1889. After various changes in ownership, the name ended up with the Italian vermouth producers Martini & Rossi, through their purchase of the MacDuff Distillery (home of the Glen Deveron single malt).

This distillery had been constructed in 1960 by a consortium of whisky blenders to a design by the innovative Welsh distillery architect William Delmé-Evans (who also designed Glenallachie, Isle of Jura, and Tullibardine distilleries). The original partners sold the business, which was eventually bought in 1972 by Martini, who expanded the distillery. Bacardi then acquired Martini & Rossi in late 1992.

Though not available in the UK, the various William Lawson's expressions sell well over one million cases annually and are extremely popular in France, where they are positioned at the top end of the "value" market. Belgium, Spain, and

Whyte & Mackay, now part of the mighty UB Group, still has its offices in Glasgow, where the firm began.

Alcohol levels in maturing spirit are regularly checked, and whisky usually diluted prior to bottling – typically down to 40% ABV.

Venezuela are also significant markets for Lawson's.

In recent years, the brand has been noted for its stylish and witty TV advertising, featuring an iconoclastic approach to the kilt in some unusual settings.

The range comprises William Lawson's Finest, which is the standard style; a 12-year-old Scottish Gold; and two premium styles. Of the premium blends, Founder's Reserve is an 18-year-old blend, first created in 2000, and Private Reserve is a limited edition 21-year-old, which launched in 2004.

Spanish sherry and American bourbon oak casks are used for maturing the whisky, with Glen Deveron Single Malt employing the highest percentage of sherry wood of any whisky in the Dewar's group. This contributes to its full flavour and rich colour.

🍷 **WILLIAM LAWSON'S FINEST**
40% ABV ● With its heart of Glen Deveron Single Malt, William Lawson's Finest blended Scotch whisky is distinguished by a satisfyingly well-balanced palate, with hints of crisp toffee apple. Its body is medium to full and the finish slightly dry, with delicate oak notes.

WINDSOR

Owner: Diageo

This premium brand of Scotch whisky, marketed by Diageo in South Korea, is not to be confused with its Canadian namesake *(see p221)*, a low-price offering, or even the company's own barely visible Windsor Castle blend. Launched in 1996, Windsor is a serious player in South Korea, one of the world's largest whisky markets. Gratifyingly, premium whisky brands account for 72 per cent of sales there, while super and ultra premium whisky

Windsor 17 Super Premium

brands take up some 26 per cent. Indeed, standard and low-price brands are virtually unknown.

Moreover, the South Korean market has been growing fast, and – though not without some alarms. Diageo faced its own problems in 2007, when Korea's tax authorities found it dealing with unlicensed wholesalers.

Assuming these local difficulties can be ironed out, Diageo's Windsor looks set for further growth. Already it is claimed to be the largest selling super premium Scotch whisky in the world, and accordingly has its own unique bottle shapes.

In keeping with the premium standards of this status-driven market, there are two expressions: a 12-year-old blend and a 17-year-old super premium. Windsor 17 features a luminous label to make it stand out in dimly lit clubs.

Windsor 12 Premium

WHISKY LIQUEURS

A liqueur is a sweetened product, in which additional flavours of spices, flowers, fruits, seeds, or roots are introduced to the spirit base through re-distillation, infusion, or maceration. Today, whisky liqueurs are a distinct category, albeit dominated by one brand – Drambuie.

Whisky liqueurs have a long historical tradition. *The Practical Distiller* of 1718 includes several recipes for making them, including one for "Fine Usquebaugh", which required the addition of spices, raisins, dates, a quantity of Lisbon sugar, and other ingredients to rectified malt spirits.

This may have had much to do with the low quality of the spirit base, but here, in the early 18th century, we see the antecedents of today's whisky liqueur.

Drambuie is produced today by an independent company controlled by the descendants of Captain John MacKinnnon. It was to MacKinnon that Prince Charles Edward Stuart ("Bonnie Prince Charlie") reputedly entrusted the secret recipe of his own personal liqueur in recognition of the captain's loyalty. Even today, the recipe is known only to the MacKinnon family, and responsibility for the elixir

Drambuie

that flavours Drambuie's whisky base lies in the hands of the senior female representative of the line.

Other brands compete for this market, which stretches worldwide. They include: Glayva, from Whyte & Mackay; Columba Cream (a cream-based whisky liqueur in the style of Bailey's); Amber, from Macallan; and a number of liqueurs based exclusively on the whisky from specific distilleries, such as Arran, Edradour, Glenturret, Old Pulteney, and Glenfiddich Liqueurs.

An interesting recent development is the introduction of Orangerie from Compass Box. Described as a "whisky infusion", this is not strictly a liqueur, as it is unsweetened, but it represents an exciting contemporary spin on a time-honoured tradition.

Edradour Distillery produces its own cream liqueur – a combination of Edradour single malt whisky and Scottish cream.

IRELAND

Sitting, as it does, in the warm damp gulf stream on the very edge of western Europe, it is perhaps not surprising that the story of Irish whiskey is something of a misty and romantic tale. It is also an astonishing and frustrating one.

To begin with, there are the enigmatic monks – the healers of western Europe who are thought to have brought distilling to Ireland in the wake of the Black Death in the 14th century. They effectively policed the production of *uisce beatha* until the Reformation, some 200 years later. With the Dissolution of the Monasteries in the mid-16th century, distilling spread into communities as a cottage industry. However, this all changed with the arrival of English law, set up at the beginning of the 17th century to exact taxation from distilling. In response, much distilling went underground, resulting in two national drinks, duty paid whiskey and illegal poteen.

Duty paid, or Parliament, whiskey (always spelt with an "e" in Ireland) went on to dominate the British Empire, as it was the Irish and not the Scots who were first to turn distilling into a global business. The golden age of Irish whiskey dawned early in the 19th century, and most of Ireland's most famous brands – Jameson, Powers, and Bushmills – date from this period. The Irish anticipated the needs of the mass market, creating a product that was consistent in terms of both quality and availability. Today, we're used to branded drinks tasting identical wherever in the world you buy them, but in the 19th century this notion of sameness was revolutionary.

However, Irish whiskey was labour intensive and expensive to produce. Pot stills were, and still are, slow and terribly inefficient. Each load is produced singly, batch by batch, and, between each run, the stills have to be cooled and cleaned.

CONTINUOUS DISTILLATION

The holy grail of distilling was a system that allowed continuous distillation – this was the way to raise the economies of scale, and so increase both productivity and profits. The goal was achieved by an Irishman, Aeneas Coffey *(see p172)*, and his Patent Still changed distilling forever.

Some Irish distilleries, especially in Belfast, did install Coffey's still, but as far as the major Dublin distillers were concerned, the problem with "Coffey's Patent Continuous Distilling Apparatus", as they referred to it, was that it didn't produce what they considered to be whiskey. "These things," they wrote in a circular, "no more yield whiskey than they yield wine or beer." The Dublin whiskey hierarchy was famous for its flavoursome, "oily" pot still whiskey.

Old Bushmills in County Antrim is Ireland's oldest surviving distillery, producing its own single malts as well as whiskey for many well-known blends.

It was the way things were done, and they weren't for changing.

The Scots and English, though, had nothing to lose by adopting the Coffey still. Although expensive to commission, they could produce in a week what a traditional pot still could make in nine months.

The Irish had taken their eye off the ball, so it's doubtful that anyone in Dublin made a fuss when changes to the law in the mid-19th century allowed whiskey to be stored and blended prior to the point of taxation, which was now only on shipment. This subtle change meant that merchants were free to buy, blend, and bottle their own whiskeys without having to pay tax up front. Silent spirit could now be blended with some very individual highland malt to produce a new kind of whisky. The quality of these Scottish blends was consistent, but unlike Irish whiskey, they were easy to make and cheap to produce. The names Johnnie Walker and Tommy Dewar are still with us, but they were not distillers – they were blenders and bottlers, and they went on to become whisky barons.

TROUBLED TIMES

The dawn of the 20th century brought little comfort for the Irish. After a long court battle, Blended Scotch was allowed to be called whisky. Then, the whole

IRELAND'S DISTILLERIES

nation was thrown into turmoil as Ireland firstly entered into a war of independence with the British, then embarked on a bitter civil war. By 1922 it was a divided country. In the south, the Irish Free State was founded, while six of Ireland's Ulster counties remained part of the UK. American Prohibition and an economic war with Britain hit the distillers hard: almost overnight their two largest export markets dried up. To make things worse, the newly free Catholic Ireland reignited the church dominated temperance movement, and the distillers found they had very few friends in government.

ACROSS THE DIVIDE

By the mid 1960s there were just two distilleries left, one either side of a bitterly sectarian border. From that nadir, however, the present state of the whiskey industry looks more promising. It centres on three distilleries: Midleton, Bushmills, and Cooley – the new addition to the two left standing in the 1960s. These three distilleries produce all of the brands and bottlings of Irish whiskey, from popular blends to single malts and the last two remaining pure pot still Irish whiskeys.

Bushmills is Ireland's oldest distillery, and its roots can be traced back to the whiskey industry's beginnings in the 1600s.

DISTILLERIES, MALTS, POT STILLS

Ireland's distilleries, though now few and far between, maintain a strong tradition of producing unique, world-class malt and pure pot still whiskeys. Ireland's blends are covered on pages 169–77.

BUSHMILLS

✉ 2 Distillery Road, Bushmills, County Antrim
☞ www.bushmills.com
🏛 Open to visitors

Of the 28 Irish distilleries recorded by the Victorian writer Alfred Barnard (see p50) in his guide to the distilleries of the United Kingdom, Bushmills is the only one where whiskey is still made. Kilbeggan and the Old Midleton distilleries now house museums; only at Old Bushmills will you find pot stills that still feel the heat of action.

For a distillery with such a long history, it is not surprising that Old Bushmills has survived by changing with the times. At one point, like just about every other distillery in Ireland, it produced pot still whiskey. But with the rise in popularity of Scotch single malts, like its near neighbours across the narrow strip of the Irish Sea, Bushmills went on to produce a peated malt. Today the distillery's malts are unpeated, and Bushmills is the only distillery in Ireland whose output is purely single malt whiskey – its blends (see p169) use grain whiskey bought in from Midleton Distillery.

BUSHMILLS MALT 10 40% ABV ● This is triple distilled and peat free, and, given how familiar its square bottles have become, it is hard to believe that this single malt was first bottled as recently as 1987.

🥃 An elegant and tasty dram, quite unlike anything else produced in Ireland – or Scotland for that matter. Malty, with a hint of nutty fudge – warms nicely on the way down.

BUSHMILLS MALT 12 DISTILLERY RESERVE 40% ABV ● The 12-year-old reserve is a small but significant malt that can only be bought from the distillery shop.

🥃 Sweet and figgy, with the signature Bushmills biscuitiness in evidence. Round, dry fruits, and a touch of liquorice.

BUSHMILLS MALT 16 40% ABV Slightly older bourbon and sherry-wood matured single malt whiskeys are vatted and aged for a further year in port pipes, resulting in an exceptional 16-year-old malt.

🥃 The colour – amber shot through with ruby – is a dead giveaway to the two-fold maturation process. An intense fusion of citrus and chocolate make this a most extraordinarily flavourful malt.

BUSHMILLS MALT 21 MADEIRA FINISH 40% ABV
The oldest Bushmills expression is a 21-year-old malt. Due to Ireland's mild climate, a 21-year-old Irish malt can be far more fragile than a similar aged Scotch, and here Bushmills have put an already old whiskey into Madeira wood for a further two to three years. Launched in 2001, this takes maturation to a new level.

Bushmills Malt 16

🥃 This is Christmas cake and waves of butter, nuts, and dried fruit. A seriously long finish.

Clontarf Single Malt

CLONTARF SINGLE MALT

Distillery: Midleton
☞ www.clontarf whiskey.com

Clontarf is a brand that started life with a unique selling point: after maturation, it was charcoal mellowed. This rather overpowered the original Cooley malt, and the current Bushmills whiskey doesn't fare any better.

🥃 **CLONTARF SINGLE MALT** 40% ABV
An incredibly sweet drink, which overwhelms whatever else the whiskey may have to offer; hard to see what the charcoal mellowing achieves.

IRISH COFFEE

Ingredients: Half a cup of good quality coffee
1 measure (25ml) of Irish whiskey
2 spoonfuls of brown sugar
20ml of freshly whipped cream

Method: Pour the shot of whiskey into a warmed stemmed glass. Pour in the coffee up to within 15mm (½ in) of the top. Put in the sugar and stir until it is dissolved. Place the spoon onto the rim of the glass, face up, ensuring that the curved part of the spoon is just touching the coffee. Pour the cream onto the spoon; it will flow over the edge and rest on the coffee.

THE BUSHMILLS STORY

The north Antrim coast is home to the spectacular Giants Causeway, a naturally occurring phenomenon of mostly six-sided basalt columns. But inland just a couple of miles, is something that is arguably even more famous: the Old Bushmills Distillery.

Old Bushmills' Cooperidge

The present distillery, with its Scottish style "pagoda" roof, dates from the late 19th century, but distilling here goes back to the very beginning of English law in Ireland at the start of the 17th century. Up until this time, Gaelic, or Brehon law, had allowed anyone to freely distil. One of the first things the new English Governor of Ulster did, however, was to introduce taxation on distilling, thereby creating a divide between legal, duty paid whiskey and illegal poteen. From 1608, anyone distilling "within the county of Colrane" had to pay Sir Thomas Phillips a royalty – indeed, that's where the term "royalty" comes from. For Phillips, it amounted to a licence to print money.

There's no record of how the locals reacted to the new state of affairs – but we can guess. This had always been whiskey country, and it remained a hot

Old Bushmills Distillery produces only single malt, and for its blends uses grain whiskey bought in from elsewhere.

bed of illegal distilling. By the 19th century, the Irish whiskey industry had greatly expanded, but little changed at Bushmills. The distillery continued distilling only malt whiskey, most of which was drunk locally. Ironically, that's what ensured Bushmills' survival. It was small enough to weather the storm that brought the major Dublin and Belfast distilleries to their knees.

It was 1964 before Old Bushmills passed out of family ownership, when it was sold to the English brewers Charrington. However, distilling was of secondary importance to the beer giant, and in the 1970s Bushmills was first bought by Seagram of Montreal before becoming a subsidiary of the Irish Distillers Group (IDG).

For a generation that's how things remained. Bushmills' fine whiskeys won plenty of accolades, but, as part of IDG, they were always in the shadow of the Jameson brand. All that changed, however, with Bushmills coming into the hands of Diageo in 2006.

CONNEMARA MALTS

Distillery: Cooley
www.connemarawhiskey.com

Of all Cooley's whiskeys, this is the one that caused the biggest stir in Ireland's whiskey industry. It seemed to contradict everything that the Irish whiskey sector held sacrosanct. Bad enough that it wasn't triple distilled in the traditional manner; worse still … it was peated.

Connemara takes its name from Ireland's western seaboard, and although it owes a lot more to Islay than to Galway, it would be wrong to think of it as "Highland light". Connemara is a more earthy malt than you'll find in Scotland, and, being warehoused in Kilbeggan – which is about as far from the sea as it's possible to get in Ireland – there's no salt or iodine. Connemara, then, is a breed unto itself – a unique whiskey that allows us to taste age-old flavours of a peated Irish malt whiskey.

As well as the standard single malt, there is a 12-year-old. This is Cooley's oldest and rarest malt simply because the distillery was mothballed between 1993 and 1995. Until stocks catch up with demand, a limited amount of casks can be released. In addition,

The Locke Distillery warehouses have been put to good use, maturing Cooley's whiskey.

Connemara also produce a cask strength monster. It is non chill-filtered, allowing this excellent whiskey to really strut its stuff on your taste buds. One for purists.

CONNEMARA SINGLE MALT
40% ABV ● A sweet whiskey, with a gentle, peaty heart and loads of malty character.

CONNEMARA CASK STRENGTH
Minty, smoky, and much oilier and mouth-coating than the original version. There's a soft chocolate finish and a distant rumble of turf embers.

COOLEY

Riverstown, Cooley, County Louth
www.cooleywhiskey.com

John Teeling knew a lot about business but little of the world of whiskey when he founded Cooley Distillery in 1987 on the site of a disused industrial alcohol producing plant. At the time, the French drinks company Pernod Richard had recently bought Irish Distillers, and Teeling knew that the French would seek to capitalize on their monopoly by pushing the Jameson brand globally. Irish whiskey then counted for 10 per cent of world sales, and Teeling saw an opportunity to succeed with the Cooley Distillery if he could just get a fraction of the Irish whiskey market.

Teeling did his homework. Whiskey needs heritage, so he bought up some old brands, such as Locke's and Tyrconnell, providing his

new whiskey with instant provenance. Better still, he leased the silent Locke's Distillery at Kilbeggan to mature his whiskey.

Having weathered some tumultuous corporate storms *(see p164)*, Cooley now produces whiskey for Connemara, as well as Greenore, Locke's, Michael Collins, and Tyrconnell malt brands *(see pp165–68)*.

The original plant on the Cooley peninsula was joined in 2007 by a micro-distillery in the old Locke's Distillery in Kilbeggan *(see p165)*.

DUNGOURNEY 1964

Distillery: Midleton

In 1994 Midleton's master distiller Barry Crockett made a once in a lifetime discovery. In a dusty corner of warehouse No. 11, he found an old cask that was not on any stock chart. It turned out to be 30 years old and had been laid down by Barry's father when he was the master distiller back in 1964.

In honour of the river that runs through Midleton and at one time was used in the making of spirit here, the whiskey has been given the name Dungourney.

An old elegant leather armchair of a whiskey, with crisp biscuity sweetness. A real charmer with a distant whiff of oak and custard.

**Connemara
Cask Strength**

COOLEY'S NARROW ESCAPE

In a world dominated by global brands and multi-national drinks companies, Cooley Distillery is that most Irish of things, a rebel. And if you're going to be an Irish rebel, then Easter Sunday is a pretty good day to step up and start the revolution.

In 1989, entrepreneur and permanent teetotaller Dr John Teeling fired up the stills in Ireland's only independent distillery. Teeling had bought the distillery on the Cooley peninsula in 1987 from the Irish State, who had originally built the plant in the 1950s to turn diseased potatoes into industrial alcohol.

The short, squat stills at Cooley tend to produce a fuller, "heavier" spirit.

The business was cash flowed for three years while the first batches of whiskey matured, and the plan was for Teeling to then sell Cooley as a going concern, complete with warehouses full of Irish whiskey ready to sell.

Initially there was plenty of interest, but by 1992 Europe was slipping into recession. The whisky industry was tightening its belt and, in a declining market, no one was buying distilleries. By 1993 the money had run out and Teeling mothballed the Cooley plant.

Then, however, a curious thing happened: Pernod Ricard made Teeling a £24.5 million offer. He would have undoubtedly accepted, but Ireland's Competition Authority was unhappy with the proposed takeover. They decided that the inflated price Pernod Ricard were willing to pay for a distillery they intended to close down implied that their interest was in shoring up their monopoly of the Irish whiskey market. The takeover was, therefore, ruled to be in breach of European Law.

With the French off the scene and no other knight in shining armour around, the Irish banks started to call in their debts. Teeling had just a week to fend off the receivers and convince Cooley's backers to pre-buy millions of pounds worth of stock. Amazingly, he did this, and in 1995 the stills fired back into life and the spirit flowed once more.

Cooley's whiskey is matured in casks in the centuries-old warehouses of the silent Locke's Distillery in Kilbeggan.

WILLIAMSTOWN

Ingredients: 1 measure (25ml) of Irish whiskey
½ measure (about 10ml) of Irish Mist liqueur
A splash of red lemonade (only available in Ireland, but try white lemonade or a dash of ginger ale)
Garnish: twist of lemon

Method: Pour ingredients over crushed ice in an old-fashioned glass. Garnish with the twist of lemon.

GREENORE SINGLE GRAIN

Distillery: Cooley

County Louth is Ireland's smallest county; it's also home to Ireland's smallest distilling group, Cooley *(see opposite & p163)*. The Cooley plant produces all of its malt and grain whiskey requirements, which is unusual in today's industry – in Scotland, grain whisky for blending tends to be bought in from specialist grain whisky distilleries. However, Cooley's grain distilling operation doesn't have the kind of economies of scale seen in Scottish grain distilleries, or even in Midleton, so consequently is very expensive to produce. However, Greenmore is the only single Irish grain whiskey available, and it is a drink of which the company is very proud and keen to keep producing.

Named after the nearby port of Greenore, the whiskey is double distilled, then matured in once-used bourbon casks for a minimum of eight years. The casks to be bottled are hand picked by master distiller and

Greenore 8-Year-Old Single Grain

blender Noel Sweeney, who has something of a soft spot for his single grain whiskey.

🍶 **GREENORE 8-YEAR-OLD SINGLE GRAIN** 40% ABV
The incredible linseed nose promises plenty, and the whiskey delivers. Gentle but firm on the tongue, with peppery cereal and darkest chocolate.

GREEN SPOT

Distillery: Midleton

There was a time, and not too long ago, when Irish distilleries simply made their whiskey, leaving the bottling and selling to independent retailers.

These were the wine and spirit merchants, and they were to be found in just about every town in the country. Most merchants sold "own brand" whiskey straight from the cask; some would even bottle it, though, back then, glass bottles were an expensive innovation that would surely never catch on!

After the foundation of Irish Distillers, sales to the country's spirit merchants were scaled back and eventually they ceased altogether – well almost. Mitchell's in Dublin is now the only remaining whiskey merchant in business, and its famous Green Spot brand is still supplied by Irish Distillers. That alone would be a good reason for getting a bottle, but this is no ordinary whiskey. It's a pure pot still, and a rather good one to boot.

This whiskey is now released as a 7 to 8-year-old pure pot still, with a juicy quarter of the vatting coming from sherry wood.

Green Spot

A strictly limited 6,000 bottles are produced each year.

Most are sold in Ireland; they never make it as far as the airport retail outlets, though it is possible to buy via online stores.

🍶 **GREEN SPOT** 40% ABV
Matured for six to seven years, Green Spot's pot-still crackle of linseed and menthol is unmistakable, and the sherry flourishes that follow are like fireworks – brief and dazzling.

THE IRISHMAN

Distillery: Bushmills

The malt here comes from Bushmills, but it is the double cask finish (a mix of whiskeys that have been matured in sherry and bourbon casks) that makes this offering very interesting. A premium bottling released in batches of 1,000 cases.

🍶 **THE IRISHMAN SINGLE MALT** 40% ABV ● Like all single malts produced by Bushmills, the soft cereal is most evident,

KILBEGGAN'S MICRO

Although the stills went cold in 1953, John Locke's Distillery is one of the most precious distilleries in the entire world. To celebrate the 250th anniversary of its foundation, Cooley started making whiskey here again in 2007. The still itself is a real piece of history – it came from nearby Tullamore and is at least 150 years old.

Currently, the first distillation happens in the main Cooley plant in Louth, with the second taking place in Kilbeggan, but there will soon be a second still in Kilbeggan, and so it won't be long before the entire distilling and maturing process takes place on site.

but here the sherry adds complexity and some sweetness, rounding off a very tasty malt indeed.

KNAPPOGUE CASTLE

Distillery: Bushmills

When Mark Andrews got to bottle the whiskey his father had bought from the Tullamore Distillery in 1951, he chose to call it after the family home. So the 36-year-old Knappogue Castle was born, and it proved so popular that Mark decided to bottle a vintage whiskey on an annual basis. The first modern bottlings were released in 1990 and came from the Cooley stable, but more recent vintages have been produced with whiskey from Bushmills Distillery.

KNAPPOGUE CASTLE '95 40% ABV
This vintage is an excellent example of the Bushmills house style. The triple distilled single malt is very approachable, with plenty of light nuts and warming toasted malt. It is, however, still quite young and so not a very complex whiskey.

LOCKE'S

Distillery: Cooley

Of all the heritages and brands that Cooley revived, surely that of John Locke was the most evocative. The Brusna Distillery in Kilbeggan survived until the 1950s and, among older people at any rate, there was a tremendous fondness for their heavy pot still whiskey. When Hollywood's John Ford and John Wayne were filming *The Quiet Man* on location in Ireland in 1951, Locke's was taken to

Locke's 8-Year-Old Single Malt

their hearts too, and became their hell-raising whiskey of choice.

Modern-day Locke's is a single malt rather than a pot still *(see p168)*, and although distilled in County Louth, like all Cooley whiskey, it is taken by tanker to be matured at John Locke's warehouses.

LOCKE'S SINGLE MALT 8-YEAR-OLD 40% ABV
Soft and clean if a little uninspiring. This vatting of Cooley's unpeated and peated malts is less than the sum of its parts.

MICHAEL COLLINS

Distillery: Cooley

www.michaelcollins whiskey.com

This range of whiskeys was designed for the American market, and it bears the name, and indeed the signature, of one of Ireland's greatest modern heroes. Michael Collins, also known as "the big fellow", spearheaded Ireland's struggle for independence and was the architect of the 1921 treaty, from which the modern Irish state emerged.

Sidney Frank is the company behind the brand, and they worked with Tim Pat Coogan, the official biographer of Michael Collins, to contact the Collins family when seeking an agreement to use Michael's name on their whiskey.

MICHAEL COLLINS SINGLE MALT 40% ABV ● Creamy biscuits, smooth vanilla, and some very decent peat; this malt is a vatting of Cooley's peated and unpeated single malts, and it hangs together most beautifully.

Michael Collins Single Malt

MIDLETON

✉ Midleton, County Cork
🖥 www.irishdistillers.ie
⛴ Old Midleton Distillery is open to visitors as a museum; the new, working distillery is not

The modern Midleton plant, which has been in operation since the mid-1970s *(see opposite)* produces the most astonishing range of whiskeys, from heavy to light, pure pot still to single malt to grain. Unlike the situation in Scotland, however, very few of these whiskeys ever get bottled in their own right. Most provide notes, colours, and flavours that are mixed and blended to produce the huge range of brands in the Irish Distillers stable, which includes Paddy, Jameson, and Powers *(see pp172–6)*.

REDBREAST

Distillery: Midleton

Redbreast 12-year-old is the oldest pure pot still whiskey on sale today. It and the younger Green Spot *(see p165)* are all that is left of Ireland's unique style of whiskey – the pure pot still *(see p168)*.

Redbreast was initially launched in 1939, when whiskey merchants Gilbey's put the label on their own particular blend from the original Jameson Distillery. The brand was so popular that it was subsequently bought from Gilbey's by Jameson, after the distiller ceased to supply the bonded whiskey trade in the 1960s.

The present Redbreast is made of heavier pot still whiskeys that are matured for at least 12 years in sherry casks and bourbon barrels. Like all good pot still whiskeys, it is strongly flavoured and assertive, making it a rare treat.

Redbreast 12-Year-Old Pot Still

THE MIDLETON STORY

There's not *one* distillery in the pretty town of Midleton, but two. The first looks as a distillery should – modest in scale, with bright paintwork – the other looks like an oil refinery. Needless to say, the former is a museum, while the latter produces some of Ireland's finest whiskeys.

To comprehend the story of what's going on in Midleton is to understand the complex history of whiskey making in Ireland.

The old Victorian distillery belongs to the heyday of Irish whiskey – when Irish, not Scotch, was the drink of

Midleton's Distillery is a high-tech operation, but its pot stills are resolutely traditional.

the British Empire. Midleton Distillery was born in 1867, when five small Cork distilleries joined forces to form The Cork Distilleries Company (CDC). Over time CDC centralized all production at the Midleton plant; it was a taste of things to come.

Fast-forward 100 years to 1966, and we find that Scotch whisky has become a global phenomenon while Irish whiskey teeters on the brink of extinction. The three Irish distilleries still remaining were fighting each other to the death in a declining market, and something needed to be

done. John A. Ryan, the Managing Director of John Power & Son *(see p176)* persuaded the boards of the Cork Distilleries Company and John Jameson & Son to bury the hatchet. After 200 years of rivalry and competition the Irish Distillers Group was formed. The old Powers and Jameson distilleries in Dublin were closed, and operations were centralized at a new super-distillery in Midleton.

Midleton's Victorian distillery was abandoned, as in 1975 the new plant set sail, carrying with it the hopes of an entire industry. The new Midleton Distillery does not have the romance of the old one, but it has been designed specifically to replicate the output of all the distilleries it replaced. As well as making vodka and gin, it has to reproduce the taste of Ireland's most famous whiskeys: Jameson, Powers, and Paddy. Today Midleton produces the widest range of whiskeys to come from Ireland *(see opposite)*.

Old Midleton Distillery, with its neat stonework and brightly painted shutters, now houses a whiskey museum.

REDBREAST 12-YEAR OLD

40% ABV • Other whiskeys may have "pot still character", but this is the real deal. It's a fat, oily riot in a glass, with the unmalted barley bringing a whole new dimension to whiskey drinking. There's a lovely long finish that resonates soundly for ages.

REDBREAST 15-YEAR OLD

40% ABV • This whiskey is a huge mouth-coating carnival of sherry and vanilla pods, but the pot still is not shy and here it is aged to perfection. Full flavoured but not assertive, this is a monster of a whiskey. Redbreast is simply one of the world's finest whiskeys.

TYRCONNELL MALTS

Distillery: Cooley
www.tyrconnellwhiskey.com

The Tyrconnell brand was one of the first things Cooley bought when the company went shopping for history *(see p163)*. First introduced in 1876 by Derry distiller Andrew A. Watt & Co., the Tyrconnell whiskey was launched to celebrate a well-known horse that made everyone but the bookies happy by winning at staggering odds of 100/1.

This unpeated single malt was the first whiskey that Cooley produced at their new distillery when they began producing in the late 1980s. It is now the company's best selling malt. Alongside the standard malt are three 10-year-old malts with different wood finishes – sherry, madeira, and port. There's nothing new about finishing whiskey in exotic casks, but this is a first for Cooley and a sign of their growing confidence.

TYRCONNELL SINGLE MALT

40% ABV • Cooley's signature boiled sweets nose is most evident here and the flowery malt is very well put together. Sweet notes of honey and jasmine combine

Tyrconnell Single Malt

to make this a very approachable malt.

TYRCONNELL 10-YEAR-OLD SINGLE MALT PORT WOOD FINISH 40% ABV • The nose is very spicy and exotic; but the port sits slightly on top of the whiskey. However, there's plenty of fig, raisins, and ripe plums, as well as a lovely warm finish.

TYRCONNELL 10-YEAR-OLD SINGLE MALT MADEIRA WOOD FINISH 40% ABV These were good Madeira casks and the flavour of warm toasted wood is very prevalent. It is sweet, but not overpoweringly so. A great rumble of a finish.

TYRCONNELL 10-YEAR-OLD SINGLE MALT SHERRY WOOD FINISH 40% ABV • It's not a radical combination, but here the flowery malt and fruity sherry fuse beautifully. The sherry butts add complexity, but leave room for the elegant whiskey to impress. The most accomplished of the three wood finishes.

POT STILL WHISKEY

Pot still whiskey is unique to Ireland. But, ironically, Ireland's most independent spirit is without a firm standing in law. While Scotland has annexed the term "single malt", Ireland has all but thrown away the unique expression that is "pure pot still", and now two contrasting definitions exist to describe what constitutes pot still whiskey.

The legal definition simply states that any duty-paid spirit distilled in a pot still can be called pot still whiskey, regardless of what it is made from. This is how Cooley's single malt is labelled as "pure pot still".

However, traditionally, the appellation was reserved for spirits distilled from malted and unmalted barley. This grain mix is unique to Ireland and this is what traditionally makes a pure pot still whiskey. The element of unmalted barley gives traditional Irish pot still whiskey a steely edge and an oily viscosity that's as flavoursome as it is unique. Once, just about every Irish whiskey was a pure pot still, but the appellation almost disappeared in the 1970s as Irish Distillers reformulated all their brands.

Today there are only a couple of pure Irish pot still whiskeys remaining, but to track them down is to taste history. Redbreast *(see p166)* is the most widely known, but Green Spot is also worth making room for, though, unless you're in Dublin, you may struggle to find a bottle *(see p165)*.

Pot stills in Ireland traditionally distilled a mash of both malted and unmalted barley; this produced the unique "pure pot still whiskey"

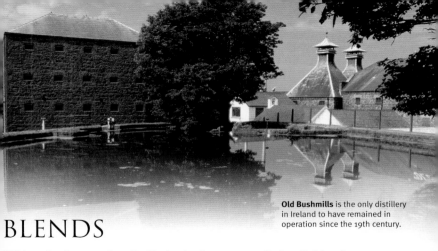

Old Bushmills is the only distillery in Ireland to have remained in operation since the 19th century.

BLENDS

With only three major distilleries in the country, Ireland's blends demonstrate the variety of whiskeys that these plants produce. Coupled with the skill of the blenders, it all results in some of the world's finest blended whiskey, some of which has a high proportion of flavourful malt.

BUSHMILLS

Distillery: Bushmills and Midleton

Old Bushmills is a single malt distillery, so the grain whiskey that is blended with their malt to produce brands like Blackbush, has always come from somewhere else. In the past it was made in the nearby Coleraine Distillery, but since the closure of that plant in the 1970s the grain has come from Midleton. So, long before the Good Friday Agreement, the two traditions on the island – Ulster malt and Republican grain – lived happily together in a glass bottle.

BUSHMILLS ORIGINAL 40% ABV
A roughly 50/50 split of Bushmills malt and Midleton grain creates a well-balanced easy-drinking blend. Sweet, with the same kind of flavours you get from fruit biscuits dunked in cocoa.

BUSHMILLS 1608 46% ABV
This new blend marks the 400th anniversary of the original licence to distil. Sweet, honeyed, and biscuity fresh on the nose. The Bushmills DNA is very evident: malted milk, but layered with subtle vanilla and raisins, maturing into

toasted almonds, hints of fine cocoa and finishing with a warming peppery tickle.

BLACK BUSH 40% ABV
An elegant, mostly malt blend, which benefits from being aged in some very juicy sherry wood. The result is a stunning desert island whiskey and the yardstick by which Irish blends are measured.

Oranges and sherry. Exotic colours from Jerez dance around the signature Bushmills malt notes. A glorious, mouth-filling experience, and one of the finest blends in the world.

CLONTARF

Distillery: Bushmills and Midleton

When Clontarf whiskey was launched in Ireland, it caused consternation for two reasons. Firstly there was the unusual bottling – three stackable mini-bottles for the price of one – but more shocking still was that Clontarf whiskey was charcoal mellowed.

Recently, however, this whiskey was taken over by Castlebrands, so it is a

product in flux, and all this may change in the future.

CLONTARF BLEND 40% ABV
The standard blend is an incredibly sweet, almost toffee-like whiskey. It's robust though, with hints of pot still whiskey and some decent lingering chocolate notes towards the end.

CLONTARF RESERVE
40% ABV ● This is quite a light whiskey and is almost overpowered by the layers of woody oak. However, without the body of the classic blend, Clontarf is tooth-meltingly sweet.

Bushmills Black Bush

CRESTED TEN

Distillery: Midleton

This is a spicy, pot still blend, available mostly in Ireland. Launched in 1963, this was the first Jameson product to be bottled solely by the distillery. Confusingly, the whiskeys in the blend are not 10 years old, and have largely matured for seven to eight years.

CRESTED TEN 40% ABV ● A fairly robust pot still flavour, with a strong sherry influence, which comes from first-fill Oloroso casks.

Whiskey drinking is a tradition that harks back to the cottage industry that distilling once was throughout Ireland.

MR AENEAS COFFEY AND HIS PATENT STILL

In less than a generation, the Coffey still completely changed the face of the whiskey business. Blenders and not distillers had the power and the money, and that's how things remained until the revival in the fortunes of single malt whiskies in the 1970s. The fact that an Irishman, Aeneas Coffey, was responsible for the rise of Scotch blends is not the only irony, for Coffey the distiller used to be an excise officer, and he led a very colourful life.

In the year 1818 in Donegal, Aeneas Coffey was struggling to control illegal distilling. This was one of Ireland's most lawless counties, and Coffey narrowly escaped death on a number of occasions. During a particularly vicious encounter, his skull was fractured and, in his own words, the poteen makers "left my body one mass of contusion and gave me two bayonet wounds, one of

A Coffey still is able to work continuously rather than in batches, as with a pot still.

which completely perforated my thigh. I owed my life to the rapid approach of the military party from which I had imprudently wandered a few hundred yards ..."

Aeneas Coffey went on to be Inspector General of Excise in Ireland and, although he didn't invent the continuous still, in 1830 he lodged a series of patents that were revolutionary. As a contemporary government publication put it, the Coffey still "is said to be the speediest and most economical device for preparing a highly concentrated spirit in a single operation."

The traditional Dublin pot still distillers derided the patent still whiskey as "silent" (tasteless) spirit, so Aeneas Coffey left Ireland for the more open and welcoming Scottish and English markets. The rest, as they say, is history.

FECKIN' IRISH WHISKEY

Distillery: Cooley
🖥 www.feckinwhiskey.com

"Feck" is a very Irish word. It sounds rude, but is in fact no more than a mild oath in Ireland – widely used and socially acceptable. This whiskey, then, is the product of one in a number of independent bottlers using Cooley whiskey to target the younger drinker.

🍶 **FECKIN' IRISH WHISKEY** 40% ABV
A light, pleasant dram with that signature Cooley sweetness. However, it lacks the depth of similar blends like Kilbeggan.

INISHOWEN

Distillery: Cooley

Inishowen is Cooley's twist on the well-worn blended Scotch. The logic is sound: people like blended Scotch, so let's give them what they want. However, it seems that Ireland's

Inishowen Irish Whiskey

whiskey drinkers have a hard time getting used to a locally produced peated blend, and this whiskey is hard to find.

🍶 **INISHOWEN** 40% ABV • This is the only Irish blend where peat openly flouts itself. But the real joy here is the dominance of some excellent grain, which gives the blend real spine and lets the turf smoke and oak do their thing.

THE IRISHMAN 70

Distillery: Bushmills and Midleton

This is a most interesting blend, put together by Bernard Walsh, whose company started life with a hot Irish whiskey mix. As the name implies, The Irishman 70 contains 70 per cent malt from Bushmills, with the remainder made up of Midleton pure pot still. There is no grain whiskey here at all.

🍶 **THE IRISHMAN 70** 40% ABV • The pot still

character is evident from the start, but it works well against the crisp malt. This a full-flavoured ball of malt, with plenty of rich Christmas cake character. A most welcome addition to the fold.

JAMESON

Distillery: Midleton
🖥 www.jamesonwhiskey.com

Jameson is the world's leading brand of Irish whiskey, accounting for nearly 75 per cent of all Irish whiskey sold globally. In its home market of Ireland, Jameson has grown over 40 per cent during the past five years – but at a cost. Jameson has succeeded at the expense of the quirkier Irish Distillers products such as Hewitt's, which has been dropped, and Bushmills, which has been sold on.

Currently Jameson is a blend of roughly 50 per cent medium-bodied pot still and 50 per cent grain whiskey, each of which has matured first-fill bourbon and sherry wood for four to seven years. The whiskey owes not a small degree of its success to a whole heap of marketing.

JAMESON 40% ABV
There is some pot still spiciness and a pleasant sweetness here, but they fade quickly, leaving short vanilla notes. There are much finer Irish whiskeys to be explored – next time use this book and live a little!

JAMESON 12-YEAR-OLD SPECIAL RESERVE 40% abv
"Special Reserve" is the new Jameson buzz word, and while some whiskeys might need that little bit of marketing dazzle on the label, this is one that certainly does not. This whiskey was Irish Distillers first attempt at a premium brand and it started life as Jameson 1780, named after the year in which the Dublin distillery was founded. Now featuring an age statement, this is still one of the best value-for-money Irish whiskeys available.
Typically 80 per cent pot still to 20 per cent grain whiskey, it is, nevertheless, the use of first-fill bourbon

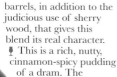

Jameson Standard Blend

barrels, in addition to the judicious use of sherry wood, that gives this blend its real character.
This is a rich, nutty, cinnamon-spicy pudding of a dram. The whiskey is very classy and the excellent wood gives the 12-year-old reserve a wonderful sherry, warm cocoa finish. For all-round value, this is the best Irish you can buy.

JAMESON 18-YEAR-OLD LIMITED RESERVE 40% abv
Jameson 18-year-old is the master blender's hand-picked selection of the very best pot still and grain whiskeys, aged in oak casks for at least 18 years. This whiskey is an excellent example of the fine wood policy employed at Midleton and the art of the blender.
The cracking nose is just the start of the adventure here. This exceptional blend is raisins and liquid velvet, maple syrup on muffins, and fudge melted over a choc-ice; an astonishing achievement and a world class dram.

JAMESON GOLD SPECIAL RESERVE 40% abv
Jameson Gold is a premium Irish whiskey developed for the airport retail and duty-free market. This is the only Irish Distillers whiskey in which virgin oak is used for maturation.
Yeasty bread and spicy honey, with some obvious vanilla and a peppery finish. Not the brightest star in the Jameson premium galaxy. It's also expensive, making Jameson 12-year-old a much smarter buy.

KILBEGGAN

Distillery: Cooley
www.kilbegganwhiskey.com

Kilbeggan is Cooley's flagship blended whiskey and is named after the midlands town where you'll find Locke's Distillery. Master distiller Noel Sweeney started working on this blend in 1994 when the distillery was still mothballed. Early examples reflected the limited range of whiskeys he had to work with, but over the years this blend has matured into a very fine whiskey indeed.

Locke's Kilbeggan Distillery gives its name to Cooley's Kilbeggan blended whiskey.

JOHN JAMESON & SON

As with most things to do with Irish Whiskey, the further back in time you go the mistier the details get. What we do know about John Jameson is that he was a Scottish Presbyterian who came to Ireland and took over an existing distillery in around 1780.

For the next 200 years – until 1988 in fact – there was always a descendant of John Jameson working for the company in the same offices at Bow Street in Dublin. Otherwise not much happened: each generation of Jameson built on the success of the last, until JJ&S was recognized as the finest whiskey that money could buy.

The Dublin distillery was very proud of its pure pot still whiskey and initially wasn't too concerned about the rise in popularity of blended Scotch. In 1890 Ireland had about 90 per cent of world whiskey exports, with the enormous Bow Street plant accounting for 10 per cent of the country's annual whiskey output.

But as outlined earlier, Prohibition in the USA, civil war in Ireland, and the rise of blended Scotch devastated the Irish whiskey industry, and, like

Jameson Tower at the old distillery is now a viewing platform.

every other distiller on the island, Jameson felt the pain.

In the mid-1960s Jameson was one of the founding members of Irish Distillers, with the Bow Street plant finally closing in 1971. Then, in 1988, Irish Distillers was taken over by the Pernod Ricard group, and the Jameson brand was singled out for greatness. In 1996, sales of Jameson finally broke through the magic one million cases a year barrier and the whiskey joined the world's top 100 spirit brands. Today Jameson is synonymous with Irish Whiskey and is sold in over 120 markets. Although now distilled in Midleton, the Old Bow Street Distillery where the whole story began now houses a heritage centre.

Jameson Distillery was situated in Dublin until the early 1970s, when the Bow Street distillery closed and operations were move to Midleton.

Kilbeggan 15-year-old

🍾 **KILBEGGAN** 40% ABV
Rich and unctuous, this predominantly grain blend is a real mouth-filling wonder of honey and oatmeal, with that now very distinctive after taste of chocolate covered coffee beans.

🍾 **KILBEGGAN 15-YEAR-OLD** 40% ABV
Kilbeggan's older brother has a lot in common with his younger sibling. There's the same unmistakable family DNA, but this guy has hormones and he's been down the gym.

This muscular specimen grips the tongue nicely before exploding into life. Now the honey (noticeable in the younger whiskey) is more defined – it's from pine trees and it's on a toasted bagel. The chocolate is still there, but it's darker and the coffee is Italian and impossibly tall, dark, and handsome. Bravo!

LOCKE'S BLEND

Distillery: Cooley

John Locke was the man who put the Kilbeggan Distillery on the map, and his name adorned the beautiful stone crocks that used to hold whiskey from this midlands distillery. Today the Locke's name is back on a whiskey – this time one produced by the Cooley camp. This blend has a higher malt content than its stable-mate

Kilbeggan, with a hint of that malt being peated.
🍾 **LOCKE'S BLEND** 40% ABV
This is an incredibly delicate creature – water kills it stone dead, so be warned. Neat Locke's blend has some charm, but it's a pale reflection of what Cooley can achieve with their malts and grainier blends.

MICHAEL COLLINS BLEND

Distillery: Cooley

A blend designed by Cooley for American importers Sidney Frank.
🍾 **MICHAEL COLLINS BLEND** 40% ABV • The start is thin enough, but the whiskey opens up into vanilla and warm oak embers.

MIDLETON VERY RARE

Distillery: Midleton

One of the most expensive whiskeys produced on a regular basis by Irish Distillers. Since 1984, no more than 2,500 cases (and usually fewer) of Midleton Very Rare have been released annually. Older vintages feature whiskey from the silent Midleton Distillery; more recent bottlings are the work of the new Midleton plant.

The whiskeys in this blend are between 12 and 25 years old, and are matured exclusively in seasoned bourbon barrels. The nature of the selection process for Midleton Very Rare means that each vintage has its own distinct character.
🍾 **MIDLETON VERY RARE 2006** 40% ABV
Beeswax and melon, with that signature cream soda softness. This is exceptional stuff, showing how

Middleton Very Rare

good Midleton whiskey can get, from inception, through maturation, to blending. It is expensive, but then it is an exceptional drop.

MILLARS SPECIAL RESERVE

Distillery: Cooley

Adam Millar & Company was a firm of Dublin whiskey bonders which sat across the road from Powers Distillery. Cooley Distillery bought them out in 1988. Millars has a 20 per cent malt content, with both grain and malt having been aged in freshly emptied bourbon barrels.
🍾 Millars is a whiskey with real character. It's a box of tricks – firm, spicy, and unapologetically tasty. The most underrated blend in Ireland.

Millars Special Reserve

PADDY

Distillery: Midleton

It's only in the past half century or so that most Irish distilleries have taken to bottling their own whiskey. In the era of the whiskey merchant, Power's Gold label (white labels were reserved for the merchants) and the Cork Distilleries Company Old Irish Whiskey were the only two proprietary brands.

Paddy Flaherty was the CDC's celebrated sales representative, and during the 1920s and 30s he was well known for his generosity, often standing the whole bar a round of drinks – whiskey of course. Before long his Old Irish Whiskey was known to locals as "Paddy Flaherty's whiskey".

Over time, CDC gradually incorporated his name and signature onto the label to authenticate it, until eventually it became known simply as Paddy.

Most recently, Paddy's more regal patronage came to light following the auction by Christies in Paris of a rare bottle from the 1920s. Bought by Irish Distillers for £1,500 in 2003, it was once owned by Edward VIII, Duke of Windsor, but was later sold by his wife, Mrs Simpson, after his death.

Today Paddy features slightly older whiskeys than are found in Jameson, and, although there is a similar wood policy, Paddy does not use as much first-fill wood. The whiskey is made up of roughly equal measures of pot still and grain whiskey.

🍶 **PADDY** 40 % ABV ● This is a malty and easy-going drink. It's light and peppery, and best served short with a drop or two of water. This opens up the spirit, yielding jasmine and buttery fruitcake. But too much water will drown its delicate nature.

Paddy Old Irish Whiskey

POWERS

Distillery: Midleton

The Powers were the other Dublin distilling dynasty. Their distillery was situated on the south side of the narrow River Liffey, facing John Jameson & Son to the north.

John Power took over the company from his father James in 1817 and became a very influential man in the capital. For a number of years, he was High Sheriff of Dublin, and he was a close friend of Daniel O'Connell, the Liberator. At the age of 64 he became Sir John Power, and could look back on a successful life having extended the distillery until it covered seven acres of the city.

The company was fond of innovation; they were the first major Dublin firm to embrace the Coffey still, albeit on a limited scale.

They moved into white spirits with Powers gin and Powers vodka, but more importantly they were first to try out in-house bottling. In an era when glass bottles were hand-made and expensive, they bottled their own "Gold Label" whiskey. They even went on to produce miniature bottles (known as Baby Powers) – an innovation, and later worldwide trend, that required an act of Parliament to allow it.

POWERS GOLD LABEL

This is a superbly made whiskey, with that distinctive high Irish pot still whiskey that now only emanates from the Midleton Distillery.

Powers is a rich, round, complex, and full-flavoured drinking experience. Selling more than six million measures each year across Ireland, it is the country's favourite whiskey.

🍶 Gulp, don't sip. Slosh it around in your mouth. Make silly gargling sounds and swallow deeply. Now try and catch all the flavours; there's heather, all spice, cloves, camphor … now take another gulp and try again. Brilliant!

POWERS 12-YEAR-OLD SPECIAL RESERVE

Powers 12-year-old Reserve is a premium edition of Ireland's favourite whiskey. This reserve is chosen from specially selected whiskeys, aged from 12 to 24 years. It's the same formulation as the regular Powers, just older.

🍶 It's amazing what a few more years in the wood will do to a whiskey. This is regular Powers on steroids: there's the

Powers Gold Label

usual assault of spice, honey, and hard custard, but this time it's layered with soft wood tones and very soothing fruit jelly.

TULLAMORE DEW

Distillery: Midleton
🖰 www.tullamoredew.com

Locke's in Kilbeggan and Daly's, up the road in Tullamore, were the last Irish distilleries to close in the early 1950s. Both were modest rural operations that had clung on long after most of their contemporaries had shut up shop. A micro-distillery has recently re-opened in Kilbeggan (see p165), but its close neighbour in Tullamore hasn't been so lucky. A shopping mall now stands where the whiskey was once made, though there is a museum in one of the old warehouses.

In its time, Tullamore was a very innovative distillery. The owners embraced the continuous still, and in the 1950s Tullamore Dew became the first Irish whiskey to be reformulated as a blend. The distillery was sited almost exactly in the centre of Ireland, but despite poor transport links to the costal ports, the company focused heavily on the export market; to this day Tullamore Dew is still the largest selling Irish whiskey in Germany.

Tullamore Dew

The company's most famous brand, Tullamore Dew, is still going strong, though it has passed through numerous hands since the distillery closed in 1954. Today it is owned by the Irish food and drink company C&C, which in turn is owned by a group of UK venture capitalists. So the fate of this brand is far from settled. All the whiskies in the Tullamore Dew range are distilled at the Midleton Distillery in County Cork.

🥃 **TULLAMORE DEW** 40% ABV
By far the lightest Irish whiskey on sale today – very grainy and lacking in much depth. Best served over ice with a sweet mixer like cola.

🥃 **TULLAMORE DEW 12** 40% ABV
Sherry wood and spicy pot still whiskey is very much to the fore here in a very classy blend, aimed at the premium airport retail market. This whiskey has much more in common with the Jameson family of premium whiskeys than standard Tullamore Dew.

TULLAMORE DEW HERITAGE 40% ABV
One of the canal-side distillery warehouses is now home to a small museum and a shop, and this is where you'll find this offering. Prior to bottling, all the whiskeys that make up the Heritage blend are married for just under a year in second-fill bourbon wood.

🥃 There are some very fine and very old pot still whiskeys making themselves known here. A beautifully balanced example of the blender's art; sweet vanilla and sherry drift on with the distant scent of old leather car seats. Very lovely.

WILD GEESE WHISKEY

Distillery: Cooley
🖥 www.wildgeese-irishwhiskey.com

Yet another blend aimed at the ex-pat market, but this one's got a bit of bite to it.

🥃 **WILD GEESE WHISKEY** 40% ABV
This whiskey is sweet at the start, but somewhere in the middle of the tongue it changes into quite a classy monster. Here the grain whiskey makes all the running, but it's good firm stuff, proving that Cooley master distiller, Noel Sweeney, is right to have such faith in his grain.

POTEEN

Poteen is Ireland's other national drink. It's the outrageous outlaw – the bad boy everybody loves. In movie terms, it is Colin Farrell to whiskey's Pierce Brosnan. But how different things could have been. You see, until 1661 *uisce beatha* (whiskey) and *uisce poitín* (poteen) were one and the same, but, after that date, duty was paid on the former and not on the latter, so making poteen illegal.

At the time, there wasn't any difference between the taste of Parliament whiskey (*uisce beatha*) and the illegal stuff (*uisce poitín*), they were both small-batch, colourless spirits distilled from native grain and drunk hot from the still. But as the centuries rolled past, the two spirits took on very different identities.

During the 19th century, distilling in Ireland moved from a cottage industry to a model of Victorian laissez-faire enterprise. Whiskey was no longer sold straight from the still; it was matured in oak wood for at least three years, which gave the spirit extra flavour and colour.

Poteen changed too, but in minor ways. It was always made from whatever was cheap and at hand, so molasses replaced barley and copper hot-water tanks replaced tin pot stills.

Despite 400 years of persecution by both Church and State, the outlaw thrived in song and folklore in the hills of Ireland until very recently. Then came prosperity. The Celtic Tiger swept all before it, bringing full employment and soaring house prices, and changing Ireland forever. The market for cheap spirits dried up and the skills that had been passed from generation to generation started to die off.

Whether this is a passing phase, or whether poteen has been fatally mauled by the Celtic Tiger, it's too early to tell. If you see a product labelled "poteen" in an airport or a bar, it's simply a white duty-paid Irish schnapps. By definition, poteen is illegal and can't be sold.

This poteen still from the early 20th century shows how basic the apparatus can be: an open fire heats the pot, the spirit condenses in the pipe and slowly dips into the standing barrel.

THE WELSH WHISKY COMPANY
150
PENDERYN
2004
THE WELSH WHISKY COMPANY
144
PENDERYN
2004
THE WELSH WHISKY COMPANY
157
PENDERYN
2004
THE WELSH WHISKY COMPANY
160
PENDERYN
2004
THE WELSH WHISKY COMPANY
147
PENDERYN
2004
THE WELSH WHISKY COMPANY
133
PENDERYN
2004
THE WELSH WHISKY
129
PENDERYN
2004

ENGLAND AND WALES

If the history of alcohol production in the UK has taught us anything about the English, it's that for them patience is not a virtue. Whisky takes time to mature, and, while it has been produced in England in the past, it has been only on a modest scale, and the general tendency is towards far faster results.

While the Scots and Irish were perfecting the art of maturation and integrating flavour into their national spirits, the scenario in England was more divided. The nobility bought in quality port, cognac, Irish whiskey, and finally Scotch for their high tables; while the majority of the population settled on a foul-tasting grain spirit, flavoured to hide its taste, and called gin. It was a variant of the sweeter Dutch spirit genever, but was a considerably poorer drink. In the 18th and 19th centuries, when gin's popularity was at its height and it was sold in "gin palaces" throughout the land, the spririt was often made with grain unfit for ale production and flavoured, not with juniper berries and botanicals as we know it today, but in some instances with turpentine.

There were a few whisky distilleries in England – Alfred Barnard *(see p50)* visited four in the 1880s – and they did produce some single malt in pot stills, but most of the output found its way into Scottish or Irish blends, or even went on to make gin. It seems that eventually the English gave up trying to make malt altogether, however, and simply conceded that the Scots did it far better.

THE WELSH PICTURE

The same conclusion would seem to have been drawn in Wales, too. Although evidence exists that whisky was made in the province, it died away more than 100 years ago, perhaps to some degree as a result of the temperance movement. The descendents of Welsh emmigrants – Evan Williams and Jack Daniel included – did make their mark across the Atlantic in America, however.

Over the last century, attempts to establish distilleries in England have mostly been half-hearted. Land has occasionally been secured and planning permission sought, but there progress has stalled. Typically, when a distillery was finally established in Cornwall, it was immediately followed by plans for a clutch of others, though so far only one other in England has actually opened – Norfolk's St George's Distillery.

Meanwhile, a very bright beacon shines in Wales, where whisky is not only being produced at Penderyn, but is also selling very successfully.

Penderyn uses ex-bourbon barrels for the maturation of its spirit, which is then transferred into Madeira casks to finish the ageing process.

DISTILLERIES

Although there are only three whisky distilleries in England and Wales, they are not here simply for novelty value. Penderyn is the most established, and is already producing a successful malt using innovative techniques, while St George's is taking advantage of great local barley.

PENDERYN

✉ Penderyn, Near Aberdare, South Wales

🖥 www.welsh-whisky.co.uk

⚓ Open to visitors

If there was a heavy dose of cynicism about Welsh whisky being nothing more than poor man's Scotch, it was dispelled almost as soon as Penderyn's first malt appeared, some four years ago. Dressed in modern and stylish packaging that was light years away from anything coming out if Scotland, it tasted other-worldly too.

Closer inspection reveals that the Welsh have pulled off a masterstroke. By teaming up with world-renowned technical experts, Penderyn

Pendryn's unusual still has a rectifying column rising up from the pot-shaped base.

has created a whole new way of making malt.

The wash is brought in from local beer brewer, Brain's, a break with recognized Scottish production methods, and is distilled once in a unique still that has a pot at the bottom and a tall recifying column above. The whisky comes off the still at 91 per cent ABV and is light and delicate.

The standard bottle commands a premium price, having been matured in top quality bourbon casks, before finishing maturation in Madeira wood.

Penderyn's managing director Stephen Davies says that, right from the start, the aim was to produce a whisky that wouldn't just survive for its novelty value. It's working. The distillery is selling about 85,000 bottles in 15 countries. The distillery has upped production, though it

ENGLISH AND WELSH DISTILLERIES

will be a while before the results of this increase will see their way into bottles.

🍾 **PENDERYN SINGLE MALT** 46% ABV
The nose offers over-ripe raisins and candy pineapple. It's zesty and fresh – very appealing. The palate is winey, malty, and then bitter fruits come through – tangerine perhaps. It's rather prickly, fruity, and bitter in the finish but, surprisingly, not unpleasantly so.

Penderyn Single Malt

St George's stills will soon be producing a variety of whisky styles, even including some that are heavily peated.

ST GEORGE'S

✉ East Harling, Norfolk
🖥 www.englishwhisky.co.uk
🏛 Open to the public

St George's Distillery is run by The English Whisky Company, which stated its intentions in 2006 with the announcement that the esteemed Scottish distiller Iain Henderson would be coming out of retirement to run England's first licensed distillery for more than 100 years. In 2007 the distillery opened a visitor centre and began laying down spirit. It's too early to know how the whisky will turn out, but the new make is impressive.

Eastern England produces some of the world's finest barley – which helps – and although some have questioned whether Norfolk water is suited to whisky production, the distillery uses a deep water table and its mineral make up has given considerable grounds for optimism. Quality pot stills and a climate favourable to maturation also play a part.

Iain Henderson retired for the third time in Autumn 2007 and has been replaced by David Fitt, a former brewer with East Anglian beer giant Greene King.

Although it's early days, all the signs are that St George's is preparing to create a large range of whisky styles and won't be shy when it comes to special finishes. Already the distillery has laid down casks of heavily peated spirit and the new make has many of the characteristics of the sort of Laphroaig Iain Henderson was making some years ago. The word from the distillery is that they have been experimenting with a triple distilled malt, and the plan is eventually to pack the shop with a range of malts, blends, and liqueurs.

THE CORNISH CYDER FARM

✉ Penhallow, Cornwall
🖥 www.thecornishcyder company.co.uk

They have been producing whisky in Cornwall for five years now, so surely that would make The Cyder Farm, and not St George's, the first English distillery for more than 100 years? But no. "We're not English, we're Cornish," says owner David Healey. A fair point, but what about the kudos of being "the first?" "We are. We're the first Cornish distillery for 300 years."

The whisky is made with wash from St Austell Brewery and is distilled in an apple brandy still. It tastes like it – or at least the earliest distillations do – thin, shapeless, appley spirit. But the younger spirit – just one or two years old – has come on leaps and bounds and is developing a pleasant personality with, yes, a green fruit character. The first batches have already been bought up, so it'll be a while before bottlings are available.

DISTILLERIES ON THE HORIZON

For some time now there have been plans for a distillery in the Lake District in northwest England, permission having been granted to Andrew Currie, formerly marketing director at the Isle of Arran Distillery. But plans for The Barley Bridge Distillery, at Stavely, next to the fast-flowing River Kent, seem to have been put on hold – hopefully only temporarily. There are also plans afoot for a new distillery in Northumbria, over on the northeast coast of England, but, as yet, they are only in the early stages.

River Kent in the Lake District has been identified as a good source of water for whisky making.

USA

When European immigrants crossed the Atlantic, they carried with them the art of distilling from grain. Many of them set up home in Maryland, Pennsylvania, and Virginia, and began to make whiskey using rye instead of barley.

R ye grew well, and German settlers in southeastern Pennsylvania had a heritage of distilling schnapps from rye. However, as more settlers moved further west, they found that the most prolific crop was maize, or Indian corn, and so they employed that in their whiskey-making.

By the late 18th century, Kentucky boasted a well-established whiskey business based on corn, and Bourbon County was renowned for the quality of its whiskey. Bourbon County is named after the French royal house of Bourbon, and earned its sobriquet because the French gave "rebel" colonists significant aid during the War of Independence. Once the war was over, gratitude was expressed by christening many new settlements and administrative areas with French names. When the then West Virginian county of Kentucky was subdivided in the 1780s, one new county was named in honour of the Bourbons, while Kentucky itself became a fully fledged state in its own right in 1792.

The limestone soil of Kentucky yields rich crops of corn, and it is no coincidence that most of the principal whiskey-producing states of the USA, both past and present, partly overlie the same limestone shelf. Limestone also produces excellent spring water, and it is claimed that the calcium content of water that flows over limestone aids enzyme action during the fermentation stage of whiskey-making.

THE FATHER OF BOURBON

Evan Williams is often credited with being the first commercial distiller in Kentucky, establishing a distillery in the Louisville area in 1783, but a Baptist minister by the name of the Reverend Elijah Craig is widely considered the "father of bourbon". According to whiskey folklore, he instigated the practice of using charred barrels for maturation – a serendipitous discovery following a fire – leading to a distinctive style that helps to define bourbon.

America soon developed a thriving commercial distilling industry, and in 1838 Samuel Morewood noted in his book *Inventions and Customs of Ancient and Modern Nations in the Manufacture and Use of Inebriating Liquors* the existence of 3,594 stills in Pennsylvania, 2,000 in Kentucky, 591 in New York (mostly producing rum and brandy), 560 in Connecticut, 343 in Ohio, and 126 in Georgia. Around the

Kentucky's Maker's Mark Distillery was established in 1805; while there are older distilleries in the USA, this one has remained on its original site the longest.

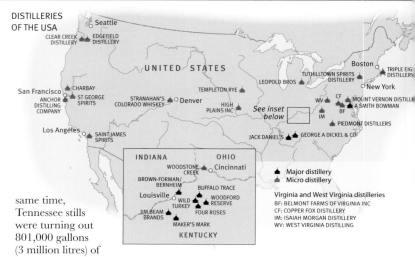

DISTILLERIES OF THE USA

Seattle

CLEAR CREEK DISTILLERY
EDGEFIELD DISTILLERY

UNITED STATES

Boston
TRIPLE EIG DISTILLERY

TUTHILLTOWN SPIRITS DISTILLERY

LEOPOLD BROS

New York

San Francisco

CHARBAY
ST GEORGE SPIRITS

ANCHOR DISTILLING COMPANY

STRANAHAN'S COLORADO WHISKEY

Denver

TEMPLETON RYE

HIGH PLAINS INC

See inset below

WV
CF
MOUNT VERNON DISTILL
A SMITH BOWMAN

BF

IM

PIEDMONT DISTILLERS

Los Angeles

SAINT JAMES SPIRITS

JACK DANIEL'S

GEORGE A DICKEL & CO

INDIANA

OHIO

WOODSTONE CREEK
Cincinnati

BROWN-FORMAN/ BERNHEIM

Louisville

WILD TURKEY

JIM BEAM BRANDS

BUFFALO TRACE

WOODFORD RESERVE

FOUR ROSES

MAKER'S MARK

KENTUCKY

▲ Major distillery
▲ Micro distillery

Virginia and West Virginia distilleries
BF: BELMONT FARMS OF VIRGINIA INC
CF: COPPER FOX DISTILLERY
IM: ISAIAH MORGAN DISTILLERY
WV: WEST VIRGINIA DISTILLING

same time, Tennessee stills were turning out 801,000 gallons (3 million litres) of whiskey per year –approximately one third of the combined output of Kentucky and Virginia.

PROHIBITION

Despite the devastation wreaked by national Prohibition *(see p210)*, Pennsylvania still had 42 working distilleries at the outbreak of World War II, but when Michter Distillery in Schaefferstown closed in 1988 the great tradition of Pennsylvanian distilling came to an end. Kentucky, too, has lost many distilleries, firstly due to Prohibition and then, in the succeeding years, as Scotch became the favoured whisky in North America.

However, growth of interest in single malt from the 1980s onwards has also led to a re-evaluation of America's whiskeys,

which have begun to regain favour. Additionally, as a significant number of consumers tire of homogenized and mass-produced food and drink, bourbon has successfully fought back against declining sales with small-batch bourbon. Bottled from the vatting of a small number of particularly fine casks of spirit, small-batch bourbons were the USA's answer to Scotland's single malt whiskies. Accompanying this trend has been a welcome, if modest, revival in rye whiskeys, which became all but extinct in the decades following Prohibition.

REDISCOVERING FLAVOUR

During the Prohibition years, rye-flavoured blends from Canada were smuggled into the USA in massive quantities, and this may have caused confusion among consumers regarding the true character of rye. It may also have been the case that, as drinkers came to prefer increasingly bland drinks, so rye, with its distinctive bittersweet style, was just too characterful.

Today, Kentucky remains the heartland of American whiskey production, with all but three of the country's 13 full-scale, commercial distilling operations based in the state. However, many other states are home to micro, or "craft", distillers *(see p205)*. Their ranks have been swelled significantly during the past few years, bringing diversity and dynamism to the American whiskey sector.

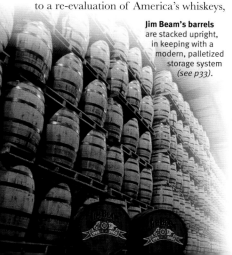

Jim Beam's barrels are stacked upright, in keeping with a modern, palletized storage system *(see p33)*.

Just 40 to 50 barrels a day are filled at Woodford Reserve, the smallest distillery in Kentucky.

DISTILLERIES

The USA has about a dozen major distilleries, most of which produce a variety of whiskeys. Some also distill for other whiskey brands, which are rounded up on pp212–17; micro-distilleries are covered on pp204–9.

A Smith Bowman moved to their new site in the 1980s, as northern Virginia grew more prosperous.

A SMITH BOWMAN

✉ 1 Bowman Drive, Fredericksburg, Virginia
🖥 www.asmithbowman.com

The current A Smith Bowman Distillery can be found on the outskirts of Fredericksburg, in Virginia. However, the original operation was established by Abram Smith Bowman on Sunset Hills Farm, the Bowmans' family property in Fairfax County. That was in 1935, soon after the repeal of Prohibition *(see p211)*.

Virginia Gentleman 90 Proof Small Batch Bourbon

In response to the rapid commercial and residential growth of northern Virginia, the distilling operation was moved in 1988 to the historic city of Fredericksburg in Spotsylvania County, 60 miles (100 km) from its original location. The semi-derelict, former FMC cellophane manufacturing plant was acquired for the purpose, and subsequently redeveloped into the new Smith Bowman Distillery.

The distillery is best known for its Virginia Gentleman Straight Bourbon Whiskey, and the plant has been owned by the Sazarac Company of New Orleans since its acquisition from the Bowman family in 2003. Sazarac also owns Buffalo Trace *(see p188)* in Kentucky.

Since the relocation to Fredericksburg in 1988, the first run of Virginia Gentleman has been fermented and distilled at the Buffalo Trace Distillery, before a second, slow run through a copper pot doubler still takes place on the Smith Bowman site. The whiskey is also matured here in charred, white oak barrels. Virginia Gentleman has a higher percentage of corn in its mash bill than many bourbons, giving it a greater degree of sweetness.

🍸 **VIRGINIA GENTLEMAN 90 PROOF SMALL-BATCH BOURBON** 45% ABV • This expression of Virginia Gentleman was launched in 1998. It features oak and corn on the nose, with oak, rye, and honey notes in the mouth. Spicy rye continues in the drying finish.

THE LAST DISTILLERY IN VIRGINIA

Until the opening of Mount Vernon Distillery in Fairfax County in 2006 *(see p206)*, the A Smith Bowman plant was the only surviving Virginian distillery, despite the state's long and distinguished whiskey-making heritage. During the first half of the 19th century, for example, Virginia produced more whiskey per annum than Kentucky.

The distilling equipment at the Smith Bowman plant survives from the 1930s.

BOURBON AND OTHER AMERICAN WHISKEY STYLES

Bourbon is the most famous style of American whiskey. It takes its name from Bourbon County in Kentucky, although it is a popular misconception that bourbon must legally be distilled in Kentucky.

In fact, bourbon can be produced anywhere in the USA provided it complies with the requirements of component grains and maturation processes. First officially defined by law in 1964, bourbon is produced from a mash of not less than 51 per cent corn grain. The raw spirit may not be distilled to more than 80 per cent alcohol by volume, and maturation must be for a minimum of two years in new white oak barrels that have been charred in order to allow the spirit to interact more easily with the wood.

Bourbon pouring into charcoal-filtering vats at the Jim Beam plant.

TENNESSEE WHISKEY As with bourbon, Tennessee whiskey is a legally-defined, distinct whiskey type, and is made from a fermented mash containing at least 51 per cent corn. It is then filtered through a layer of maple charcoal before being aged for a minimum of two years in new, charred oak barrels.

RYE WHISKEY In the USA rye whiskey has to be made from a minimum of 51 per cent rye, and distilled at no more than 80 per cent alcohol by volume.

There is no legal minimum maturation period, but it cannot be termed "straight rye" unless it has been aged for at least two years. Like bourbon, rye is aged in new, charred oak casks.

WHEAT WHISKEY Made with more than 51 per cent wheat in its mash bill, wheat whiskey is very rare, but the inclusion of wheat as one of the subsidiary grains in the mash bill – usually in place of rye – gives a sweetness and mellowness to whiskey.

CORN WHISKEY Legally, corn whiskey has to be made from not less than 80 per cent corn and be matured in un-charred new barrels or used bourbon barrels. There is no specified minimum ageing period, and it is associated with "moonshine whiskey" *(see p206)*, which is usually sold fresh and new.

BLENDED WHISKEY American blended whiskey comprises a proportion of rye or bourbon whiskey mixed with "grain neutral spirit", or "light whiskey", which has been matured in new, uncharred barrels or used oak barrels. The proportion of rye or bourbon may be as little as 20 per cent.

The small-scale Woodford Reserve Distillery produces some of Kentucky's most highly regarded bourbon whiskey.

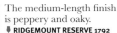

Barton Distillery's buildings date from the 1940s, but distilling has been carried out here for considerably longer.

🥃 **VIRGINIA GENTLEMAN STRAIGHT BOURBON** 40% ABV • Aged for at least four years, Virginia Gentleman offers a light, sweet, toasted nut aroma. Spicy rye, sweet corn, honey, caramel, and cocoa are present on the smooth, well-balanced palate. The finish is complex, with rye, malt and vanilla.

BARTON

✉ 1 Barton Road, Bardstown, Kentucky, PO BOX 40004
🖥 www.bartonbrands.com

Barton Brands Ltd is a distilling subsidiary of the international Constellation Brands Inc. and is situated at Bardstown in Nelson County. Bardstown lies in the true heartland of bourbon country, and once boasted more than 20 distilleries. Today, the town hosts a week-long annual Kentucky Bourbon Festival every September.

Barton has what is probably the lowest profile of all the working distilleries in Kentucky, and has no visitor facilities. The present buildings date principally

from the 1940s, although distilling was taking place in the immediate vicinity in the 1880s, and local distillers Tom Moore and Ben Mattingly established the Tom Moore Distillery in 1889. This was one of the many casualties of Prohibition, but in 1934 the plant was acquired and modernized by Harry Teur. A decade later it was purchased by the Oscar Getz family, whose collection of Kentucky distilling memorabilia was formerly displayed at the distillery but now forms part of the Oscar Getz Museum of Whiskey History, which is located in Bardstown.

Barton's whiskeys are characterized by being comparatively youthful, dry, and aromatic, and the standard mash bill is made up of 74 per cent corn, 16 per cent rye, and 10 per cent malted barley.

🥃 **KENTUCKY GENTLEMAN KENTUCKY STRAIGHT BOURBON WHISKEY** 40% ABV • Made with a higher percentage of rye than most Barton whiskeys, Kentucky Gentleman offers caramel and sweet oak aromas, and is oily, full-bodied, spicy, and fruity in the mouth. Rye, fruits, vanilla, and cocoa figure in an assertive finish.

🥃 **KENTUCKY TAVERN KENTUCKY STRAIGHT BOURBON WHISKEY 4-YEAR-OLD** 40% ABV • Assertive and oaky on the nose, with apples and honey. Spices, oak, more apples, and a note of rye on the palate.

The medium-length finish is peppery and oaky.

🥃 **RIDGEMOUNT RESERVE 1792 SMALL-BATCH BOURBON 8-YEAR-OLD** 46.85% ABV This comparatively delicate and complex bourbon boasts a soft nose with vanilla, caramel, leather, rye, corn, and spice notes. Oily and initially sweet on the palate, caramel and spicy rye develop along with a suggestion of oak. The finish is oaky, spicy, and quite long, with a sweet lingering hint of caramel.

Incidentally, the "1792" in the name refers to the year in which Kentucky became a state.

Ridgemount Reserve 1792 Small Batch Bourbon

🥃 **TEN HIGH KENTUCKY STRAIGHT SOUR MASH BOURBON** 40% ABV Grainy and slightly oaky on the nose, Ten High is notably malty on the palate, almost like a young malt Scotch, and has notes of vanilla and caramel. The finish is quite short and drying.

🥃 **TOM MOORE KENTUCKY STRAIGHT BOURBON WHISKEY** 40% ABV • Distinct notes of rye and herbs on the nose, along with vanilla, oak, and cooked berries. Medium-bodied, the palate is a blend of sugary sweetness and spicy rye bitterness. Toffee and ginger dominate the finish.

🥃 **VERY OLD BARTON KENTUCKY STRAIGHT BOURBON WHISKEY 6-YEAR-OLD** 40% ABV At a modest six years of age, this is comparatively old for a Barton whiskey, hence its name. The nose is rich, syrupy and spicy, with a prickle of salt. Big-bodied in the mouth, it is fruity and spicy, with spices and ginger in the drying finish.

Very Old Barton Kentucky Straight Bourbon

BERNHEIM

See Heaven Hill

BOSTON

See Jim Beam

BROWN-FORMAN

✉ 850 Dixie Highway, Louisville, Kentucky

🖰 www.brown-forman.com

The Brown-Forman Corporation, which dates back to 1870, also owns the Jack Daniel's and Woodford Reserve distilleries. The company's Louisville facility was established in 1935, when it was known as the Old Kentucky Distillery. Brown-Forman acquired it in 1940 and subsequently rebuilt the plant, ultimately re-christening it the Early Times distillery. Brown-Forman also owned the Old Forester Distillery in Louisville. That

In the fermenter (this one is at the Brown-Forman plant) yeast turns sugars from the grain into alcohol.

DISTILLERY ROW

The Brown-Forman Distillery is situated in the area of Louisville, Kentucky, known as "Distillery Row", where half a dozen distilleries once operated. Today, only the Brown-Forman plant and Bernheim (*see p192*) survive, but a century ago Louisville was awash with whiskey and home to more than 20 distilleries.

Early Times Kentucky Whisky

closed in 1979, after which production of Old Forester bourbon was switched to the Early Times Distillery. Today, Early Times Kentucky Whisky and Old Forester Kentucky Straight Bourbon Whisky are the principal output of that plant, and Brown-Forman favours the Scottish spelling of "whisky". It also favours the "Brown-Forman" name to the previous "Early Times".

The Early Times name lingers on, however, in one of the distillery's whiskies – which is a good thing as the brand name has been around since the 1860s and stems from an early settlement situated near Bardstown. Until the Prohibition period, Early Times was a blended whisky – that is a mixture of straight whisky and neutral spirit – but was subsequently produced as a straight whisky.

Generally, it cannot be classified as a bourbon simply because some of the spirit is filled into used barrels, whereas bourbon legislation insists that all spirit must be matured in new charred oak (*see p186*). Early Times is therefore marketed as a "Straight Kentucky Whisky". The method of maturation – using spirit aged in used barrels for a minimum of three years blended with 5 to 7-year-old whisky from new barrels – makes for a lighter bodied, less woody spirit. This version of Early Times whisky was introduced in 1981 in order to compete with the increasingly popular light-bodied Canadian whiskies, but some "straight" Early Times is sold in overseas markets.

The Early Times mash bill is made up of 79 per cent corn, 11 per cent rye, and 10 per cent malted barley, while Old Forrester is made with around 72 per cent corn; the remainder of the mash bill comprises 18 per cent rye and 10 per cent malted barley.

🥄 **EARLY TIMES KENTUCKY WHISKY OVER 3 YEARS-OLD** 40% ABV
Quite light on the nose, with nuts and spices. The palate offers more nuts and spices, together with honey and butterscotch notes.

🥄 **OLD FORESTER KENTUCKY STRAIGHT BOURBON WHISKY OVER 8 YEARS-OLD** 50% ABV
Much more complex than Early Times, with pronounced floral notes, vanilla, spice, fruit, chocolate, and menthol on the nose. Old Forester is notably fuller and fruitier than Early Times in the mouth, where rye and peaches vie with fudge, nutmeg, and oak. The finish offers more rye, toffee, liquorice, and drying oak.

BUFFALO TRACE

✉ Sazerac Company Inc., 1001 Wilkinson Boulevard, Frankfort, Kentucky

🖰 www.buffalotrace.com

⛰ Open to visitors

Buffalo Trace Distillery is located at a crossing point where, in times past, herds of migrating buffalo forded the Kentucky River. The trail these animals followed was known as the Great Buffalo Trace. A settlement grew up here, starting in 1775, and the first formal distillery was established in 1857 by the Blanton family. From 1886 it was owned by the "bourbon aristocrat" Edmund Haynes Taylor Jr, who christened the plant

Old Forester Straight Bourbon

Buffalo Trace is known for its sweet flavoured bourbon, due to high corn levels in the mash bill.

OFC – initials which stand for Old-Fashioned Copper Distillery.

Another Kentucky gentleman, Colonel Albert Bacon Blanton, rose from office clerk in the 1890s to become distillery manager and part owner with George T Stagg. He retired in 1952 after 55 years of service to the company, and is commemorated by a statue at the distillery and Blanton's Single Barrel Bourbon. This was the first commercially available single barrel bourbon, and was introduced in 1984 by then master distiller Elmer T Lee, who now also has a whiskey named in his honour.

The distillery has an annual capacity of 54 million litres (12 million gallons), and the house style is notably sweet, due to the inclusion of a high percentage of corn in the mash bill. Heavily charred barrels are used for maturation, and the spirit is chill-filtered before bottling rather than employing the more usual method of charcoal filtering.

The Four Roses brand has been around since the late 19th century.

Buffalo Trace Straight Bourbon

According to the company, this leads to a more flavoursome whiskey.

Buffalo Trace offers the broadest range of aged whiskey (from four to 23 years) in the USA, and is the only US distillery using five recipes for whiskey products – namely two straight bourbons, one barley whiskey, one rye whiskey, and one wheated bourbon.

As well as the popular Buffalo Trace Kentucky Straight Bourbon, the distillery also produces several other brands, including Ancient Age *(see pp212)*, which was in fact the name of this distillery until 1999. Since 2002, the distillery has also produced spirit for the Van Winkle brand of whiskeys *(see p217)*.

🍸 **BUFFALO TRACE KENTUCKY STRAIGHT BOURBON** 45% ABV
Aged for a minimum of nine years, Buffalo Trace has an aroma of gum, vanilla, mint, and molasses. Sweet, fruity and notably spicy on the palate, with emerging brown sugar and oak. Water releases intensive, fruity notes. The finish is long, spicy, and comparatively dry, with developing vanilla.

FOUR ROSES

✉ **1224 Bonds Mill Road, Lawrenceburg, Kentucky**
🖥 **www.fourroses.us**
🏛 **Visitor centre at bottling and warehousing facility: 624 Lotus Road, HWY 1604, Cox's Creek, Kentucky**

Built to a striking Spanish Mission-style design in 1910, Four Roses Distillery is situated near the town of Lawrenceburg and takes its name from the brand

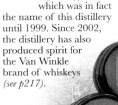

These barrels at Four Roses are vatted (combined with other barrels), prior to bottling.

trademarked by Paul Jones Jr in 1888. Jones was born in Georgia, and legend has it that his fiancée wore a corsage of four red roses to indicate acceptance of his marriage proposal, hence the name given to his bourbon.

In 1922, the Paul Jones Company purchased the Frankfort Distilling Company, one of only six distilleries granted permission to operate through Prohibition in order to produce bourbon for medicinal purposes. Four Roses became the best-selling bourbon in the US in the years following Prohibition, and in 1943 the Canadian-based Seagram organization purchased Frankfort, principally to acquire the Four Roses brand. However, for many years they used the Four Roses name for a blended whiskey in the US market, rather than a straight bourbon.

In February 2002, the Tokyo-based Kirin Brewery Company bought the Four Roses brand trademark, along with the production, bottling, and warehousing facilities, naming their new acquisition Four Roses Distillery LLC. Two years later they added a visitor centre and shop. Kirin also reintroduced Four Roses into the USA in the as a straight bourbon.

Four Roses is unique in having used the same grain source for 45 years, and two mash bills are in daily production. One mash bill contains significantly more rye (35 per cent) than any other bourbon, resulting in a spicy, full-bodied taste. Five proprietary yeast strains are used, and the combination of two mash bills and five yeasts gives 10 different bourbon flavours, which are usually blended to create one bottling style. Four Roses is also the only distillery that uses single-storey rack warehouses in order to minimize variations in temperature. This promotes a more even maturation process.

Four Roses Single Barrel Bourbon

❦ **FOUR ROSES KENTUCKY STRAIGHT BOURBON WHISKEY** 40% ABV The original Four Roses offering, Yellow Label, is aged for five to six years and is a comparatively light-bodied bourbon, with honey, burnt sugar, and wood varnish on the nose. Water releases attractive orange and cream notes. Fresh fruits, spice, and oak characterize the palate, while ginger nuts and drying oak figure in the medium finish.

❦ **FOUR ROSES SMALL BATCH BOURBON** 45% ABV • The most recent addition to the Four Roses range, Small Batch is mild and refined on the nose, with nutmeg and restrained honey. Water releases delicate, toasty, floral notes. Bold and rich on the well-balanced palate, with spices, fruit, and honey flavours. The finish is long and insinuating, with developing notes of vanilla.

❦ **FOUR ROSES SINGLE BARREL BOURBON** 43% ABV • Single Barrel was launched in 2004, and offers a rich, complex nose, comprising malt, fruits, spices, and fudge. Long and mellow in the mouth, with vanilla, oak, and a hint of menthol. The finish is long, spicy, and decidedly mellow.

Four Roses Small Batch Bourbon

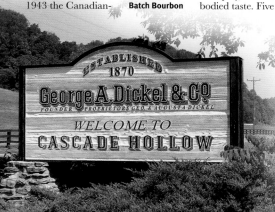

George Dickel Distillery was built in the late 1950s, close to the site of the original Cascade Distillery.

GEORGE DICKEL

✉ **1950 Cascade Hollow Road, Normandy, Tennessee**

⛬ Open to visitors

Along with Jack Daniel's, George Dickel is the only surviving licenced, full-scale distillery in the state of Tennessee. Tennessee whiskey has enjoyed its own legal designation since 1941, and is characterized by the Lincoln County Process of charcoal mellowing, which sees the new spirit, or "white dog", filtered through a deep bed of sugar maple charcoal for several days before being filled into barrels. This process removes some of the heavier fusel oils, giving a cleaner spirit.

George Dickel Distillery is much smaller in scale than its neighbour Jack Daniel's, located some 10 miles (16 km) away, and lies 6 miles (10 km) northeast of the town of Tullahoma, between Nashville and Chattanooga. The distillery uses the Scottish "whisky" spelling because founder George A Dickel insisted that the spirit he made was as smooth as the finest Scotch.

Dickel was German by birth, and was operating as a merchant in Nashville when he discovered Cascade Hollow and decided to make whisky there. The firm of George A Dickel & Co. was registered in 1870, and the Cascade Distillery was founded seven years later.

1910 saw the onset of Prohibition in Tennessee, and the Dickel operation moved to Kentucky, where distilling took place for a time at the Stitzel Weller plant in Louisville. In 1937, George A Dickel & Co. was acquired by Schenley Distiling Co., who moved

Bust of George Dickel

production to the Ancient Age Distillery – now known as Buffalo Trace *(see p188)*.

In 1958, Schenley decided that George Dickel should return to its roots, and a new distillery was built three-quarters of a mile (about 1 km) from the old Cascade Hollow location. Through a series of mergers and acquisitions, the Dickel Distillery and brand name subsequently came into the possession of Diageo. In character, George Dickel whiskies tend to be lighter, more aromatic and less oily than those produced by neighbour Jack Daniel's.

🍶 **GEORGE DICKEL NO 8** 40% ABV
Sweet on the nose, with aromas of chocolate, cocoa, and vanilla. The palate of this whisky is quite sweet and well-rounded, with fresh fruit and vanilla notes. The short finish features spices and charcoal.

MATURATION

When new white oak barrels are charred, compounds in the wood change and become "active", lending sweetness and colour to the spirit, while the char itself removes "off notes". During maturation, usually in racked warehouses where barrels are stacked up to 24 high, the spirit experiences significant seasonal changes of temperature, with barrels high up in the warehouses subject to most heat, and therefore maturing faster than those lower down. Overall, the comparatively high levels of heat and humidity experienced in American warehouses mean that the spirit matures earlier than it would in countries such as Scotland and Ireland.

Barrels at a low level in the storehouse mature more slowly than those higher up.

🍶 **GEORGE DICKEL NO 12** 45% ABV
The nose is aromatic, with fruit, fresh leather, butterscotch, a whiff of charcoal, and vanilla too. The palate is also rich and complex, with rye, chocolate, fruit, and vanilla. The finish offers vanilla toffee, and drying oak.

HEAVEN HILL

✉ **Bernheim Distillery, 1701 West Breckinridge Street, Louisville, Kentucky**

🖰 **www.heaven-hill.com**

⛬ Heaven Hill Distilleries Bourbon Heritage Centre, 1311 Gilkey Run Road, Bardstown, Kentucky

For most of its existence Heaven Hill has focused on its flagship bourbon labels, Evan Williams and Elijah Craig *(see pp213–14)*. However, it is also now a major supplier of own-label whiskey to other customers. The company's speciality is older, higher proof bourbons, which are traditional in character,

HEAVEN HILL AND THE BERNHEIM DISTILLERY

A Heaven Hill Distillery had been built in 1890, but the present Heaven Hill company was established in 1935, soon after the repeal of Prohibition, by five Shapira brothers. They constructed a distillery close to the Loretto road, just south of Bardstown.

Descendants of the Shapira brothers control the firm to this day, and Heaven Hill is the USA's largest independent producer of distilled spirits to remain in family ownership. It is also the last family-owned distillery in Kentucky.

The history of whiskey-making features many distillery fires, but the most spectacular and destructive in recent times occurred on 7 November 1996, when the Heaven Hill Distillery and warehouses were almost completely destroyed by fire, and over 340,000 litres (75,000 gallons) of maturing spirit was lost.

While future plans were being considered, production capacity was provided for Heaven Hill by Brown-Forman and Jim Beam, and eventually it was decided that rather than rebuild on the old site, Diageo's Bernheim Distillery in Louisville would be purchased instead.

Bernheim was built in 1992, and is one of the most technologically

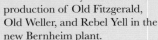

Bernheim Original

advanced distilleries in the States. It was constructed on the site of the old Astor and Belmont distilleries (respectively home to Henry Clay Bourbon and the Old Charter and IW Harper brands), which the Guinness subsidiary United Distillers had purchased and subsequently demolished. United Distillers also closed the Stitzel-Weller Distillery in Shively and concentrated production of Old Fitzgerald, Old Weller, and Rebel Yell in the new Bernheim plant.

In 1997 Guinness merged with GrandMet to form the giant Diageo organization. Bourbon was not a global priority for Diageo, whose US distilling interests were soon concentrated around the George Dickel brand of Tennessee whiskey *(see p191)*, along with a number of bourbons that were made under contract. This paved the way for Heaven Hill's acquisition of the Bernheim Distillery in 1999.

A stylish new heritage centre now stands close to the site of the old Heaven Hill Distillery.

full-bodied, and complex. Heaven Hill is also the only remaining national producer of corn whiskeys, including both aged brands, such as Mellow Corn, and un-aged bottlings such as Georgia Moon. While fermenting, mashing, and distilling the Heaven Hill range occurs at Bernheim, ageing, bottling, and shipping still take place in Bardstown. The Bourbon Heritage Centre is also located there, amongst Heaven Hill's "rickhouses", where the world's second-largest stock of bourbon (as many as 600,000 barrels) matures.

Alongside Bernheim Original Straight – the only straight wheat whiskey in the US market – the distillery also produce a couple of interesting rye whiskeys. Rittenhouse Rye, once associated with the rye whiskey-making heartland of Pennsylvania, now survives in Kentucky, its mash bill comprising 51 per cent rye, 37 per cent corn, and 12 per cent barley. Complementing Rittenhouse's "Pennsylvania style", a "Maryland", or "Potomac style" of rye also survives in the shape of Pikesville Supreme Straight.

Among the Heaven Hill bourbons is Very Special Old Fitzgerald – a complex and well-balanced spirit, made with some wheat in the mash bill rather than rye. Another in the range is Henry McKenna Single Barrel, which uses a family recipe brought by McKenna from Ireland in 1837 and first used in America when he settled in Fairfield, Kentucky and founded a distillery in 1855.

BERNHEIM ORIGINAL STRAIGHT WHEAT WHISKEY
45% ABV ● Bernheim exhibits toast and butter on the spicy nose, with freshly sawn wood, toffee, vanilla, and a hint of mint on the palate. The finish is good and long, drying, and nicely spicy.

GEORGIA MOON 40% ABV
Bottled in a mason jar, and with a label that promises that the contents have spent less than 30 days maturing, Georgia Moon harks back to the old moonshining days. Consequently, drinkers should not expect something sophisticated from this one! After an initial tang of sour liquor on the nose, the smell of sweet corn follows. The palate suggests cabbage water and plums, plus developing sweeter "candy corn" notes. The finish is extremely short.

HEAVEN HILL OLD STYLE BOURBON 4 YEAR-OLD
40% ABV ● This is an excellent and competitively priced "entry level" bourbon, with a nose of oranges and corn bread, a sweet, oily mouth-feel, with vanilla and corn featuring on the well-balanced palate.

HENRY McKENNA SINGLE BARREL KENTUCKY STRAIGHT BOURBON WHISKEY
10 YEAR-OLD 50% ABV
This single barrel whiskey boasts an interesting blend of citrus fruits, charcoal, vanilla, and caramel on the nose. The contrasts continue in the palate, where spices and charred oak vie pleasingly with mint and honey.

Heaven Hill Old Style Bourbon

Heaven Hill racks its barrels three high on 16 floors; summer temperatures reach 48.9°C (120°F) at the top.

MELLOW CORN KENTUCKY STRAIGHT CORN WHISKEY 50% ABV
Wood varnish and vanilla, along with floral and herbal notes, are what greet you on the nose. The palate is big and oily and fruity, with toffee apples. More fruit, cinder toffee, and an understated trace of vanilla complete the finish. Young and boisterous.

PIKESVILLE SUPREME STRAIGHT RYE WHISKEY 4 YEAR-OLD 40% ABV
The nose presents bubble gum, fruit, and wood varnish, while on the palate there is more bubble gum, spice, oak, and an overt vanilla theme. The finish mixes more lingering vanilla with ripe oranges.

RITTENHOUSE RYE WHISKEY
50% ABV ● The nose is notably spicy, with nuts and oranges. On the palate, powerful spices and oak meet lemon and then a much sweeter note of lavender and violet. As for the finish: it is a long, bitter rye classic.

VERY SPECIAL OLD FITZGERALD KENTUCKY STRAIGHT BOURBON WHISKEY 12-YEAR-OLD 45% ABV
The nose is rich, fruity, and leathery, while the palate exhibits sweet and fruity notes that are balanced by spices and oak. The finish is long and drying, with vanilla fading to oak.

Rittenhouse Rye Whiskey

There are **76 barrel houses** at Jack Daniel's, holding 190 million litres (42 million gallons) of spirit.

JACK DANIEL'S

✉ 280 Lynchburg Road, Lynchburg, Tennessee
🖱 www.jackdaniels.com
🚪 Open to visitors

The Jack Daniel's enterprise operates on a grand scale, with a distillery output of some 90 million litres (20 million gallons) of alcohol per annum. Ten million cases of whiskey are exported annually to 150 different countries, with around 50 per cent destined for Europe. Seventy-six warehouses contain 190 million litres (42 million gallons) of maturing spirit, and seven on-site bottling lines are in operation.

The Jack Daniel's mash bill is high on corn, which constitutes 80 per cent of the total; the remainder comprises 12 per cent rye and eight per cent barley malt. Like George Dickel, Jack Daniel's uses a version of the Lincoln County Process of charcoal mellowing prior to being filled into barrels.

Jack Daniel's Old No. 7

Jack Daniel's was able to resume distilling in Tennessee in 1938.

Every year, hundreds of thousands of visitors flock to Lynchburg in pilgrimage to Jack Daniel's – the man and the whiskey. Ironically, while they are able to purchase any number of varied souvenirs emblazoned with the Jack Daniel's name, they cannot buy the whiskey. Lynchburg is situated in Moore County, which is officially "dry".

Gentleman Jack

In fact, of Tennessee's 95 counties, spirits may legally be distilled only in Moore, Coffee, and Lincoln counties.

🥃 **JACK DANIEL'S OLD NO. 7** 43% AbV
Jack Daniel's presents a powerful nose of vanilla, smoke, and liquorice. On the palate it offers oily cough mixture and treacle, with a final kick of maple syrup and burnt wood in the surprisingly long finish. Not particularly complex, but muscular and decidedly singular.

🥃 **GENTLEMAN JACK** 40% AbV
Gentleman Jack is characterized by being charcoal-mellowed twice: once before barrelling and again after ageing for about four years. The result is a nose that is considerably more mellow, muted, and fruity than that of Old No. 7. The palate yields more fruit, along with caramel, liquorice, vanilla, and a whiff of smoke.

🥃 **JACK DANIEL'S SINGLE BARREL TENNESSEE WHISKEY** 47% ABV
Introduced in 1997, Single Barrel is charming and smooth on the nose, with notes of peach, vanilla, nuts, and oak. The comparatively dry palate offers depth, richness, and elegance, with oily corn, liquorice, malt, and oak. Malt, oak, and a touch of rye spice are present in the lengthy finish.

JIM BEAM

✉ Clermont and Boston Distilleries Clermont Distillery, 149 Happy Hollow Road, Clermont, Kentucky
🖱 www.jimbeam.com
🚪 Open to visitors

The principal Jim Beam Distillery is located at Clermont, in Bullit County, 25 miles (40 km) south of Louisville in Kentucky, and not far from the "bourbon capital" of Bardstown.

THE JACK DANIEL'S STORY

Jack Daniel's has become a truly iconic brand, known all over the world. It is America's best-selling whiskey, and is famous as the rock star's drink of choice. Often consumed with cola, "JD" is one of the few brown spirits consistently popular with younger drinkers.

The story of Jack Daniel's begins with the birth of Jasper Newton Daniel in Lincoln County, Tennessee in 1846. Legend has it that "Jack" did not get on with his stepmother, and at the age of six left home. He eventually came to live with local farmer and Lutheran lay preacher Dan Call. Call ran a whiskey still, and one of his slaves, Nearest Green, taught young Jack the art of distilling. When pressure from Call's congregation led him to choose religion over whiskey making, he sold the still to Jack, who was aged just 14 at the time. Despite his youth, Jack Daniel clearly already possessed the sharp business brain that was to see him succeed so well in the future. He soon moved the still, settling on a site next to Cave Spring, in an area close to Lynchburg known as The Hollow. Jack was drawn to the area by the spring's abundant supply of pure limestone water, and he christened the new plant the Jack Daniel Old Time Distillery.

In 1887 Jack was joined in the business by his nephew, Lem Motlow, and it was Lem who was responsible for moving the distilling operation to

Jack Daniel's statue now resides in the visitors centre.

St Louis in 1910, when Tennessee went "dry". Jack died shortly after, in 1911, following a bizarre accident in which he kicked a stubborn safe door in temper and got a foot infection, which led first to amputation, then to gangrene, and finally to death. The distillery continued to operate in St Louis until 1919, when National Prohibition intervened. It was not until 1938 that Motlow and his sons were granted permission to recommence distilling at the Old Time Distillery. They developed the company extremely successfully in the difficult years after the repeal of Prohibition, and in 1956 sold the enterprise to the Brown-Forman Distillery Corporation for $18 million.

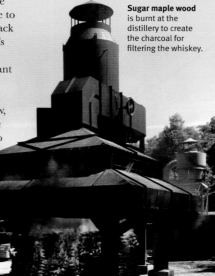

Sugar maple wood is burnt at the distillery to create the charcoal for filtering the whiskey.

THE JIM BEAM STORY

The origins of Jim Beam date back to the 18th century, when German-born farmer and miller Jacob Boehm travelled west into Bourbon County from Virginia, carrying with him his copper pot still. There he settled down and created a small-scale distillery.

Jacob is reputed to have sold his first barrel of whiskey for cash in 1795. He subsequently moved his distilling operation to Washington County when he inherited land there from his father-in-law.

Jacob had two sons, named John and David, and during David Beam's time at the helm, the distillery adopted the "Old Tub Distillery" name. In 1854 David's son, who was also named David, moved the venture to Nelson County, where the Clear Springs Distillery was established close to a railroad.

Jim Beam himself was Jacob Boehm's great-grandson, and was christened James Beauregard Beam. He entered the family firm in 1880 at the age of 16, and trade prospered for the distillery in the years before Prohibition forced the closure of Clear

Jim Beam and associates at the Clermont Distillery in Kentucky.

Springs. Jim Beam established the present Clermont Distillery close to Clear Springs soon after the repeal of Prohibition at the end of 1933, despite being 70 years old at the time. Jim died in 1947, five years after the Jim Beam name began to be used on the bottle labels. The family connection carries on to this day through Fred Noe, great-grandson of Jim and a seventh generation Beam family member. Fred's father was the late, legendary Booker Noe, a larger than life figure who is acknowledged as one of the true greats of bourbon distilling, and the man responsible for developing small-batch bourbon.

In contrast to the company's industrial-scale distilleries, the Jim Beam American Outpost recalls the older traditions of distilling at a leisurely pace.

The Jim Beam American Outpost is a major tourist attraction, though the Clermont Distillery itself is staunchly industrial in appearance and scale.

Jim Beam is the best-selling bourbon brand in the world, and the James B Beam Distilling Company has belonged to Fortune Brands Inc. (formerly American Brands) since 1967. It was formerly in family ownership for around 150 years before being sold in 1945 to Harry Blum of Chicago, previously a partner in the company for several years.

Illinois-based Fortune Brands actually operates two Jim Beam distilleries: at Clermont and in nearby Boston, where the distillery dates from 1953. Together, the two plants have an annual capacity of 40 million litres (nearly 9 million gallons). All of the spirit bottled as Booker's (see p213) is distilled at the Boston Distillery and Jim Beam White Label is a 50/50 mix of bourbon from Clermont and Boston.

In 1987, American Brands acquired Frankfort-based National Distillers, and with it the Old Crow, Old Taylor and Old Grand-Dad distilleries and brands (see p216). The three distilleries

Jim Beam White label

were closed down, and their whiskeys are now distilled in Jim Beam's distilleries at Clermont and Boston.

The Jim Beam house style is characterized by high proportions of rye and corn in the mash bill; the rest is made up of malted barley. In addition to the White and Black labels, and the Kentucky Straight Bourbon and Straight Rye, the distillery also produces a range of specialist whiskies, such as Baker's Kentucky, Booker's Kentucky, Basil Hayden's, Knob Creek, Old Crow, Old Grand-Dad, and Old Taylor. Information about these bourbons can all be found in the Brands section (pp212–17).

🥃 **JIM BEAM WHITE LABEL KENTUCKY STRAIGHT BOURBON WHISKEY 4 YEAR-OLD** 40% ABV Vanilla and delicate floral notes on the nose. Initially sweet, with restrained vanilla, then drier, oaky notes develop, fading into furniture polish and soft malt in the finish.

Nosing is vital to monitor consistency in any distillery, and Jim Beam is no exception.

🥃 **JIM BEAM BLACK LABEL KENTUCKY STRAIGHT BOURBON WHISKEY 8 YEAR-OLD** 45% ABV Greater depth than White Label, with more complex fruit and vanilla notes, along with liquorice, vanilla, and sweet rye.

🥃 **JIM BEAM'S CHOICE KENTUCKY STRAIGHT BOURBON WHISKEY 5 YEAR-OLD** 40% ABV In the style of Tennessee whiskey, this is charcoal-filtered, after maturing. It is soft and silky, with caramel notes.

🥃 **JIM BEAM STRAIGHT RYE WHISKEY** 40% ABV Light, perfumed, and aromatic on the nose, with lemon and mint. Oily in the mouth, with soft fruits, honey, and rye on the palate; the finish is drying and spicy.

Jim Beam Black Label

Jim Beam's Clermont Distillery is industrial in look and scale.

MAKER'S MARK

✉ 3350 Burks Springs Road, Loretto, Kentucky

🖰 www.makersmark.com

⚜ Open to visitors

Maker's Mark Distillery is located on the banks of Hardin's Creek, near Loretto, in Marion County, and was established in 1805 as a distillery and grist mill. It is the USA's oldest working distillery on its original site and in 1980 was declared a National Historic Landmark.

Exactly two centuries earlier, Robert Samuels had migrated to Kentucky, where he farmed and distilled whiskey. In 1844 Robert's grandson, TW Samuels, built a commercial distillery at Deatsville, Kentucky, and the "secret" family mash recipe was subsequently handed down from one generation of distillers to the next.

In 1943, the old Deatsville distillery was sold, and a decade later Bill Samuels Sr purchased the dilapidated Star Hill Farm and the Happy Hollow Distillery near Loretto. He was keen to create a particularly smooth and refined bourbon, and using the example of the Old Fitzgerald brand, he developed a new recipe based on locally grown maize and malted barley, coupled with red winter wheat, rather than the traditional rye. This had the effect of reducing the "burn" left by many bourbons of the time, and resulted in a comparatively soft and gentle spirit, which becomes very mellow as it matures. Samuels perfected the recipe, not in a distillery but in the family kitchen, baking bread and experimenting with different grains.

The Scottish spelling of "whisky" has been employed since the outset in recognition of the family's Scottish ancestry. It is Bill Samuels' wife, Marge, who is credited with naming the new whisky. As a collector of pewter, she was accustomed to searching for "the mark of the maker". She was also a collector of

Every aspect of Maker's Mark, right down to these spirits safes, was duplicated to enlarge the distillery in 2001.

Maker's Mark Straight Bourbon

MAKER'S MARK BOURBON MANHATTAN

Ingredients:
2 measures (50 ml) of Maker's Mark bourbon
1 measure (25 ml) of sweet vermouth
2 dashes of Angostura bitters.
½ (about 10 ml) of maraschino cherry syrup (from the jar)

Method:: put all ingredients into a mixing glass filled with ice; stir thoroughly for about 30 seconds. Strain into a cocktail glass, and garnish with a twist of orange (squeezed) and a maraschino cherry.

The original barrel warehouses at Maker's Mark Hardin's Creek site are about 100 years old.

bottles of cognac, many of which were sealed with colourful wax, and the hand-dipped red wax seal was soon adopted for Maker's Mark bottles.

In 1981 Maker's Mark passed out of family ownership to Hiram Walker & Sons, and ultimately came into the hands of Allied Domecq. Since 2005, however, Maker's Mark has been owned by Fortune Brands Inc., who also own Jim Beam.

Due to the growing popularity of the whisky, the Hardin's Creek site was expanded in 2000–2001, duplicating, in exact detail, the distillery as it had been restored in the 1960s. This effectively doubled production capacity.

MAKER'S MARK KENTUCKY STRAIGHT BOURBON WHISKY
45% ABV • A subtle, complex, clean nose, with vanilla and spice, a delicate floral note of roses, plus lime and cocoa beans. Medium in body, Maker's Mark offers a palate of fresh fruit, spices, eucalyptus, and ginger cake. The finish features more spices, fresh oak with a hint of smoke, and a final flash of peach cheesecake. A delicate and circumspect bourbon.

Wild Turkey Distillery has been owned since 1980 by the French drinks company Pernod Ricard.

WILD TURKEY

✉ **US Highway 62 East, Lawrenceburg, Kentucky**
🖰 **www.wildturkeybourbon.com**
🏛 **Open to visitors**

Wild Turkey's Boulevard Distillery is situated on Wild Turkey Hill, above the Kentucky River in Anderson County. The plant was first established in 1905 by three Ripy brothers, whose family had been making whiskey in the nearby distilling centre of Tyrone since 1869.

Today, Wild Turkey is created under the watchful eye of legendary master distiller Jimmy Russell – one of the great characters of the bourbon world, and now

TURKEY COLLINS

Ingredients:
2 measures (50 ml) of Wild Turkey
1 measure (25 ml) of lemon juice
1 measure (25 ml) of sugar syrup
5 measures (125 ml) of soda water

Method:
Mix the ingredients in a shaker, then pour into a tall (Collins) glass over ice. Garnish with a maraschino cherry, an orange slice, and a lemon slice.

a leading ambassador for the bourbon industry all over the world. James C Russell, to give him his full name, has worked at Wild Turkey since 1954, and both his father and grandfather were also distillers. Fittingly, Jimmy's son Eddie has followed in the family tradition too.

Wild Turkey uses the smallest percentage of corn of any Kentucky bourbon, with greater quantities of rye and malt to achieve a fuller bodied and generally more flavoursome whiskey. The same mash bill and yeast strain is used for the entire Wild Turkey range.

The spirit is distilled at a comparatively low proof (56–57.5 per cent) because Jimmy Russell likens making great whiskey to making great soup: "If you cook it longer at a lower temperature, you retain the best flavours." An additional influence on the character of the matured spirit is that the "white dog" (the new make, clear spirit) is filled into heavily charred barrels. The heavy charring contributes significantly to Wild Turkey's signature flavour.

The most readily available expression of Wild Turkey in most markets, "101", is notable for possessing a remarkably soft yet rich aroma for such a high proof

THE WILD TURKEY NAME

The Wild Turkey brand was conceived in 1940, when Thomas McCarthy, president of Austin Nichols (a specialist wine and spirits business), chose a quantity of 101 proof (50.5 per cent ABV) straight bourbon from his company stocks to take along on a wild turkey shooting weekend. For many years what is now the Wild Turkey Distillery was JTS Brown Distillery, and produced Wild Turkey bourbon under contract. Then, in 1971, it was acquired by Austin Nichols Distilling Co., and the name was changed.

The Wild Turkey brand has been owned by Pernod Ricard since 1980.

Wild Turkey's spirits safe, where the stillsman can test the flowing spirit and make the "cut".

whiskey – no doubt due in part to its eight years of maturation. Wild Turkey "80" was introduced to the range in 1974, and, according to Jimmy Russell, this expression is ideal served on the rocks, and perfect for drinkers who enjoy their bourbon with a mixer.

The Kentucky Spirit is a single barrel whiskey, with each barrel being personally selected by Jimmy Russell, who sets out to choose examples that are fuller bodied than normal, with rich vanilla flavours and a hint of sweetness. Jimmy maintains that 50.5 per cent (101 proof) is the optimum bottling strength for Wild Turkey whiskey.

Launched in 1991, Rare Breed comprises whiskeys aged from six to 12 years. Russell himself believes that

10 years is a wonderful stage of maturity for a bourbon. His son Eddie agrees, and indeed it was Eddie who suggested offering the 10 year-old expression.

🍂 **WILD TURKEY KENTUCKY STRAIGHT BOURBON WHISKEY 80 PROOF** 40% ABV ● The soft, sweet nose hints at corn, while on the palate this is a very traditional whiskey, nicely balancing sweet caramel and vanilla flavours.

🍂 **WILD TURKEY KENTUCKY STRAIGHT BOURBON WHISKEY 101 PROOF 8-YEAR-OLD** 50.5% ABV The nose offers caramel, vanilla, fresh, soft fruits, and a touch of spice, while in the mouth this is a decidedly full-bodied, rich, and robust bourbon, with more vanilla, fresh fruit, and spice, as well as brown sugar and honey. Notes of oak develop in the long and powerful, yet smooth finish.

🍂 **WILD TURKEY KENTUCKY SPIRIT** 50.5% ABV ● The nose is fresh and attractive, with oranges and notes of rye, while on the palate it is complex, with almonds, honey, toffee, more oranges, and a hint of leather. The finish is long

Wild Turkey 8 Year-Old Bourbon

and initially quite sweet, gradually darkening and becoming a little treacly.

🍂 **WILD TURKEY RARE BREED** 54.2% ABV ● As with "101", both the aroma and flavour are notably smooth for a high-strength bourbon. The complex nose is initially slightly assertive, with nuts, oranges, spices, and floral notes. Honey, oranges, vanilla, tobacco, mint, and molasses make for a complex palate to match the nose. The finish is long and nutty, with spicy and peppery rye.

🍂 **WILD TURKEY RUSSELL'S RESERVE 10 YEAR-OLD** 50.5% ABV ● The nose boasts toffee, vanilla, oak, rye, and a hint of worn leather, while the massive body gives spicy and citric notes in the mouth, with traces of cumin and almonds.

🍂 **WILD TURKEY KENTUCKY STRAIGHT RYE** 50.5% ABV ● Wild Turkey's offering of a straight rye has a pleasingly firm nose that's crammed with fruit. The body is full and rich, while the well-balanced palate offers intense spices and ripe fruit. The finish is profoundly

WOODFORD'S PEPPER AND CROW

Woodford Reserve traces its origins back to 1797, when Elijah Pepper moved from Virginia to Versailles, where he made corn whiskey in a small distillery behind the county courthouse. In 1812 he moved his operation to the present site on Glenn's Creek in order to take advantage of the excellent supply of pure limestone water.

Two years after Elijah Pepper's death in 1831, his son Oscar hired Scottish-born chemist James Crow to work at the "Old Pepper Distillery" (later christened the "Oscar Pepper Distillery"). The bourbon industry owes much to the work of Crow. He recognized the importance of consistency in whiskey making, perfected the "sour-mash" process, and discovered the benefits of maturing spirit in charred oak barrels. Crow worked as head distiller for 29 years.

The whiskey produced on the stills at Woodford Reserve became a favourite of writers Mark Twain and Walt Whitman, and of the 7th US president, Andrew Jackson.

Woodford Reserve is the new incarnation of a distillery that had lay silent since the early 1970s.

WOODFORD RESERVE

✉ 7855 McCracken Pike, Versailles, Kentucky
🖰 www.woodfordreserve.com
⛴ Open to visitors

Woodford Reserve is the smallest distillery operating in Kentucky, and is unique in using a triple distillation method. This employs three copper pot stills – built in Scotland by the renowned Speyside coppersmiths Forsyth's. Woodford is the only bourbon distillery to use exclusively copper pot stills in the distillation process, the last having been the Old Crow distillery prior to its closure during Prohibition.

Woodford Reserve is operated by the Louisville-based Brown-Forman Distillery Corporation, which also owns Jack Daniel's. The plant stands on the banks of Glenn's Creek, near the late 19th-century town of Versailles, in the heart of Kentucky's bluegrass thoroughbred racehorse breeding country.

The distillery was in the Pepper family from the late 18th century until the 1870s, when it was acquired by Frankfort banker James Graham and French wine merchant Leopold Labrot. Apart from during the hiatus of the Prohibition years, they ran the plant until 1940.

Then in 1941 Brown-Forman bought the site and more than 25,000 barrels of high quality bourbon from Labrott & Graham for an extremely modest $75,000. However, in the postwar years bourbon sales went into decline, and many distilleries closed down. The small distillery by Glenn's Creek was no exception, and in 1972 it was sold to a company called Freeman Hockensmith, who proceeded to make the car fuel substitute gasohol in the distillery for a short period. When that venture failed, the distillery lay silent for the next 23 years.

However, when the distillery had been sold to Hockensmith, it was with the proviso that Brown-Forman could buy it back at a future date. So when, in 1994, Hockensmith died – and with interest in small-batch bourbon rising – Brown-Forman bought back the semi-derelict site, and went on to spend $10.5 million restoring it.

After almost a quarter of a century, the Labrott & Graham distillery reopened, and in 2003 the present Woodford Reserve name was adopted for the distillery and its whiskey. Between 40 and 50 barrels a day are filled here, and to ensure consistency, the Woodford spirit is blended with a quantity of Old Forrester Straight Bourbon from Brown-Forman's Louisville Distillery (*see p188*); the resultant whiskey is bottled at six to seven years of age. The mash bill comprises 72 per cent corn, 18 per cent rye and 12 per cent malted barley.

MINT JULEP

Woodford Reserve was introduced to the UK in 1998, and soon became a favourite with cocktail makers. Here's the distillery's recipe for a classic Mint Julep.

Ingredients:
2 measures (50 ml) of Woodford Reserve
2 heaped teaspoons of caster sugar
10–12 mint leaves

Method: into a large glass, pour the sugar, a splash of the Woodford, and the mint leaves. Muddle the mint (using the end of a rolling pin or similar object) to release the oils. Fill the glass with crushed ice and pour in the rest of the bourbon. Stir briskly and top up the glass with more crushed ice if necessary. Garnish with a couple of large sprigs of mint.

🍸 **WOODFORD RESERVE DISTILLER'S SELECT KENTUCKY STRAIGHT BOURBON** 45.2% ABV
Elegant yet robust on the nose, perfumed, with milk chocolate raisins, dried fruit, burnt sugar, ginger, and a little saddle soap. Complex palate: fragrant, fruity with raspberries, camomile, and ginger. The finish displays lingering vanilla notes and peppery oak. Cognac-like until the vanilla kicks in.

Woodford's Distiller's Select Bourbon

The fertile fields of Kentucky form the heartland of American whiskey production, providing the grain for distilling as well as the pure spring water that is so essential to whiskey making.

St George Spirits was established in 1982 after its founder Jörg Rupf gave up studying law at the University of California.

MICRO-DISTILLERIES

A micro-distillery, or craft distillery, is defined as one that manufactures fewer than 500 barrels of spirit per year. A decade ago there were only a handful, while today there are more than 60, producing a wide range of spirits.

ANCHOR DISTILLING COMPANY

✉ 1705 Mariposa Street, San Francisco, California
🍶 www.anchorbrewing.com

Fritz Maytag is one of the pioneers of the American micro drinks movement. As the man who's been largely responsible for the revival of craft brewing in the USA, he has been running San Francisco's historic Anchor Steam Brewery since 1965. He also makes York Creek wine and port at his vineyard, which straddles the famous Napa and Sonoma wine-producing areas just to the north of San Francisco.

In 1994 Maytag added a small distillery to his brewery on San Francisco's Portrero Hill. His aim in doing this has been to "re-create the original whiskey of America". And by that, he means making small batches of spirit in traditional pot stills, using 100 per cent rye malt.

🍶 **OLD PORTRERO SINGLE MALT WHISKEY** 62.1% ABV ● Aged for one year only in new, lightly-toasted oak barrels, Old Portrero Single Malt is described by Maytag as having an "18th-century style". It is floral and nutty on the nose, with vanilla and spice. Oily and smooth on the palate, with mint, honey, chocolate, and pepper evident in the lengthy finish.

🍶 **OLD PORTRERO SINGLE MALT STRAIGHT RYE WHISKEY** 62.6% ABV Aged for a little longer – three years in this case – in new, charred oak barrels, this "19th-century style" whiskey, to quote Maytag again, boasts nuts, buttery vanilla, sweet oak, and pepper on the nose. Complex in the mouth – oily, sweet and spicy, with caramel, oak, and spicy rye notes in the finish.

BELMONT FARMS OF VIRGINIA, INC.

✉ 13490 Cedar Run Rd, Culpeper, Virginia
🍶 www.virginiamoonshine.com

For the past 15 years, corn grown on Belmont Farm has been used to make Virginia Lightning Corn Whiskey (50 per cent ABV). The mash is cooked to an old family recipe, and is then distilled in a 9,000-litre (2,000-gallon) copper still that dates back to the 1930s. Finally, it passes through a "doubler" ("analyser still" in the UK) to increase its strength and remove impurities before being bottled.

CHARBAY

✉ 4001 Spring Mountain Road, Napa Valley, St Helena, California
🍶 www.charbay.com

Father Miles and son Marko Karakasevic are 12th and 13th-generation winemakers and distillers. Among their spirits is Charbay Double Barrel Hop-Flavoured Whiskey, which is double distilled using European malted barley in the mash, and hops for aromatic effect. This is true small-batch distilling, with just 24 barrels being filled from the first batch of spirit, which is offered at barrel strength.

🍶 **CHARBAY DOUBLE-BARREL RELEASE ONE** 64% ABV ● Honey, vanilla, oranges, oak, and smoky spice on the nose; citrus spice and honey on palate; long, vanilla and dried fruit finish.

CLEAR CREEK

✉ 2389 NW Wilson Street, Portland, Oregon
🍶 www.clearcreek distillery.com

Steve McCarthy established Clear Creek Distillery more than 20 years ago because he wanted to find the best use for fruit from the

Clear Creek's McCarthy's Single Malt

McCarthy family's orchard. During his travels in Europe he became acquainted with a number of traditional European spirits, among them an *eau de vie* (spirit) made from Williams pears. He has now been distilling for 10 years, and his whiskey is made from peat-malted barley bought in from Scotland. In fact, he claims that "the whiskey would be a single malt Scotch if [only] Oregon were Scotland."

McCarthy's Oregon Single Malt Whiskey is close in style to Lagavulin single malt from Islay *(see p104)*. It is initially matured in ex-sherry casks for two or three years, then for six to 12 months in barrels made from air-dried Oregon oak.

🍂 MCCARTHY'S OREGON SINGLE MALT WHISKEY 40% ABV
Kippery and spicy on the nose – with a hint of sulphur, peat, and vanilla – Oregon is big-bodied and oily. The meaty palate is smoky-sweet, with dry oak, malt, spice, and salt in the lengthy finish.

COPPER FOX

📬 9 River Lane, Sperryville, Virginia
🔗 www.copperfox.biz

In 2000 Rick Wasmund paid a visit to Scotland with the idea of starting up his own micro-distillery back in Virginia on his return. He spent six weeks working at Bowmore Distillery on Islay *(see p99)*, then purchased an existing Virginia distillery to launch Copper Fox Whisky in the spring of 2003. Wasmund malts barley in the traditional Scottish manner, on a malting floor, and then dries it, not using peat, but with the infusion of apple, cherry, and oak wood. It is distilled twice in one-barrel batches.

Wasmund has developed a unique "chip and barrel ageing process", which consists of bags of charred chunks of apple, cherry, and oak wood being suspended in the spirit as it ages in the barrel. The effect serves to speed up maturation dramatically, and the whisky is usually aged for just four months prior to bottling. Copper Fox moved to its present new-build site at Sperryville in 2005, and 2006 saw the release of the first single malt using Wasmund's malting and maturing innovations.

🍂 WASMUND'S SINGLE MALT WHISKY 48% ABV ● A nose of honey, vanilla, leather, and watermelon. The palate offers a well-balanced blend

Wasmund's Single Malt

of sweet and dry flavours, with notes of smoke, nuts, spices, and vanilla.

EDGEFIELD

📬 2126 SW Halsey Street, Troutdale, Oregon
🔗 www.mcmenamins.com

Located in a former dry store for root vegetables, Edgefield distillery is operated by the McMenamin's hotel and pub group. The distillery has been in production since February 1998, producing not only whiskey, but also brandy and gin. According to McMenamin's, the copper and stainless-steel

THE MICRO PHENOMENON

During the 1980s and 90s, Scotch whisky producers developed a growing market for single malts, and it wasn't long before the large, commercial US distillers began to emulate them by developing small-batch bourbons. Similarly, micro, or "craft", distillers saw the opportunity to create notably characterful and individual whiskeys on a small scale.

Not bound by convention, and with flexibility due to the size of their operations, they could experiment with ingredients and processes. With a blend of historical reverence and modern science, they have taken up the baton of the rye revival and also championed single malts – one of the most interesting developments on the scene. Hop-flavoured and fruit-flavoured whiskeys have appeared on the market, along with "legal moonshine" and something very close to an Islay single malt.

The phenomenon began in California and Oregon, often on the back of micro-brewing enterprises, but has since spread out to embrace a number of states, including Kansas, Massachusetts, New York, and Ohio – states that either have very little heritage of distilling or lost their distilleries many years ago. It seems likely that the trend will continue, too, as the desire to seek out all things quirky, niche, and hand-crafted continues unabated among discerning drinkers.

Clear Creek distills with peat-malted barley from Scotland to create an Islay-like American whiskey.

still they use "resembles a hybrid of a 19th-century diving suit and an oversized coffee urn". Its design was the work of Holstein in Germany, the world's oldest surviving manufacturer of spirit stills.

HOGSHEAD WHISKEY 46% ABV
Banana and malt are evident on the sweet, floral nose, with sweet vanilla and caramel notes on the palate. Barley, honey, and oak come into play in the medium-length finish.

HIGH PLAINS INC.

✉ 1807 South 2nd Street, Leavenworth, Kansas
🖰 www.highplainsinc.com

Seth Fox, a former process engineer and amateur distiller, converted the profitable electronics company he started in 1984 into High Plains in 2004, producing the first liquor to be distilled legally in Kansas since the state banned its manufacture in 1880. Fox is the seventh generation of a family with a history of illicit distilling in the hills of North Carolina. "I'm not the first to do it in my family," he says, "but I am the first to do it legally."

Having initially specialized in vodka, marketed under the Most Wanted brand, Fox introduced Most Wanted Kansas Bourbon Whiskey and Most Wanted Pioneer Whiskey in 2006.

ISAIAH MORGAN

✉ 45 Winery Lane, Summersville, West Virginia
🖰 www.kirkwood-wine.com

Isaiah Morgan is notable for being the first legal distillery in southwest Virginia. It was established by Rodney Facemire in 2002, and now produces Isaiah Morgan Rye Whiskey and Southern Moon Corn Liquor. Both whiskeys are bottled white and unaged in the best moonshining traditions.

MOONSHINE

The term "moonshine" refers to illicitly-distilled liquor, usually made from corn and sugar. The sooner the spirit was removed from its place of production, the safer for all concerned, so the luxury of a period of maturation in oak barrels was eschewed in favour of filling it into mason jars while it was fresh and clear – hence the nickname "white lightning". The southern states formed the principal moonshine territory, and the craft continues to this day. The drink enjoys a rebellious reputation, and to buy a jar is to defy authority – though today it is possible to purchase "legal moonshine", such as Catdaddy (*see opposite*), Georgia Moon (*see p193*), Mountain Moonshine (*see p209*) and Southern Moon Corn Liquor (*see below*). Despite this niche market for lawful moonshine, the clichéd image persists of "good ole boys" loading up pickups and "running shine" on the dirt back roads of Tennessee and Georgia.

An illicit still is seized by officers of the law during Prohibition.

LEOPOLD BROS

✉ 523 South Main Street, Ann Arbor, Michigan
🖰 www.leopoldbros.com

Leopold Bros is a family operated small-batch distillery located in an old renovated brake factory. Its vodka, gin, and flavoured whiskeys are produced in a hand-hammered pot still.

PEACH WHISKEY 40% ABV
The juice of Rocky Mountain peaches are blended into this whiskey, resulting in a peachy-sweet spirit, with underlying oak, vanilla and raisin notes.

BLACKBERRY WHISKEY 40% ABV
Blackberry juice is added to whiskey and racked into ex-bourbon barrels for up to a year. The sweetness of the blackberries is immediately apparent, but oak and vanilla also develop, giving the whiskey complexity.

MOUNT VERNON

✉ Mount Vernon Estate, 3200 Mount Vernon Memorial Highway, Virginia; the distillery is on Route 235, 3 miles (5 km) south of Mount Vernon

🖰 www.mountvernon.org
🏛 Open to visitors

The first president of the United States, George Washington, was also a whiskey-maker, and built a distillery on his Mount Vernon estate in 1798. With five stills producing some 50,000 litres (11,000 gallons) of whiskey per year, it was one of America's largest and most profitable distilleries.

As a military man, Washington had firmly advocated the supply of spirits to his troops to combat the effects of inhospitable weather and fatigue. "The benefits arising from the moderate use of strong

At the Mount Vernon Estate a recreation has been made of George Washington's distillery.

liquor have been experienced in all armies and are not to be disputed," he wrote.

In 1939 a still believed to have come from Washington's original distillery was seized by revenue officers. It bore the legend, "Made in Bristol, England, 1783", and was discovered during a raid on an illicit whiskey-making venture run by an African-American family who were descendents of slaves on Washington's Mount Vernon estate.

Excavation and restoration work began on the distillery site during 2000, and reproduction 18th-century stills were subsequently installed in the reconstructed buildings, which opened to the public in September 2006. The stills produce 135° proof (67.5 per cent ABV) spirit to the recipe developed by James Anderson, Washington's Scottish-born farm manager, who was responsible for the construction and operation of the distillery, along with his son, John. The mash bill consists of 60 per cent rye, 35 per cent corn and 5 per cent malted barley.

In 2003 a number of distillers combined to produce a batch of whiskey in a replica 18th-century still using Washington's

rye mash bill. This was matured at Mount Vernon and is now on sale in commemorative bottlings, along with miniatures of the "new" Mount Vernon spirit.

PIEDMONT DISTILLERS INC.

✉ 203 East Murphy St, Madison, North Carolina
🖰 www.catdaddymoonshine.com

Piedmont is the only licensed distillery in North Carolina, and its Catdaddy Moonshine celebrates the state's heritage of illicit distilling. It was in 2005 that ex-New Yorker Joe Michalek established Piedmont Distillers –the first legal distillery in the Carolinas since the days before Prohibition kicked in.

"According to the lore of moonshine, only the best moonshine earns the right to be called the Catdaddy," says Michalek. The whiskey is distilled in a copper pot still and is made in very small batches that yield just 1,500 bottles each year. It is a flavoured moonshine, which uses secret ingredients that, according to Joe Michalek, are unique to his moonshine whiskey.

🍾 **CATDADDY CAROLINA MOONSHINE** 40% abv
Triple-distilled from corn, Catdaddy Moonshine is a sweet and spicy whiskey, with notes of vanilla and cinnamon.

Catdaddy Moonshine

ST GEORGE SPIRITS

✉ 2601 Monarch Street, Almeda, California
🖰 www.stgeorge spirits.com

St George Spirits was established by Jörg Rupf in 1982 to distil *eau de vie*. Brought up in the Black Forest region of Germany, Rupf moved to the USA in 1978 to study law at the University of California. He gave up a legal career, however, in favour of craft distilling. As one of the pioneers of the American micro-distilling movement, he is a widely respected figure and something of a mentor. His distillery employs two Holstein copper pot stills and uses a percentage of heavily roasted barley and some that

THE AMERICAN WHISKEY TRAIL

Mount Vernon is the only operating 18th-century-style distillery in North America. It functions as a national distilling museum and is also the gateway to the American Whiskey Trail, which encompasses historic distilling-related sites in New York, Pennsylvania, Virginia, Kentucky, and Tennessee. The Mount Vernon project has been financially supported by The Distilled Spirits Council of the United States, which represents the interests of many of the country's distillers. Its website (www.discus.org/trail) has information about the trail.

Mount Vernon estate

The handsome copper still made by Holstein is kept in sparkling condition at St George Spirits.

is smoked over alder and beech wood. Most of the single malt is matured in ex-bourbon barrels for three to five years, though a proportion is put into French oak and former port casks.

🍸 **ST GEORGE SPIRITS SINGLE MALT WHISKEY** 43% ABV • The nose offers fresh floral notes, with fruit, nuts, coffee, and vanilla. Quite delicate on the palate – sweet, nutty, and fruity, with a hint of menthol and cocoa. Vanilla and chocolate notes figure in the finish, with the merest wisp of smoke.

SAINT JAMES SPIRITS

✉ 5220 Fourth Street Unit 17, Irwindale, California
🖳 www.saintjamesspirits.com

In 1995 Jim Busuttil founded Saint James Spirits to produce a range of premium liquors. Busuttil's family has a long history of wine production, and Jim learnt his distilling skills in Germany and Switzerland. He also manages to combine running the distillery with his career as a teacher. Since 1997 he has been making a single malt whiskey called Peregrine Rock. It is produced from peated Scottish barley and matured in bourbon casks for a minimum of three years.

🍸 **PEREGRINE ROCK CALIFORNIA PURE SINGLE MALT WHISKEY** 40% ABV • Floral on the nose, with fresh fruits and a hint of

smoke. The palate is delicate and fruity, with a citric twist, while sweeter, malty, and new-mown grass notes develop in the slightly smoky finish.

STRANAHAN'S COLORADO WHISKEY

✉ 2405 Blake Street, Denver, Colorado
🖳 www.stranahans.com

Stranahan's distilling enterprise had an unlikely beginning, when volunteer fire-fighter Jess Graber tackled a neighbour's barn fire. The neighbour, George Stranahan, was a drinks connoisseur, and the result of their subsequent friendship was the establishment in March 2004 of the first licensed distillery in Colorado.

Three barrels of whiskey are produced each week, using a four-barley wash from the neighbouring Flying Dog Brewery. The spirit is filled into new, charred American oak barrels, and is aged for a minimum of two years. Each batch bottled comprises the contents of between two and six barrels.

🍸 **STRANAHAN'S COLORADO WHISKEY** 47% ABV • The nose is quite bourbon-like, with notes of caramel, liquorice, spice, and oak. The palate is slightly oily, big and sweet, with honey and spices. The comparatively short finish is quite oaky.

Stranahan's Colorado whiskey

TEMPLETON RYE

✉ Templeton Rye Spirits, Templeton, Iowa
🖳 www.templetonrye.com

Scott Bush's Templeton Rye Single Barrel Rye Whiskey came on to the market in 2006, and is distilled in a 1,400-litre (308-gallon) copper pot still before being aged in new, charred oak barrels. Bush boasts his rye is made to a "Prohibition-era recipe", and the story of the origins of Templeton Rye is an extraordinary one.

In the years of the Great Depression, a group of farmers in the Templeton area started to distil a rye whiskey illicitly in order to help boost their faltering agricultural incomes. Templeton Rye earned a widespread reputation for being a high quality spirit, and, during Prohibition, it apparently came to the attention of cohorts of Al Capone. Capone's gang began bootlegging hundreds of kegs of Templeton Rye per month, distributing it to speakeasies throughout New York and Chicago, and as far west as Denver. The story goes that Capone even orchestrated a mission to have a case of Templeton Rye smuggled to him while incarcerated in Alcatraz.

Scott Bush grew up in Western, Iowa, where his great-grandfather had an illicit still on his farm and his grandfather was one of the originators of Templeton Rye. This pedigree proved useful when Bush decided to recreate the spirit on a legal basis, and enabled him to discover the original recipe from a number of "old-timers" who were reluctant to discuss the subject with anyone else.

🍸 **TEMPLETON RYE SINGLE BARREL RYE WHISKEY** 40% Abv • The revived Templeton Rye is bright, crisp, and mildly sweet. The finish is smooth, with a long, warming finish.

TRIPLE EIGHT

✉ 5&7 Bartlett Farm Road, Nantucket, Massachusetts

🖰 www.ciscobrewers.com

Dean and Melissa Long started up their Nantucket Winery in 1981, and added the Cisco Brewery in 1995. Two years later they established the region's first micro-distillery, which takes its name from its water source – well number 888. The first single malt whiskey was distilled in 2000 and is called Notch Whiskey – "Notch" because it is not Scotch, but is produced in the Scottish style. George McClements – former distilling consultant to Bowmore distillery on Islay – was involved with the whiskey's development.

Notch is made by distilling Whale's Tale Pale Ale from the Cisco Brewery in a pot still; it is then matured in ex-bourbon barrels for five years.

TUTHILLTOWN SPIRITS

✉ 14 Gristmill Lane, Gardiner, New York

Based in a converted granary which adjoins a historic gristmill dating back to 1788, Tuthilltown distillery was set up in 2005 and is operated by Brian Lee and Ralph Erenzo.

In 1825 New York State had more than 1,000 working distilleries and produced a major share of the nation's whiskey, but today, Tuthilltown is New York's only distillery.

It produces Hudson Baby Bourbon (46 per cent ABV), made with 100 per cent New York State corn. This is the first bourbon to be made in New York, and the first legal pot-distilled whiskey to be produced in New York since Prohibition. It is described as "a mildly sweet, smooth spirit with hints of vanilla and caramel." Hudson Manhattan Rye (46 per cent ABV) is "floral, fruity, and

smooth" and works as "a perfect complement to sweet vermouth". Government Warning Rye (46 per cent ABV) – made from a mash of 100 per cent rye – is described as "grassy and soft – perfect sipping rye."

WEST VIRGINIA DISTILLING

✉ 1425 Saratoga Ave, Suite C, Morgantown, West Virginia

🖰 www.mountainmoonshine.com

Lawyer and entrepreneur Payton Fireman and his friend Bo McDaniel run West Virginia Distilling. They are dedicated to producing legal moonshine in the best traditions of West Virginia, which boasts a distilling heritage dating back to the late 1700s. Payton's operation is West Virginia's first licensed distilled spirits plant, and Mountain Moonshine Old Oak Recipe Spirit Whiskey (50 per cent ABV) is distilled from fermented corn mash. It is then aged with roasted oak chips for a short period

to remove the harsher flavours and "change the complexion of the whiskey from white lightning to smooth sipping," as Payton Fireman puts it.

WOODSTONE CREEK

✉ 3641 Newton Avenue, Cincinnati, Ohio

🖰 www.woodstonecreek.com

Woodstone Creek is Ohio's first micro-distillery. It is owned and run by husband-and-wife team Don and Linda Outterson. In 2001 the couple added a pot still operation to their urban winery, producing vodka, rum, and three whiskies.

The whiskies (employing the Scottish spelling) are produced in a rare, direct-fired pot still, and will all be marketed as single barrel expressions, though they are currently still maturing. Don Outterson has distilled a straight bourbon from a five grain recipe and a malt whisky; a small-batch blended whisky will also be on offer in due course.

THE WHISKEY REBELLION

General George Washington was an accomplished distiller.

In 1791 the first tax was imposed on distilled spirits in the USA. Commercial producers were assessed at a rate of six cents per gallon, but smaller, farm-based distillers were assessed at nine cents per gallon. Those most affected by this apparently unfair discrepancy were western settlers of Scottish and Irish origin, who often had little choice but to convert the grain they grew into whiskey to use as a form of currency. Unrest spread among farmers along the western frontier, from Pennsylvania to Georgia, with many refusing to pay their taxes. In the summer of 1794 this manifested itself in what became known as the Whiskey Rebellion, when excise officers were assaulted and armed groups threatened to march on Pittsburgh. The rebellion was only quelled when 13,000 troops were assembled and marched along the course of the Monongahela River, under the command of future president and distiller General George Washington (see also p206). It is sometimes claimed that it took more troops to defeat the distillers than it had to beat the British during the War of Independence!

PROHIBITION

The growth in commercial whiskey production during the 19th century meant that by 1874 in excess of 200,000 retailers across America sold whiskey, 120,000 more than just a decade previously. The Prohibitionist Party was formed in 1869, and the temperance movement became ever more influential in the face of a perceived over-consumption of alcohol.

Al Capone flouted Prohibition laws.

In 1909 no fewer than 120,000 saloons were closed down and by 1910 more than 45 per cent of the country was "dry". Many Tennessee distillers were forced to move their operations to Kentucky in order to continue. Nine years later, however, in the aftermath of World War I, Prohibition became a national issue.

Temperence posters such as this used sentiment to warn against the intoxicating effects of liquor.

NATIONAL PROHIBITION

The National Prohibition Act of 1919 enabled federal enforcement of the 18th Amendment to the American Constitution, which banned the "manufacture, sale, or transportation of intoxicating liquors". While wooing "dry" voters during the 1928 presidential election campaign, Herbert Hoover declared: "Our country has deliberately undertaken a great social and economic experiment, noble in motive and far-reaching in purpose." Its stated aims were "to reduce crime and corruption, solve social problems, reduce the tax burden created by prisons and poorhouses, and improve health and hygiene in America."

Prohibition came into force in January 1920, but far from bringing about a decline in drinking, alcohol consumption actually rose by 15 per cent. Prohibition was also the trigger for large-scale criminality, with gangs led by high-profile figures such as Al Capone making fortunes smuggling alcohol into the USA and supplying it to illegal drinking dens, known as speakeasies. New York alone was home to some 32,000 speakeasies.

Even before Prohibition bars were being closed down and stills such as this one in North Carolina were being confiscated by sheriffs.

In the period just prior to Prohibition, the city had boasted less than half that number of legal bars.

AN ALCOHOLIC CRIME WAVE

Large quantities of home-made alcohol, often disparagingly referred to as "bathtub gin", were distilled. Some of it was merely unpalatable, while the worst was lethal. A drink known as Jake, made from high-strength alcohol fluid extracted from Jamaican ginger with added wood alcohol, is estimated to have caused permanent paralysis in some 15,000 people. An astonishing 172,537 illegal stills were captured in 1925 alone, and five years later the figure rose to 282,122.

Concealed pockets were used to smuggle and sell illicit liquor.

Safer was the branded alcohol imported illegally by the likes of Captain William McCoy, who used his schooner *Arethusa* to run spirits from Nassau in the Bahamas to the coast near Boston. McCoy specialized in genuine Scotch whisky, and his name ultimately entered the English language, with "the Real McCoy" becoming synonymous with authenticity. Vast amounts of Canadian whisky were smuggled across the border into the USA, and gangster Lucky Luciano claimed that during Prohibition Sam Bronfman, president of the Seagram Company, was "bootlegging enough whisky across the Canadian border to double the size of Lake Eyrie!"

The American whiskey industry was forced to close down or diversify, with the exception of six Kentucky distilleries, which were granted licenses to produce "medicinal whiskey". Between them, they turned out 5.3 million litres (1.4 million gallons) per year of spirit, which was just as well, since Chicago doctors alone prescribed some 760,000 litres (200,000 gallons) of "medicinal" spirit in 1922.

PROHIBITION'S LEGACY

The "noble experiment" of Prohibition was manifestly a failure, and the public mood, which had initially been supportive, changed significantly as the years passed. December 1933 saw the repeal of Prohibition, after which consumption of alcohol in the USA actually fell by a quarter. As the Scottish writer Neil M Gunn wrote, "the American experiment proved that you cannot legislate a people into sobriety."

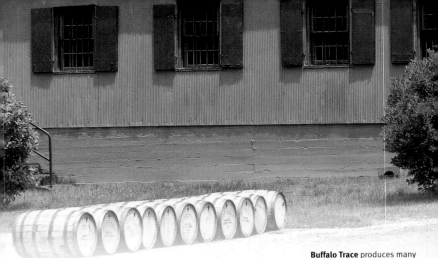

BRANDS

The USA has many brands with distinct identities that stand apart from the distilleries that produce them. Indeed their ownership and provenance may have changed over the years, reflecting the industry's fluctuations.

ANCIENT AGE

Distillery: Buffalo Trace

Operated by the Leestown Distilling Company Inc., the Ancient Age Distillery was renamed Buffalo Trace in 1999 (see p188). The Ancient Age brand is, therefore, a homage to the former distillery name.

🍶 **ANCIENT AGE 10-YEAR-OLD** 43% ABV ● Complex and fragrant on the nose, with spices, fudge, oranges, and honey. Medium-bodied and, after a slightly dry opening, the oily palate sweetens with developing notes of vanilla, cocoa, and a light char.

BAKER'S KENTUCKY BOURBON

Distillery: Jim Beam

Baker's Kentucky Straight honours Baker Beam, former Clermont distiller and cousin of Booker Noe (see over), the high profile distiller who instigated small-

batch bourbon distilling in the 1980s. It is distilled using the standard Jim Beam formula, but aged longer and offered at a higher strength.

🍶 **BAKER'S KENTUCKY STRAIGHT BOURBON 7-YEAR-OLD** 55.3% ABV Baker's is a fruity, toasty expression of the Jim Beam formula: medium-bodied, mellow, and richly flavoured, with mainstream notes of vanilla and caramel.

BASIL HAYDEN'S KENTUCKY BOURBON

Distillery: Jim Beam

Named after a pioneering Kentucky distiller, Basil Hayden's is produced to a high rye formula, as also used for Old Grand-Dad (see p216).

🍶 **BASIL HAYDEN'S KENTUCKY STRAIGHT BOURBON 8-YEAR-OLD** 40% ABV ● The nose of Basil Hayden's is light, aromatic, and spicy, with soft rye, wood polish, spices, pepper, and vanilla on the palate.

Basil Hayden's Straight Bourbon

Blantons Single Barrel Bourbon

BLANTON'S SINGLE BARREL BOURBON

Distillery: Buffalo Trace

Colonel Albert Bacon Blanton was part-owner of what is now Buffalo Trace Distillery, where he worked for 55 years. And that's reason enough for this commemorative bourbon, named in his honour.

🍶 **BLANTON'S SINGLE BARREL BOURBON 6–8 YEARS-OLD** 46.5% ABV ● The nose of Blanton's is soft, with toffee, leather, and a hint of mint.

The Buffalo Trace motif recalls the distillery's origins, at a Kentucky River crossing for herds of buffalo.

Full-bodied and rounded on the palate, this is a sweet bourbon, embracing vanilla, caramel, honey, and spices. The finish is long and creamy, with a late hint of spice.

BOOKER'S KENTUCKY BOURBON

Distillery: Jim Beam

Named after Jim Beam's grandson, Booker Noe *(see p196)*, this bourbon is made to the same Jim Beam formula as Baker's Bourbon, and is bottled unfiltered and undiluted to maintain its natural barrel favours.

BOOKER'S KENTUCKY STRAIGHT BOURBON 6 TO 8-YEAR-OLD 61.5%–63% ABV ● Big, fruity, and spicy on the nose, Booker's is sweet and slightly nutty on the palate, with heat and spiciness in the oaky finish. A big, traditional bourbon.

BULLEIT BOURBON

Distillery: Four Roses

Bulleit Bourbon originated in the 1830s, where Augustus Bulleit was a tavern-keeper and small-time distiller. His whiskey became well known in Kentucky and Indiana, but production ceased with Bulleit's death in 1860.

However, Bulleit Bourbon was revived in 1987 by family member Tom Bulleit, who began to make the whiskey to the original recipe in association with Seagram Co. Ltd in their Four Roses Distillery. Seagram subsequently took over the brand and, ultimately, it passed to Diageo. Bulleit Bourbon is now distilled for Diageo by Four Roses, and has a high rye content of 29 per cent.

BULLEIT BOURBON FRONTIER WHISKEY 45% ABV ● Rich, oaky aromas lead into a mellow flavour, gathered around vanilla and honey. The medium-length finish features vanilla and a hint of smoke.

EAGLE RARE SINGLE BARREL BOURBON

Distillery: Buffalo Trace

EAGLE RARE SINGLE BARREL KENTUCKY STRAIGHT BOURBON 10-YEAR-OLD 45% ABV ● Soft and delicate on the nose, with honey, leather, vanilla, and oak. Sweet corn and stewed fruits hit the palate, with spices, vanilla, and rye notes. The finish is long and quite sweet, with a hint of ginger.

ELIJAH CRAIG BOURBON

Distillery: Heaven Hill

Baptist minister Reverend Elijah Craig *(see p183)* is widely regarded as the "father of bourbon". The expression that honours him is produced from no more than 100 barrels. It can justifiably be considered the first "small-batch" bourbon, although it actually predates the term.

Booker's Straight Bourbon

ELIJAH CRAIG KENTUCKY STRAIGHT BOURBON 12-YEAR-OLD 47% ABV ● Elijah Craig is a classic bourbon, with sweet, mature aromas of caramel, vanilla, spice, and honey, plus a sprig of mint. Rich, full-bodied, and rounded on the mellow palate, with caramel, malt, corn, rye, and a hint of smoke. Sweet oak, liquorice, and restrained vanilla on the finish.

ELIJAH CRAIG SINGLE BARREL VINTAGE KENTUCKY STRAIGHT BOURBON 18-YEAR-OLD 45% ABV The oldest single barrel bourbon on the market, this expression has an aroma of caramel, vanilla, and oak. Almost cognac-like on the palate, it is medium-bodied, with oak, honey, and rye. The finish is long, slightly smoky and dry, with oily rye notes.

Elijah Craig 12-Year-Old

ELMER T LEE SINGLE BARREL BOURBON

Distillery: Buffalo Trace

ELMER T LEE SINGLE BARREL BOURBON 45% ABV ● Produced at Buffalo Trace and named in honour of its former master distiller, Elmer T Lee Single Barrel is aged for six to eight years. This expression offers citrus, vanilla, and sweet corn on the fragrant nose, while the palate is full and sweet, where honey and lingering caramel and cocoa notes are much in evidence.

EVAN WILLIAMS KENTUCKY BOURBON

Distillery: Heaven Hill

The second-biggest selling bourbon after Jim Beam, Evan Williams takes its name from the man considered to be Kentucky's first distiller. Evan began distilling on the banks of the Ohio River in

1783. It is the flagship brand in the Heaven Hill portfolio.

🍶 **EVAN WILLIAMS BLACK LABEL KENTUCKY STRAIGHT BOURBON 7 YEAR-OLD 43% ABV** • The nose is quite light yet aromatic, with vanilla and mint notes, while the palate is initially sweet, with caramel, malt, and developing leather and spice notes.

🍶 **EVAN WILLIAMS SINGLE BARREL VINTAGE KENTUCKY STRAIGHT BOURBON 43.3% ABV** • This is the world's only vintage-dated single barrel bourbon. It boasts an aromatic, malty nose and is medium-bodied, due to its comparatively high corn content. Vanilla, light caramel, marshmallow, and mild oak characterize the palate. There is a whiff of smoke, plus almonds and honey in the spicy, satisfying finish.

GEORGE T STAGG BOURBON

Distillery: Buffalo Trace

This bourbon is named in honour of George T Stagg, who owned what is now the Buffalo Trace Distillery in the late 19th and early 20th centuries.

🍶 **GEORGE T STAGG KENTUCKY STRAIGHT BOURBON 71.35% ABV** • Offered unfiltered, at cask strength, and at 15 years old, George T Stagg boasts a big, rich Christmas cake nose, along with a hint of mint. Complex in the mouth, with oranges, spices, and lots of sweetness. The finish is long and sweet.

HANCOCK'S PRESIDENT'S RESERVE BOURBON

Distillery: Buffalo Trace

🍶 **HANCOCK'S PRESIDENT'S RESERVE SINGLE BARREL BOURBON 44–45% ABV** • Oily on the nose, with liquorice, caramel and spicy rye. Sweet in the mouth, with malt, fudge, and

vanilla notes. Drying in the finish, with notable oak notes, but the whiskey's residual sweetness remains to the end.

AH HIRSCH BOURBON

Distillery: Michter's

Hirsch Reserve represents a remarkable piece of American distilling history, as the whiskey was actually distilled back in 1974 in the last surviving Pennsylvania distillery. Michter's Distillery at Schaefferstown had its origins in a farm distilling operation that was in existence since at least 1753. In the years leading up to Prohibition in the 20th century, Michter's turned out significant quantities of rye whiskey. During the 1950s copper pot stills were installed, and pot still whiskey with a high rye content was produced. Sadly, Michter's closed in 1988, but a former Schenley Co. executive, Adolf Hirsch, had acquired quantities of the spirit some years previously, and after they had been matured for 16 years they were filled into

Four Roses Distillery provides the whiskey for IW Harper President's Reserve Kentucky Bourbon.

stainless-steel tanks to prevent further ageing. This whiskey is now available from Preiss Imports (www. preissimports.com) of California.

🍶 **AH HIRSCH RESERVE STRAIGHT BOURBON 16-YEAR-OLD 45.8% ABV** Caramel, honey, and rye dominate the complex nose, with a whiff of smoke also drifting on through. Oily corn, honey, and oak are evident on the rich palate, with rye and oak in the drying finish.

IW HARPER PRESIDENT'S RESERVE BOURBON

Distillery: Four Roses

The historic and once best-selling IW Harper brand was established by Isaac Wolfe Bernheim, a major figure in the bourbon business at the turn of the 19th century. It is now distilled for Diageo by Four Roses Distillery, and is one of the leading bourbons in the Japanese market.

🍶 **IW HARPER PRESIDENT'S RESERVE KENTUCKY STRAIGHT BOURBON 43% ABV** • Pepper combines with mint, oranges, and caramel on the nose, while caramel and oak feature on the elegant palate. The finish is dry and smoky.

JOHNNY DRUM KENTUCKY BOURBON

Distillery: Kentucky Bourbon Distillers

Johnny Drum is reputed to have been a Confederate drummer boy during the American Civil War, and latterly a pioneer farmer in Kentucky. He started to distil his corn to generate extra income, and developed a reputation for making excellent whiskey. Johnny Drum bourbon was formerly produced in the Willet

Hancock's President Special Reserve

Evan Williams Bourbon Whiskey

Distillery, located just outside Bardstown in Kentucky. It was established by the Willet family in 1935 and closed in the early 1980s when the last Willet retired. The plant was later acquired by Kentucky Bourbon Distillers Ltd, which now has a range of whiskies distilled under contract.

JOHNNY DRUM KENTUCKY STRAIGHT BOURBON 12-YEAR-OLD 43% ABV
Smooth and elegant on the nose, with vanilla, gentle spices, and smoke. This is a full-bodied bourbon, well-balanced and smooth in the mouth, with vanilla and a hint of smoke. The finish is lingering and sophisticated.

KESSLER BLENDED WHISKEY

Distillery: Jim Beam

One of the best known and most highly regarded blended American whiskeys, Kessler traces its origins back to 1888, when it was first blended by one Julius

Jim Beam Distillery produces several well-known brands, as well as its own range.

Kessler, who travelled from saloon to saloon in the old West, selling it as he went.

🍶 **KESSLER BLENDED AMERICAN WHISKEY** 40% ABV • This whiskey has carried the "smooth as silk" slogan for more than 50 years, and certainly lives up to its billing. The nose is light and fruity; the palate sweet, with just enough complexity of liquorice and leather to highlight the fact that the bourbon in this blend has been aged for at least four years.

Knob Creek Straight Bourbon

KNOB CREEK BOURBON

Distillery: Jim Beam

Knob Creek is the Kentucky town where Abraham Lincoln's father, Thomas, owned a farm and worked at the local distillery. This bourbon is made with the same high rye formula as the Basil Hayden and Old Grand-Dad whiskey brands *(see pp212 & 216)*.

🍶 **KNOB CREEK KENTUCKY STRAIGHT BOURBON 9-YEAR-OLD** 50% ABV
It has a nutty nose of sweet, tangy fruit and rye, with malt, spice, and nuts on the palate, drying in the finish with notes of vanilla.

NOAH'S MILL BOURBON

Distillery: Kentucky Bourbon Distillers Ltd

Like Johnny Drum, Noah's Mill was formerly distilled in the now silent Willet Distillery, and is currently produced under contract. It is a hand-bottled, small-batch bourbon.

NOAH'S MILL BOURBON 15-YEAR-OLD 57.15% ABV • Elegant and well-balanced on the nose, with caramel, nuts, coffee, dark fruits, and oak. A rich texture and notably dry on the palate, with nuts, spice, and background notes of soft fruit. Long, oaky finish.

OLD CHARTER BOURBON

Distillery: Buffalo Trace

Buffalo Trace produce several expressions in the Old Charter range, including 8, 10, and 12-year-old bourbons, plus the elegant 13-year-old Proprietor's Reserve.

🍶 **OLD CHARTER KENTUCKY STRAIGHT BOURBON 8 YEAR-OLD** 40% ABV • Initially dry and peppery on the nose, with sweet and buttery aromas following through. Mouth-coatingly rich, with fruit, vanilla, old leather, and cloves on the palate. A long and sophisticated finish.

OLD CHARTER PROPRIETOR'S RESERVE KENTUCKY STRAIGHT BOURBON 13-YEAR-OLD 45% ABV

Initially dry and peppery on the nose, with developing buttery and sweet notes. Big-bodied and viscous, with fruit, vanilla, and worn leather on the palate. The finish is long, complex, and, as you'd expect of a 13-year-old bourbon, sophisticated.

OLD CROW BOURBON

Distillery: Jim Beam

Named in honour of the 19th-century Scottish-born chemist and Kentucky distiller James Christopher Crow *(see p200)*, Old Crow is well rounded for a three-year-old whiskey. Along with Old Grand-Dad and Old Taylor, this brand was acquired by Jim Beam from National Distillers in 1987, and the three individual distilleries associated with these bourbons were closed. All production of these whiskeys now takes place in Jim Beam's distilleries at Boston and Clermont.

OLD CROW KENTUCKY STRAIGHT BOURBON 3-YEAR-OLD 40% ABV

Complex on the nose, with malt, rye, and sharp fruit notes that combine with gentle spice. The palate follows through with spicy, malty, and citric notes – the citrus and spice to the fore.

OLD GRAND-DAD BOURBON

Distillery: Jim Beam

The Old Grand-Dad formula, with its high percentage of rye, gives a drier, more heavily-bodied spirit than most Jim Beam whiskeys.

OLD GRAND-DAD KENTUCKY STRAIGHT BOURBON 4-YEAR-OLD 50% ABV ● Oranges and peppery spices on the nose, while the taste is full yet surprisingly smooth, considering its strength. Fruit, nuts, and caramel are foremost on the palate, while the finish is long and oily.

Old Grand-Dad Straight Bourbon

OLD TAYLOR BOURBON

Distillery: Jim Beam

Old Taylor is named after Colonel Edmund Haynes Taylor Jr – the man responsible for the Bottled-in-Bond Act of 1897, which guaranteed that bottles of whiskey bearing an official government seal would be 100 proof (50 per cent ABV) and at least four years old.

OLD TAYLOR KENTUCKY STRAIGHT BOURBON 6 YEAR-OLD 40% ABV

Old Taylor is light and orangey on the nose,

Old Crow Straight Bourbon

with a hint of marzipan; sweet, honeyed, and lightly oaky on the palate.

REBEL YELL BOURBON

Distillery: Heaven Hill

Produced at the Bernheim Distillery in Louisville for St Louis-based drinks company Luxco, Rebel Yell is made with a percentage of wheat in its mash bill instead of rye. A whiskey was first made to the Rebel Yell recipe back in 1849, and the whiskey has enjoyed popularity in the southern states for many years. The brand was finally released on an international basis during the 1980s.

REBEL YELL KENTUCKY STRAIGHT BOURBON 40% ABV ● A nose of honey, raisins, and butter leads into a big-bodied bourbon which again features honey and a buttery quality, along with plums. The finish is long and spicier than might be expected from the sweet palate.

ROCK HILL FARM BOURBON

Distillery: Buffalo Trace

ROCK HILL FARM SINGLE CASK BOURBON 50% ABV

Oak, raisins, and fruity rye on the nose, with a hint of mint. Medium to full-bodied, bittersweet, with rye

A wide array of whiskeys pass through the bottling plant at Buffalo Trace, from Blanton's Single Barrel to Weller's Special Reserve.

fruitiness, fudge, and oak. A long, sweet rye finish with a suggestion of liquorice.

SAZERAC RYE WHISKEY

Distillery: Buffalo Trace

There are two Sazerac expressions: a young and feisty 8-year-old and a complex 18-year-old.

🍷 SAZERAC STRAIGHT RYE WHISKEY 18-YEAR-OLD 45% ABV • The oldest rye whiskey on the market is big and spicy on the nose, with molasses, sultanas, vanilla, and lanolin. It coats the mouth with intense and oily rye, conveying dry spices and a hint of liquorice, then sweetens, with ripe bananas. The finish is long, with a sprinkling of pepper; lightly oaky and very dry.

SEAGRAM'S SEVEN CROWN

Distillery: Four Roses

One of the best known and most characterful blended American whiskeys, Seven Crowns survived the break up of the Seagram empire and is now produced at Four Roses Distillery.

🍷 SEAGRAM'S SEVEN CROWN BLENDED WHISKEY 40% ABV • A delicate nose with a hint of spicy rye; clean and well structured on the spicy palate.

WL WELLER BOURBON

Distillery: Buffalo Trace

William LaRue Weller established the original WL Weller Bourbon brand in 1849. It is made using wheat rather than rye as the "small grain", which is combined with corn and a proportion of malted barley. This mash bill tends to produce big-bodied yet soft whiskeys.

🍷 WL WELLER SPECIAL RESERVE KENTUCKY STRAIGHT BOURBON 7-YEAR-OLD 45% ABV
Oranges, honey, and vanilla on the nose, sweet in the mouth, with more vanilla, butterscotch, fruit, and spices. The finish is long, with pepper and fruity spice.

VAN WINKLE WHISKEYS

Distillery: various

Since 2002 Buffalo Trace Distillery has partnered the Julian Van Winkle brand in a joint venture whereby the distillery makes, bottles, and distributes the Van Winkle range of older whiskeys. The whiskeys are then matured at Van Winkle's now silent Old Hoffman Distillery at Lawrenceburg.

Julian Van Winkle specializes in small-batch, aged whiskeys, with as few as three or four barrels going into some bottlings. His bourbons are made with wheat, rather than the less expensive rye, to give them a smoother and sweeter flavour. Van Winkle also favours a long maturation period, and all whiskeys in the range are matured for at least 10 years in lightly charred mountain oak barrels. Though Van Winkle is a partner of Buffalo Trace, the current expressions were actually produced at a number of different distilleries.

Van Winkle 15-Year-Old Family Reserve

🍷 OLD RIP VAN WINKLE KENTUCKY STRAIGHT BOURBON WHISKEY 10-YEAR-OLD 53.5% ABV
Caramel and molasses on the nose, followed by honey and rich, spicy fruit on the profound, mellow palate. There follows a long finish, with coffee and liquorice.

🍷 PAPPY VAN WINKLE'S FAMILY RESERVE KENTUCKY STRAIGHT BOURBON WHISKEY 15-YEAR-OLD 53.5% ABV
A sweet nose of caramel and vanilla, plus charcoal and oak. Full-bodied, round, and smooth in the mouth, with a long and complex finish of spicy orange, toffee, vanilla, and oak.

Van Winkle 13-Year-Old Family Reserve

🍷 PAPPY VAN WINKLE'S FAMILY RESERVE KENTUCKY STRAIGHT BOURBON WHISKEY 20-YEAR-OLD 47.8% ABV • Notably old for a bourbon. A sweet vanilla and caramel nose, plus raisins, apples, and oak. Rich and buttery in the mouth, with molasses and a hint of char to balance the sweetness. The finish is long and complex, with a touch of oak charring.

🍷 VAN WINKLE FAMILY RESERVE RYE WHISKEY 13-YEAR-OLD 47.8% ABV
Very old for a rye. The nose is powerful, with fruit and spice, while vanilla, spice, pepper, and cocoa dominate the complex palate. The long finish balances caramel against black coffee.

🍷 VAN WINKLE SPECIAL RESERVE KENTUCKY STRAIGHT BOURBON WHISKEY 12-YEAR-OLD 45.2% ABV
Caramel, vanilla, honey, and oak figure on the nose, while the sweet and full-bodied palate exudes caramel, vanilla, and wheat. The finish is long, well-balanced, and elegant.

PAPPY VAN WINKLE

Julian Van Winkle is the grandson of legendary bourbon figure Julian P "Pappy" Van Winkle Sr, who started working as a salesman for WL Weller & Sons in Louisville in 1893 at the age of 18. He went on to become famous for his Old Fitzgerald Bourbon, distilled in the now lost Stitzel Weller Distillery in Louisville.

CANADA

Historically, Canada is one of whisky's biggest players. And while it still commands loyal support, the fact remains that it has slipped from the top flight of whisky-producing nations. But why is this so, and can the glory days return?

C anada has probably produced whisky since the 1760s, with early distillation based around an area in the south of Ontario on Canada's east coast. By the mid-1800s, about 200 distilleries were established, and the country's reputation grew throughout the late 19th century and on well into the 20th. That was the period of Canadian whisky's golden age, as the spirit flowed across the American borders. Whisky makers such as Hiram Walker, who had created the Canadian Club brand in the 1880s, and later Sam Bronfman at Seagram created vast commercial empires. As the golden age progressed into the mid-20th century, companies such as Seagram and Hiram Walker & Sons dominated not just the American market but that of the entire world, with Seagram even building its own distilleries in Scotland, at Allt a' Bhainne and Braeval *(see pp49 & 53)*.

The initial fortunes of the country's whisky industry had been greatly aided by Prohibition in the USA. During that time, consignments of whisky would sail down the rivers and through the Great Lakes into America, where bootleggers

used it to slake the inexhaustible thirst for whisky in the many speakeasies that sprung up across the States. It was the theft of a shipment of Canadian whisky that prompted the infamous St Valentine's Day Massacre in 1929.

END OF THE GOLDEN AGE

From such a high point, the fall of Canadian whisky in world terms has been a marked decline. For several decades now, Canadian whisky has had a much lower profile and operated on a far more modest scale.

On the face of it, the future of the industry in Canada doesn't look particularly rosy. Where once 200 distilleries produced rivers of whisky to serve an all but insatiable American market, now Canada is like a broken jigsaw, with just 10 distilleries, a sizeable number of them owned by Kentucky bourbon companies or international spirits producers. Dig a little deeper, though, and there are burning embers in the ashes. And the good news for lovers of Canada's unique whisky styles – note the plural – is that Canadian whisky producers aren't going to give up without a fight.

Although there were economic reasons for the industry's decline, there are two principal explanations for its continued

Many Canadian distilleries make use of pure glacial water that flows down from the country's Rocky Mountains in fast-flowing rivers.

comparatively lowly state, and part of the trouble is self-inflicted. Crucially, the industry has done little to sell itself in recent decades. While Scotch, Irish, American, and Japanese whiskies have all been promoted in terms of their intrinsic national and regional characteristics and subtle distinctions from one another, little attempt seems to have been made to champion the unique qualities of Canadian whisky to the rest of the world.

CANADIAN DISTILLERIES

Secondly, when Canadian whisky has been praised, those extolling it have tended to be working in the cocktail sector, where the nature of the spirit has been celebrated for its mixing qualities. Quite rightly, as it happens, but that's not the whole story. And, because few people have explained Canadian whisky's other virtues, it has all too often been accepted only as a cocktail whisky – smooth, rounded, bland even, and best mixed with additional flavours.

SETTING THE RECORD STRAIGHT

Let's dismiss a couple of popular fallacies concerning the style of Canadian whisky: it isn't bland, and nor is it an imitation of either Scotch blended whisky or American bourbon. While Canada's distillers may well produce individual whiskies that bear a resemblance to

whisky from elsewhere, the country's distillate is uniquely Canadian.

Rye is at the heart of Canadian whisky, but it's quite unlike the kind of rye whiskey you'll find in the USA. Canadian whisky uses a complex mix of strongly flavoured malted and unmalted rye whiskies combined with a far greater amount of smooth and light grain whisky.

An additional quality of Canadian whisky is that it can include a small percentage of flavourings, such as fruit, sherry, or bourbon *(see p222)*, further distinguishing its character, and usually contributing to its rounded and fruity character. It's the ability to blend all these elements harmoniously that marks out the most sophisticated Canadian whiskies.

It is high time that the country's whisky was re-evaluated in international terms. As to whether a change of fortune is just around the corner, only time will tell.

Massive silos, such as these in Alberta, store the raw grain ingredients – wheat, corn, rye, and barley – for use in the whisky-making industry.

DISTILLERIES

Seagrams is no more, but in the mid-20th century it was one of the giants of the industry.

Canada's whisky industry has blending at its heart. Because its distilleries can produce the variety of constituent whiskies that contribute to a blend's mix, distilleries are intrinsically linked to the brands they produce.

ALBERTA

✉ Calgary
🔗 www.albertadistillers.com
⛴ Open to visitors

Calgary sits on the verdant plains of Alberta, where some of the world's finest rye is cultivated, and beneath the awesome Rockies, from which pure mountain spring water can be drawn. Ideal, then, for a rye-producing distillery such as Alberta.

The distillery can produce in batches or continuously and has a pot still, used for making speciality whiskies. There are two principal whisky types distilled in the production process. The bulk of the distillery's blends are made up of a base spirit, unusually made with rye rather than the traditional corn. It is first distilled in a beer still and then again in a continuous rectifier *(see p28)*. It is distilled to an alcohol level of around 95–96 per cent ABV.

A second whisky is made from rye, but this time it is distilled only once, the effect of which is to produce a spirit with a relatively low ABV of about 65 per cent. One distillation means that oils and congeners are left in the spirit, making it heavy, oily, and rich in flavour.

The two spirits are blended and maturation then takes place in first-fill bourbon casks, or even in unused new white oak casks.

ALBERTA PREMIUM 5-YEAR-OLD 40% ABV • It tends to be that the longer rye is in the cask, the mellower it becomes, so the younger expressions of Alberta's output are the most aggressive, uncompromising, and impressive. For this reason, Alberta Premium, at just 5 years old, is held up in some quarters as a world-class whisky.

ALBERTA SPRINGS 10-YEAR-OLD 40% ABV • Having been aged for 10 years, the Alberta Springs expression from the distillery is softer and sweeter. It therefore harks back to a more recognizable style of Canadian whisky.

TANGLE RIDGE 40% ABV This is the distillery's most commercial product; it contains 10-year-old whisky, but in this case it is blended with sherry and fruit flavourings – as permitted under Canada's whisky laws *(see p222)*.

WINDSOR 40% ABV • This is a fairly aggressive, rye-dominated blend.

ALBERTA'S OUTPUT

Alberta Distillery was founded in 1946 and for the last 20 years has been owned by American giant Jim Beam. It is capable of producing about 20 million litres (about 4.5 million gallons) of alcohol per year. It's not the biggest producer in Canada – not by a long shot – but that's still twice what Scotland's biggest malt distillery, Glenfiddich, produces per annum.

Despite its formidable size and its international owner, Alberta has preserved its reputation as a maverick, producing an unconventional group of whiskies dominated by rye. You might think that geography would have explained this, as rye grows easily here. These days, however, the obstacles to converting to other grain types have all but disappeared, so today's whisky is made through choice, not circumstance.

Rye is the grain that grows best in Alberta, whereas, because of the temperature, corn fares less well.

THE CHARACTER OF CANADIAN WHISKY

That there is a big market for whisky in Canada is no great surprise. Just consider the large number of early settlers who were forced to make the journey to North America from Scotland, and you'll understand why the nations' drinking tastes are linked.

However, while there are clear cultural links, as well as many similarities in the climate and terrain of the two countries, the whisky bond is not such a snug fit. It is true that a small amount of pot-still produced malt is made in Canada today, but the greater part of the country's whisky output is a very different beast.

What is widely accepted as the country's trademark style of whisky is defined, not by its malted barley content, but by rye. And even in this regard it's in a category of its own because, unlike American straight rye, the style most closely associated with Canadian whisky is, in its simplest form, a mix of a light base-grain whisky (produced in a continuous still) mixed with a small proportion of rye whisky.

In practice, Canadian whiskies are complex and sophisticated, blending several different styles of rye with the base spirit. And to differentiate

Highwood Centennial Whisky

Canadian whisky still further, Canadian law permits a fraction over nine per cent of the final whisky to be made up of other flavourings, such as sherry or fruit – or indeed foreign whisky. A handful of Canadian whiskies contain some Kentucky bourbon, for example.

Canadian whisky produced this way is notable for its smooth, rounded, and fruity style. It has been dismissed by some critics for being light and inconsequential, but, at its best, a Canadian whisky offers a subtle and sophisticated master class in blending.

There is one other key aspect to the final whisky's flavour – the impact of oak from maturation. The blending process may take place before or after maturation in oak casks, but, like Scotch whisky, the minimum maturation period is three years, rather than the two favoured in the USA.

White oak barrels such as these from the Canadian Mist Distillery add flavour to the whisky over a minium three-year maturation period.

CANADIAN CLUB

See Hiram Walker & Sons

CANADIAN MIST

✉ Georgian Bay, Collingwood, Ontario

⏣ By appointment only

Canadian Mist is a testament to the boom times for Canadian whisky, built with haste to catch the last wave of demand before it entirely passed by. It was built in the 1960s and, from foundation stone to working distillery, the construction took just five months.

The plant sits in the heart of Ontario by Collingwood, a small town close to the freshwater beach of Georgian Bay. It is one of the few Canadian distilleries that produces only whisky, as it was set up by the Kentucky bourbon makers Barton Brands *(see p187)* to expand upon the success they were already having with the Canadian Mist whisky brand.

The distillery's location was just about ideal: close to communication channels for both Canada and the United States; close enough to the grain-producing regions; endowed with great stocks of water; and with a depressed economy that ensured favourable tax breaks for businesses from the government.

Canadian Mist has enjoyed continued success since the plant started up, and was in fact America's top-selling Canadian whisky for many years. These days the distillery is owned by another Kentucky-based company, Brown-Forman *(see p188)*, who also own Jack Daniel's and Woodford Reserve. It remains a big brand in the American market.

🍸 **CANADIAN MIST** 40% ABV
The nose offers light fruit, a hint of toffee, and a little spice. Rich, sweet, and fruity on the palate, with toffee and vanilla too. The finish is soft, rounded, and pleasant.

Canadian Mist

GIMLI

✉ Gimli, Manitoba
🖥 www.crownroyal.com
🍷 Open to visitors

Gimli stands close to the edge of Lake Winnipeg, about 100 miles (160 km) north of the town of Winnipeg, amid a large Icelandic community. It is now owned by drinks giant Diageo, and in some ways its history is a microcosm of Canada's whisky history as a whole. Gimli was built in 1968 to catch the same wave of popularity for Canadian whisky that Canadian Mist was riding, and its modern design is a testament to just how high Canadian whisky flew in relatively recent times.

It was one of a number of distilleries owned by Seagram, each of them producing spirit for the world's markets.

A DISTILLERY LIKE NO OTHER

Canadian Mist is a continuous distillation plant. It is neither particularly pretty nor, on the face of it, particularly exceptional. Until, that is, you look at it purely from a whisky enthusiast's technical point of view, for it has three peculiarities that make it unique. In fact, this distillery is a phenomenon that turns conventional whisky lore on its head.

Firstly, Canadian Mist is made without any exposure whatsoever to copper. The production equipment is entirely made from stainless steel, and purists will tell you that the finished whisky should be sulphurous as a result. More than two million cases sold in America each year argue rather emphatically that it's not.

Secondly, it is the only Canadian whisky made with a mash of corn and malted barley. Malted barley is often used as the catalyst to help other grains begin to ferment, and in this plant the process just wouldn't happen without it. It adds flavour, too, though that is incidental to the Canadian Mist operation.

And thirdly, the distillery does not produce any rye for flavouring. Instead it brings in rye from one of Brown-Forman's Kentucky distilleries, as well as an amount of Kentucky bourbon, which is allowed under Canadian law *(see opposite)*. Canadian Mist is not to everyone's taste, but it is an enigma – and quite literally goes against the grain.

Candian Mist Distillery uses stainless steel throughout, including these fermenters.

Samples of whisky are selected from casks for appraisal at the former Seagram's Distillery.

One by one, however, the distilleries fell by the wayside, and Gimli was Seagram's last whisky-producing plant before the company itself finally succumbed to the fall in the fortunes of the Canadian whisky industry.

Gimli remains a monster of a distillery, however. Visit the website and you can find

Crown Royal

out exactly how much corn and water are used in making the whisky. Suffice to say that there are 1.25 million barrels stored on the site, a similar quantity to the number stored at Jack Daniel's Tennessee Distillery.

Gimli is also home to one of Canada's most iconic brands, Crown Royal. The brand was launched in 1939 to mark the visit to Canada of King George VI and Queen Elizabeth of Great Britain, and the blend has contributed significantly to Canada's whisky exports ever since.

The base whisky is made in three primary beer stills and a complex four-column rectifier, while bourbon and rye flavouring whiskies pass through a simpler two-column continuous still. No other non-whisky flavourings are added.

The resulting whisky is almost archetypally Canadian, its rich fruitiness and touch of spice blended to perfection. The special

and limited editions of Crown Royal contain older and rarer whiskies. They may contain up to 50 whiskies in the mix, and a distinctly bourbony flavour emerges.

Gimli also produces a number of smaller brands, including Seagram's 83 and Seagram's Five Star, a wistful nod to the distillery's history.

🥃 **CROWN ROYAL** 40% ABV • Rye spice, honey, and red fruit combine on the nose. It has a rounded, balanced palate, with fruit, spice, and oak; the finish is soft, sweet, and pleasant – fair to middling.

🥃 **CROWN ROYAL XR** 40% ABV A nice wave of spicy rye, and then bourbony vanilla, polished leather, and musk body spray. Decidedly male. The palate offers up-front rye and wood, and the polite bourbon taste expected from the nose, but gives ground easily and settles for a gentle caress rather than a hefty Kentucky slap – intriguing. As for the finish, well, the rye stays around longer after the whisky, oiled to the sides of the mouth.

CANADA DAY COCKTAIL

Canadian whisky remains very popular with modern mixologists because it is versatile and ideal for making modern and unusual cocktails, such as this one, which celebrates Canada Day.

Ingredients:
½ measure (10 ml) of Crown Royal whisky
½ measure (10 ml) of sloe gin
½ measure (10 ml) of triple sec
½ measure (10 ml) of Galliano
About 2 measures (40–60 ml) of orange juice

Method: Stir all the ingredients over cracked ice. Strain over ice in to a highball glass and garnish with lemon and lime slices.

THE PROCESS OF MAKING CANADIAN WHISKY

To achieve a perfectly balanced whisky, Canadian distilleries make a range of different whiskies at each plant. This will include using a variety of grains, varying the fermentation period and the mash bill, and employing different distilling techniques.

Although the basic method of production involves mainly column still distillation, copper pot stills often feature to make heavy, flavouring whisky. Complicated combinations are employed, making Canada's production process among the most sophisticated in the world.

Unusually, it is common to distil with malted rye (rather than the more common unmalted form), and most distilleries will also produce a version of bourbon. Even basic Canadian whiskies will use around 15 different whiskies; some have well in excess of 20, and they can have up to as many as 50. Although

Schenley's huge column stills produce the bulk of the distillery's output.

the character of Canadian whisky is defined by the spicy and dominant rye, malted rye is a crucial component for the smoothness and fullness of flavour in a Canadian whisky. Despite its dominance, however, rye may only account for about 10 per cent of the spirit in the mix, and that figure can often fall to as low as five per cent.

Some single malt whisky does exist in Canada, as do some single grain whiskies, and generally the standard is very high. That quality, coupled with a renewed interest in rye among whisky lovers, could prompt a reappraisal of Canadian whisky.

Vast grain fields in Saskatchewan and other parts of Canada produce plenty of top-quality grain for Canada's whisky industry.

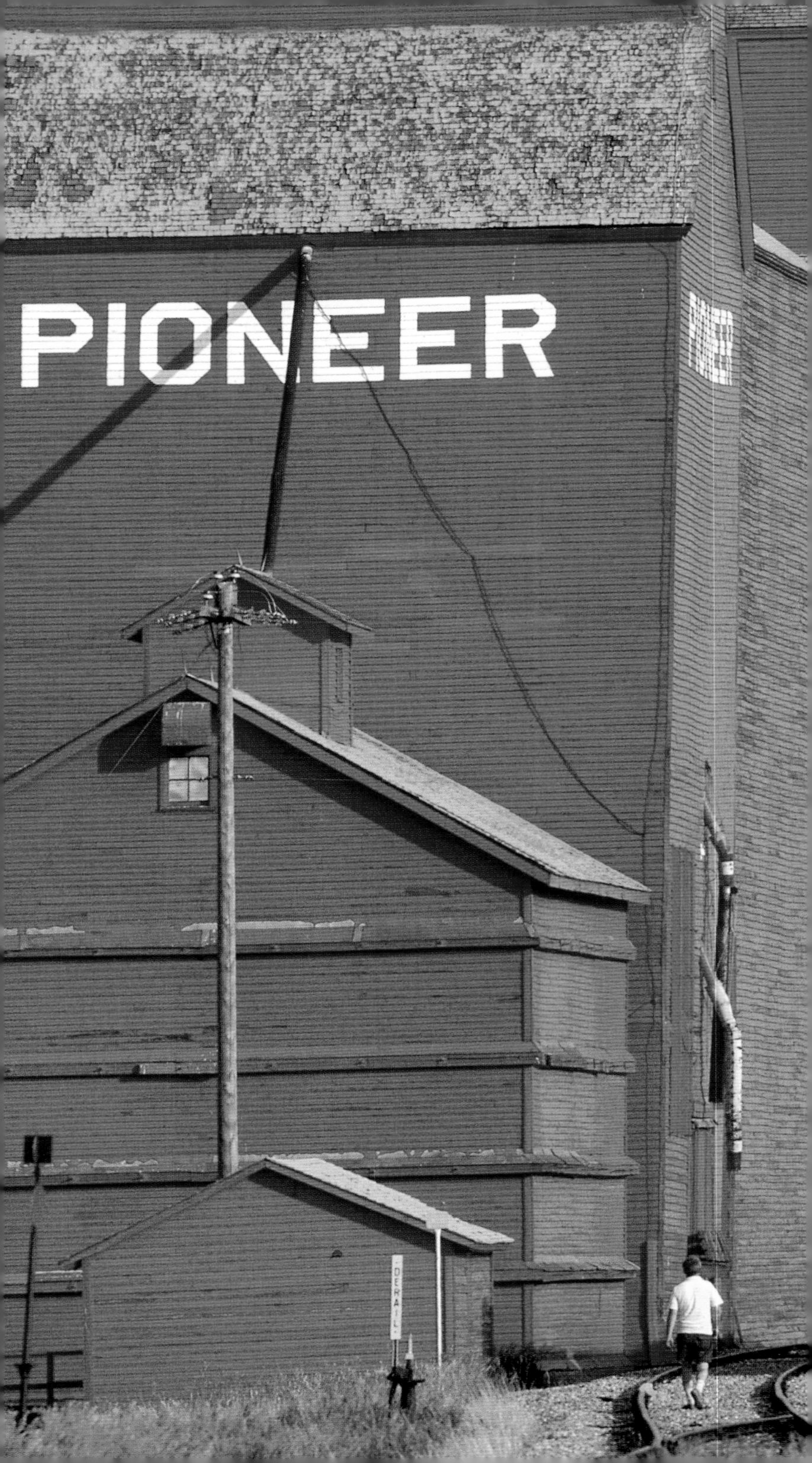
PIONEER
PIONEER
DERAIL

The grain silos in Alberta are vast, and give an indication of just how fertile the terrain is, especially for growing rye.

GLENORA

✉ Glenville, Cape Breton, Nova Scotia

🖰 www.glenoradistillery.com

⚓ Open to visitors

Nova Scotia means "New Scotland", and when people draw comparisons between Scotland and Canada, it's often of Nova Scotia that they are thinking. It should, therefore, come as no surprise to find Canada's only single malt distillery, complete with imported copper pot stills, right here in Cape Breton.

Indeed, so close is the link between Cape Breton and the Scottish Highlands that Glenora has managed to upset the Scotch Whisky Association. It claimed the distillery's Glen Breton whisky caused confusion over its origin by the use of the word "glen", so common to famous Scotch malts such as Glenlivet. It's a claim that's undermined, however, by the prominent maple leaf on the bottles.

Glenora has chalets for visitors close to the plant; they overlook the beautiful valley where the distillery is located.

Glen Breton Ice Whisky

Glenora Distillery has been making whisky for just under 20 years, and was the brainchild of Canadian businessman Bruce Jardine. The site was chosen because of the purity of its water source – a burn flowing over granite. However, within a few weeks of production starting, it stopped when the money ran out. After two stuttering years, it was sold to another local businessman, Lauchie MacLean, whose ancestors hail from Scotland. Bruce died in 1994 before he could see his vision and investment bear fruit. But, from a tentative start, the distillery started to get its act together. Poor early spirit was redistilled, producing a triple-distilled whisky. In the past few years it has continued to evolve nicely, and is now being bottled as an 8 or 9-year-old whisky.

The distillery itself is built on a 300-acre (120-ha) site, comprising seven buildings.

Glenora is a high-tech distillery, but produces that most traditional of whiskies, single malt.

glenora distiller

It has a wash and a spirit still imported from Scotland and is capable of producing a modest 250,000 litres (55,000 gallons) of spirit a year – though the owners point out that the site has been designed to allow improvements that would quickly increase output to as much as twice that amount. The distillery has imported barley from Scotland in the past and has experimented with a range of peat levels, while favouring just lightly peated whisky for its core expression, which is matured in bourbon barrels.

At present the distillery's main bottling is called Cape Breton Rare Canadian. It's an 8-year-old whisky with a distinctive butterscotch and orange flavour. The distillery has also recently launched an expression called Glen Breton Ice, which is the same spirit, but matured in ice wine barrels – the world's first whisky to be aged this way, it is claimed.

If you are thinking of making the journey out to this beautiful part of the world, consider staying at one of the nearby chalets, which are advertised on the distillery's website.

HIGHWOOD

✉ High River, Alberta
🖰 www.highwood-distillers.com
⚓ Open to visitors

Highwood is a remote, independent operation that nestles in the middle of some of Canada's most fertile grain-producing land. This seems to be a distillery on the up, albeit from a fairly low starting point.

In fact, it's effectively two distilleries for the price of one, because, back in 2005, Highwood bought Potter's

Distillery – at the time, British Columbia's only surviving distillery. The Potter's name recalls one Ernie Potter, who founded the distillery in 1958. When Highwood bought Potter's, it brought all the brands associated with that distillery under the Highwood wing.

The plant was in fact first established as Sunnyvale Distillery in 1974, another distillery created to take advantage of the booming Canadian whisky market. It changed its name in 1984 in recognition of the region within which it is producing, and now boasts a portfolio of some 50 different products, including premixed drinks and liqueurs. It has several little-known whisky brands that sell mainly in the west of Canada, although there has been some expansion to the east and down to America. It also bottles spirits for other companies.

Its point of difference from other Canadian distilleries is that it is the only one in Canada to produce its neutral base spirit from wheat rather than corn.

The trouble is, wheat produces a lighter spirit that is ideal for vodka production – which is key to the distillery's output – but is not necessarily so good for whisky. Those who have tried the new make report that it is not only characterless but also just about tasteless – and that, of course, doesn't augur well for the mature whisky.

That said, however, the 13-year-old and 15-year-old

Highwood's Potter's Rye Whisky

Highwood Rye Whisky

whiskies produced under the Century Reserve label are single cask pure rye whiskies. They have a great deal of personality, and hint at the premium direction in which this distillery could well move in the near future.

HIRAM WALKER & SONS

✉ Walkerville, Windsor, Ontario
🖰 www.canadianclubwhisky.com
⚓ Open to visitors

Founded in 1858, Hiram Walker's distillery was expanded in 1894, with great fanfare, and a town grew up around it to accommodate distillery employees. Known as Walkerville, the area is still home to the original distillery and much of it is a throwback to Hiram Walker's time. The production methods haven't changed significantly either, and much of the old equipment remains in place, though not necessarily in use.

The Hiram Walker Distillery has long been associated with the Canadian Club brand *(see over)*, although ownership has recently been split, with the distillery now falling under the Pernod Ricard umbrella; and Canadian Club now being part of Jim Beam Global.

Canadian Club has, of course, remained a world-famous brand, but under the one name is a range of distinct whiskies. Mostly they are distilled and then

Canadian Club whisky

HIRAM WALKER AND CANADIAN CLUB WHISKY

There are some legendary names scattered through the history of Canadian whisky, but none are bigger than Hiram Walker. Through the methods he used and through his Canadian Club brand, he more than any other was responsible for putting Canada on the whisky map.

While it might be stretching it a little to credit him with inventing Canadian whisky as we know it today, Hiram Walker's influence on its development is immense, and his way of producing whisky has been emulated across the country ever since.

Early references to Canadian whisky mention the wild and pioneering times of the 18th century, when distilled grain was consumed by trappers, hunters, and settlers to get inebriated. It would have been an unrefined hooch far removed from the smooth and sophisticated product it is today.

By the 1840s there were 200 distilleries in Canada, but it wasn't until 1858 that Walker, a businessman with interests in shipping and tobacco, founded a mill and distillery at a site near Windsor, Ontario.

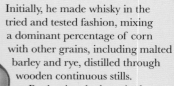

Canadian Club Special Reserve

The Hiram Walker Distillery pioneered the distinctive style of Canadian whisky, marrying grain whisky with a flavourful oil-rich rye.

Initially, he made whisky in the tried and tested fashion, mixing a dominant percentage of corn with other grains, including malted barley and rye, distilled through wooden continuous stills.

By the time he launched what was to become known as Canadian Club in 1884, though, the production method had changed to one that is now recognizably a Canadian style. The whisky was made up of very strong base spirit mixed with a considerably weaker flavoured spirit, often made with rye. For this, a copper pot still was used to make a heavy, oil-rich rye.

The result was lighter and cleaner whisky than others of the time, and it was an immediate success, particularly across the border in the northern industrial cities of America.

Its success prompted other producers to turn to the same production methods and so it was that the Canadian boom began.

Canadian Club, as advertised in this French-Canadian poster, was popularized around the world as a mixing whisky for cocktails.

blended before maturing. The standard Canadian Club is a 6-year-old, but Canadian Club Reserve is a 10-year-old and contains a higher proportion of rye. The Classic 12-year-old has a higher proportion of malted barley. Best of the range, though, are the 100 proof version and the Canadian Club Sherry Finish, which is an 8-year-old and benefits considerably from the additional fruitiness the second cask imparts.

CANADIAN CLUB 40% ABV
Spirity and winey on the nose. The palate is sharp and oily, with a splash of vanilla and then a spicy finish, which is both short and sharp.

CANADIAN CLUB CLASSIC 40% ABV • Toffee and vanilla aromas on the nose, and a palate that offers a big dose of fruit, some oak spice, and then a rich caramel hit. The finish is drier, spicier, and longer than many Canadian whiskies.

WISER'S WHISKIES
Hiram Walker is now also home to some of the whiskies that used to be produced by the Corby Distillery, which closed in the 1990s. They include the highly respected range that appear under the Wiser's label (owned by Pernod Ricard), which have been distilled at Hiram Walker's for about 10 years.

WISER'S DE LUXE 40% ABV
The nose is solid, with rye and fruit, and the palate both grainy and oily, with some toffee and vanilla notes. There's lots going on, with oak and grain in attendance, and the finish is full and embracing. Distinctly moreish.

WISER'S 18-YEAR-OLD 40% ABV
Shy but complicated nose, with prune, overripe peach, polished leather, and honey. On the palate, this is whisky's version of a sugar-coated candy, with a grain and oak coating and a chocolate and fruit centre. The finish lashes out with a sharp prod at the end, then smoulders in the mouth for a while. Not totally expected, but captivating all the same.

KITTLING RIDGE

✉ Grimsby, Ontario
🖥 www.kittlingridge.com
🚪 Open to visitors Mar–Oct, or by appointment

Canadian Club Classic

If it is a dramatic location you want for your distillery, then Kittling Ridge Estate Wines and Spirits fits the bill perfectly. It sits close to the beaches of Lake Erie and about 40 miles (65 km) away from Niagara Falls.

Chances are, you haven't heard of it. Kittling Ridge is a small, independent company, founded in 1971 by a Swiss stillmaster in order to make European-style fruit brandies. The operation was expanded soon after to produce other spirits. Despite the vineyard-sounding name – introduced no doubt to attract the growing number of Canadian wine enthusiasts – wine has been a relatively late addition to the company's offering.

The wine link came when original founder Otto Reider retired and winemaker John Hall took over. It is his precise and wine-like approach to whisky making that has helped define this distillery's products – in particular Forty Creek Barrel Select, one of Canada's most appealing and intriguing whiskies.

Forty Creek is made using three grains, but there is no mash bill for them. That is because they are fermented in batches separately, and then individually distilled in copper stills. Each of them is then matured in white oak casks that have been selected specially for the individual spirits, and each cask has a different level of charring. Only when the whiskies have been aged for between six and 10 years are they blended and finished for a further six months in oak casks that have previously contained sherry made by Hall himself.

MAPLE LEAF

Ingredients:
A little over 1 measure (30 ml) of Canadian Club Classic whisky
A third of a measure (8 ml) of lemon juice
1 tsp of maple syrup

Method: Fill a mixing glass with ice. Add the whisky, lemon juice, and maple syrup, then shake. Strain into a cocktail glass.

Valleyfield, Canada's only French-speaking distillery, was once part of a strong whisky-making region.

The resulting whisky puts to rest once and for all the erroneous assumption that Canadian whiskies are bland and uninteresting. It has a varied and impressive taste profile that makes it not just unique to Canada but unique in the entire world of whisky. If you're looking for hope for the future of Canadian whisky, this distillery is surely it.

Kittling Ridge does also produce a couple of more conventional whiskies, in the shape of Pure Gold and the recently released Mountain Rock. The latter comes in an unbreakable plastic bottle – its sales pitch being that it is "easy to pack when travelling".

🍶 **FORTY CREEK BARREL SELECT** 40% ABV ● Assertive and inviting on the nose, Forty Creek Barrel Select is full of plummy sherry and fruity promise. The palate is fullsome, with chunky orange fruit, chocolate, and spice, followed by a satisfying and quite intense finish. Impressive stuff.

PALLISER

✉ **Lethbridge, Alberta**

Palliser Distillery lies about two hours' drive from the American border and is the home of the Black Velvet Distilling Company – a subsidiary of Gilbey, the gin makers. Gilbey launched Black Velvet Whisky just after World War II, and opened the Palliser plant as the demand for Canadian whisky exploded. As we know, though, the boom days weren't set to last, and Gilbey's original whisky distillery was shut down and production of other spirits brought to Palliser.

Now the plant is best known for making Smirnoff. Black Velvet is also produced here again, and still enjoys considerable success, selling in the region of two million cases worldwide. However, it very much plays second fiddle to the world-famous vodka brand.

The base neutral spirit for Black Velvet is produced

Black Velvet Canadian Whisky

from a three-column continuous still and aged for about three years. The flavouring spirits are distilled in a one-column still and matured for about six years. In a break with conventional practice, the 6-year-old flavouring whiskies are mixed into the base spirit when it is newly distilled and before it is matured.

The resulting whisky is pleasant enough, without setting the world on fire.

🍶 **BLACK VELVET** 40% ABV
The nose is malty, fresh, and spicy; the palate clean and with a nice balance between sweetness and spice. As for the finish, it heads for the exit signs almost immediately.

VALLEYFIELD

✉ **Valleyfield, Quebec**

Quebec is, of course, the French-speaking part of Canada, and Valleyfield is the world's only French-speaking distillery outside France. Maybe the French influence has rubbed off on the whisky production, because several of this large distillery's whiskies are of the highest quality.

Also known as the Old Schenley Distillery, Valleyfield lies about 30 miles (50 km) outside Montreal. It was once part of a proud distilling region in Quebec, where there were eight distilleries 45 years ago. Now Valleyfield is the last one.

Originally a brewery, it was acquired by Schenley – which had been successfully producing spirits in Pennsylvania – at the end of World War II. New stillhouses and warehouses were built and, as the demand for Canadian whisky soared, it was expanded in the 1960s. As early as 1950, the distillery was producing 8-year-old whiskies which are said to have been of exceptional quality. They included Gibson Straight Rye and a straight bourbon.

The distillery is now capable of producing about 25 million litres (5.5 million gallons) of spirit each year. Not all of it is whisky, however. Vodka and rum have been produced at the distillery, which is now owned by Kentucky bourbon producers Barton Brands, who bought it just before the end of the millennium.

Barton own Black Velvet and so have a sister distillery (Palliser, *see above*) in Alberta. Quebec is well placed to meet the demands of America's eastern seaboard; while Alberta can satisfy the needs of the west.

That's only part of the story though. The distillery has been designed with flexibility in mind, and can produce a range of different styles of whiskies. It boasts

In the early 1980s, Valleyfield Distillery filled its three millionth barrel of whisky.

large open-top fermenters, and produces its flavouring rye in copper pot still doublers. The system seems to have been tailor-made to produce a surprisingly characterful corn spirit, and it's this that lies at the heart of some of its award-winning whiskies. These include the Gibson's range and the Schenley whiskies.

🍸 **SCHENLEY GOLDEN WEDDING** 40% ABV ● One of Canada's best-sellers, Schenley Golden Wedding is a young and stylish, but ordered, whisky. Everything about it is light, smooth, and impeccably well behaved.

🍸 **SCHENLEY OFC** 40% ABV ● The name OFC stands for Original Fine Canadian, a whisky produced for the domestic market as an 8-year-old, as opposed to the 6-year-old version that is exported to America. OFC is defined by its rich toffee and vanilla characteristics.

WINCHESTER CELLARS

✉ Vancouver Island
🖳 www.winchestercellars.com
🍷 Open to visitors

It is fitting that the last of the distilleries to be featured in the Canadian section is Winchester Cellars, because it is from micro-distillers like this that the future of Canadian whisky might well develop and be defined.

Winchester Cellars is a highly respected wine producer on Vancouver Island, the biggest wine growing area in Canada. Established by Ken Winchester 25 years ago, it has expanded gradually and is now turning its attention to single malt whisky, though it has some way to go before it produces its first bottle for consumption.

Ken Winchester has a long history in distilling, but mainly of brandy and grappa. Now he is intent on producing premium single malt whisky commercially.

Ken Winchester and the German pot still that he is using to distill peated malt from Scotland.

Ken has a 250-litre (55-gallon) German pot still, which he says is "small but sophisticated". With it, he is experimenting with unpeated and lightly peated Scottish malt, though he is in talks with local Canadian barley producers and plans to experiment with peat from the island. In time, he says, he wants the whisky to be made entirely with produce from the island. He will mature the spirit he produces in the finest French oak casks, which he has already sourced for his wine making.

A new distillery is always a cause for celebration. And one that adds more variety into the market place is even greater reason to cheer. As to the future of Canadian whisky, it's further proof that the embers still burn brightly.

JAPAN

The first grain spirit made in Japan would possibly have been a form of *shochu* made in Kyushu (where a barley-based spirit is still made today), and there are records of *yoshu* (foreign spirits) being made at the end of the 19th century in Japan.

One of the firms experimenting with *yoshu* was Gisuke Konishi, which was selling something that it called whisky in the late 1880s. Shinjiro Torii, a nephew of its owner, was employed at the firm before he left in 1899 to establish his own liquor retail and importing venture, Kotobukiya. By 1919 his brand, "Tory's Finest Liqueur Scotch Whisky", was being sold. Torii had the whisky bug – now he needed a distillery. By the start of the 1920s, Torii had bought a large tract of land between Kyoto and Osaka to build his distillery. All that was missing was a whisky maker. Enter Masataka Taketsuru.

A scion of a *sake* brewing family from Hiroshima, Taketsuru was sent to Glasgow in 1918 to study whisky making by Kihei Abe of Osaka-based distiller Settsu Shuzo. Although Takesuru studied chemistry at Glasgow University, he gained his whisky-making experience at first hand, with apprenticeships at Longmorn and Hazelburn distilleries *(see also p248)*. In 1920 he returned to Japan, along with his Scottish wife, and was soon snapped up by Torii as manager of Yamazaki, Japan's first malt distillery.

Advertised here in Tokyo, Suntory was the first whisky produced in Japan and remains a leading brand, famous at home and abroad.

In 1929, Japan's first whisky was introduced. Called Shirofuda ("White Label"), it was a blend of Yamazaki malt and grain spirit from the firm's Osaka distillery. By the start of the next decade, Yamazaki's whiskies were being exported. Then, in 1934, Taketsuru left.

It appears that he and Torii were suffering from the distilling equivalent of musical differences. Taketsuru argued that the distillery should be located in the cool north, not in the middle of humid Honshu. His preference was for peaty whiskies, whereas Torii felt that a lighter style would better suit the Japanese palate and have greater commercial appeal.

COOL NORTHERN CLIMES

Taketsuru founded Dai-nippon-kaju. To locate the perfect spot for a distillery, he followed his instinct and went to Japan's northernmost island, Hokkaido. Here, at Yoichi, he found everything he felt he needed to make whisky his way: peat, barley, a cold climate, and plentiful water supplies. In 1934, Yoichi Distillery started its production. Torii's firm Kotobukiya now had a rival, and this duopoly has dominated Japanese whisky ever since.

Kotobukiya pressed on with a raft of new brands, though it wasn't until the end of World War II that the Japanese whisky industry could start in earnest.

By then Taketsuru had changed the name of his firm to Nikka, while, in 1952, Torii founded a chain of bars, called Tory's, to promote its whiskies.

By now, other distillers were joining in. Hombu began distilling in Kagoshima Prefecture in the early 1950s, while in 1956 Daikoku-budoshu converted a winery on the slopes of Mount Asama into its Karuizawa Distillery. *Shochu* distiller Takara also got in on the act, making whisky for its King brand at the Shirakawa Distillery in Fukushima *(see p251)*.

It was around this time that the *mizuwari* style of drinking whisky long and heavily diluted became the preferred way to imbibe among the "salarymen" who helped fuel Japan's postwar economic boom. They also helped to fuel a boom for Japanese whisky.

THE RISE OF SUNTORY

New brands continued to appear, along with a new dominant personality. Keizo Saji, Shinjiro Torii's son, took over as president of Kotobukiya in 1963 and renamed the firm Suntory (a combination of the firm's port brand Akadama, which translates as "red ball", aka "sun", and Torii's surname). Under his stewardship, new brands Suntory Royal, Red, White, and Reserve all appeared – the last in 1969, the same year that Taketsuru's firm (now called Nikka) started whisky production at its new Sendai Distillery.

In 1973 a further two plants opened: Gotemba, a joint venture between Kirin breweries and Seagram; and Suntory's Hakushu, one of the world's largest malt distilleries.

By the end of the 1980s the industry was in expansionist mode and needing to guarantee supplies of Scotch to be

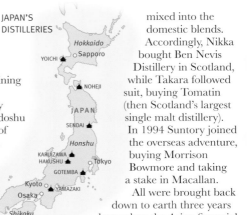

JAPAN'S DISTILLERIES

mixed into the domestic blends. Accordingly, Nikka bought Ben Nevis Distillery in Scotland, while Takara followed suit, buying Tomatin (then Scotland's largest single malt distillery). In 1994 Suntory joined the overseas adventure, buying Morrison Bowmore and taking a stake in Macallan.

All were brought back down to earth three years later when the Asian financial crisis hit. Sales plummeted and, against expectations, did not bounce back. Like their colleagues in Scotland, Japanese distillers believed that each new generation would consume whisky in ever-larger quantities. The decline may have been initiated by a financial crisis, but it was also due to a generational shift away from dark spirits and towards lighter alternatives. In Britain and the US, vodka was in the ascendency; in Japan it was the turn of *shochu*.

The downturn in sales put most distilleries in mothballs; others closed forever. The consequent whisky surplus forced distillers to find new ways to sell their stock. As in Scotland, single malt was the answer, and that is what is leading the Japanese revival.

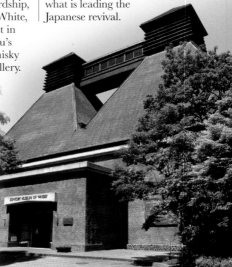

Hakushu, which is owned by Suntory, was the world's largest malt distillery in the mid-1980s.

DISTILLERIES AND MALTS

Despite the industry's setback in the mid-1990s, there are signs of a new confidence in Japanese whisky making. With greater interest in quality malts, it is clear that Japanese whisky is unique and can exist on its own terms.

GOTEMBA

✉ Shibanta 970, Gotembashi, Shizuoka
🖰 www.kirin.co.jp
⚑ Open to visitors

At 620 m (2,000 ft) above sea level, Gotemba is cool, and the maturation profile is, therefore, similar to that of Suntory's Hakushu Distillery (see p239). That is beneficial, the firm believes, for longer ageing. There's a further similarity with that alpine distillery, as both were built in 1973, during the Japanese whisky boom. Gotemba is, however, the only example of a foreign firm – in this case the Canadian distiller Seagram – investing in the infrastructure of the Japanese distilling industry.

The style is similar to that of Hakushu, though whether this is due to altitude or a result of the "Seagram template" is unclear. What is certain is that Kirin (the present owner) believes that it is making a genuine Japanese style – delicate and light, and designed to accompany the country's cuisine.

Not overly constrained by space considerations, the site is sprawling. The production unit is surprisingly small, however, with a malt plant in one room and a grain distillery in another. Four types of malt, from unpeated to heavily peated, are used, and the Japanese model of crystal clear wort and a long, cool fermentation in stainless steel (using, in this case, one of three yeasts cultured at the plant) is employed to assist in the creation of all-important esters.

The four pot stills were modelled on those at

Scotland's Strathisla Distillery (see p74), an ex-Seagram plant. The distillation is run so as to maximize the interaction between vapour and copper, which assists in the creation of a light spirit.

The grain distillery houses three different types of still:

Gotemba Distillery was built in 1973 by Canada's Seagram.

a single column still, a linked column still, and a doubler (as used by Kentucky whiskey makers) to produce three very different styles of grain whisky. All the spirits are aged in American oak barrels.

Today, Gotemba is Japanese-owned. When Seagram sold its distilling interests, the drinks firm Kirin bought back its share of the business – and snapped up the Four Roses

FINDING THE RIGHT LOCATION

Picking a site for a distillery is never an easy task. A number of different criteria need to considered. Water is an obvious one; ease of access to market is another. Space comes into the equation too. This last issue is of no concern to Kirin, the brewer that owns Gotemba. If you stand on the viewing platform on the top of the distillery, there is nothing in front of you but the slopes of Mount Fuji. The area behind is also clear, as it is used as a Japanese Defence Force training site. While many distillers may balk at building their still between an active volcano and a bombing range, it doesn't appear to concern the workers at Gotemba. The main issue for choosing the site was the plentiful supply of lava-filtered snow melt, which flows from Fuji-san. Its location, between Tokyo and Osaka, allowed the firm quick access to Japan's two largest conurbations. It took three years of searching to find the site.

The snow-covered slopes of Mount Fuji provide water for Gotemba.

THE HAKUSHU STORY

Hakushu is spectacularly situated in the "Japanese Alps", a three-hour bullet train ride from all the bustle of Tokyo. Above the distillery rise the granite slopes of Mount Kai-Komagatake, while opposite it looms the active volcano Mount Yatsugatake.

The air at Hakushu is clean and cool, the first indication that the distillery sits at 700 m (2,300 ft) above sea level – more than twice as high as Scotland's highest single-malt distillery. The maximum summer temperature reaches 28°C (82°F) – one reason why this part of the country is a popular destination for city-bound people seeking a short respite from the stifling summer plains.

Despite the distillery site covering 850,000 sq metres (9 million sq ft), there is an absence of any thoughts of industrialization. Hakushu, for all its size, blends into the deep green forests. Over half of the site is kept as a nature reserve, and the distillery's (extremely soft) process water is also bottled and sold by owner Suntory (therefore making the perfect dilutant for the single malt). It was the

Hakushu
10-Year-Old

water that attracted Keizo Saji (son of Suntory's founder, Shinjiro Torii) to the location, not only for its purity and softness, but also because of the volumes that could be captured from the rivers that flow off the surrounding mountains.

Hakushu was one of the distilleries built as a result of the Japanese whisky boom and it was built on a grand scale. Even so, in 1983 Suntory decided to build a second wing, Hakushu East, which made it the largest malt whisky producer in the world. These days, things have been reined back considerably. The original distillery, with its large pot stills, remains mothballed, and production centres on Hakushu East. Even so, the multiple variations on a theme, which typify Japanese whisky making, remain the central distilling ethos. Two types of barley are imported, unpeated and heavily peated. This, in theory, will allow the distiller to blend barleys to produce even more variations.

Hakushu employs a great variety of pot stills to create many different distilling conditions and therefore a wide range of whiskies.

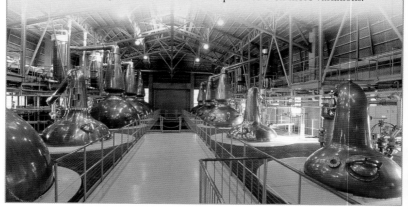

Distillery *(see p189)* as well. Since then, a new brand, Fujisan, has been launched as both a single malt and a blend. Hopefully, this will signal the start of a concerted push behind Gotemba's whiskies.

🍶 **FUJI-GOTEMBA 18-YEAR-OLD** 43% ABV
Classic Gotemba lightness of character on the nose, with biscuit and pear hints. The same leathery note as Fujisanroku, but slightly more oily. The palate is dry and slightly tannic, with some sweet biscuit notes and tobacco. The finish is nutty.

🍶 **FUJI-GOTEMBA SINGLE GRAIN 15-YEAR-OLD** 43% ABV ● One of a very limited number of Japanese single grains available. The Gotemba Distillery uses maize for the base cereal. The whisky is very sweet, almost like a liqueur, with some honey, sesame, and plenty of coconut from ageing in American oak barrels. The palate is extremely soft, with a mix of succulent spirit and buttery wood.

HAKUSHU

✉ Torihara 2913–1, Hakushucho, Komagun, Yamanashi
🌐 www.suntory.co.jp
🚪 Open to visitors

The key to Hakushu lies in the stillhouse. The assortment of equipment at this distillery is nothing short of astonishing. There are six wash stills and five spirit stills – all bar one direct fired – but of a wide variety of type, size, and shape. They run from minuscule "Macallan-type" pots to large "lamp-glass" monsters.

Lyne arms stretch upwards, dip gently,

or fall abruptly. There's even one spirit still with a detachable lyne arm – one arm points up, another goes down. The different distilling conditions created by this set-up will yield dramatically different spirits … and that is the point. Hakushu was not built as a distillery to produce one style of bottled single malt, but was developed to make as wide a variety of flavouring whiskies as possible for Suntory's range of blends.

Fuji-Gotemba 18-Year-Old

It is impossible for a visitor to make sense of the complicated set-up here. A quick look below the stills, for example, reveals twice the number of receiving tanks that you would expect. Whatever their methods, Suntory are keeping them to themselves.

An on-site cooperage carries out recharring and repair work on different types of cask, all of which are held in 22 warehouses. It is estimated that 160 million litres (35 million gallons) of whisky are maturing on site.

Hakushu's whiskies are a crucial component of Suntory's blends, but the distillery is also building a reputation for its single malt. It first appeared as a "Pure Malt" with no age statement in 1988, but today the range comprises 10, 12, and 18-year-old expressions. The distiller claims that its reputation is partially due to the altitude of the distillery, which encourages low-pressure distillation, which allows fewer heavier elements into

Hakushu 12-Year-Old

the spirit. All this esoteric distilling theory becomes academic, however, once the single malt is tasted.

🍶 **HAKUSHU 10-YEAR-OLD** 43% ABV
Light in character with a slight floral, almost pine-like aroma, and just a hint of smoke.

🍶 **HAKUSHU 12-YEAR-OLD** 43% ABV
This is in many ways the perfect introduction to the Hakushu style. Clean and pure, with touches of light grass, cut flowers, pine, and a little peach juice. A hint of linseed oil indicates its relative youth. The palate starts very sweet, and then the peachy note returns before nuts come back towards the (very clean) finish. A light whisky, but a well-balanced one.

🍶 **HAKUSHU 18-YEAR-OLD** 43% ABV
The oak is extremely well balanced – almost restrained in the distillery's older expression. The flowers have shifted to a more general vegetal character, alongside some green plum. The peach juice has moved into mango, while the green grass has shifted to dry hay. There's a fresh acidity cut with a delicate sweetness. The palate shows more toasty oak. Best drunk with water on the side.

Hakushu 18-Year-Old

Hakushu Distillery handles the important process of charring its casks at its on-site cooperage.

HANYU

www.onedrinks.com

Even in the complicated world of Japanese whisky, Hanyu occupies a special place. This is a distillery whose single malts – masterminded by master distiller Ichiro Akuto – have exploded onto the world whisky scene, picking up rave reviews and international prizes. Yet, there is currently no Hanyu Distillery.

Akuto's family started in the liquor trade in the early 17th century when it established a *sake* brewery in Chichibu. In 1941, the decision was made to expand into other areas, and Ichiro's grandfather, Isouji Akuto, built a new *sake* brewery and *shochu* distillery in the town of Hanyu. Five years later his firm, Toa Shuzo, began to blend whisky, though it was not until the early 1980s that the firm began to distil its own whisky. The Japanese obsession with the right water resulted in supplies being trucked 50 km (31 miles) from Chichibu to the distillery.

The firm's style (sold under the Chichibu and Golden Horse labels) was in the

Karuizawa is a small-scale, boutique distillery that focuses on one particular style of whisky.

Yoichi/Karuizawa vein of fuller-bodied, peated whiskies. This adversely impacted on sales, though, as in the 1980s Japanese whisky drinkers tended to knock back their drams *mizuwari* style *(see p236)*. Though Ichiro Akuto had plans to launch a range of single-malt expressions, a downturn in the market bankrupted Toa Shuzo. In 2000 it was sold to a *sake* and *shochu* producer, and the distillery dismantled.

Thankfully, Ichiro Akuto received backing from *sake* brewer Sasanogawa Shuzo to buy back much of the whisky stocks, which he began releasing under the Ichiro's Malt label *(see p251)*, as the Card Series.

The reaction, particularly on the export market, has been astonishing. The whiskies are revealed as being highly complex, medium to full bodied, but with classic Japanese precision of flavour. The happy ending to the story is that, in 2007, Ichiro Akuto began distilling at his new purpose-built distillery in Chichibu. The Card Series will be eked out until his new malts are mature.

🥃 **HANYU VINTAGE 1988, NUMBER 1 DRINKS COMPANY** 55.6% ABV ● This was bottled for Hanyu's UK importer. The whisky was aged in an American oak

Hanyu Single Cask 1988

KARUIZAWA'S BARLEY

This could be the only malt distillery in the world still insisting on using Golden Promise barley exclusively. Karuizawa's whisky makers believe that this barley strain gives a heavier and more oily character and is better suited for extended maturation. These days, the barley is unpeated. Until the mid-1990s, however, heavily-peated malt was used, and this type still appears in the older bottlings.

hogshead and then given a period of finishing in Japanese oak. The nose is a mix of the softly fragrant (vanilla pod, lemon zest, white chocolate) and the exotic – even some black olive tapenade. Light smoke adds another layer. The palate follows in this vein and demonstrates the ability of the best Japanese whiskies to have complexity while retaining a very bright character. The finish is slightly tarry.

KARUIZAWA

✉ Maseguchi 1795–2, Oaza, Miyotamachi, Kitasakugun, Nagano
www.mercian.co.jp
🚪 Open to visitors

"Boutique" is the term that best describes Karuizawa. While most of Japan's other distilleries sprawl over huge sites, it is squeezed into a few buildings on the outskirts of Miyota-cho. Behind it rises the smoking cone of Mount Asama. Originally, this site was a vineyard and the buildings housed a winery. After World War II its then owner, Daikoku-budoshu, in common with a number of other domestic liquor producers decided to join Japan's nascent whisky business. In 1962, it merged with Mercian, another drinks business.

JAPANESE WHISKY: WHAT MAKES IT DIFFERENT?

Strip away all the clues that you are in Japan – cicadas, shrines, *bento* boxes in the café, the signage – and a visit to a Japanese distillery is rather familiar for the visitor already well versed in Scottish malt distillation. There are mash tuns, washbacks, double distillation in pot stills, and maturation (predominantly) in the same mix of woods.

How do Japanese distillers manage to craft a style of whisky that, though similar to its Scottish cousins, has its own individual – Japanese – character?

To start, maybe it is best to define that Japaneseness. The difference was best expressed by Dr Mas Minabe at Suntory, who talked of a "transparency"

Suntory is the best-known producer of Japanese whisky.

of flavour that exists in Japanese malts and is not present in Scottish ones. On one hand this means a precision of character, an ordered array of aromas and flavours that seem to line up on the palate and can be tasted almost individually while still making up a complex whole. This isn't to say that these are light whiskies. Transparency is spot on. You can see into them.

Another defining element is that Japanese single malt is not malty.

Suntory uses wooden mash tuns, like these, as well as more modern stainless-steel tuns to create further variety in the spirit they produce.

There are no cereal notes. Even a non-malty Scotch will seem to be filled with cereal notes when compared to a Japanese malt. In order to achieve this, Japanese distillers avoid any solids from the grist being brought through from the mash tun to the washback. Scottish distillers talk of clear and cloudy worts, but none have the clarity of wort achieved in Japan.

A wide mix of yeasts, some unique to a single distillery, is also employed, allowing the creation of distinct flavours, while the widespread use of long fermentation helps to build complexity and aromatic elements and reduces cereal elements.

Japan itself has a part to play. Its climate has an influence on the manner in which the whisky matures. In the words of Masataka Taketsuru: "whisky making is an act of co-operative creation between the blessings of nature and the wisdom of man."

The differences between Karuizawa and its colleagues is clear from the start. No creation of a range of flavours here. The distillery is set up to make one style of malt whisky, end of story.

The fermentation process is intriguing and appears to take its inspiration from *sake* brewing. A small percentage of wort is pumped into a tank and yeast is added. Only once this "starter" is active it is transferred to the washback where the rest of the worts and a small extra amount of yeast is added.

The stillhouse – actually, it is more of a stillroom – gives the impression of being slightly too small for the pots it contains, even though they could hardly be described as gigantic. The necks of the two pairs of wash and spirit stills arch into the wooden rafters. Distillation is relaxed, and maturation in the ivy-festooned, fungus-blackened stone warehouses is predominantly in European oak ex-sherry barrels, which have been remade to hold 400 litres (88 gallons) – less to do with wood interaction and more to do with fitting into the racks.

The Japanese climate has its part to play too. Winters can be very cold – the train from Tokyo is often filled with skiers then – but summers are sultry and humid, causing the maturation to vary its pace markedly – another Japanese twist in what at first seems a classic, old-style Scottish set-up.

Taste Karuizawa and the terms "fat", "full", "power", "sweet", and "weight" appear regularly. These are robust but balanced whiskies. A range of aged malts and vintage-dated bottlings is available as well as occasional releases by other bottlers.

SENDAI'S SETTING

Nikka's second malt distillery is set among the mountains on the road to the cherry orchards, mountain temples and hot springs of Tone, in Miyagi Prefecture to the northeast of Tokyo. Its large buildings are scattered across the river plain, separated by mini plantations of pine and cradled by the waters of the Nikkawa and Hirose rivers.

It was the confluence of these two rivers at this point that prompted Masataka Taketsuru to start building here in 1969, at the end of a three-year search for a suitable location for a second distillery. Company legend has it that Masataka came here, tasted the water and pronounced it good. In an echo of the founding of Yamazaki, he also felt the humidity from the rivers was conducive to a good maturation profile.

Sadly, Karuizawa has been mothballed for a number of years. There was a frisson of hope in 2007 when Mercian was bought by Kirin, though it appears the brewer was more interested in that firm's wine business. Hopefully this will change. The full-blooded Karuizawa style would make a wonderful counterpoint to the delicate Gotemba malts.

KARUIZAWA VINTAGE 1988
59.8% ABV ● A rich melange of fruits (black cherry, green fig) alongside chocolate, and a vegetal aroma that recalls wet grass or bamboo. The palate is where the deeper notes begin to show. Tongue-coating with layers of flavour and good weight. Long finish.

KARUIZAWA 15-YEAR-OLD 40% ABV This runs counter to most of the distillery's bottlings as it appears to have come from an American oak (ex-bourbon) cask. Lighter in character with some grassiness but a soft, fruity weight as well: ripe pear, baked peach, honey. Karuizawa's chewy quality is there on the palate along with coffee and some smoke (the malt was peated until 1994).

KARUIZAWA 17-YEAR-OLD 40% ABV This is more in line with what is thought of as the classic

Karuizawa 17-Year-Old

Karuizawa style: huge and meaty with truffle/dried shiitake mushroom, even hints of balsamic – a sure indication of greater age. The smoke is slightly sooty along with roast chestnut and a slight earthy note. The sheer weight and heaviness of character is slightly atypical of most Japanese malts. One for after a meal.

SENDAI (MIYAGIKYO)

✉ Nikka 1, Aobaku, Sendaishi, Miyagiken

🔗 www.nikka.com

⛴ Open to visitors

There is some confusion as to what this site is actually called. The distillery's name originally was Sendai, because that is the nearest major city. This was of no concern until Nikka decided to start bottling it as a single malt. Calling your brand after a city with over one million people is akin to a Scottish distiller naming its single malt "Glasgow". A new name was devised: Miyagikyo. Kyo is Japanese for "valley", Miyagi is the name of the prefecture, so the name could be loosely translated as "Glen Miyagi", which is more appropriate. These days, the single malt is called Miyagikyo, while the distillery itself remains as Sendai – though some early bottlings of the malt have Sendai on the label.

The plant has been expanded twice (in 1979 and 1989) since its founding, and now has malt and grain distilleries and extensive warehousing. Though the capacity of the malt site is 600,000 litres (132,000 gallons) a year, it is currently operating at just one third of that. The whole process is computerized and monitored from a central control room.

As far as malt production goes, variety is the key, and the approach is similar to the one taken at Yoichi, though here only unpeated and lightly peated malt is used. Two lauter tuns produce worts that run as clear as the Nikkawa's water. Different yeasts are used to help produce a range of flavours in the wash, which ferments slowly in 22 stainless-steel washbacks.

Distillation takes place in eight stills (four from the original distillery and a second quartet), which are set up to run in pairs. They are large and heavy-bottomed, with fat necks that allow plenty of time for the vapour to interact with the copper, helping to create a light style of spirit.

Ageing takes place in 18 warehouses scattered around the site. American oak hoggies are the favoured type of cask, though some European butts are still used. They are only ever stored two high as this is an earthquake zone.

THE MIYAGIKYO WHISKIES

Five types of whisky are made, but the standard Miyagikyo is fruity with an aromatic, estery lift. It's a lighter dram than Yoichi, with less peat and a floral edge that drifts into soft stone fruits: fresh in younger examples; dried or caramelized in older expressions.

The grain plant contains two Coffey stills for continuous distillation of grain spirit. The stills were installed in 1999, and provide spirit for Nikka's blends. A number of styles are made: a malt/corn blend, a 100 per cent corn distillate, as well as one from 100 per cent malted barley. The firm has launched, in limited quantities, a "Coffey Grain".

Malt devotees who taste this whisky are usually pleasantly surprised.

In the export markets, Miyagikyo is somewhat overshadowed by its more robust northern brother, Yoichi, but its make is more in keeping with the Japanese style of estery and lightly fruity whiskies. And these single malts possess an appealing depth of character.

Miyagiko 15-Year-Old

Miyagiko 12-Year-Old

🥃 **MIYAGIKYO 10-YEAR-OLD** 45% ABV
The standard bottled product shows Miyagikyo to be a gentle and fruity malt with light floral touches and good depth. The 10-year-old is light and aromatic with hints of lily, broom, and fennel on the nose, alongside a butterscotch nuttiness. Very clean and precise. This is a medium-bodied malt with a clean, light texture, touches of tangerine, and a pine-like finish.

Sendai has a beautiful setting on a watery plain where the Hikkawa and Hirose rivers meet.

🜋 MIYAGIKYO 12-YEAR-OLD 45% ABV

By the time the whisky has reached 12 years old, the flavour has filled out with dried peach and heavy vanilla overtones. Medium-bodied, it also shows a little more oaky grip than the younger example.

🜋 MIYAGIKYO 15-YEAR-OLD 45% ABV

By 15 years everything has deepened and softened. Toffee, chocolate, and ripe soft fruits on the nose. There's also a touch of raisin on the palate. The most complex of the three, though the fresh grassy notes of youth are still discernable.

YAMAZAKI

✉ Yamazaki 5-2-2, Honcho, Mishimagun, Osaka

🜊 www.suntory.co.jp

⛴ Open to visitors

Arriving at Yamazaki is unlike the approach to any other distillery. You exit at a small railway station,

surprised at being in what seems to be the country after the clustering chaos of Kyoto. The noise of cicadas is deafening as you walk through narrow streets to the level crossing and, on the other side, a looming brown building. Over the tracks you arrive in a wooded and landscaped garden. There, one path leads to the huge distillery, while another takes you through the *torii* gate to a Shinto shrine high in the trees.

The shrine is an indication of the auspicious nature of this location, which is one reason why, in the 16th century, it was chosen as the site of the first tea house built by Sen no Rikyu, the creator of *chanoyu* (the tea ceremony). He was drawn by the fact that Yamazaki is at the confluence of four rivers: namely Katsura, Kamo, Uji and Kizu; all four flow into the Yodo river.

Yamazaki 25-Year-Old

While Rikyu came looking for tranquillity, Yamazaki's founder, Shinjiro Torii *(see p238)*, was more excited by the misty humidity generated by the river waters. These, he felt, would assist with maturation at this, Japan's first malt whisky distillery.

The main distillery buildings that can be seen today were built when Yamazaki was doubled in size in 1958. They are not at all pretty, and are topped with two rounded pyramidal protuberances that give the plant the air of a stylized frog. Rather than being in any way decorative, though, they originally had a functional use as pagoda-style chimneys for the distillery's on-site maltings. The maltings closed in 1972, and now, in common with every other Japanese distillery, Yamazaki imports its malted barley, either from Scotland or Australia.

There were further expansions in 1980 and 1989 as the Japanese whisky boom took hold. If you had visited over the last decade or so, however, you would have found a very different sight. Like every other Japanese distillery, Yamazaki was on an enforced cut-back in production as its owner Suntory tried to balance its stock surplus.

The tough times appear to be receding, however, and in 2005 Yamazaki had yet another makeover, conceivably its most radical yet. While the first Yamazaki had large steam-fired stills, and the 1989 rebuild saw medium-sized steam-fired stills being brought in, the new Yamazaki has small, direct-fired stills. These have been introduced with the aim of making a heavier style of whisky. A mix of condensers and worm tubs are also used. Production is now half of the previous capacity, meaning that only one of the distillery's two mash tuns is being used.

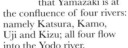

A NEW AGE OF CONNOISSEURSHIP

The slump in sales of Japanese blended whisky from the late 1990s left distillers with excess whisky. Suntory had launched Yamazaki as a single malt in 1984, but the firm's main business was blend based. Now, however, premium whisky and malt were to receive ever-greater focus as Suntory tried to persuade a new generation of drinkers to drink less quantity but better quality.

This necessitated creating brands that would appeal to this new consumer. The malt-drinkers' palate, as they discovered, is different to that of the blend lover. The old ways of *mizuwari* (lots of ice, lots of water) with whisky as a thirst quencher was being replaced by a new connoisseurship where malts (and top blends) were served as shots with glasses of iced water on the side. *Mizuwari* drinkers needed light flavoured whisky; the new premium drinkers demanded flavour above all else.

A change in approach by the consumer, Suntory felt, justified a change in approach at the distillery. Scottish distillers may tweak their plant or wood policy to cope with shifts in demand. Suntory changed the stillhouse.

Yamazaki's 1984 Single Malt

A PLETHORA OF STYLES

Unlike their Scottish counterparts, Japanese distillers do not exchange whiskies for their blends. The onus is, therefore, on the firm's distilling teams to make a number of different styles at each site. Suntory's way is to introduce as much variation in the stillhouse as possible. Japanese distillers become rather secretive when asked about how many flavouring whiskies they make, and Yamazaki is no exception in this regard.

The stillhouse remains one of the most remarkable in the whisky world. There are six pairs of stills, mostly running in tandem, but all are differently shaped.

The make that appears as a single malt is a medium-bodied, fruity malt with a subtle depth in the middle of the palate. (You might pick up some smoke on future bottlings). Like all the country's whiskies, Yamazaki has a clarity of flavour that clearly differentiates it from Scottish single malt.

In recent years Yamazaki has launched a range of single-cask whiskies from a wide variety of wood types: the standard American oak barrel and hoggie and European oak butts; but also new oak and, most exciting for whisky enthusiasts, Japanese oak (see p249). The originator remains at the forefront of the new age of Japanese whisky.

YAMAZAKI'S HOUSE STYLE
The first malt distillery in Japan, Yamazaki produces a wide range of styles for Suntory's blender, Seiichi Koshimizu, to work with. The core style, however, is a sweet, fruity single malt, which almost seems to slow down in the middle of the palate to reveal its full complexity. It is a malt that appears to benefit from a slightly longer period in the cask.

Yamazaki 12-Year-Old

🥃 **YAMAZAKI 10-YEAR-OLD**
40% ABV ● The lightest of the range, at 10 years of age, this Yamazaki expression has yet to develop its defining succulent fruitiness. There's a spicy note in here, along with some oak. A light lunchtime drink.

🥃 **YAMAZAKI 12-YEAR-OLD** 43% ABV
● This expression is very clean and crisp with touches of pineapple, citrus, flowers/ blossom, dried herbs, and a little oak. The palate is quite sweet with a hint of smoke before the dense and fruity character hits in the middle of the tongue, followed by the spices surging through. Very precise and classically Japanese. There's some raisin and coconut as well, suggesting a variety of casks have been used in the mix.

🥃 **YAMAZAKI 18-YEAR-OLD**
43% ABV ● With greater age, Yamazaki acquires more influence from oak. The estery notes of the younger variants have been replaced with ripe apple, violet, and a deep, sweet oakiness that's reminiscent of a walk in an autumn forest. This impression continues on the palate, where a mossy, pine-like character is evident, along with the classic Yamazaki richness in the middle of the mouth. An extremely classy whisky.

Yamazaki 18-Year-Old

The stills at Yamazaki Distillery are in six pairs of varying shapes and sizes, and lyne arm angles.

Pure snow melt from the slopes of Mount Fuji supplies the water for Gotemba Distillery.

TAKETSURU'S SCOTTISH TRAVELS

Taketsuru's experiences in Scotland were of profound importance to his approach to whisky making. His travels, all meticulously recorded in a series of notebooks, centred around a short period at Longmorn in Speyside, and a longer spell of work experience at Hazelburn in Campbeltown.

Masataka Taketsuru

He returned to Japan convinced of a number of basics that he felt were essential in making great whisky. Water and barley were both a given. What was more important was peat and a cold temperature for long, steady maturation. Taketsuru had experienced big, rich whiskies in Scotland – even today, Longmorn is one of the richer Speysiders, and though Hazelburn has long since gone, the distillery was known for

making a classic oily, smoky, and rich "Campbeltown" style. If that was his template, it was one that ran counter to the vision of his first boss in Japan, Shinjiro Torii, who wanted a more delicate whisky and was happy with maturing in the warmer locations closer to the main markets of Osaka, Kyoto, and Tokyo.

It is not surprising therefore that after helping to establish Yamazaki, Taketsuru headed north to Hokkaido. It is a fanciful notion, but maybe the sight of the herring boats heading off into the Sea of Japan near Yoichi reminded him of Campbeltown. More prosaically, there was water and barley, peat near at hand, oak forests close by, and the temperature was as close as he could find to that of Scotland.

YOICHI

✉ Kurokawacho 7–6, Yoichimachi, Yoichigun, Hokkaido

🖥 www.nikka.com

⛴ Open to visitors

Japan's most northerly distillery is situated in a small fishing port of 24,000 people on the east coast of the island of Hokkaido. Mountains rise around it on three sides, and on the other is the Sea of Japan. If you were to sail due west you would reach Vladivostok on the coast of Russia. Not surprisingly, perhaps, the setting is reminiscent of Scotland, particularly if you

head here in the winter when snow lies thick on the ground and covers the red-roofed pagodas of the kiln.

This is where Masataka Taketsuru headed when he left Kotobukiya (now Suntory) to set up on his own in the 1930s (*see also p235*).

Building started on the Yoichi Distillery in 1934 and the first spirit ran from the stills two years later. By 1940 Yoichi's whiskies were on the Japanese market. On the face of it, little has changed since then. Sadly, though, the kiln has been silent since the 1960s. No longer is it being fired with peat cut for it in Ishikari.

Now the barley arrives ready peated from Scotland. Malting in Japan is simply too expensive an option for the country's distillers, who are already faced with higher fixed costs than most whisky makers elsewhere.

In common with its great rival, Nikka needs to produce a wide selection of different flavoured whiskies at this one site, though the approach is different to that taken by Suntory. Although the single-malt bottlings are

Yoichi Distillery was founded in the 1930s, and is Japan's most northerly whisky-making plant.

all peaty, there is unpeated barley used here as well. In addition, Nikka uses different strains of yeast in order to create a range of flavour profiles, while fermentation times (always on the long side), are varied to assist in this process.

The stills are all large and plain – similar, Nikka likes to say, to the stills with which the founder first worked at Longmorn in Scotland. Direct firing is used and the distillate is condensed in worm tubs. Varying cut points will also assist in widening the flavour spectrum, but the key at Yoichi is weight on the palate. These are deep whiskies that need cool maturation – in a variety of casks from both European and American oak – to demonstrate their full complexity. Nikka has regular (though limited edition) bottlings from a wide range of the different styles made at the distillery.

Yoichi -Year-Old

YOICHI'S WHISKIES

It was a Yoichi whisky that helped to trigger the worldwide interest among malt connoisseurs for Japanese whisky. In 2001, the 10-year-old cask strength won the inaugural "Best of the Best" blind tasting organized by *Whisky Magazine*. A year later, the Scotch Malt Whisky Society broke with tradition and bottled a single cask.

From these two small events, the start of Japanese whisky's acceptance across the world started. Yet although these whiskies are among the fullest that are created in Japan, they still have the precision of flavour that defines the essential Japanese whisky character. Taketsuru may have been

aiming to recreate whisky from Scotland. What he actually succeeded in doing was to give birth to an entirely new and subtly different family of whiskies.

YOICHI 10-YEAR-OLD 45% ABV
A rare creature in Japanese whisky, Yoichi 10-year-old is a slightly malty dram. The peated element is quite light on the nose, though giving a salty note. Sweet toffee notes balance things well. The palate is slightly oily with sooty smoke on the back palate along with muted dried flowers. Deep and full-flavoured, but with the energy of youth.

YOICHI 12-YEAR-OLD 45% ABV • Here, the full Yoichi character is on

Yoichi 15-Year-Old

show: rich deep flavours with an earthy, almost dusty, quality. The sooty smoke remains, though by now the fruits are beginning to emerge. The palate has an interesting mix of burnt heather, liquorice, and cooked fruits. Robust, yet elegant.

YOICHI 15-YEAR-OLD 45% ABV • By this stage, the whisky has added another layer. The rough edges of the 12-year-old have been thoroughly smoothed off, and this is as sleek as Yoichi gets. Citrus notes, light tannin, plenty of rich oak, and the ever-present smoke, but there's sufficient weight to give balance. A big whisky.

THE WEIRD WORLD OF JAPANESE OAK

The aroma was familiar, yet alien – in its acidity and zestiness reminiscent of a young rye whisky, yet more perfumed and greatly more intense. It's rare that you come across a completely new aroma in whisky, but this was one such moment. Seiichi Koshimizu, chief blender at Suntory, explained: "we say it smells of temples". It was spot on. The aroma was of Japanese incense, with the heady aromas of *oudh*, or aloeswood.

It transpires that this whisky (a single cask from Yamazaki) had been matured in Japanese oak (*Quercus mongolica*). This is rare, as most Japanese oak has already been felled (some say to make coffins for British soldiers in World War II, others maintain as the result of the clearance programme in Hokkaido to create pasture land). Distillers didn't particularly like Japanese oak casks, as they tended to leak, though they had to be used after World War II as there was no alternative. In addition, blenders didn't like the strong aroma the oak imparted, and as soon as ex-bourbon and ex-sherry casks were available, the industry switched. Suntory coopered its last Japanese oak cask in 1975.

Now, however, with the rise of single malt and of flavour, it is slowly finding favour once again. Suntory has its own new plantation and has started a very limited coopering programme. Koshimizu-san is using Japanese oak as part of his blending palette, while Ichiro Akuto is also laying down stock of new barrels. The startling aroma may yet have a future.

Ichiro's Two of Clubs Malt, 2000 was finished in Japanese oak, giving an acidic finish to the whisky.

BRANDS AND BLENDS

Japanese blends have made a great impact internationally in the last decade, winning acclaim and awards. Unlike distilleries in most other countries, those in Japan do not trade with competitors, so one distillery will produce a wide range of whiskies to make up its blends.

FUJISANROKU

Distillery: Gotemba

The newest brand to appear from Kirin's Gotemba Distillery, Fujisanroku is bottled both as a blended whisky and a single malt, so read the label carefully. The distillery style is light and estery. The single malt has older malts up to 24 years old blended in with it.

FUJISANROKU SINGLE MALT 18-YEAR-OLD 43% ABV • The aroma shows good age: there is a slight leathery note combined with dried peach.

At Suntory's Yamazaki Distillery, the emphasis is on producing a variety of flavours for the blends.

The wood element appears as notes of pine sap. Water releases citrus oils, elderflower, honeycomb, and lime blossom. Estery and perfumed. A delicate palate, but still offering a complex array of flavours. A slight waxy note allows it to hold to the tongue.

GOLDEN HORSE

Distillery: Hanyu

This is the brand name originally used by Toa Shuzo, which owned the old Hanyu Distillery. The trademark has now passed to the new owner of the company, which continues to bottle some old stock. Golden Horse is not to be confused with the Ichiro's Malt range *(see opposite)*.

GOLDEN HORSE 8-YEAR-OLD 40% ABV • A youthful and quite energetic attack on the nose with an aroma rarely seen in Japanese whisky – a touch of bran-like maltiness. Some nutty oak as well. The palate is light and crisp with some grip from the oak, which is, at this point in its life, still fighting with the inherently sweet spirit rather than working in harmony with it.

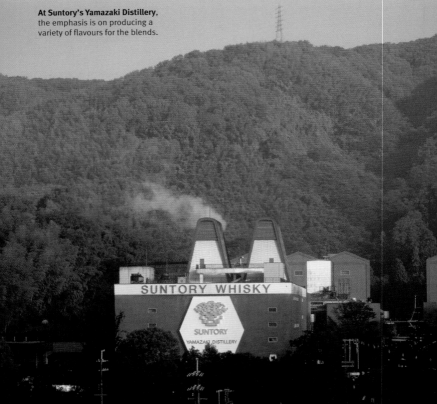

Hibiki 30-Year-Old

HIBIKI

Producer: Suntory

Suntory's flagship premium blended whisky was launched in 1989 to commemorate the 90th anniversary of the company's founding. The 21-year-old followed in 1994. A decade later the 30-year-old won the Trophy at the International Spirits Challenge, the first Japanese whisky to do so. The same whisky beat all-comers to win best blend in the World Whisky Awards in 2007.

HIBIKI 17-YEAR-OLD 43% ABV
There is a distinct fruitiness to the nose mixed with some more delicate estery notes, a smooth, creamy tablet-like sweetness, and a hint of citrus. The palate is rich and filled with vanilla, rosehip, black cherry, and a touch of firm oak. Good complexity and balance.

HIBIKI 17-YEAR-OLD 50.5% ABV
Suntory also bottles Hibiki

17-year-old at a higher strength. The sweetness is accentuated, touching on golden syrup. There's also some dried orange peel and an aromatic note reminiscent of cocoa butter. Bigger in the mouth (thanks to the higher alcohol) with a mix of raspberry and peach, caramel toffee, and a nuttily sweet finish.

HIBIKI 30-YEAR-OLD 43% ABV The multi-award winner is huge in flavour with quite assertive wood at first on the nose. A polished walnut table somehow springs to mind. There are caramelized fruits and a touch of aniseed. On the palate the flavours go deep, recalling Oxford marmalade. The effect is velvety and rich. Not shy.

Suntory's sponsorship of golf tournaments began in the early 1970s, and has done much to popularize the brand image.

Hokuto Pure Malt 12-Year-Old

coming into whisky through *shochu*. The key production quirk that sets it apart lies in the fact that it has been filtered through bamboo.

HOKUTO PURE MALT 12-YEAR-OLD 40% ABV
This blended malt is very gentle on the nose, with some banana, pear, and cut flowers. A very soft palate too, with touches of sweet spice, particularly on the finish.

ICHIRO'S MALT

Distillery: Hanyu

This selection of single-cask bottlings is drawn from the stock of whisky that Ichiro Akuto managed to buy back when his family distillery was sold in 2000. He is releasing these slowly on to the market to bridge the period between the end of the old distillery and the release of whiskies from his new site (scheduled to be complete in 2007). The whiskies were distilled between 1985 and 2000 and each cask has been named

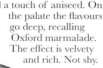

HOKUTO

Producer: Suntory

This blended (vatted) malt was created by Suntory to try and appeal to a new generation of drinkers who were

Hibiki 21-Year-Old

Hibiki 17-Year-Old

after a different playing card; collectively they are referred to as the Card Series. Most of them have been given a period of secondary maturation in a selection of different casks: American, European, and Japanese oak.

🍶 **ICHIRO'S MALT, TWO OF CLUBS, 2000** 55% ABV ●
Distilled in the Hanyu Distillery's final year, this young whisky has been finished in Japanese oak. The nose is very intense with some vanilla as well as a cherry-like/maraschino lift. The palate

OTHER DISTILLERIES

Situated in the town of Miyata in the Kiso mountain range, **Shinshu Distillery** is Japan's highest. Owned by **Hombu**, a *shochu* and liqueur producer, this small distillery with two pots was built in 1985 and sells its malt under the Komagatake label. The distillery is currently silent. Hombu actually had been making whisky off and on since the early 1950s. Its first distillery was in Kagoshima, on the southerly island of Kyushu, the spiritual home of *shochu*. It was making whisky until 1984, but the plant has now reverted to the production of sweet potato *shochu*. The Satsuma single malt from the distillery is still available. **Shirakawa Distillery** in Fukushima is long silent. It was owned by Takara Shuzou, whose only interest in whisky distilling these days comes from its ownership of Tomatin Distillery in Scotland (*see p97*) and co-ownership of the Blanton's range of small-batch bourbons (*see p212*). It's King blend is still available in Japan.

is very soft and smooth initially, and water brings out a creamy character. This then gives way to the fragrant, quite acidic finish that typifies Japanese oak. Young, but with bags of character.

🍶 **ICHIRO'S MALT, QUEEN OF HEARTS, 1990** 54% ABV ● This French-oak finished member of the series shows an interplay between the fat and the lean. The nose is round and plump with light red fruits and a touch of sweet wood. A light touch of smoke with an estery lift gives an added perfume. The palate is lighter than expected, though there is a succulent quality to the middle palate. The French oak gives a spicy kick to the finish.

🍶 **ICHIRO'S MALT, KING OF DIAMONDS, 1988** 56% ABV
One of the most complex of the Card Series, the King of Diamonds was finished in ex-sherry barrels made from American oak. The nose is a mix of cream and toasted almond, with some dry sacking notes indicative of age. As usual there's light smoke and when

Ichiro Akuto is seen here taking delivery of a copper pot still for his new distillery in 2007.

water is added there's a fragrant sandalwood edge alongside pineapple, lemon, and pine sap. The palate is equally complex. Though old, it has a floral freshness and the smoke and oak are never dominant. Balanced.

🍶 **ICHIRO'S MALT, ACE OF SPADES, 1985** 55% ABV ●
One of the oldest in the series, the Ace of Spades (or the Motorhead malt, as some call it) was finished in ex-sherry barrels made from Spanish oak. This has given it an aroma of chocolate-covered raisin, and treacle with a hint of creosote-like smoke. The palate is very thick and chewy, like melting toffee in the mouth. The finish recalls prunes macerated in brandy. Not a shy beast.

Ichiro's Malt, King of Diamonds

Ichiro's Malt, Ace of Spades

NIKKA

Distilleries: Sendai (Miyagikyo), Yoichi

This major distiller, now part of Asahi Breweries, was founded by

Nikka Pure Malt Series, Black

Nikka From the Barrel Malt

Masataka Taketsuru *(see p235)* and is Suntory's main (some would say only) rival on the domestic market. As well as a range of single malts from its two distilleries, Yoichi and Sendai (Miyagikyo), the firm produces blends, blended malts, and single grain under its own name and proprietory brands.

PURE MALT SERIES: RED 43% ABV
Red is the lightest of the colour-coded series, using a high percentage of Miyagikyo malts. Estery with the aroma of apple, powdered almond, and a crisp oakiness. The palate is light and floral with a zesty citric lift. Good as an aperitif.

Sendai Distillery provides malt for many brands, notably the Nikka and Taketsuru pure malt series.

PURE MALT SERIES: WHITE 43% ABV ● White is the most phenolic of the trio, moving into a perfumed zone with hints of dried lavender along with light nutty notes. Slightly herbal on the nose, there is a slight soapiness on the palate.

PURE MALT SERIES: BLACK 43% ABV ● Black is the biggest of the three with a deep, chocolatey, almost leathery nose. The smokiness gives it an earthy quality. Dry for a Japanese whisky, the high proportion of Yoichi malt used here adds density and weight, though there is a blackcurrant sweetness in the centre and a peppery finish.

NIKKA ALL MALT 40% ABV ● A blend of pot still malt and 100 per cent malt from a Coffey still. An intriguing mix of sweet and dry oak on the nose alongside some banana, the palate is soft and unctuous with silky, juicy fruits to the fore.

FROM THE BARREL 51.4% ABV ● A blend of grain and malt, which have been vatted together and then given a period of

secondary ageing in barrel. It is bottled at cask strength. This has the most intense nose of the Nikka range with a resinous perfume intensity hinting at rosemary oil while some dried chocolate and cherry adds interest. The palate is a mix of sweet and savoury with a heavy dose of spices on the finish. Complex.

TAKETSURU

Distilleries: Sendai (Miyagikyo), Yoichi

A duo of vatted malts from Nikka are named after the legendary founder of the company. The constituent parts are drawn from the multitude of whiskies made at their two distilleries.

TAKETSURU PURE MALT 17-YEAR-OLD 43% ABV ● A highly complex whisky, this leads with marzipan, light smoke, polished wood, and tobacco. In time a tropical fruit note emerges alongside eucalypt and vanilla. The palate is very juicy and the vanilla deepens into cocoa. There's oak but sufficient clean pure fruit to balance. Very precise and complex.

Taketsuru Pure Malt 17-Year-Old

TAKETSURU PURE MALT 21-YEAR-OLD 43% ABV ● Winner of best blended malt in the 2007 World Whiskies Awards, beating rivals from Scotland, this older expression has more smoke on show, along with layers of sweet toffee, sultana, and rich oak, and a slightly fungal note that you get from mature whiskies. Tropical fruits seen in the younger expression (conceivably part of the Miyagikyo contribution) are more concentrated in this expression.

Taketsuru Pure Malt 21-Year-Old

EUROPE

Although Ireland and Scotland are generally recognized as the cradle of whisky distilling, at the same time that their industries were forming in the 17th, 18th, and 19th centuries, distilling was in full swing elsewhere in Europe – but not whisky.

D ue to the climate, the southern part of Europe concentrated on distilling fruits into a variety of *eaux-de-vie*, whereas the north used barley to brew beer, or distilled gin and vodka from other grains, usually flavoured with herbs, spices, and fruits. Austria for instance is famous for its wide variety of schnapps, flavoured with whatever berries the makers can lay their hands on. France's most noble distillates are Cognac, Armagnac, Calvados, and Mar, each made in specific regions. The Germans also provide the lover of strong liquor with a variety of schnapps, while Scandinavian countries have been enjoying aquavit for ages. The Dutch have their own sort of gin, "genever"; the process for making this comes closest to the making of whisky if flavouring were left out and maturation introduced.

In the last 10 years or so, however, the interest in making whisky has grown slowly but surely on the Continent. Companies have kept a watchful eye on the development of whisky in particular, since it was the only liquor showing growth figures, whereas drinks like genever, schnapps, and Cognac showed

a marked decline in sales. Typically distilleries were started by existing companies, either producers of *eaux-de-vie* or brewers of beer. After all, without the hops, whisky is distilled beer.

Today Austria is home to five whisky distillers, Germany ten, France eight, and the Netherlands three. Several other countries have just one or two whisky-making distilleries. Spain, for example, has been making a blended whisky since 1959 at DYC. The distillery is owned by Fortune Brands, which also owns the Islay single malt Laphroaig, the bourbons Maker's Mark and Jim Beam, and Teacher's blended Scotch.

Continental European whisky-distilling history is in most cases a short one and whisky needs time to mature. Currently the Continentals offer rather young whiskies to the market in order to make an early return on their investments. Most whiskies in this section are less than 10 years old and some have just passed the legal minimum of three years' maturation. Those young ones are hard to judge and it will take another 10 to 15 years to see how they develop and which distilleries survive. In any case, aficionados follow them with great interest and can hardly wait to taste fully matured 12 to 18-year-old European single malts.

Zuidam Distillery in the Netherlands, which has this attractive windmill on site, introduced their Millstone 5-Year-Old Malt in 2007.

DISTILLERIES AND BRANDS

A growing number of European distillers are turning their hands to whisky, producing an intriguing mix of styles. Time will tell how well these spirits develop with age, but there are plenty of signs of promise.

BAUERNHOF

Switzerland:
✉ Talacher, 6340 Baar
🖳 www.swissky.ch

Brennerei Zentrum Bauernhof produces a wide variety of fruit liquors and has recently started to venture into whisky distilling. Their first product is a single malt called Swissky with no age statement. The latest expression is St Moritzer Single Malt. Apparently, the malt used is *rauchmalz*, a local variety from Bamberg in southern Germany, but the distillery tends to be secretive about its casks and maturation methods.

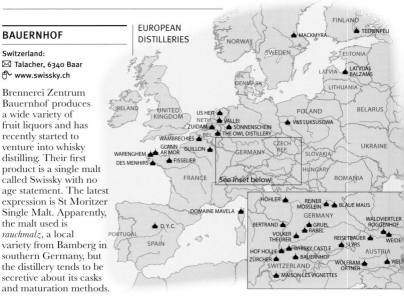

EUROPEAN DISTILLERIES

See inset below.

BERTRAND

France:
✉ 3 Rue du Maréchal Leclerc, Uberach
🖳 www.distillerie-bertrand.com
🍷 Open by appointment only

Uberach is a small village in the north of the Alsace and its distillery was founded in 1874, mainly to produce brandy and liqueurs. Whisky production started in 2002. Since Bertrand also owns a brewery, malt is shared between the beer and whisky producers. Bertrand has two expressions. Uberach Single Malt is a blend using different casks (ex-Banyuls sweet wine and new wood), aged between three and four years. Uberach Single Cask Malt is a non-filtered whisky,

Bertrand's Uberach Single Malt

and is matured exclusively in Banyuls casks for three years.

🥃 **UBERACH SINGLE MALT** 42.2% ABV • This straw-coloured malt is young leather and cut grass, hay, light honey, becoming waxy. Dried fruits (apricots) and a spicy, peppery finish.

🥃 **UBERACH SINGLE CASK MALT** 43.8% ABV • Amber with pink tones. Chocolate aromas, with hints of old plum and a little peat; deep, with a fruity roundness.

BLAUE MAUS

Germany:
✉ Bamberger Strasse 2, Eggolsheim-Neuses
🖳 www.fleischmann-whisky.de
🍷 Open by appointment only

Robert Fleischmann started in 1980 with a brandy wine distillery on the premises of

the original family company – a grocery and tobacco shop. Three years later he attempted for the first time to make pure malt whisky. Many attempts would follow, honouring his motto: "Practise, practise, practise". Fleischmann began selling his whisky in 1996. In 2000 his son Thomas and wife Petra took over the company.

The current offerings number five different single malt whiskies.

🥃 **GRÜNER HUND VINTAGE 1991** 40% ABV • At first slightly sour, almonds, then floral, fragrant, nutty. Toasted almonds, slightly bitter, though creamy, with a malty sweetness. The finish is warming and medium long.

🥃 **BLAUE MAUS VINTAGE 1993** 40% ABV • Malty with oak notes. Sweet-sour with a slightly spicy and peppery finish.

🥃 **KROTTENTALER VINTAGE 1994** 40% ABV • Sweet, malty with

a decent oaky note. Creamy, slightly sweet vanilla oak. A medium to long finish ends in a beautiful taste of almonds.

🥄 **SCHWARZER PIRAT VINTAGE 1995** 40 % ABV
Dry, peaty, and sweet, with an almond flavour which echoes sweetly in a medium finish.

🥄 **SPINNAKER VINTAGE 1997** 40 % ABV
Malty, lightly nutty, and creamy. Sweet like marzipan, with a short, dry-sweet finish in which the marzipan lingers on.

DES MENHIRS

France:
✉ Pont Menhir, 29700 Plomelin
🖳 www.distillerie.fr

This distillery was built in Brittany in 1986 to distil apple cider. In 1998 a separate still was installed to produce whisky, solely made from buckwheat.

The whisky is called Eddu (Breton for buckwheat) and available in three expressions. Eddu Silver is double-distilled and matured in French oak casks, though the maturation period is not specified. Eddu Gold is similar, only higher in alcohol. Eddu Grey Rock is a blend, with 30 per cent buckwheat whisky.

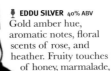

Des Menhirs'
Eddu Grey Rock

🥄 **EDDU SILVER** 40% ABV
Gold amber hue, aromatic notes, floral scents of rose, and heather. Fruity touches of honey, marmalade, and spicy notes of nutmeg. Velvety on the palate with pleasing touches of vanilla oak.

🥄 **EDDU GREY ROCK** 40% ABV ● Amber gold, woody and with broom-flower flavours. Orange and apricot notes, slight mineral sea breeze aromas with a touch of cinnamon. A balance of flavours and an astounding persistence on the palate.

DOMAINE MAVELA

France:
✉ Brasserie Pietra
Route de la Marana
20600 Furiani Corsica

🖳 www.brasseriepietra.com
🍷 Open to visitors

Brasserie Pietra and Domaine Mavela on the French island of Corsica have been cooperating for a number of years to present their P&M whisky to the market. Pietra, which was founded in 1996 and was originally a brewery, makes the wash and Mavela distils.

Pietra offers three expressions: P&M Blend, P&M Blend Supérieur, and P&M Pure Malt. This

malt matures in casks that are made of oak sourced from the Troncet forest. The casks are primed first with malmsey and muscatel. The spirit matures for an unspecified period of time after which it is vatted in barrels that have previously contained *eaux-de-vie* originating from Domaine Mavela.

🥄 **P&M BLEND SUPÉRIEUR** 42% ABV
Strong, fruity, and with a beautiful amber colour. This is a rich, complex, and very imaginative whisky, and the flavours linger for a long time in the mouth.

🥄 **P&M PURE MALT** 42% ABV
A subtle aroma of honey, apricot, and citrus fruit on the nose. A very complex and aromatic bouquet.

French oak is used for the casks at Des Menhirs, which makes its whisky using buckwheat.

Glann ar Mor is a Breton phrase meaning "beside the sea", which describes its location perfectly.

DYC

Spain:
✉ Beam Global España SA
Pasaje Molino del Arco,
Palazuelos de Eresma, Segovia
🖱 www.dyc.es

This was the first Spanish distillery, founded in the 1950s near Segovia. It was built by the Eresma River – famous for its excellent water quality – and whisky started to flow in 1959. The distillery is now owned by Fortune Brands, who put all its wines and spirits under its subsidiary Beam Global.

DYC, which stands for Distilerias Y Crianza del Whisky, comes in three versions, a 5-year-old and an 8-year-old expression, both blends of various grains, and a malt whisky with no age statement. The spirits mature in American oak barrels. They are primarily sold on the home market. The Spanish drink it in a mix with cola and ask at the bar for a "whisky-dyc" (pronounced "dick").

🍾 **DYC 5 40% ABV** ● A pale straw colour, clean, with a hint of fruit, spice, and toasted wood. Malty, spicy, with a smooth, creamy mouthfeel and a smoky, spicy finish.

🍾 **DYC 8 40% ABV** ● Golden amber with a floral, spicy, smoky, grassy nose, and hints of honey and heather.

A smooth, creamy mouthfeel, malty, with vanilla, marzipan, and apple and citrus fruits. A long, bittersweet, smooth finish.

🍾 **DYC MALT 40% ABV** ● A fragrant, golden amber malt, with hints of citrus, sweetness, and vanilla, making a sophisticated bouquet. A full-bodied, rich malt flavour, and a long, subtle, finish.

FISSELIER

France:
✉ 56 rue du Verger, Chantepie
🖱 www.jacques-fisselier.com

Fisselier was founded in 1968 as a producer of fruit liqueurs. However, for the past few years, the distillery has produced two whiskies: Gwenroc Whisky Breton and Whisky de Bretagne. Both are blended whiskies, with the latter containing a higher percentage of malt.

GLANN AR MOR

France:
✉ Crec'h ar Fur, Pleubian
🖱 www.glannarmor.com

Glann ar Mor Distillery opened in 2005 after eight years of planning. In 1999 a small amount of spirit was distilled and matured in ex-Bordeaux casks for five years. It was eventually bottled as

Taol Esa in 2004, just before the distillery proper opened.

In June 2006 the second "first" new make ran from the stills. The spirit is made from 100 per cent malted barley in a peated and an unpeated version. The first 3-year-old single malt from this Breton distillery is due to appear in the summer of 2009.

Taol Esa is Breton for "the essay". Let's hope it grows into a novel in years to come!

GRUEL

Germany:
✉ Neue Strasse 26, Owen

Christian and Inge Gruel were inspired to start making whisky having visited distilleries in Scotland in the 1990s. So far they have produced three expressions – all single grain whiskies. Named Gruel Single Grain Whisky, they are aged at five, seven, and nine years.

GUILLON

France:
✉ Hameau de Vertuelle, Louvois
🖱 www.whisky-guillon.com
🏛 Open to visitors

The Guillon Distillery is located in the Champagne region and was purpose-built in 1997 to make whisky. The first spirit flowed from the stills in 1999. Annual production in 2007 was about 400,000 bottles.

Guillon offers an impressive range of different expressions. The single malts include Le Single Malt Guillon No. 1, Le Single Malt de Louvois Champagne, and Le Single Malt de Louvois Banyuls. Guillon's blend, called Le Premium Blend, consists of 50 per cent malt and 50 per cent grain whisky. The whiskies are quite fruity and elegant –

Le Single Malt Guillon No. 1

the result of maturation in ex-burgundy casks first, followed by a six-month finish in a sweet wine cask, most notably former Sauterne, Maury, and Banyuls casks. Guillon chose not to use more traditional casks, such as ex-sherry, port, or American bourbon.

HOF HOLLE

Switzerland:
✉ Hollen 52, Lauwil
🖥 www.single-malt.ch
🚪 Open by appointment only

The Hollen is a farm in the country near Basle. It has had its own little distillery for fruit liquor for a long time. Until 1999 in Switzerland it was strictly forbidden to distil spirit from grain, since it was considered a food staple. The day the law

Guillon Distillery chooses its casks to impart a fruity flavour to the finished whisky.

changed (1 July 1999), the Bader family started to distil from grains and thus became the first whisky distillery in Switzerland.

The whisky is mainly sold as single cask malt, therefore the taste differs slightly with each bottling. The most mature expression available is just over five years old. Maturation takes place in French oak casks that previously held either white or red wine.

🍷 **HOLLE SINGLE MALT WHISKY**
42% ABV • Delicate, not smoky, unobtrusive aromas of malt, wood, and vanilla combine with a flavour of wine. There is also a cask-strength version, which is bottled at 51.1 per cent ABV.

HÖHLER

Germany:
✉ Kirchgasse 3, Aarbergen
🖥 www.brennerei-hoehler.de
🚪 Open to visitors

Höhler originated in 1895 as a fruit liquor distillery. The current owner, Holger, is the fourth generation Höhler. Since 2001 he has made small batches of whisky from a recipe of corn, wheat, and malted barley. They mature for three years and when bottled sell out almost at once. Höhler sometimes calls his product Whessky – a fusion of Whisky and

Höhler whisky is produced in small, distinctive batches that are in great demand.

Hessen, the province where the distillery is located.

Currently the following expressions are maturing in his warehouse: Dinkelwhisky 2004, Haferwhisky 2004, and Brauer-Whisky 2005. They are difficult to find, since the product is not sold in shops and demand is larger than output.

Previous expressions from 2003 were a rye Whessky and an Irish-styled Whessky made from barley, malted barley, rye, and oats.

🍷 **WHESSKEY, IRISH STYLE** 44.5% ABV
Light gold in colour, with cereal grains on the nose and bitter lemon, grains, and sour peppermint on the palate. Thin body, short finish.

🍷 **WHESSKEY, SCOTTISH STYLE SINGLE MALT** 45.7% ABV • Aromas of stables, tea, straw, and cedar wood. The taste: stewed earl grey tea and peppermint, but slightly honeyish. Thin in body, and the finish has notes of bitter lemon.

🍷 **WHESSKEY, RYE STYLE** 45.7% ABV
Menthol and grains on the nose, with old strawberry candies. Peppermint, dried fruit, apricot, and strawberry on the palate. Slightly oily, with a pleasant, warm finish.

🍷 **WHESSKEY, BOURBON STYLE**
45% ABV • Nose: cooked grains, cooked pear, apple, apricot jam. Taste is a bit musty: mushrooms, cardboard, cherry bubble gum.

WHISKY, BOURBON STYLE, CASK STRENGTH 61% ABV • Fuller than the 45 per cent ABV, with citrus zest and a hot finish. With water: much flatter.

LATVIJAS BALZAMS

Latvia:
✉ A. Caka iela 160, Riga
⌂ www.balzams.lv

Latvia's only distillery is in the capital of this tiny Baltic state which joined the EU in 2004. The Latvian term for whisky is *viskij*. It comes in two expressions, "Alexandrs" and LB. Both are made from local rye and have a very smooth, light taste that is unusual for rye-based whisky.

MACKMYRA

Sweden:
✉ Bruksgatan 4, Valbo
⌂ www.mackmyra.se
🏛 Open by appointment only

Swedish engineer Magnus Dardanell founded Mackmyra in 1999 with a group of friends. The stills were made by Forsyth's of Rothes, in Scotland. Swedish washbacks and a German mash tun complete this truly European distillery. In 2006 Mackmyra launched the first bottling in a limited series, Preludium 01. Preludium 02, 03, 04, and 05 soon followed. Their latest is Preludium 06. Each is bottled at a high 52–55 per cent ABV.

The whisky comes in different expressions.

Mackmyra Distillery creates its individualistic whiskies using equipment from many countries.

"Elegant" is the original recipe. "Smoke" is spiced with herbs and so cannot really be called whisky. Mackmyra Reserve matures in exceptionally small 30-litre (6.5-gallon) casks, speeding up the maturation process hugely.

Individuals can buy their own spirit and select a cask (ex-bourbon, ex-sherry, or new Swedish oak) in which to have their whisky matured.

MACKMYRA, PRELUDIUM 05 48.4% ABV • Marzipan, custard, and a light citrus note on the nose. Taste: crème brûlée, bitter chocolate, lemon zest. A bit oily; slightly metallic and grainy in the finish – creamier with water.

MAISON LES VIGNETTES

France:
✉ Les Vignettes 6, Ardon
⌂ www.swhisky.ch
🏛 Open to visitors

Les Vignettes has distilled whisky since December 2000. The product matures

Belgian Owl Single Malt

in ex-Burgundy casks. Currently, three ranges are offered. Each range has various expressions.

The Collection Club range consists of "Challenge" and "Skipper". The Collection Prestige range consists of Annouim, Abred, Gwenwed, and Keugant. The Collection Must range has "1825" and Grand Crû.

All expressions are labelled as "Glen Vignettes Single Malt Swhisky"; cask-strength is 56.2 per cent ABV. They are exported to France, Belgium, Germany, and Japan.

ANNOUIM 45% ABV
Light, fruity – an aperitif.

GWENWED 45% ABV
Lively, fruity, hints of prunes and toast. Makes for a pleasant evening.

ABRED 45% ABV
Smoky. Fresh leather. For the unconditioned…

KEUGANT 56.2% ABV
Cask strength. Powerful, with tones of pepper and ginger. Be sure to have a bed nearby!

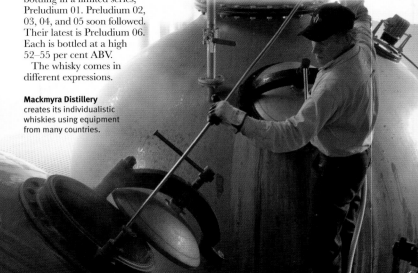

THE OWL

Belgium:
✉ Rue Sainte Anne 94, Grâce-Hollogne
🖥 www.belgianwhisky.com
🍷 Open by appointment only

Founded in 2004, the distillery has already changed names a couple of times in its short history – it was previously known as the Lambicool and Pur.E. Distillery. Master distiller Etienne Bouillon uses only home-grown barley (Scarlet and Prestige) and first-fill bourbon casks to age his spirit, which is known as Belgian Owl.

The entire production process takes place on the premises. Bouillon bottles his whisky at the legal age of three years. He also provides professional tasters with new make from 6, 12, and 18 months old to let them discover for themselves how the spirit matures.

The first cask was filled in October 2004. The 3-year-old Belgian Owl Single Malt Whisky, released in the autumn of 2007 is bottled at 46 per cent ABV, unfiltered.

🥃 **BELGIAN OWL 17-MONTH SPIRIT**
Fresh, direct, white and green flowers in the nose. Apple-cinnamon, pear, and a whiff of banana, developing into aromas of plum pudding and pearl sugar, with a malty fruity finish.

RABEL

Germany:
✉ Berghof, 73277 Owen-Teck
🖥 www.berghof-rabel.de

Originally a schnapps distillery, Rabel has started making Schwäbischer whisky. It is a blend of barley and wheat. Whisky von der Alb is matured for

eight years in oak casks. The water used runs through limestone – like a lot of American whisky *(see p183)* – and owner Thomas Rabel describes the whisky he produces as a cross between Scotch and bourbon.

REINER MÖSSLEIN

Germany:
✉ Untere Dorfstrasse 8, Zeilitzheim
🖥 www.weingeister.de

This is a winery that also produces various schnapps and one malt whisky. The whisky matures in oak casks for five years and has a smoky aroma. It is labelled Fränkischer Whisky.

Reiner Mösslein Malt Whisky

REISETBAUER

Austria:
✉ 4062 Axberg 15
🖥 www.reisetbauer.at

Originally a producer of fruit distillates, Hans Reisetbauer ventured into whisky distilling in 1995. He planted four hectares of summer brewing barley, dedicated to the making of single malt. In 2002 the first Reisetbauer bottling appeared as a 7-year-old expression. For maturation, Reisetbauer uses casks that contained Chardonnay and Trockenbeerenauslese wines.

Reisetbauer 7-Year-Old Single Malt

THE CZECH REPUBLIC

Once, when still called Czechoslovakia, this country harboured four whisky distilleries. Two of them, Tesetice and Dolany, are now mothballed. The former used to make King Barley, the only Czech single malt. The two distilleries currently producing are **Rudolf Jelinek** (www.rjelinek.cz) and **Stock Plzen** (www.stock.cz), both founded in the late 19th century. Jelinek bought the brand Gold Cock, previously owned by Tesetice. For its two expressions Jelinek uses Moravian barley and water that comes from an underground well, rich in minerals. Its two whiskies are: Gold Cock Red Feathers, 3-year-old blended whisky; and Gold Cock, 12-year-old malt. Stock Plzen distils Printer's, a 6-year-old malt whisky. They also use this whisky for a cream liquor.

🥃 **REISETBAUER 7-YEAR-OLD** 56% ABV ● Delicate, multi-layered on the nose with roasted hazelnuts and dried herbs; notes of bread and cereals, slightly smoky with fine spice; aged, yet full of verve.

SLYRS

Germany:
✉ Bayrischzellerstrasse 13, Schliersee-Ortsteil Neuhaus
🖥 www.slyrs.de
🍷 Open to the public

Slyrs was founded in 1999 and makes a decent whisky, which is distributed by Lantenhammer, a schnapps distillery in the same village. Slyrs Bavarian Single Malt is matured for an unspecified time in new 225-litre (50-gallon) American white oak barrels. The supply is limited and bottles can be purchased only via a select number of

TURKEY'S TEKEL

Tekel Distillery is owned by the Turkish government and produces a whisky called Ankara. It is bottled as a 3-year-old and a 5-year-old. There is some confusion as to whether it is real whisky. The former is made from malted barley and rice, so it cannot be called whisky. The latter however states on the label that it is manufactured from malted barley only.

retailers. Since 2002, a 3-year-old has been bottled and sold each year; in 2015 the company plans to present a 12-year-old single malt.

SONNENSCHEIN

Germany:
✉ Alter Fährweg 7–9, Witten-Heven
🖰 www.sonnenschein-brennerei.de

Sonnenschein started in 1875 with the production of fruit liquors and brandy wine. In 1990 a single malt was distilled in readiness for the plant's 125th anniversary celebrations in 2000. The whisky was matured in oak casks from Scotland and finished in sherry wood. It is no longer available, but Sonnenschein continues to make a Sonnenschein 10-year-old single malt, still using casks originating from Scotland. It comes in a nifty 50cl bottle.

Valley Single Malt Spirit

TEERENPELI

Finland:
✉ Hämeenkatu 19, Lahti
🖰 www.teerenpeli.com
⛴ Open to visitors

Teerenpeli is a brewery and a bar. The company started to import Scotch whisky in

2000 and gave it a second maturation in Finland, with their own wood finish. Apparently a couple of years in the Finnish climate enhances the flavours of the original whisky, resulting in a full, round, and slightly spicy taste. Recently, Teerenpeli has started to distil whisky as well, although it is not yet bottled as a single malt.

US HEIT

Netherlands:
✉ Snekerstraat 43, Bolsward, Friesland
🖰 www.usheitdistillery.nl
⛴ Open to visitors

Friesland (or Fryslân) is one of the northern provinces of the Netherlands and considers itself a country within a country. Its language, Frysian, comes from a different root to the Dutch language. Frysk, as it is properly spelled in the "native" tongue, is officially recognized as the second language in the Netherlands. The province of Friesland also has its own flag, parliament, and broadcasting company, but not currency. Us Heit, meaning "our father", was originally a brewery. Owner Aart van der Linde used his brewing skills to make the first Dutch whisky, but gave it a Frisian name: Frysk Hynder – which honours a famous Frisian horse, apparently. Frysk Hynder is sold as a 3-year-old and comes in two different expressions. One has been matured in wine casks and the other matured in sherry casks.

🍶 **FRYSK HYNDER WINE MATURED**
43% ABV • A sweet character, surprisingly smooth considering its young age. Pleasant and fruity.

US Heit is the first Dutch whisky; the expression shown here is matured in wine casks.

🍶 **FRYSK HYNDER SHERRY MATURED** 43% ABV • Sweetish, and soft for a 3-year-old whisky. Tasty, with full wood notes from the sherry cask.

VALLEI

Netherlands:
✉ Asschatterweg 233, JP Leusden
🖰 www.valleibieren.nl/whisky
⛴ Open by appointment only

The Dutch word Vallei means "valley" or, even better, "glen". In 2002 owner Bert Burger started some distilling experiments

POLISH WHISKY

Although some whisky writers have referred to a product called "Dark Whisky" as a Polish whisky, the parent company, Polmos Zielona Gora (part of the Swedish-based V&S group), clearly states that its brand is in fact a blend of Scotch whiskies. The Polish distillery itself, based at Zielona Gora, produces a wide variety of spirits, including vodka, gin, rum, and several liqueurs. Therefore, strictly speaking, there is no such thing as genuine Polish whisky ... yet.

Volker Theurer is one of Europe's older spirit makers, but its whisky distilling began relatively recently.

at home in his kitchen. His neighbour, a farmer, supplied him with barley and allowed him to convert a calf barn into what is a true farm distillery. The official founding year was 2004.

Burger single-handedly malts, mashes, ferments, distils, fills casks, and bottles his product. To make some money, the first spirit was released as a malt whisky liqueur in November 2006. Currently, larger quantities of spirit are in the process of maturing, closely monitored by Burger.

The new make spirit has pleasantly surprising fruity aromas, but we'll have to wait to sample a mature whisky from this one-man-band.

VALLEY SINGLE MALT SPIRIT 43% ABV • A cask sample offered a spiry and fruity nose, with hints of apricots and cloves. Liquorice and dried fruit on a slightly metallic palate, and the finish was dry, with liquorice again and spice.

VOLKER THEURER

Germany:
✉ Jesinger Hauptstrasse 55/57, Tübingen
🖰 www.lamm-tuebingen.de
🏛 Open by appointment only

The host of the Hotel Gasthof Lamm apparently enjoys distilling very much. A large assortment of schnapps is available to guests and, for the whisky

devotee, Mr Theurer offers Original Ammertal Whisky, which is also known as Black Horse Original Ammertal Whisky.

WALDVIERTLER ROGGENHOF

Austria:
✉ 3664 Roggenreith 3
🖰 www.roggenhof.at
🏛 Open to visitors

This company claims to be the first whisky distillery in Austria and was founded in 1995. Besides distilling, owner Johann Haider has also created the "Whisky Experience" in his premises, which consists of a permanent exhibition all about whisky and a seminar room. Seminars are regularly given and are based on Haider's own book *Fascination Whisky*.

Roggenhof produces five different whiskies. All of them mature for a period of between 3 and 12 years in Manhartsberger summer oak casks. The whisky is bottled exclusively as a single cask offering, with the alcoholic strength varying between 41 and 54 per cent ABV.

Volker Theurer's Ammertal Whisky label

RYE WHISKY JH • Made from 60 per cent rye and 40 per cent malt, this whisky is harmoniously balanced by the two corn varieties. It has a light vanilla flavour, and matures in Manhartsberger summer oak.

PURE RYE-MALT WHISKY JH A gentle, sweet taste of honey harmonizes perfectly with light vanilla in this 100 per cent malted rye whisky. Like the mixed rye, it is matured in Manhartsberger summer oak.

PURE RYE-MALT WHISKY JH "NOUGAT" • The malted rye is roasted to a darker shade, which gives the whisky an intense malty taste with a touch of both chocolate and nougat.

SINGLE BARLEY MALT WHISKY JH Made from 100 per cent lightly malted barley, this whisky offers a light, crisp, and, of course, malty caramel flavour.

SINGLE BARLEY MALT WHISKY JH "KARAMELL" Made from 100 per cent dark malted and roasted barley, the Karamell whisky is both smoky and dry, and has an intense flavour of – yes, you've guessed it – caramel.

Waldviertler Roggenhof Distillery produces five different whiskies using rye and barley.

WAMBRECHIES

France:
- ✉ 1 rue de la Distillerie
  59118 Wambrechies
- 🖥 www.wambrechies.com
- ⛪ Open by appointment only

Wambrechies was founded in 1817 as a genever (gin) distillery and still produces an impressive range of genevers. Some are called Pur Malt and Vieux Malt (old malt), but are not to be confused with malt whisky. The distillery produces one whisky: Wambrechies Single Malt, which is bottled without an age statement.

WARENGHEM

France:
- ✉ Route de Guingamp
  22300 Lannion
- 🖥 www.distillerie-warenghem.com
- ⛪ Open to visitors in summer only

Warenghem was founded in 1900 to produce apple cider and fruit liquors. In its 99th year of existence the distillery ventured into whisky production. It now makes two varieties: Armorik Single Malt, which is released without an age statement; and Breton Whisky WB, a 3-year-old blend of 25 per cent malt and 75 per cent grain alcohol. Both are released at 40 per cent ABV.

Spelt is closely related to common wheat, but is higher in protein and has a nuttier taste; Weidenauer Distillery use it for Dinkel Whisky.

Whisky Castle have added to their core distilling business with a new events facility.

WEIDENAUER

Austria:
- ✉ Leopolds 6, 3623 Kottes
- 🖥 www.weidenauer.at
- ⛪ Open by appointment only

This 19th-century fruit liqueur distillery has produced whisky since 1998. Their Hafer Whisky is made of oats, while their Dinkel Whisky is made from spelt (a type of wheat, ancestor to many modern wheats).

WEUTZ

Austria:
- ✉ St Nikolai 6
  8505 St Nikolai im Sausal
- 🖥 www.weutz.at
- ⛪ Open by appointment only

About 15 years ago this fruit liqueur distillery started to experiment with distilling

from grains. Currently it produces five different single malts – marketed as Hot Stone, White Smoke, Maroon, Moonshine, and Franziska – and one corn whisky, which is known as Sugar Corn. Weutz calls the Sugar Corn "bourbon new make", though technically this is incorrect, since bourbon can only be manufactured in the USA.

WHISKY CASTLE

Switzerland:
- ✉ Schlossstrasse 17
  5077 Elfingen
- 🖥 www.whisky-castle.com
- ⛪ Open to visitors

Käsers Schloss, as the Whisky Castle is called in Swiss, is owned by Ruedi and

THE RUSSIAN BEAR

Russia is a large, growing market for (Scotch) whisky but does not have a whisky distillery yet. It did try in the past, however. During the reign of Stalin, a whisky devotee himself, a plan was developed to build a whisky distillery that would use potatoes and sugar beet as its base product. Since whisky, whether it is Scotch, bourbon, blend, or rye, has to be made from grains, the Russians would not have qualified as whisky distillers, but the question is academic as the project never got off the ground. Nevertheless, this market is potentially so large that several Scottish distillers have been enlarging their capacity to meet the expected demand. No doubt the Continental distillers will try to conquer a small piece of that emerging market in times to come, and maybe in the near future a vodka producer will venture into whisky distilling.

Wolfram Ortner offers tours of its distillery and sells a range of luxury items in its shop.

Franziska Käser. They started to produce whisky in 2000 and expanded their business in July 2006 when a brand new building was opened where whisky-related events can be hosted. The Käsers organize four-course dinners, whisky-jazz brunches, and the like.

Whisky Castle produces single malts as well as blends that are made from rye, wheat, and oats.

WOLFRAM ORTNER

Austria:
✉ Untertscherner Weg 3
9546 Bad Kleinkirchheim
🖥 www.wob.at
🚪 Open by appointment only

Wolfram Ortner specializes in luxury products – especially cigars, glasses, chocolates, coffee, and fruit liqueurs. The distillery was founded in 1989 and the company started to produce Nockland Whisky in 1996.

The whisky is also referred to as Wob Dö Malt. It is matured exclusively in new casks. For these, Ortner makes his choice from a wide variety of European oak, including casks that come from wine producing regions, such as Limousin, Allier, Nevers, and Vosges. He also uses some American white oak casks.

🥃 **NOCKLAND WHISKY** 48% ABV
Sweet and malty on the palate, with flavours of spice and tobacco adding to the whisky's complexity.

ZUIDAM

Netherlands:
✉ Weverstraat 6
5111 PW, Baarle Nassau
🖥 www.zuidam-distillers.com
🚪 Open by appointment only

Zuidam is renowned for its excellent genevers and *korenwijn* – a variety of genever that's matured in oak casks for up to 10 years. In 2007 brothers Gilbert and Patrick Zuidam, sons of the founder, introduced a 5-year-old single malt called Millstone, which is aged in ex-bourbon, ex-sherry, and new American oak casks. Around 5,000 bottles have been sold, and there are plans to release a similar quantity as a 10-year-old.

Wolfram Ortner Nockland Whisky

MILLSTONE 40% ABV

🥃 **MILLSTONE** 40% ABV
Sweet and fruity, with aromas of honey, vanilla, wood, and grain. It tastes beautifully woody, sweet, a bit spicy, and spirity, with notes of honey and citrus. The finish is lightly drying, with notes of fruit, honey, vanilla, wood, and a touch of coconut.

ZÜRCHER

Switzerland:
✉ Nägeligässli 7, Port

Brennerei Zürcher started distilling whisky in 2003 and launched its first in 2006. It is called Single Lakeland Malt Whisky – not to be confused with the whisky that may or may not eventually emerge from the English Lakeland *(see p181)*. It is matured for three years in Oloroso sherry casks.

🥃 **SINGLE LAKELAND MALT WHISKY** 42% ABV
Pure, nice and woody; aromatic, with a taste of sweetish grains and a slightly astringent finish.

Zuidam Distillery has had considerable success with its Millstone 5-Year-Old Single Malt.

AUSTRALASIA

Clean water, fresh air, and quality barley ought to make for a perfect whisky-producing environment. Yet it is really only in recent years that Australia and New Zealand have begun producing and exporting quality malts of their own.

New Zealand's very first distillery, simply named the New Zealand Distillery Company, opened as long ago as 1869, in response to a change in legislation that reduced the levy on locally distilled spirits to just half that of imports. However, pressure from Scottish distillers and concern about the drop in excise revenue forced the government to increase duty six years later. Conditions became too difficult for the new distillery, and it was forced to close.

Around the same time, a man from Aberdeenshire in Scotland started a new brewery in the New Zealand town of Dunedin. He went into partnership with his brother-in-law James Wilson, a fellow Aberdonian, who in turn enlisted the help of his son Charles. It was Charles who made the malt extract Maltexo a staple part of the New Zealand diet. It wasn't until 13 years after his death in 1951, however, that his successors took the link between malt and brewing a step further to transform the company into Wilson Distillers Ltd in 1964. It became the country's first legal distiller in almost a century. In those intervening years, a prolific and illicit "moonshining" tradition had erupted.

Hobart in Tasmania is home to the Lark Distillery, the first modern Australian whisky producer. The distillery has a harbourside location.

Australia tells a similar tale, beginning with the opening of the Sorrell Distillery in 1822. The output of this legal distillery was augmented by a plentiful supply from illicit stills – Tasmania (then Van Diemen's Land), especially, was awash with them. In response to the illicit trade, Lieutenant Governor Franklin introduced legislation in 1939 that required distilleries to have a minimum wash capacity of 2,700 litres (594 gallons), which put an end to the Tasmanian distilling industry in favour of ale production.

It wasn't until the mid-1980s – when Bill and Lyn Lark had to change federal legislation to allow them to operate their own still on the island state of Tasmania – that Australia saw production of its first legally produced single malt in more than 100 years. Made with a specially developed strain of barley to tolerate the cool Tasmanian climate and local peat for the malting, the Larks' first whisky was released in 1998.

To best accommodate the fact that the domestic industry has only been operating for such a short time, many distilleries opt to use smaller casks than their Scottish counterparts, which results in the spirit maturing much faster. The result of this is whisky that has been favourably compared with some of the best malts from Scotland.

DISTILLERIES

In the 1980s and 90s, whisky distilleries finally became fully established
in Australia and New Zealand with some degree of permanency.
Many now produce fast-maturing single malts of high quality.

AUSTRALASIAN DISTILLERIES

At Nant Distillery the barley is
grown, malted, distilled, and
matured all on the one site.

BAKERY HILL

✉ Balwyn, Victoria, Australia
🖐 www.bakeryhilldistillery.com.au

David Baker began making
his own malt in the late
1990s, hoping that he could
craft something reflective of
the "Australian Spirit". With
a scientific background that
included years investigating
fermentation, and after
many visits to Tasmanian
distilleries, David set out to
prove that Australia could
produce a malt to match the
Scottish product. He's had
great success, with distillery
awards as well as a number
of gold and silver medals for
his whisky at blind tastings
by the Malt Whisky Society

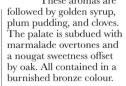

At Bakery Hill the spirit is distilled
in a copper pot still and passed
through a locked spirit safe.

of Australia.
All the whiskies
released are single cask
offerings. Some of the
bottlings are diluted with
spring water to reduce
them to a traditional
strength, one is finished
in a wine cask to impart
a slightly different
flavour, while the
others are bottled at a
powerful 60 per cent
ABV. The malts are
free from the addition
of any caramel so the
flavour you get is purely
from the production and
maturation processes.

CASK STRENGTH PEATED
60% ABV • Golden cedar
in colour; a sharp
peat on the nose with
crisp salt and dark
cherry notes. Toffee and
honeycomb on the palate
along with rich malt and
a rounded lingering finish.

CASK STRENGTH CLASSIC
60% ABV • Rich amber to gold
colour, with overtones of
vanilla, orange, and bitter
dark chocolate. It's mouth-
cleaning on the tongue with
hints of spiced orange
Turkish delight intertwined
with cereal and oak.

CLASSIC SINGLE MALT 46% ABV
Green apples, spiced honey,
and cider on the nose, while
on the palate the flavours
move through nutmeg,
spiced honey, and on to
cereal and malt to finish.

**Bakery Hill
Cask Strength
Peated Malt**

PEATED MALT 46% ABV
A rich gold colour with
a subdued peat aroma.
Kumquat and fruit
mince tart scents give
it a sweetness. On the
palate are hints of
tobacco leaf along
with the smoky peat.
This malt carries
with it a long finish.

DOUBLE WOOD MALT
46% ABV • Matured in
former Jack Daniel's
barrels, and then
finished in French
oak previously used
for wine. The nose
opens with apricot,
coconut, and plum.
These aromas are
followed by golden syrup,
plum pudding, and cloves.
The palate is subdued with
marmalade overtones and
a nougat sweetness offset
by oak. All contained in a
burnished bronze colour.

GREAT SOUTHERN

✉ Albany, Western Australia,
Australia
🖐 www.distillery.com.au

This distillery is temporarily
set up on the outskirts of
the Western Australian town
of Albany while the owner,
Cameron Syme, awaits the
completion of his purpose-

built distillery and visitor centre. So new is this distillery that production barrel numbers are still under 100 at the time of writing, but as soon as the new facility is up and running, the output is expected to grow rapidly. The southwestern location not only provides pristine source material for making spirits, but also supplies 75 per cent of their electricity via wind power.

Having learnt the trade in Scottish and Tasmanian distilleries, Cameron runs the business with day-to-day distillery manager Tony Browne. Great Southern will be bottling its first expression, "Limeburners", in the second quarter of 2008. Currently the whisky is being matured in a combination of ex-bourbon, ex-brandy, and rejuvenated American and French oak casks.

HELLYERS ROAD

✉ 53 Old Surrey Road, Burnie, Tasmania, Australia
🖰 www.hellyersroaddistillery.com.au
🚢 Open to the public

The largest single malt distillery in Australia is a highly automated site, everything being computer controlled and capable of being remotely monitored from the home of the head distiller. Hellyers Road is a subsidiary of Betta Milk Co-operative Ltd, and years of running a successful milk processing plant has given owner Laurie House a wealth of experience in maintaining constant environments, critical temperature points for liquids, controlled storage, and a sizeable level of capital to establish a distillation plant. With what could possibly be the largest single investment in a distillery in the southern hemisphere, Hellyers have also opened up a 60-seat café and visitor information centre, and offer tours of the distillery 7 days

a week. Things have come a long way since they distilled their first whisky in 1999, and they now have over 2,600 casks maturing.

🍶 **ORIGINAL PURE AUSTRALIAN MALT**
46.2% ABV ● A pale straw-coloured liquid offering vanilla, citrus, and floral scents on the nose. Mouth-warming, it opens with sweet cereal flavours followed by bitter dark chocolate and just a hint of smoked oak.

LARK

✉ 14 Davey Street, Hobart, Tasmania, Australia
🖰 www.larkdistillery.com.au
🚢 Open to the public

Having opened the first legal distillery in Australia in the last 100 years, Bill and Lyn Lark are considered by many to be the modern pioneers of the Australian whisky industry. Bill pondered why it was that, with such an abundance of quality raw material and ideal conditions, Australia was not producing a single malt of its own. The idea gained support, and eventually the government was persuaded to overturn an 88-year-old piece of legislation that stood in the way of founding a new distillery. Bill's experience

Lark Single Malt Whisky

has led him to be involved in the setting up and production of a number of the malts now being produced in Australia, while his wife Lyn has found inventive ways to include local fruits in the production of unique liqueurs. Their new harbourside location offers visitors a chance to walk through the distilling process, sample a few drams at the whisky bar, or simply take in the atmosphere.

🍶 **TASMANIA SINGLE MALT**
40% ABV Malty and lightly peated on the nose, it is complemented by the peppery spices that follow, with hints of butterscotch. More malt on the tongue, offset with a clean, fruity flavour and powdery oak to offer further complexity. The finish is spiced and delicate.

NANT

✉ Bothwell, Tasmania, Australia
🖰 www.nantdistillery.com.au

The entire operation here is situated on a large riverside farm, allowing Nant to control the process from barley to bottle. Franklin barley is grown on the farm and ground in a former flour

Lark Distillery on Hobart Harbour has a specialist whisky bar with indoor and outdoor seating.

mill (originally built by convicts). Mashing, brewing, distilling, and ageing are all carried out here, and the first bottles will be ready in 2008. Visitors have the chance to stay overnight and experience a fully Scottish-inspired whisky experience that extends to a round of golf on the adjoining course and fly fishing in the on-site stream.

SMALL CONCERN

✉ Ulverstone, Tasmania, Australia
🖰 www.tasmanianwhisky.com.au

As its name suggests, this was a little distillery. The water for its whisky came from a stream that begins in the nearby Cradle Mountain National Park and flows along volcanic paths that are scattered across the island. Such purity of water ensured a clean crispness in the final whisky once produced here.

Unfortunately production of their malts ceased in the late 1990s, and the distillery equipment was sold. Supply is obviously limited, but two Small Concern whiskies can be found. Cradle Mountain Single Malt is triple distilled and smoother than most in the region. Cradle Mountain Double Malt is a blended malt, made by combining the Cradle Mountain Single Malt with Springbank Single Malt from Campbeltown in Scotland, which adds a little coastal saltiness.

CRADLE MOUNTAIN SINGLE MALT 43% ABV ● Citrus notes on the nose with hints of nuts and honey. The mouthfeel is clean, as is the finish.

CRADLE MOUNTAIN DOUBLE MALT 46–54.4% ABV ● Lightly peaty, with fruit, possibly pear, followed by honey. The Springbank imparts an obvious saltiness on the nose and the palate, with a soft finish.

SMITH'S

✉ Angaston, South Australia, Australia
🖰 www.yalumba.com

In the late 1990s, Samuel Smith & Sons decided to make use of a pot still formerly employed to produce brandy at their Yalumba winery. On a handful of occasions in the late 1990s and again in 2000, it was used for making whisky. It has since been decommissioned, which is a terrible shame as it produced a fine whisky that was similar in quality and taste to that of Wilson's Lammerlaw *(see opposite)*. The spirit was distilled from wash made from local barley, and was aged in old sherry, old French, old American, and new American casks.

SMITH'S ANGASTON 7-YEAR-OLD 40% ABV ● This is a blend of the various casks from the same distillation run. It has a sweet, fruity nose with hints of spice and nuts. The palate is buttery in the mouth with chocolate and sherry flavours. It is followed by a toffee and honey finish.

Smith's Angaston 7-Year-Old

THE SOUTHERN DISTILLING COMPANY

✉ Stafford Street, Timaro, New Zealand
🖰 www.hokonuiwhiskey.com

Sadly this is the only distillery still actively producing new whisky in New Zealand. Thankfully Malcolm Willmott and Peter Wheeler, the founders of the distillery, are using it to keep the traditional spirit of the New Zealand whisky alive. Using a recipe dating back to the late 1800s, the distillery has tried to keep a whisky that is true to its moonshining roots. This moonshine is now bottled and sold legally by the distillery as "Old Hokonui", and despite the skull and crossbones on the bottle's label and the somewhat intimidating packaging, it is a pleasant drink with a smooth, sweet finish. The rest of the whiskies from this distillery take on a more traditionally Scottish style with an island-

The mill house where the distilling process takes place at Nant Distillery.

The MacKenzie Blended Whisky

style level of peatiness. Southern adopts a unique approach to charring their oak barrels to impart the distillery's own special characteristics into the malt. Driftwood and seaweed are burnt to smoke the barrels prior to use, adding an extra level of complexity to the smokiness – a light saltiness, as you may imagine.

THE COASTER 40% ABV • A single malt with a deep amber colour. The nose is full of cereal in addition to the light smoke and peat notes. The palate has a light brine note followed by rich malt and smoky caramel. Smooth and lasting finish.

THE MACKENZIE 40% ABV • A light golden blend with caramel and oak on the nose. Across the palate it is light and carries the caramel and cereal flavours. The finish is again quite smooth.

TASMANIA

✉ 1/14 Lamb Place, Cambridge, Tasmania, Australia

🖰 www.tasdistillery.com.au

A boutique distillery that has changed hands and locations numerous times over the past 10 years, Tasmania Distillery employs only two people on a full-time basis. Patrick Maguire is quick to admit that early batches of their whisky left something to be desired. However, the 7-year-old has since been awarded gold and silver medals in blind tastings by the Malt Whisky Society of Australia. With such a small distillery, though, it is difficult to spread focus and Patrick has decided for the time being to

close the bar, shop, and museum and concentrate on producing a quality product. That being said, getting your hands on a bottle of this non-peated malt can be incredibly difficult.

SULLIVAN'S COVE SINGLE BARREL CASK STRENGTH A powerful nose offers a strong malt scent. As the whisky hits the tongue, there is an immediate rush of malt yet again, quickly followed by oak and sweet vanilla and chocolate notes. The finish is smooth and lingering.

SULLIVAN'S COVE SINGLE BARREL CASK STRENGTH PORT FINISH A surprisingly floral nose on this malt is followed by a deep, rich aroma of a Guinness-like stout. Across the palate it is dry but warming, with a sweet finish.

WILSON'S

✉ Dunedin, New Zealand

Wilson's had the good fortune to be the first legalized distillery in New Zealand in the past 100 years. But that is pretty much where the good fortune ended. After producing Lammerlaw, a quality single malt, Seagram's purchased the company in 1994 and before long all its stills were dismantled. It officially closed in 2000.

Lammerlaw was quite highly acclaimed and did well to set a benchmark for other up-and-coming producers in the region. Bottles of Lammerlaw are rarely available, but a collection of unbottled casks

Tasmania Distillery's Sullivan's Cove range of whiskies

have made their way into the Milford Whisky range, and continue to be aged and bottled under the Milford brand until stocks run out.

LAMMERLAW 40% ABV Similar in style to a lowland Scottish malt, it has light citrus notes on the nose and a touch of honey. The palate is again light, with lemon and caramel notes, and a smooth, lasting finish.

MILFORD 10-YEAR-OLD 43% ABV A dry nose but one that really opens up with a dash of water to offer vanilla, marmalade, and peaches. Across the tongue, it recalls the citrus notes of the marmalade again, but with a creaminess and malt added to the mix.

MILFORD 12-YEAR-OLD 43% ABV Light cereal aromas and a hint of wet straw. The taste is of orange and nuts with a peppery aftertaste.

MILFORD 15-YEAR-OLD 43% ABV Creamy cereal and custard when first nosed, it develops into a slightly sour kumquat scent. In the mouth it is smooth, the fruitiness becoming more pear-like, with ginger and spice opening up. The finish is warm, with a hint of aniseed.

ASIA

Asia continues to be not only the largest growth market for whisky, but also the largest consumer. India alone consumes over 60 million cases each year, accounting for around 47 per cent of global whisky consumption.

The definition of whisky can be very different in Asia to that generally accepted elsewhere. This is to such an extent that some spirit produced in the region and labelled as whisky is derived from alcohol made from molasses or sugar cane (much like rum) combined with additives and spices to impart a whisky-like flavour and colour. And what is termed blended whisky may have only a passing inclusion of malt whisky (legally as little as 4 per cent), with the rest made up of what's known as extra neutral spirit *(see p276)*, which could be distilled from molasses or a variety of grains that grow well in the region but are unusual to whisky, such as rice.

Asian whisky is rarely aged, partly because the region's climate is disadvantageous to maturation. The higher temperatures mean that the angels' share (whisky lost from the cask due to evaporation while maturing) can be as high as 15 per cent each year. Therefore, the whisky needs to be bottled early to be at all profitable. By the time the whisky has been casked for its traditional minimum 3-year maturation, the distillery could have lost 40 per cent of the original volume. The increased heat

does partially offset this disadvantage, however, by allowing the maturation to occur more quickly, giving Asian whiskies a complexity that belies their age.

A few distilleries have attempted to replicate the Scottish conditions more closely. Mohan Meakin's Kasauli Distillery, originally founded by an Englishman in the 1820s, is located in the cooler climes of the Himalayas. Less is lost to the "angels", and traditional barley, more suited to cooler temperatures, can be used in the production.

WHISKY IN A DRY STATE

Also to be found in Asia is one of the few distilleries operating in an Islamic country. The Murree Brewery in Pakistan is permitted by the local government to produce alcohol for non-Muslims and foreigners. Although it started up in 1860, it wasn't until a century later, in the 1960s, that the distillery began producing a single malt.

Scottish distillers have had difficulty selling whisky in much of Asia, but eastern Asia has been a considerable consumer, and South Korea leads the way with their consumption of the major premium export Scotch blends, such as Chivas Regal and Johnnie Walker. Surely it won't be long before they have a distillery of their own.

Barley grown in the fertile plains at the base of the Himalayas is used for whisky making by Amrut Distillers; they also source their water from the region.

DISTILLERIES AND WHISKIES

Asia has many distilleries, most of which produce ENA (extra neutral alcohol) from molasses and other agricultural by-products *(see p276)*. Those selected here, however, focus at least part of their output on whisky made from barley or grain using traditional methods and ageing.

AMRUT

India:
✉ 36, Sampangi Tank Road, Bangalore
🖰 www.amrutdistilleries.com

In Indian mythology, the meaning of the word Amrut is similar to "ambrosia", or "the elixir of life". Although the distillery was founded in 1948, it was not until the 1980s that Amrut included malt whisky in its list of distilled products. With assistance from some Scottish experts, and a business plan crafted by the British-educated grandson of the founder, Amrut has managed to position itself quite prominently in the Scottish market. In particular, it has gained a grip in the numerous Indian restaurants in Glasgow and elewhere in Scotland. It was the tactic of the ever-creative Rakshit Jagdale to trial miniatures of the distillery's single malt in 85 Indian restaurants throughout the United

INDIA AND PAKISTAN'S DISTILLERIES

Amrut Single Malt

Kingdom that proved the feasibility of his product in one of the toughest whisky markets. Having satisfied himself that Amrut's product was viable in the UK market, Rakshit promptly returned to India to become Executive Director of Amrut and to commence exporting.

Amrut Single Malt Whisky is made from select Indian barley, grown in the foothills of the Himalayas, and cultivated by old and traditional agricultural practices. The barley is carefully malted and mashed in water flowing from the Himalayan mountain range. Distillation, in traditional pot stills, occurs in small batches and maturation takes place in oak barrels, for a minimum of 3 years.

The maturation site, which is situated at an altitude of 1,000 m (3,300 ft) above sea level in Bangalore, the garden city of India, has a unique tropical condition. During maturation, the whisky loses almost half its volume as "the angels' share".

As well as Amrut Single Malt, the distillery also produce MaQintosh

Premium Malt Whisky, which uses 5-year-old Scotch blended with ENA.

🍸 **AMRUT SINGLE MALT**
40% ABV
Flowery and fruity on the nose, there is just a light spice added by some ginger and aniseed notes. The palate is smooth with a surprising amount of spice and malt, while the finish is short and sweet.

JAGATJIT

India:
✉ 4th Floor, Bhandari House, 91 Nehru Place, New Delhi
🖰 www.jagatjit.com

Jagatjit Industries was founded in 1944 by the late LP Jaiswal in the erstwhile state of Kapurthala. The distillery was set up under the patronage

Jagatjit Aristocrat

Amrut operates in a warm, humid climate, and consequently much of its maturing spirit evaporates.

McDowell's has headquarters and distilleries in Bangalore and at Ponda (pictured) in Goa.

of its Maharajah, Jagatjit Singh. Today, the plant produces a variety of ENA spirits and blended whiskies, as well as one malt whisky, which is called Aristocrat Premium Malt Whisky.

KASAULI

See Mohan Meakin

MCDOWELL'S

India:
✉ 51 Le Parc Richmonde, Richmond Road, Bangalore
🖥 www.clubmcdowell.com

These days McDowell's, India's biggest brand of whisky, is owned by United Spirits (a division of the mighty UB Group), but the original company was first established in 1898. The name McDowell is derived from Macdougall, which came from the Gaelic *Dubh gall*, meaning "dark stranger", and almost certainly referred to the Danish Vikings that began to settle in Scotland 1,000 years ago.

Whatever the etymology, it was one Angus McDowell who started the firm in Scotland to market products to Britons staying in various corners of the Empire. In India, the McDowell base had its warehouses north of Fort St George in Madras.

From its beginnings in 1898 as a small importer of wine and spirits to India, McDowell grew to become the subcontinent's undisputed leader in the spirits market. In 1951, the late Mr Vittal Mallya, founder of the UB Group, acquired McDowell. The

UB Group grew rapidly and expansively by several mergers and acquisitions. Along with many whisky brands, it now owns the famous Scottish distillers and blenders Whyte & Mackay *(see p154)*.

The malt whisky arm of the UB Group has always followed the "Scottish Rite", with distillation in pot stills and maturation in oak casks under the strict observation of traditional periods of ageing. McDowell's also carry out their malting and kilning on site.

Locally cultivated barley and water of the utmost purity contribute to the shaping of a unique base product such as McDowell's Single Malt, made at the group's distillery at Ponda, in the province of Goa.

One of the largest distilleries in India, Ponda is responsible for the production of a range of malts and blends for both domestic and international markets. The most successful of these is the No. 1 McDowell's Whisky, which, according to the company's sales figures, is the 5th best selling whisky in the world; it is also quite possibly the fastest growing. The distillery uses traditional pot stills, and the whiskies are usually aged for no more than 3 years, because of the fact that they mature quickly in the warm climate.

🍾 **MCDOWELL'S SINGLE MALT**
42.8% ABV • A very light nose, with just a hint of grain and malt

MacDowell No 1

SATISFYING THE LOCAL MARKET

The lion's share of Asian distilleries are either converted ethanol factories or ethanol factories that also distil some neutral alcohol as a side operation. Few were initially set up as sole producers of alcohol for consumption, with the exception of those established by British expatriates.

At the time of writing, only a handful of Asian whisky producers distil spirit that passes international guidelines for what constitutes whisky *(see p276)*. Consequently, Asian whiskies seldom find their way onto the supermarket shelves of the global market. Local whisky-like products rarely travel beyond their national borders, except as tourist souvenirs.

UNDERSTANDING ASIAN WHISKY

The Asian spirits industry was established by expatriates in the 18th, 19th, and 20th centuries to distil and bottle alcohol primarily for the British forces. Western types of alcohol such as brandy, gin, rum, vodka, and whisky became collectively known as "LMFL".

The initials LMFL stood for "locally made foreign liquor". The term was used widely in Asia, though in India the term IMFL, or "Indian Made Foreign Liquor", was preferred. This categorization became primarily an instrument to balance the domestic alcohol industry against the import trade. No national rules defining raw material and process were, or indeed are, attached to the LMFL/IMFL. However, if production is destined for export aimed at a specific market, such as the European Union, then regulations prevailing at the target market have to be followed. With tight EU rules for whisky designation, very little Asian spirit reaches this market.

MacDowell's Vintage

DEFINITIONS

ENA WHISKY Extra Neutral Alcohol (ENA) is fermented and distilled in continuous stills using molasses, rice, millet, buckwheat, or any other fermentable agricultural product. ENA whisky is usually colour adjusted with spirit caramel, and is not matured. Most Asian whiskies belong to this category.

BLENDED WHISKY Asian blended whiskies are a mix of ENA whisky and a varying portion of either locally produced malt whisky or bulk imported Scotch whisky. Sometimes an age statement is given. In such cases it is the age of the bulk imported whisky that is presented. However, as the product contains ENA, it does not meet EU whisky regulation.

PURE MALT WHISKY These are blends of 100 per cent malt whiskies stemming from two or more domestic or foreign distilleries. Any pure malt whisky matured in oak casks for 3 years or more qualifies for the EU classification.

SINGLE MALT WHISKY As with a Scottish malt, this is a pure malt whisky from a single distillery.

The bottling plant at the Jagatjit Distillery produces a wide variety of spirits, but just one malt whisky, Aristocrat Premium.

MacDowell's Single Malt

that combine to form a creamy note. The palate is soft and somewhat reminiscent of stewed peaches. A short, sweet finish.

Among the other whiskies produced by McDowell's are: McDowell's Vintage, which is a pure malt whisky, matured in oak casks; McDowell's Premium Blended, a blend of pure malt whiskies; and No. 1 McDowell's Centenary Blended, which is a traditional blended Scotch, using malt and grain whisky.

MOHAN MEAKIN

India:

✉ Solan Distillery and Brewery, Shimla Hills, Solan, Himachal Pradesh; Kasauli Distillery, Solan District, Himachal Pradesh

🖳 www.mohanmeakin.com

The origins of Mohan Meakin go back to the mid-19th century and to an Englishman named Edward Dyer. He set up the first brewery in India at Kasauli in 1855, and made indigenous beer available to Indians as well as Britons. The Kasauli plant switched to distilling when the brewery moved to nearby Solan, and Dyer went on to set up furhter breweries at Simla, Murree, Rawalpindi, and Mandalay.

Another entrepreneur from the UK, HG Meakin, came to India and bought the old Simla and Solan breweries from Edward Dyer. He added more breweries at Ranikhet, Dalhousie, Chakrata, Darjeeling, and Kirkee in the early 20th century. The Dyer and Meakin businesses merged in 1937. Following India's independence in 1947, NN

When he built his distillery, Edward Dyer had to sail the British-made equipment the entire length of the River Ganges (pictured) to reach Kasauli.

Mohan became the majority shareholder in the company and then its managing director in 1949. The firm eventually changed name to Mohan Meakin in 1967.

Today, the company has two distilleries, one at Solan and the other at Kasauli, in the Himalayas. At an altitude of over 2,000 m (6,600 ft), Kasauli is the highest distillery in the world.

When he established the distillery, Dyer brought with

him distillation equipment from England and Scotland that had to be shipped the full length of the Ganges River before being carted up the Himalayas to its current location. Some of the same equipment is still in use today.

The difficult location was selected not just because of the abundance of fresh spring water and because the climate was similar to the cooler climes of Scotland, but also because it was then ruled by the British, so there was a ready market for those that were stationed abroad and homesick for their traditional spirit.

It was the growth of the town of Kasauli that precipitated the move to Solan, as demands on the mountain spring water grew. But while the brewery was forced to move, it left room for the distillery

to develop. It is, in fact, the oldest whisky distillery in all of Asia, and one of the oldest continuously operating distilleries in the entire world.

Among the whiskies produced by Mohan Meakin are Colonel's Special Whisky and Solan No. 1 Whisky, both of which are blends.

MURREE

Pakistan:
✉ National Park Road, PO Box No. 13, Rawalpindi

🌐 www.murreebrewery.com

As well as founding the Solan and Kasauli distilleries, Edward Dyer also established the Murree Brewery, which was originally constructed in 1860. It is now situated in Rawalpindi, though its name recalls a hill station near the earlier plant, built by Dyer, at Ghora Galli

Murree 8-Year-Old

TAIWAN'S NEWEST DISTILLERY

A Scottish design and manufacturing firm has recently (in 2006) completed a £15 million project to create Taiwan's first-ever malt whisky distillery. Forsyth's, which has its headquarters in Rothes, Scotland, was heavily involved in the successful construction and design of the distillery, which is located in northeast Taiwan.

Working in association with the distillery's owners, King Car Food Industrial (www.kingcar.com.tw), a Taiwanese soft drink and food firm, Forsyth's built and installed the milling, mashing, and distilling equipment. It produced the four-tonne stainless-steel mash tun, with a copper cover, two 11,000-litre (2,500-gallon) wash stills, and two 6,500-litre (1,450-gallon) spirit stills, complete with their condensers and spirit safes. In addition, Buhler UK supplied the milling system, whilst all other equipment, vessels, and pipework, were designed by Forsyth's and built in Taiwan. Casks acquired for maturation are predominantly ex-bourbon. Maturation will be be performed in line with Scottish guidelines.

The fully automated distillery, which took a year to design and build, is set to produce one million litres (220,000 gallons) of alcohol every year. All the operations at the distillery can be remotely monitored from Grants engineering firm at Dufftown in Scotland. There, staff will be able to keep a check on all the distilling processes right around the clock. Grants (not to be mistaken with WM Grant & Sons) is part of the Forsyth group.

DRINKING IN PAKISTAN

Under the laws of Pakistan, Muslims are prohibited from consuming alcoholic drinks. Non-Muslims and foreigners require a consumption permit which is issued by provincial governments and Islamabad (for the capital territory). However in most cases a liquor retailer will assist in obtaining a permit.

in the Pir Punjal range of the Western Himalayas. The original intention for the brewery was to supply locally produced alcohol to British troops stationed in India, but the beer also became a local hit and was in high demand with the rest of the populace.

Providing a steady supply proved to be difficult, however, as a series of earthquakes and fires caused interruptions to the production process. Scarcity of water at Ghora Galli became an emerging problem also, and by the 1920s production was mostly transferred to the Rawalpindi Brewery, though the malting continued at Ghora Galli until the 1940s. The Rawalpindi site is blessed with aquifers delivering water of a very high quality.

In 1947, when the new state of Pakistan was formed, Murree became the country's first and only legal single malt whisky distillery. The distillery, designed as a classic scotch malt whisky distillery, underwent several modernizing programs from the 1960s onwards. In 1967 a German brew house was installed, followed by a box maltings system in 1971. More recently, the distilling capacity was increased in the 1990s by the installation of two alcohol rectification columns for producing alcohol from molasses.

An ambitious long-term – and still ongoing –

programme to mature malt whiskies was introduced in the late 1960s. Over the past four decades oak casks and vats have been acquired, not only from North America and Spain, but also from Australia. Murree's two underground cellars now hold over half a million litres (110,000 gallons) of malt whisky under controlled temperature conditions. The whisky is ageing for varying periods of maturation, some of it for up to 20 years.

A somewhat aspect to this distillery, due in part to the rather diversified interests most of the major distilleries in Asia have, is that the company produces its own glass bottles within its glass division.

MURREE'S PREMIUM MALT WHISKIES

The premium malt expressions from Murree are produced from a malt mash, distilled in traditional pot stills, and matured in imported oak-wood casks for guaranteed periods. The range includes the Millennium Reserve 21-Year-Old Single Malt, Murree's Millennium Reserve 12-Year-Old Single Malt, and Murree's Classic 8-Year-Old Single Malt.

Radico Khaitan's Whytehall

PONDA

See McDowell's

RADICO KHAITAN

India:
✉ Plot J-I, Block B-I,
Mohan Co-operative Industrial Area,
Mathura Road, New Delhi
🖰 www.radicokhaitan.com

Radico Khaitan is one of India's oldest and largest liquor manufacturers. Formerly known as Rampur Distillery, it was established in 1943, but it wasn't until 1999 that the company remarketed itself and produced the 8PM brand, designed to appeal to a more international customer base.

Prior to that, the products were mostly spirits made using ENA (extra neutral alcohol), in which molasses or other flavourings were added; rectified alcohol;

Radico Khaitan's 8PM Royale

Radico Khaitan's 8PM

as well as ethanol and gasoline for an industrial market. The distillery's brands now include the previously mentioned 8PM, 8PM Royale Whisky, Whytehall, and Royal Cambridge. Its smaller, regional brands include 8PM Contessa Deluxe, Crown, and Golfinger. All are blended whiskies.

Since 1999, Radico Khaitan has started to produce a decent range of blended whiskies, and is having success with 8PM brand.

Glossary

ABV (alcohol by volume) This is the proportion of alcohol in a drink, expressed as a percentage. Whisky is most commonly bottled at 40% or 43% ABV.

analyser still *see* continuous still

angels' share The expression given for the amount of liquid that evaporates from the cask during the period of *maturation*.

batch distillation Distillation carried out in batches, as opposed to *continuous distillation*. Each batch may be marginally different, which gives the method an artisanal quality.

barrel *see* cask

cask The oak container in which whisky is matured. There are many different styles and sizes of cask, as well as a principle distinction between the type of wood used: American or European oak. In the USA, whiskey is most commonly matured in barrels (180–200 litres). American barrels are re-used elsewhere; in Scotland, they are often broken down and re-assembled as re-made hogsheads (250 litres). Butts and puncheons (both 500 litres) are the largest casks used for maturing whisky, having first been seasoned with or used to age sherry.

cask finishing Using a different cask for the final period of maturation, such as port, madeira, or French wine casks.

cask strength Whisky that is bottled straight from the cask rather than first being diluted. It is typically around 57–63% ABV.

clearic *see* new make

continuous distillation The process of creating spirit as an ongoing process as opposed to *batch distillation*. It cannot be carried out in a pot still and requires instead a *continuous still*.

condenser Vaporized spirit driven off the stills is turned into liquid in a condenser. Traditionally, these were "worm tubs" – a tapering coil of copper pipe set in a vat of cold water outside the still house. Worm tubs have largely been superseded by shell-and-tube condensers, usually inside the still house.

continuous still A continuous still (also known as a Coffey, Patent, or column still) consists of an analyser and a rectifier. *Wash* enters the analyser and is heated by steam, vaporizing the alcohol. The alcoholic vapour leaves the analyser and enters the rectifier. There, it goes through a process of heating and partial condensing until it reaches the top of the still, where the vapour leaves to be condensed as a very pure (90+%ABV) spirit.

cut points In the process of pot still distillation, the operator divides the *run* into three "cuts" to separate useable spirit from rejected spirit, which must be re-distilled. The first cut contains the *foreshots*; the middle cut is the section of useable spirit; the end cut contains the *feints* or aftershots.

draff The Scottish name for the remains of the grain after mashing. It can be dried and used for cattle feed.

eau de vie Literally, "water of life", and usually used in reference to grape-based spirits. Compare with *uisge beatha*.

expression The term given to a particular whisky in relation to the overall output of a distillery or spirits company. It may refer to the age, as in a 12-year-old expression, or to a particular characteristic, such as a cask strength expression.

end cut *see* cut points

feints The final fraction of the spirit produced during a distillation *run*. Feints (also called tails) are aromatically unpleasant, and are sent to feints and foreshots receiver to be mixed with low wines and re-distilled with the next run.

fermenter Another name for a *mash tun*.

first fill The first time a cask has been used to hold whisky other than bourbon, it is referred to as a first-fill cask. A first-fill sherry cask will have held only sherry prior to its use for maturing whisky; a first-fill bourbon cask will have been used once only to hold bourbon prior to its use in maturing whisky.

foreshots The first fraction of the distillation run in pot-still distillation. Foreshots (also known as heads) are not pure enough to be used and are returned to feints and foreshots receiver to be re-distilled in the next run.

grist Ground, malted grain. Water is added to grist to form the mash.

heads *see* foreshots

high wines (US) A mix of spirit that has had its first distillation and the *foreshots* and *feints* from the second distillation, at around 28% ABV. High wines undergo a second distillation to create *new make*.

kilning Heating of the "green malt" to halt its germination and thereby retain its starch content for turning into sugars in the mashing stage and, ultimately, alcohol.

low wines The spirit produced by the first

distillation. It has a strength of about 21% ABV. Compare with *high wines*.

lyne arm (or "lye pipe") The pipe running from the still to the condenser. The lyne arm's angle, height, and thickness all have a bearing on the characteristics of the spirit.

malting The process of deliberately starting and then stopping germination in grain. As the grain begins to germinate (through the influence of heat and moisture), it becomes "green malt" (grain that has just begun to sprout). The green malt undergoes *kilning* to produce malt.

marrying This refers to the mixing and maturing of whiskies. It most often applies to blends, where whiskies of different types and from several distilleries are combined for a period in vats or casks prior to bottling.

mash The mix of *grist* and water.

mash tun The vessel in which the grist is mixed with hot water to convert starch in the grain into sugars, ready for fermentation. The fermentable liquid that results is known as *worts*; the solid residue (husks and spent grain) is *draff*.

maturation For *new make* spirit to become whisky, it must go through a period of maturation in oak casks. The length of time varies; in Scotland and Ireland, the minimum period is three years.

middle cut *see* cut points

new make The clear, useable spirit that comes from the spirit still. It has a strength of about 70% ABV, and is dilluted to around 63–64% before being put into casks for *maturation*. In the US, new make is called white dog.

peating Adding peat to the kiln ovens when malting barley to impart a smoky, phenolic aroma and taste to the whisky. Barley that has undergone this process is known as peated malt.

poteen *see* uisce poitín

pot still The large onion-shaped vessels, nearly always made of copper, used for batch distillation. Pot stills vary in size, and these variations affect the style of whisky.

proof The old term for the alcoholic proportion of a spirit that has been superseded by *ABV* in most countries. The American proof figure, which is different to Imperial proof, is twice that of the ABV.

rectifier still *see* continuous still

reflux The process by which heavier alcoholic vapours fall back into the still

rather than passing along the lyne arm to the condenser. By falling back, these vapours are re-distilled, becoming purer and lighter. Certain shapes of still contribute to the degree of reflux, which may or may not be desirable, depending on the style of whisky being made. Long-necked stills have a greater degree of reflux and produce a lighter style of spirit than squatter stills, which tend to make heavier, "oilier" whiskies.

run In batch distillation – as carried out using pot stills – the extent of a distillation is referred to as a run. The spirit produced during the run is variable in quality, and is divided by *cut points*.

silent distillery a distillery in which whisky making has stopped, but possibly only temporarily.

silent spirit neutral-flavoured spirit.

spirits safe a glass-fronted cabinet through which the distilled spirit passes and which is used to monitor the purity of the spirit. The stillman operates the spirits safe during a *run* to make *cut points*.

still The vessel in which distillation takes place. There are two basic types: a *pot still* and a *continuous still*.

tails *see* feints

triple distillation Most batch distillation involves two distillations: in a wash still and in a spirits still. Triple distillation, the traditional method in Ireland, involves a third distillation, which is said to produce a smoother spirit.

uisge beatha / uisce beatha The Scots gaelic and Irish gaelic terms, respectively, from which the word whisky derives. The term means "water of life", and so is synonymous with *eau de vie* and *aqua vita*.

uisce poitín Historically, the Irish gaelic term for non-licensed whiskey, usually known as poitín or poteen.

wash The resultant liquid when yeast is added to *worts*, fermenting into a kind of ale. Wash has an alcoholic strength of about 7% ABV. It passes into the wash still for the first distillation.

washbacks tThe fermenting vessels in which yeast is added to the *worts* to make *wash*. Called "fermenters" in the US.

white dog *see* new make

worm / worm tubs *see* condensers

worts The sweet liquid produced as a result of mixing hot water with *grist*.

Index